LOOK AT HAZARDS, LOOK AT LOSSES

BY GROUP FOR CONCEPTUAL POLITICS,
DANNY HAYWARD, ANTHONY ILES, LISA JESCHKE,
BENJAMIN NOYS, EIRIK STEINHOFF
AND MARINA VISHMIDT

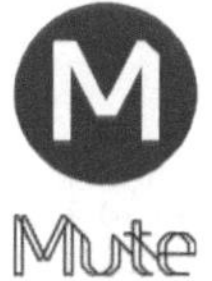

Mute

kuda.org

Publication version 1.0
GitHub commit SHA-1 ID 5603dfc – 5603dfc232d1154fedce2b65f939d9cb95a0667a

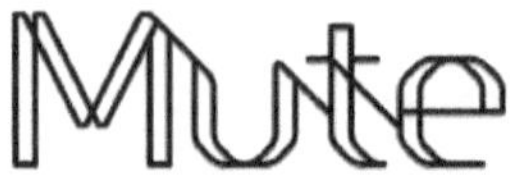

kuda.org

Look at Hazards, Look at Losses

Editors: Anthony Iles, Marina Vishmidt, New Media Center_kuda.org and Group for Conceptual Politics

Contributors: Group for Conceptual Politics, Danny Hayward, Anthony Iles, Lisa Jeschke, Benjamin Noys, Eirik Steinhoff and Marina Vishmidt

Publishers
New Media Center_kuda.org, Novi Sad
http://kuda.org
Mute Books, London
http://metamute.org

Please email services@metamute.org and office@kuda.org with any details of republication.

Mute Publishing – London | Berlin
http://metamute.org | @MuteMagazine | simon@metamute.org

Mute Books is an imprint of Mute Publishing

New Media Center_kuda.org, Novi Sad http://kuda.org | office@kuda.org

ISBN paperback (kuda.org): 978-86-88567-21-3
CIP – Cataloguing in Publication of The Matica Srpska Novi Sad
COBISS.SR-ID _313731335
ISBN eBook: 978-86-88567-22-0

Free to download in a variety of digital formats and also available in print through pay channels http://metamute.org/lookathazards

Distribution Anagram Books http://www.anagrambooks.com

The publication of this book is part of the project 'Aesthetic Education Expanded' realised in collaboration with kuda.org Novi Sad; Multimedia Institute, Kulturtreger/Booksa Zagreb; Kontrapunkt Skopje and Berliner Gazette Berlin, and supported by the EU cultural programme Creative Europe.

Year of publishing: 2017
Languages of the reader: Serbo-Croatian and English
Translation & proof-reading: Anthony Iles, Marina Vishmidt, kuda.org & GCP
Graphic layout: Simon Worthington and Hybrid Publishing Group https://hpg.io
Printer: Lightning Source LLC
Print run: 500

The project is supported by program Creative Europe (2014-2020) of the European Union, Ministry of Culture and Informing of Republic Serbia, European Cultural Foundation Amsterdam – BAC program, Ministry for Culture of Province Vojvodina and Ministry of Culture city of Novi Sad. This publication reflects the views only of the authors, and the European Commission cannot be held responsible for any use which may be made of the information contained therein.

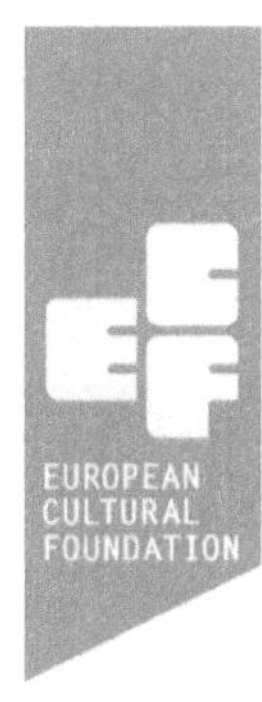

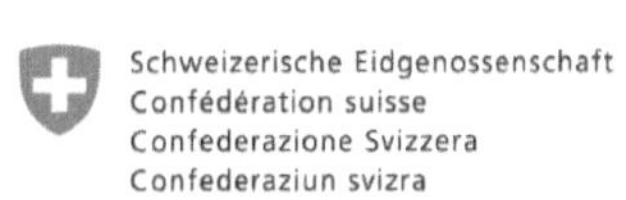

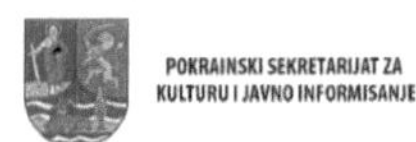

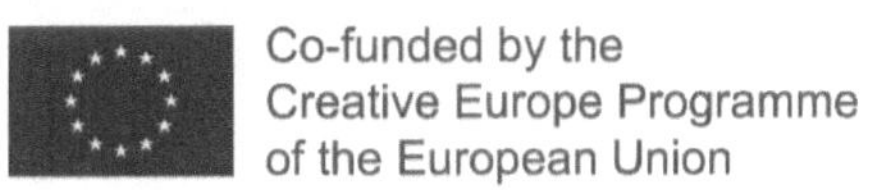

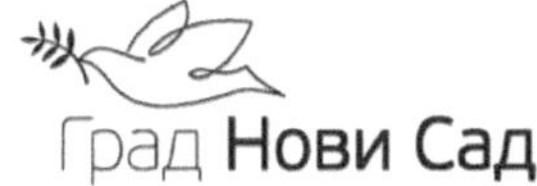

TABLE OF CONTENTS

PREFACE

THE EDITORIAL COMMUNE

We've been standing in the middle of a panoply of broken social forms for a long while now, and we've both watched and been watched as they formed constellations of crisis – financial, social and existential. The question of what mode of articulation critique could adopt remains suspended because the nature of the crisis has not yet been decided or convincingly narrated, so the crisis moment stretches indefinitely. This is to say that if there isn't yet a common narrative of the sequence of which 2007/2008 is the fulcrum, we then cannot say even if this is the finale, let alone what shape or meaning it might have, or even if it will resolve into something we can call a narrative at all.[1] Therefore, just as the gears of the global economy in decline have continued to spin without meshing, artists and writers have struggled to discern or communicate what message, if any, the crisis contains. Its movement has compassed a crisis of accumulation; debt crisis; a crisis of the wage; crises of the welfare state; of the family; of the nation; of social control; of whiteness; of masculinity; of borders, and of climate. Such an array of crises propels fears of dispossession, actual and imagined. In this sense crisis tracks the restlessness of capital, 'capital is capital in that it moves', capitalism is crisis, crisis is capitalism.

Look at Hazards, Look at Losses developed out of a series of conversations, exchanges and visits between kuda.org, Anthony Iles and Marina Vishmidt over the period of 2015-2017 through which different approaches to common problems of cultural production in early-21st century Europe and its peripheries were debated and conceptually probed. The hypotheses shared between us ranged from the incompatible to the non-contemporary. Place gathered them, neither only in space, nor exclusively in time. We believe in a thesis that contemporaneity is out-of-space and out-of-time, therefore we work in some form of non-contemporaneity. Those were moments of meetings and something which could be auto-ironically called the beauty of discussion. Setting out from Theodor W. Adorno's idea of 'the aesthetic relations of production', these discussions proceeded to explore problems bearing upon organisation in small groups in the field of culture, philosophical idealism and materialism, poetry, error, and crisis. Does aesthetic judgement still act as a condemnation of art, travelling through the ascription of aesthetic functions until the

---

1. Joshua Clover, 'Autumn of the System: Poetry and Finance Capital', *Journal of Narrative Theory,* Vol.41, No.1, Spring 2011, pp.34-52.

practice of art becomes irreducible to other practices and meets the creation of the autonomy of the world in its singularity? We count on deinstantionality (to think about reality without concepts at all), although this deconceptualises thought, it opens up the space for something other than a narrative. Fortunately, friendships sparkle in contemporaneity. The anthology reflects these concerns through engagement with the writing of ourselves and others who have helped orientate us through these discussions. It consists of eight original contributions by poets and theorists which attempt to move beyond 'crisis as a way of life' (Benjamin Noys) towards an 'expressively open radical culture' (Danny Hayward).

Crisis as a way of life has generated manifold forms of silence and states of inarticulacy, forcing 'something bad into our mouths' (Noys) resulting in a generalised 'recession in argument' (Hayward). The crisis has made us drunk (Lisa Jeschke) if not, yet, terminally stupid. With parties of opposition in crisis and the veneer of the liberal state cracking under internal and external pressures, smaller, anti-authoritarian group formations also fracture in ways both general and specific to their contexts. Without the ability to turn the crisis outward, as a question of systematic responsibility, it has turned upon us, our responsibilities are reconfigured as personal debts (Group for Conceptual Politics). From struggles to reverse the privatisation of higher education or to end police killings the road towards any gain at all has been apparently blocked, therefore several of the contributions here scan speculatively for paths out of a blocked present. Subterranean labours struggle to pose again the question of organisation in new terms (GCP) even while ciphers of regression push up against previous emancipatory forms, distorting and deforming them (Anthony Iles). Despite poetic slippages which threaten to lurch from the unprecedented to the unpresidented (Steinhoff) it is with manifold methods of management that the crisis continues to be contained within the new strange norms of neoliberal command and control (Marina Vishmidt), such as the popular management diagram that envisions risk as movement through successive layers of swiss cheese. There's an imposed necessity to reckon with how notions around contingency, irrationality, and chaos are currently operationalised with the rise of memetic forces from the far-right chthonic places of the internet to the highest levels of political power and popular consciousness alike. Where does that leave the exception, the event, and the incalculable that have been (dis)orienting political thought on the left for some time now, defining the 'open space' created by the crisis but unable to synthesise forces to act within it in anything but ephemeral ways? Here suggestions about radical poetry as a world-making and world-cracking (Noys) form of metabolic exchange through language (Steinhoff) can have some traction. Another set of connections between the contingent and the strategic desperately need to be drawn from sources such as the 'incomputable', or the working of contingency towards determinate emancipatory ends rather than the contemplative paranoia of sublime witnessing of our 'own destruction as an aesthetic pleasure'.[2] Looking at hazards and losses, in this light, would entail taking stock of the situation and checking the damage, but also being prepared for the unexpected, assessing what can yet be hazarded – to say something in a tentative way and put it at risk of being lost – as the situation continues to unfold.

2. Walter Benjamin, 'The Work of Art in the Age of Mechanical Reproduction', *Illuminations*, (Trans. Harry Zohn), New York: Schocken Books, 1969.

MANAGEMENT AND MAINTENANCE

MARINA VISHMIDT

You'll be taken care of.
    – The Management (apocryphal)

This text marks an initial foray into a line of research about the relationship between maintenance and management, and an attempt to displace some of the calcified modes of apprehending and discussing these categories.

We could begin by looking at this as a relation grounded in the seeming opposition of both of these activities to production, or to 'production proper'. The register of maintenance is decidedly not that

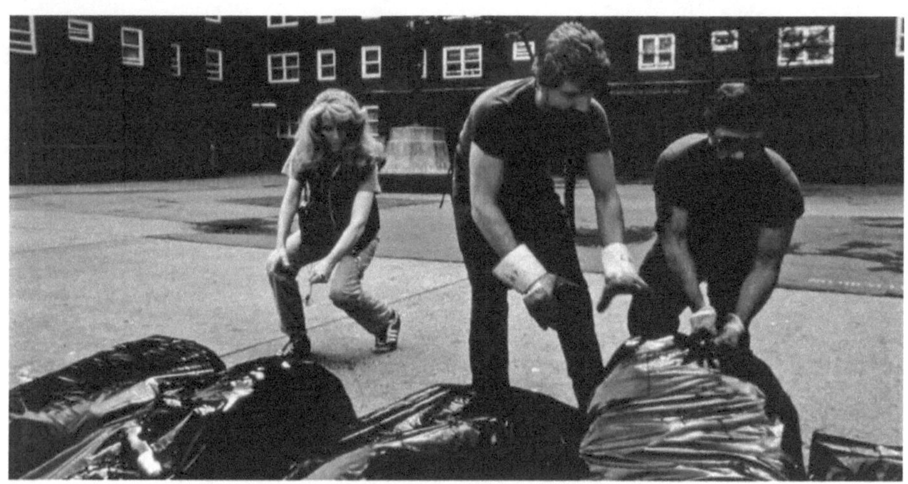

Mierle Laderman Ukeles, with two unidentified workers,
Touch Sanitation Performance, 1979.

which can be associated with the 'pure individual creation' as feminist artist Mierle Laderman Ukeles wittily frames it in her 'Maintenance Art Manifesto' in 1969. The 'pure individual creation' seen as the ex nihilo act of conceiving and putting something in the world that was not there before, a heroic production, with maintenance suborned to this as reproduction – making sure this object or entity or relation is enabled to continue existing over time, despite time's ravages on its existence and persistence. Likewise, management is not the modality of creating, inventing, producing anything but guiding, organising and optimising the activity of others. Notably, unlike the parallel status of entrepreneurship, defined by Joseph Schumpeter as neither an act of invention nor the form of ownership, but a co-ordination of existing resources in a new way, there is no initiative to management, which consists of implementing a plan developed elsewhere, be it directly down a chain of command or operationalising a more diffuse ideological climate ('managerialism').

In this typology, which can be said to feature elements of ontology and semiotics, both maintenance and management seem to suffer from a derivative quality. They require a prior signification in order to signify in their own right (which is never really their own), exhibiting a dependent status vis-à-vis the more valued term. Thus from the vantage of social or, more narrowly, workplace hierarchy, maintenance is at the bottom and management is elevated over it. This is in line with how the social division of labour in capitalist (and perhaps more generically in all class) societies establishes a steep gradient between manual and mental labour. This verticality is less secure economically as differentials in income between the two can be negligible, or even inverted (compare the earnings of a successful plumber and a duty manager at a cinema, to take two, rather difficult to meaningfully compare, lines of work).

The two registers additionally start to blur as soon as we take them into the space of 'immaterial' upkeep, that is, of brand equity or a public profile; corporate, personal, or the often vanishing border between the two. The management of perception, self-maintenance, even self-care, all emerge as indexes of the blur between the productive body and the signifying one, which can also be considered from the standpoint of human capital: the self is hived off into a portfolio of assets, and the subject-brand controls its investments, like a shell company.[1] This is one line of analysis given us to consider here - the zone of indistinction between maintenance and management which the era of social media platforms and personal brands makes unavoidable, both as imperative and as analysis. Everyone has a business inside them to share with everybody else.

---

1. See Michel Feher, 'Self-Appreciation; or, The Aspirations of Human Capital' *Public Culture*, 21:1, pp.21-41. For a counter-argument, see Dick Bryan, Randy Martin and Mike Rafferty, 'Financialization and Marx, Giving Labor and Capital a Financial Makeover', *Review of Radical Political Economics*, 41:4, pp.458-472, itself usefully critiqued by Sam Williams at his *A Critique of Crisis Theory* blog: https://critiqueofcrisistheory.wordpress.com/responses-to-readers-austrian-economics-versus-marxism/financialization-and-marx-%e2%80%94-pt-1-do-skilled-workers-own-human-capital/

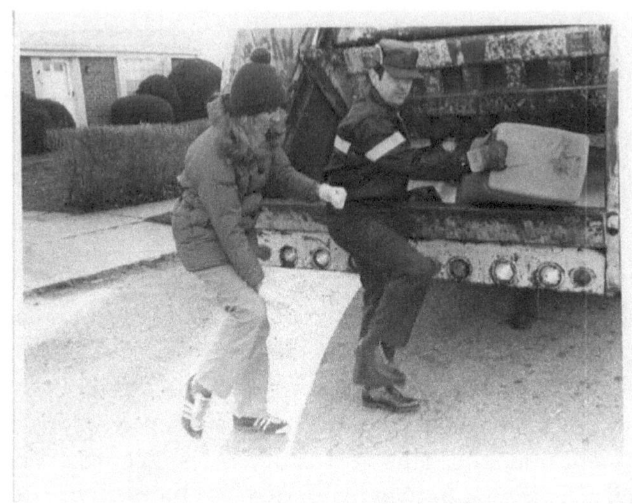

Mierle Laderman Ukeles, Touch Sanitation,
1979–80. Photo: Marcia Bricker.

Another one, which the reference to Ukeles and reproduction already hinted at, is the materialist feminist troubling of the classic political economic division between production and reproduction (a division which of course also recurs in the critique of political economy), in which reproduction is invariably the devalued term. Ukeles pointed out that most art is not pure autonomous sovereign creation, just like most work isn't, but is 'infected by strains of' maintenance activity. In this she was challenging a certain orthodox, patriarchal or Oedipal anxiety about autonomy and influence in modernist art, and pointing also to the undoubted fact that it took a lot of cleaning to keep the white cube white (in all its senses, e.g. institutional violences of exclusion such as racism, even if she didn't directly address this at the time of the Maintenance Art Manifesto but would go on to do this in later work), and that if all the unwaged, naturalised, feminised, racialised labour were to stop from one day to the other, so would the conditions for the display and appreciation of the sovereign act of art (and, going back into the 'hidden abode' of the family and the studio, probably of its production as well). This point about how constitutive the work of 'reproduction' was to all official economic, measured and recognised activities of production traversed the political spectrum of materialist feminism from the 1970s onwards, and was especially pronounced in groups like Wages for (Against) Housework, one of the tendencies that brought Marxist value categories to the debate. Doubtless one can even look to the early writings of Karl

Marx and his insistence that labour is a metabolism with nature to understand how production is always already reproduction in principle. The metabolism with nature here refers to how human activity is thoroughly co-constitutive with the affordances of its environment rather than opposed to it in the way a machine 'stands over and against' the worker in the factory. Thus the production of the means of life and the reproduction of social relations are entangled if not continuous, and nature and the social are at best heuristic distinctions rather than anthropologically given ones. Such a 'metabolic' understanding brings us close to the universality of 'individuation' as the reproduction of self-consistent entities in the ideas of engineer-philosopher Gilbert Simondon, which will recur later in the text. At the same time, this conception's bias to a kind of organicism can be kept in check by dint of the more specified sense of the continuity of production and reproduction that Marx elsewhere addressed – that all production is at the same time a reproduction of capital, both as accumulation and as a set of social relationships.

Likewise, and this is something I've developed at greater length elsewhere, insofar as the institution of art provides a safety valve to an oppressive, instrumentalised society, it legitimates that society (in the double sense of the autonomy of art Theodor W. Adorno talks about) and is thus itself a reproductive institution in Louis Althusser's terms: legitimating the state of things by seeming to be transcendent of the state of things, like other institutions of the state that mediate the social relations of the commodity in indirect and sometimes contradictory ways.[2]

Discussions of maintenance and reproduction, often under the aegis of 'care' have featured prominently in feminist art-theoretical and political discourse of late. The work of Mierle Laderman Ukeles in particular, with its conceptual clarity and accessible form, has been examined from a variety of angles. I would therefore like to turn to the less examined term here so far: management. Management is something which becomes increasingly interesting from the perspective of scale, which is to say, as it is rooted in the capitalist labour process but also radiating outwards from it.

---

2. For the most recent discussion, see Marina Vishmidt, 'The Two Reproductions', *Third Text*, forthcoming 2017.

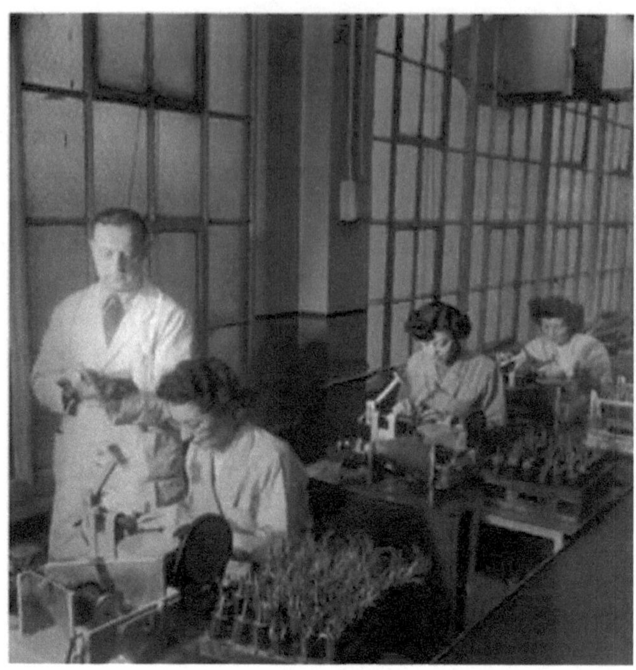

Time and motion study, Hoover factory,
Perivale, West London, 1948.

A standard labour process approach to management differentiates it from labour. Management appears in a sequence punctuated by abstractions of skill: appropriation, standardisation, and domination. As one of the most well-known analyses shows, that of Harry Braverman, the worker's know-how is studied (say, in the canonical Taylorist, assembly line scenario), broken down and codified into a set of routines, and then either imposed uniformly on the workers as a plan or used to engineer a machine which can eventually replace the worker. This process of learning from and power over is the role of the manager, and *management* is simply a description of a specific location in the production apparatus.[3] The question of domination here has been painted on a wider socio-historical canvas recently with research into the ideological commitments and the applied practices of early management theorists such as Elton Mayo in the 1920s.[4] So we are used to thinking of management in terms of labour process, with a separation of who gives orders and who executes them – who is tasked

---

3. Harry Braverman, *Labor and Monopoly Capital: The Degradation of Work in the Twentieth Century*, New York and London: Monthly Review Press, [1974] 1998.

with conceptualising the work process and who with merely implementing the directions as closely as possible. The teleology of the process, however, in both cases, is *constitutively* always elsewhere, i.e. beyond the scope of question or intervention. This can be viewed quite directly as an alienation of knowledge in a process of rationalisation meant to enhance accumulation; it is a harnessing and weaponising, as it were, of subjectivity itself. A common contemporary discussion invokes affective, cognitive, and performative modes of labour; yet this discussion is prone to overlook the centrality of these valences in the expropriation of agency within the capital-labour relation per se, whatever the technological or organisational variation.

Here, albeit parenthetically, we could touch on an significant point in Jacques Rancière's book *Disagreement*, in which he suggests that the basis of social equality appears precisely in the scenario of greatest hierarchy: the giving of orders.[5] To understand the order and have a reasonable prospect of carrying it out as anticipated, the one who obeys must be at least the equal of the one who commands in terms of understanding. This epistemic equality exists in a state of contradiction and overdetermination by social inequality, which is justified in ontological terms, as, for example, in Aristotle's theory of the slave as a 'speaking implement' in a prosthetic relation to the master.

Yet it is when we turn to management on different scales – ecologies of management, perhaps – that we start to get at some more surprising aspects of what can be called, for convenience, the logic of management. Management can also be thought of in terms of grappling with a mobile and erratic milieu, of the projection of a world view onto contingent materialities as a first step in getting them under control towards a predetermined end. This idea is fleshed out in a text published recently by the architectural theorist Maria Giudici which discusses the role of popular technical schools in the Italian

---

4. Gerald Hanlon, *The Dark Side of Management: A Secret History of Management Theory*, New York: Routledge, 2015. This book undertakes a genealogy of the role of management theory in neoliberal re-structuring, suggesting that looking at the therapeutic and data-driven discourse of management that can help focus how 'managers have acted as neoliberalism's executioners in ensuring that contemporary workers exist in a precarious world without control, democracy or power'.
5. Jacques Rancière, *Disagreement: Politics and Philosophy*, (Trans. Julie Rose), Minneapolis: University of Minnesota Press, 2008.

renaissance.[6] Her account of the emergence of the 'project' in the 15th century Italian engineering schools called *abaco* (computing, i.e. at that time using the abacus) makes the following conjecture:

> project does not necessarily imply a formal resolution: it is a term that is more concerned with the management of things to come. Project implies shaping a direction by handling, influencing, and steering a number of factors we do not necessarily fully control. It is necessarily managerial, and it is more focused on the process rather than the result.

This priority of process over result can be telescoped forward in time and shifted laterally to the sphere of contemporary art, and the resulting overlaps between management and the norms of artistic production and curation were the topic of an essay which can be seen as the remote predecessor of this one.[7] It has also been observed that the influence has gone the other way, with the focus on process associated with the arts used as a positive example in management theory seeking to appropriate for the figure of the manager the virtues of spontaneity, sovereignty, and creativity associated with the artistic genius.[8]

Giudici goes on to emphasise the role of technical rather than just humanistic education in the culture of the Renaissance in early modern Italy especially, and notes that accounting methods and managerial techniques were fundamental to the economic success of the Italian city-states and thereby their geopolitical reach and influence – and instrumental to the rise of capitalism in that region. Yet more systemically and consequentially, the *abaco* schools

---

6. Maria S. Giudici, 'Learning by Numbers', *e-flux Architecture conversations*, March 2017, http://conversations.e-flux.com/t/architecture-conversations-maria-s-giudici-responds-to-zeynep-celik-alexander-mass-gestaltung/5784
7. Marina Vishmidt, 'Everyone Has a Business Inside Them', *Mute*, 12 March 2012, http://www.metamute.org/editorial/articles/everyone-has-business-inside-them.
8. One publication from a plethora exploring these themes is Jörg Reckhenrich, Martin Kupp and Jamie Anderson, 'The Manager as Artist', *Business Strategy Review*, Summer 2009. A good discussion and bibliography of this literature can be found in Sarah Brouillette's 'Academic Labor, the Aesthetics of Management, and the Promise of Autonomous Work', *nonsite* journal, Issue 9, http://nonsite.org/article/academic-labor-the-aesthetics-of-management-and-the-promise-of-autonomous-work

introduced a different understanding of the relationship between man and the world. [...] The universe of the *abaco* schools is made of quantifiable entities, of objects that the student-subject is supposed to tame, manage, re-produce, and control. The focus is neither on form nor design, but, rather, on the strategic choreography of goods, monetary exchange and labor provision. It is a universe that for the first time is conceived of as without shadow zones: calculable, knowable, open to the preying eye of man.

A set of pedagogical methods for the production of subjectivities of quantification which are as adaptable to commercial enterprise as to military engineering, taking in historical moments of (ir)rationalisation like perspective in painting, land surveying, and chattel slavery. A parallelogram of control not so dissimilar from the quasi-Platonic reality of the exchange principle grounding Alfred Sohn-Rethel's yoking of currency and conceptuality in the logic of 'real abstraction'.[9] But this is quantification with a qualification. Managing materials and space was one thing, human behaviour another – this was the world of approximation, of rule-of-thumb techniques, of contingency management: 'School problems explicitly asked students to calculate the cost and duration of a specific job depending on whether the workers are "lazy" or not.'[10]

Thus, management is seen here as a (conjunctural) frame for containing uncertainty. As we see, Giudici opposes the 'project' to design, which is understood as a kind of exhaustive formalisation, shaping the self recursively in tandem with the environment. The project, on the other hand, is specifically managerial as a mode, since it is presented as a more inductive way of proceeding – not so much about elegant formulas as about the efficacity of control over unstable circumstances. This idea of management as an approach to contingency seems to have something reminiscent of maintenance about it on the one hand – not so much an organising of activity according to a plan as

---

9. It could be useful to elaborate on the historical circumstances of this sweeping conception, namely the massive expansion of white-collar clerical and managerial employment in Weimar-era Germany when Sohn-Rethel was writing his *Intellectual and Manual Labour: A Critique of Epistemology*, Atlantic Highlands, N.J: Humanities Press, 1977. See also Siegfried Kracauer, *The Salaried Masses: Duty and Distraction in Weimar Germany*, (Trans. Quintin Hoare), London and New York: Verso, 1998. Originally *Die Angestellten*, 1930.
10. Giudici, op.cit.

a series of ad hoc adaptations that develop in line with a chaotic plenum of forces and tendencies with a view to operation rather than

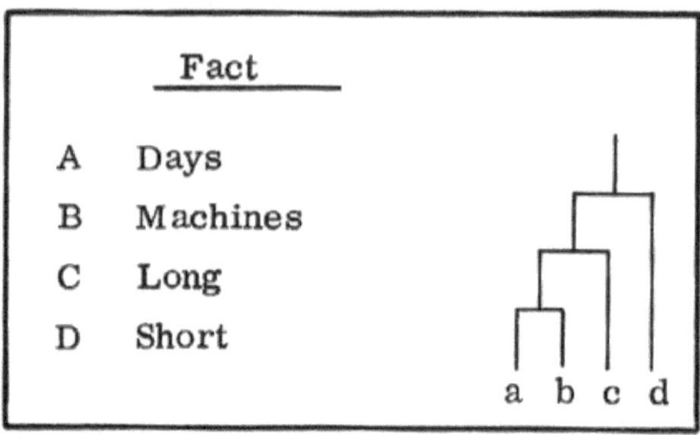

style. And yet as a species of managerial control which gave rise to adaptations like linear perspective and its unfolding in the logistical operations of warfare and colonisation, the management of contingency is no less violent if decidedly more prosaic than the ethereal, absolutist principles of total design. Giudici, however, wants to draw attention to the untapped potential of management as a prosaic and metabolic activity, in Marx's terms, a logic which can be divested of its grounding in projects of extractive domination. Thus, management was a project

> born as a historically-placed response to the emergence of capitalism, where it made it possible to organise labor and reify life into a commodity. If this is a negative heritage we now reject, there are also aspects of the project that can be rethought as means of resistance: the idea that creating a future does not mean necessarily to impose a form, but rather to imagine a set of relationships that can change, shift, readjust.[11]

Thus, by going through management as an array of dispositions and knowledges, we find the project on one side, design on the other, and, at least *in nuce*, a more materialist idea of abstraction as a shifting diagram shaped reflexively by the volatility of its (human) terrain. A quick link can here be drawn to ecology and ecological trouble as occasions for projects of management characterised by reciprocity and reflexivity. This entails comprehending management on a planetary

---

11. Ibid.

scale, in the sense of 'planetarity' recently formulated by Gayatri Spivak as an ethics of alterity in the annihilating sense she derives from the encounter and affinity between Ahab and the white whale in *Moby Dick*. A planetary scale of management then implies managing as a somewhat doomed but nonetheless collective attempt to 'handle' the uncontrollable eventualities of ecological damage and a will to persist in projects of maintenance: maintaining liveability for different human and non-human entities in a context rendered 'alien' by damage, and thus one where alienations all too familiar, along with ones hitherto little imagined, do prevail. More simply, planetarity refigures management as maintenance in and of (the conditions for) resistance, once the known quantities of 'resources' comprising management's field of action can no longer be counted on, while maintenance, with its dogged orientation to survival can emerge as a creative encounter with the truly eco-systemic unknown, necessitating newer (or older) co-operative social forms.

This starts to give us some of the tools to re-imagine maintenance not just as reproduction – as maintaining what is to remain as self-similar as possible and thus cut off from any idea of novelty or disruption – but to begin working towards a notion of maintenance as resistance. Another impulse in this direction can be drawn from an idea of technological knowledge as a processual relation to contingency which turns into 'management' when it hits the ground, so to speak, and into 'maintenance' when the ground shifts. In other words, the management of quantities and behaviours, of objects, subjects and their transitions and transversalities across scale, again, is faced with an unknowability that repels domestication, at a level of damage both granular and planetary where old exploitations dwindle or perhaps more virulent and makeshift new ones take hold. Here there is a partial correspondence to the notion of the 'incomputable' that theorists Antonia Majaca and Luciana Parisi propose in one of their recent texts.[12] They suggest that instrumentality can be re-assessed not as an independent cultural logic tending towards a totalitarianism of things, a fully quantified and (ir)rationalised dystopia in the style of the

---

12. Antonia Majaca and Luciana Parisi, 'The Incomputable and Instrumental Possibility', *e-flux journal*, No.77, http://www.e-flux.com/journal/77/76322/the-incomputable-and-instrumental-possibility/ November 2016; last accessed 22 March 2017.

Dialectic of Enlightenment, but rather that technology embodies the socio-historical values of a period.

While this sounds like a banality, the more intriguing dimension here is that instrumentality is biopolitical and that the machine itself can be the source of 'alien modes of subjectivation', which can be touched by inhabiting the perspective of the machine and not that of

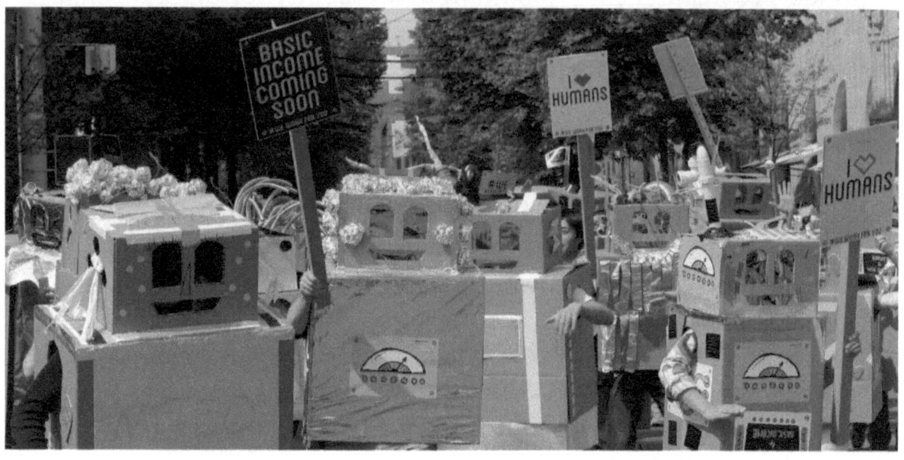

Robots for Basic Income Demo, Zürich, 30 April 2016.

the engineer, architect, designer, user, security analyst, or manager. How can this be envisioned, and in the service of what? In other words, how do we go from the scale of planetarity as the name for alterity in Spivak's political ecology to the initmacy of alterity in everyday technology? In both scenarios, the question of alterity is formulated in terms of an enabling alienation, which both defeats imagination as currently constituted and as something which 'forces us to think' (Deleuze) and act in political and affective response to a genuine novelty which cannot be 'managed away'. After alienation comes the intimacy of maintenance, which may yet entail a recalibration of the subject-object relation which commercial forms of 'techno-animism' that we experience with our gadgets nowadays block rather than enable. Also, given that, in Parisi and Majaca's terms, these devices foster 'paranoid' forms of surveillance and control rather than a reckoning with the shaping influence of algorithmic cognition on human thinking and sociality, such a reckoning would entail biopolitical inhabitation of these technologies rather than the projection of police logic upon and with its usage.

The suggestion is that 'thinking from within the machine and from within the very logic of the instrument' may provide us, especially the gendered, racialised, classed, de-abled and abjected among 'us', some resources to evacuate the self-sustaining forms of algorithmic control pervading current models of cybernetic governance and extraction. It would be primarily by overhauling the means-ends hierarchy embedded in technology as a repository for naturalised social relationships of competition, efficiency and control, and coming to it rather as a space of intimate alienation where the meaning of functionality itself can be exceeded, turned around and re-invented as part of a transformative social process. Ultimately what this would have to mean is that the persistent, if philosophically discredited, duality between technicity and nature can no longer be perpetuated, that nature is not a set of timeless meanings that technology allows us to standardise and systematise. Central to this discussion as well is the idea of the instrument possessing its own ends, its own history of subjectivation:

> The new subject can only be constructed from the hard labor of alienation, which includes understanding the logic of instrumentality, politicising it, and transcending it through usage itself. This requires building a non-paranoid imagination, and a readiness for a radical denaturalisation of both humanness and subjectivity as we know it [...].

These insights plumb, if without quite fleshing out, philosophical depths which remain beyond the scope of proximal techno-feminist positions such as 'xenofeminism', with their crude recycling of cyberfeminist tropes with an accelerationist agenda. In this light, Majaca and Parisi's work evokes that of Gilbert Simondon, and his book *On the Mode of Existence of Technical Objects*, in which he discusses a schema of co- and trans-constitution between humans, milieus, and technical objects.[13] Technical objects should not be degraded and dominated by the ends of profit, fashion, or control, but rather their technicity should be allowed to develop to ends currently deemed non-functional or desirable. This entails granting an autonomy to the technical which is less like the autonomy of capital and more like the autonomy of art, in its alignment with the social autonomy experienced

---

13. Gilbert Simondon, *On the Mode of Existence of Technical Objects*, (Trans. Cecile Malaspina and John Rogove), Minneapolis: Univocal, 2016.

by humans no longer subjugated to the naturalised despotism of the technical. In an interview, Simondon opined on the proximity between this notion of the autonomy of the technical and the ideas around maintenance discussed so far: 'I believe there are humans in the technical objects, and that the alienated human can be saved on the condition that man is caring for them.'[14]

Scale is a question for Simondon as well when he reflects on 'orders of magnitude', between which relation is fundamental. This amounts to a 'realism of relations'. The individual, of whatever ontological status – for Simondon an individual is the outcome of a process of individuation, which is myriad, it can be a mental, biological, chemical or social process, among others – is not *in* relation but *is* relation, foremost with its milieu. An individual is a composite and container of relations, which exist at different scales: the scale of an individual, the scale of the pre-individual, the scale of the milieu. The individual thus can be seen as a phase of consistency in a landscape of relations. Proceeding from this to the organisational and social scales at which we first encountered the dyad of management and maintenance, the intellectual/manual division which underpins the exercise of management is disallowed by such a conception, rather creating a panoply of scales across which consistency and responsibility may form and dissolve – something closer to the logic of maintenance, attuned as it is to ad hoc operations whose creativity is geared towards the amplification of effects and connections rather than efficiency and control for remote but unquestionable ends.

Thus, management across scales here can also imply management *of* scales, in the sense that management has the chance to develop into care: a reflexive rather than crudely operational undertaking of optimising activity or processes for predetermined ends (efficiency, performance). In this way it comes back to questions of scale from the standpoint of the project at hand. Scale is an artefact of the productive imagination and the specific engineering process in question, not at all a pre-existing frame of reference keeping a predetermined order that technology is designed to respond to, whether amelioratively or punitively. If, as Majaca and Parisi offer, instrumentality is subjectivity

---

14. 'Save The Technical Object: Interview with Gilbert Simondon', English translation of interview, (Trans. Andrew Iliadis), *Esprit* No.76, Vol.04, 1983, pp.147-52, http://linkme2.net/wh

in practice, this is a practice that travels into the object and abandons
the subject, but only at the (disavowed) cost of overcoming the
'empirico-ontological' doublet of capitalist social relations that the two
authors do not engage with directly, unlike, to take one prominent if
selective example, the Adorno in *Negative Dialectics.* Rather, they turn
their attention to noting how contemporary developments in artificial
intelligence and machine learning operate with notions of
incompleteness, error, and contingency which are ripe for re-
appropriation by a feminist technics, pursued through concepts such as
Peirce's 'abduction' (a form of logical reasoning that does not function
inferentially, but fantastically). Abduction, in distinction from the more
established modes of induction and deduction, is a way of trying to
account for the unprecedented with a series of consequences that
imply, or, rather, project a world in which that new event would make
sense. Abduction is addressed here as an 'alien mode of cognition', as it
starts with unknown or at least temporarily unknowable premises,
fusing the energy of the speculative with the tidiness of formal logic.

Such a mode of cognition would be able to make sense of 'the
generation of new hypotheses of instrumentality, one that
acknowledges the history of techne whereby the machine has been able
to elaborate strategies of autonomy from and through its own use.'[15] In
this, the xenogenetic scenarios of science fiction could be both an
example and a methodology, leading us to approach this autonomy of
the technical as an 'ironic political myth' (as Haraway begins *The Cyborg
Manifesto*). That kind of move would mean coming back to our original
categories of maintenance and management with a politics not rooted
in the productive subject vis-à-vis the derivative object – even if this is
a reproductive subject – but by displacing subjectivity to the object,
and then to the process of unknowability that the autonomy of a
technical object can bring into focus (such as when it 'breaks'). More
concretely, if we started out by looking at maintenance as the care of
what is, enabling it to develop and become, and management as the
optimisation of what is, enhancing its productivity for pre-determined
ends, perhaps we have now shifted the view in a sense by moving to
inhabit the alienation from creativity and productivity implied in both.
This enables us to see how that separation is predicated on social
hierarchies of command and control where the creativity on one side is

---

15. Parisi & Majaca, op. cit.

fostered by instrumentality on the other, and that instrumentality is first and foremost the fate of some subjects who are not considered properly human, even prior to there being anything like non-organic mechanism.

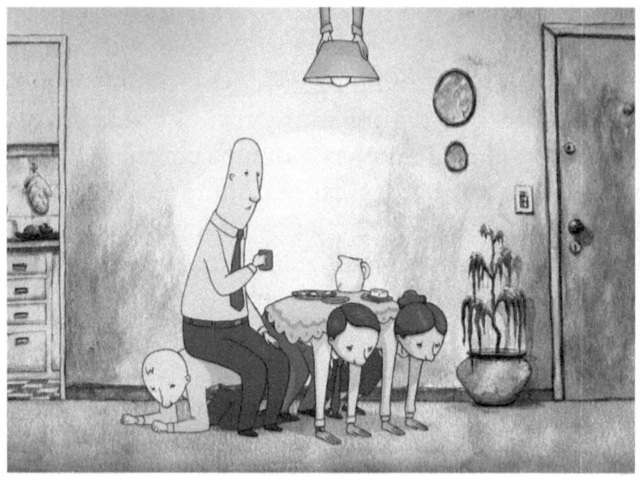

Santiago Grasso, still from *El Empleo*, 2008, Argentina.

Yet in this discussion of inhabiting mechanisms, the question of the social mechanisms of institutions can fall by the wayside, the speculative energies of the former foundering in the inertias of the latter. But a tracing of the relations between maintenance, management and resistance should also touch down in the institution. What remains perhaps to be determined is how in the present moment, all management tends towards crisis management, and thus, by default, to converge with the communal and emancipatory-minded 'politics of care'. Nowadays management is concerned to be seen to care – to make sure everything is all right, that everyone has their voice heard, that everyone feels safe, especially in workplaces exposed to more or less intensive cycles of precaritisation and proletarianisation, such as educational institutions. This concern to ensure normality at all costs has not borne the name of repressive tolerance without justification, with the 'tolerance' part always dwindling in favour of repression, as security-minded governance bodies show their eagerness to invite police and other agents of the state to 'take care' of labour or student matters on campuses. But perhaps more insidious than such not-unexpected phenomena is the discourse of care that licenses aspirations to absolute control – where dissent is painted as not a matter of antagonism but of insensitivity, organising made into a blow against dialogue rather than an attempt to foster one.

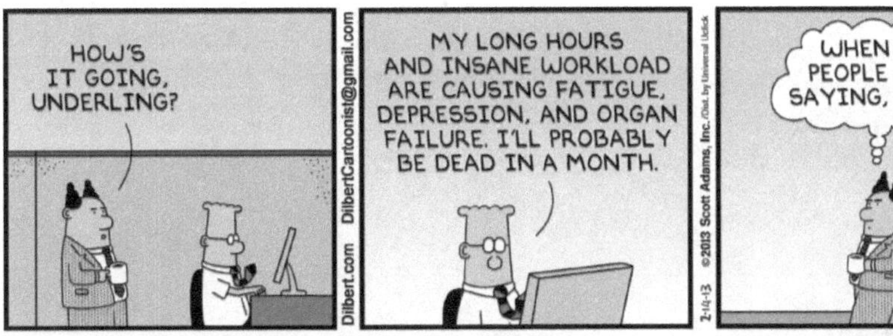

Power re-configured as care can be seen as a kind of 'reproductive realism' that appears to affirm the invisible labour of maintenance and survival, but for decisively conservative ends. In its crude dissociation of maintenance and resistance, it ends up with management. This entails the suppression of any disruption or discomfort as an unjustified exercise of power and privilege – those who want to resist are pitted against those who just want to persist, as if these were not implicated. Thus a continuum can be drawn between moments on this spectrum: the cosmetic care routines of institutional management, the ruthless denial of political questions in favour of an etiolated ethics of care that somehow always affirms market subjectivity,[16] and the 'maintenance art' of the middle-class 'broom brigades' that took to the streets of London in the aftermath of the riots of summer 2011 to flaunt their race and class hatred in fits of photogenic compulsive cleaning – an ironic inversion, to be sure, of Ukeles' 'the sourball of every revolution – who cleans up the next day?'

This short circumnavigation of some of the more dubious corners of the maintenance-management complex had the purpose of diffusing some of the sanctimony that tends to collect around the 'politics of care', as if there were just one politics and the invocation of care was adequate to signal its nature. The point must be rather that in order to re-evaluate and not just revalorise the activities of maintenance and management, there would need to be the kind of displacement of

---

16. Although widespread, such phenomena are often encountered in situations where credibility is accumulated through radical discourse but hazarded by political activity, such as the space of contemporary art. It is also a sphere where opportunism has been enshrined as survival politics, with the pretext of precarity often called upon to deflect critique for all kinds of reactionary activities, when it is not used to indict the privilege of the critics.

agency from human subjects to technical objects Majaca, Parisi and Simondon talk about, but only as part of a larger transvaluation of

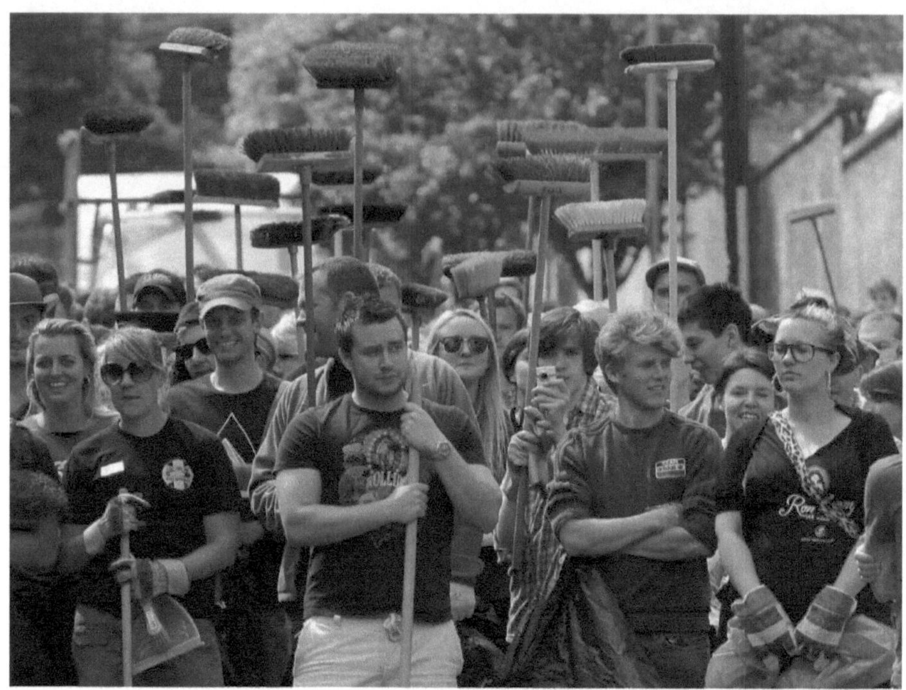

Volunteers queue to help cleanup in wake of rioting in
London's Clapham Junction, 9 August 2011.

abjected forms of labour and existence which seem technically obvious but remain socially opaque. The manoeuvre of naturalising the technical as the opposite of a reified nature only means that the social content of nature is always already functionalised – whereas what is urgent now is re-assessing the means-ends relationships of capitalist techno-science that are driving towards ecosystemic annihilation – not by rejecting the scientific or the instrumental per se but by rejecting the social relationships that perpetuate their mythologised versions as simple realism. Something the performativities of feminist art – as with Ukeles and her transvaluation of maintenance as a *non*-progressive form of life – science fiction and philosophies of technology can help us start to unpack, even as the pieties of 'care' always threaten to close it down.

INSTITUTIONAL COMMUNES: RECUPERATION OR REPRODUCTION?

GROUP FOR CONCEPTUAL POLITICS

We tend towards scandalising: all those employed at this moment can be regarded as cops. To work has become a privilege; this is a heavy blow to the politics which followed the path of workers' emancipation and workers' struggle because it put on the table both work and its refusal. How to refuse it today when nobody offers it to us? How and what to refuse in terms of what an employed worker thinks of him(or her)self? How to think about the condition that one does not work, except as a form of privilege? Whatever one thinks, an employed worker knows to appreciate it: he thinks in a statist way and the thought cannot be excluded that he will take on the idea of the public good, but it needs to be nicely packaged for him if he is not working inside the state. With state employees it will go more easily. The possibility cannot be excluded that the whole periphery, where only the state works, will easily transition to a new socialist regime of organisation and reproduction of capital. That is the hope of the left involved in parliamentary preparations, and already established on the ground in Slovenia. You do not need to be paranoid to see this, since there is no need to search for an individual who prepares for us the socialisation of debts and of the costs of maintaining debts. The public good will first appear to us in the form of debt and liturgical responsibility, as often happens in the affair of managing peripheral provinces.

Today we are facing the dilemma that some set in terms of pacifism and radicalism. Pacifism and its lies and self-deceptions, occur in the form of *public discussions* which are held for the sake of political struggle, while radicalism is that which has a high value among left activists and that has no other function except to provide grounds for exclusion. As a result we have *parliamentarism* and *conferencialism*. Most often they overlap and so we get *congressalism* followed by publicistic development of what should be theory and science. All this happens in the service of social mobility and buttering one's bread inside the state. Over the years a hunger for recognition is developed and therefore activism *in time* turns into the accumulation of symbolic and social capital.

We have some experience of struggle in this field and we have passed through many conflicts on the independent left. These are conflicts of our time, although these are not necessarily historical, considering the possible criteria of future historians who will still look for phenomena in the domain of the objective, and which is always and in the last instance the domain of the state. We went through the tears and splits and imputed the experience of self-exclusion and resentment – of cheap psychologising.

We felt on our own skin how micro-fascism and the state machine works, even when it mobilises itself under the flags of anti-fascism. Academism has proved to us that the classes can be held and in spare time lessons can be shared, even while the rules of the game remain the same. Academics, hungry for public presentation, spoke out about the public good primarily because they consider themselves to be the good which is public, and that this should be retained as the apple of everyone's eye.

Today we are no longer only exasperated, but are also 'pests'. Pests, since we work in the local community as activists in the field of local government. The project is called Local Politics and Urban Self-management. We however see problems such as this: the de-politicisation of local government and its extinguishing takes place through the disappearance of civil society at the local level. More specifically, what has disappeared at the local level is non-political-party organising which the socialist local community offices prepared the way for and we witness today, after the socialist period when the local community offices had their councils in the municipal assemblies, the presence of the state and the party in our very homes. Boards and administration in the local community office serve the party, and our homes are behest to the party because they can be maintained only if we work in the state, which always goes through the party or some other form of submission to the state, since the state is the only company that does work. The company is in crisis, but that is still working in terms of its withdrawal from the market, even if this no longer happens in order to make room for business to operate in. What created this space? This remains to be seen only in the dark of our contemporary moment.[1]

---

1. The crisis of the state (see Nicos Poulantzas) in the time of its domination by attenuation theoretically is explained. Domination of the state, this means that economical function of the state overdetermines the others. According to our theoretical remembrance, thus also was the socialist party-state treated by the concept of the mode of production, which in both East and West lit the thoughts of people while not making them contemporaries. The economic functions of the state are reflected in its interventions which are conducive for the expansion of the market as the very idea of regulation. Could we say that the market is the same as the regulation and orderliness in the way of invisibility of the hand as a decision (a prescription), and not to be understood as ideologists of political economy? Could we say this although it is again and again unclear that we are clear about what was criticism from the time of The Critique of Political Economy? (See also Foucault – Biopolitics).

Why are we therefore told that we are 'pests'? Well, because we do the job of the state. So we are told. Besides being saloon-activists preaching self-organisation, we are also told that we meanly sell an idea of indebtedness and recommend taking bank loans. We tell stories, though imagining we mobilise people to organise themselves in terms of the maintenance of the housing stock. It should be done by the State, left-oriented intellectuals (academics and journalists) apprise us. We see a paradox in this: pests because we do the job of the state, thus releasing the state from obligation to do it itself? Therefore this task is supposed to be done by the State, and not by us? So, in fact we're carrying out something that looks more like a 'Big Society' programme? Should the State be compelled to do 'its job'? Therefore we shouldn't do anything? We will not do anything in its stead, but we will enter into it and through this entrism get it done when we are in power or in a position to exercise at least a part of the power of the state. That part would probably depend on our coalition potential, if we aren't able to establish a majority and to make the State completely ours. Until then we have to wait. And that's not all.

So we are pests because we do the work of the State, which is bad because it doesn't do it. And not only that. It needs to be compelled, but one needs to know that it's bad precisely because of this, since there are pests that think they can do it without it. And this is exactly the concept of the 'Big Society', i.e. neoliberal governance or the police, a police neoliberal state. So, by no means do nothing, because every action that is not statist and not directed towards the state as something we need to work with, is pestilential and produces a state that is not doing its job. The good state therefore is the one in which we are, and quite a good one in which only are we. And since we are leftists or even socialists, such a state then does its job. And how? It is well-known: professionally and in qualified way, because when we have a functioning state we'll have professionals too.

Ok, we are not exactly accused of driving this ideology (Big Society), since we are not in the UK, but we wonder why not tighten this thing conceptually? Workers' signifiers, or signifiers of the working ideology, can overdetermine ruling ideologies which still remain bourgeois. All that springs up in the field of ideology contributes to its strengthening – and this is the way we understand the concept of hegemony. So, not only is the issue the ideological rule or the rule by ideology, but we think that at stake is also its strengthening – the strengthening of power – through resistance and the compensation of absent signifiers that could very well come to patch holes later. This is why today it seems to us that the prospect of 'flight' might be more accurate for what we want to do. Since by it we open up, according to one's taste, a perhaps too poetic and romantic route, the road of auto-theorisation and politics by which one avoids hegemony. Since the words are not just words, but also practices and acts that resonate, this approach should always look for the relations which we enter by speaking. In this sense we speak of *institutional communes.* So let's be radical without flirting with radicalism and stick to the concept of historical materialism consistently: the state is not only in the institutions that are considered to be the state - the government institutions and the political system - but the apparatuses of the state are also enterprises, cultural institutions, the tenants' assemblies, households, and families. We see apparatus as an historical materialistic concept of the institutions in which measure (also always political) is taken (like a tailor measuring cloth) concerning the function of reproduction which it performs in one mode of production. This was Althusser's question based on the answer which sociologists symptomatically gave when tending to establish the object of their science, which they would like to call a social fact. Taking apart 'the social deed/acting', which is then 'stable and established', is only a continuation of the tautological treatment of the concept of opium which opiates because it has opium power – in other words, institutions institute because they have institutional power.[2] Only bringing institutions into relation with the relations of production can tell us more about them and in this way we arrive at the concept of the apparatus which is always an apparatus of the state. Thus, the complaint is already in place: *not only that we do the work of the state, but also we make something that is the apparatus of the state and we are in the order of the state as long as there is a relation of production that is a relation of exploitation.* And is this all we can and could say? Could we think that in this way we dismantle it? How else do we imagine its withering away? Could we say it is in crisis and that before our eyes, in the dark of contemporaneity, hypnagogically possible categories are illuminated, foremost among these the category

---

2. 'virtus dormitiva, coined by Molière in *The Imaginary Invalid.* In the play, he lampoons a group of physicians providing an explanation in macaronic Latin of the sleep-inducing properties of opium as stemming from its "virtus dormitiva".' https://en.wiktionary.org/wiki/dormitive_principle

of the possible? Is calling people to take part in the State's functioning whilst keeping their distance from existing apparatuses – in the case of local government, at a distance to the party organisation that cross-links also with the domain of local government – possible? By encouraging people to self-regulate relations in which they step through processes of decision-making and the production of ideology (if they go through self-organising and the invention of institutions and organisational forms), can these actions be interpreted and performed in a different way?

In mind we have an idea we have heard from associations of citizens that we know as The Ignorant Schoolmaster and His Committees. Their goal was to encourage people to take part in the distribution of the resources of civil society. We think that this was the formulation. It seems to us that this is a good way for people to go through the invention of institutions, because, finally, at a distance from the state (although conceptually and objectively they still produce an apparatus) they still do not have to follow the patterns of the division of labour and distribution that are supported by the ruling ideology and by rationalisations seeking a foothold in the technology of the production process. The fact that one operation can be divided into a set of actions and activities, does not mean that people also have to be divided, or pinned down to certain activities. Subjectivisation is possible also in subjectivity, not only in the objective method by which one knows society and a man's world. Knowledge in subjectivity is about thinking and finding what is possible in a given situation, not seeking another basis for its existence than the one in itself and in what we can do without the state. Without state power and its conquests which logically leave on hold everything for which we would need it. Because, if we think that one problem could be solved only with the help of the existing state power and from its position, then the solution of the problem is delayed until we can win power and thus it becomes clear that our problem is actually gaining power rather than solving a specific problem.

Citizens' associations, if tautology is driven out into the open of repetition, are none other than associations of citizens. From this perspective, *associated citizens* do not represent anybody, and every question and problematisation of representativeness or answering people's concerns falls away: people are associated so no one could or should represent them. Associated people do something and what they do depends on whether and how they agree. The whole question is in how much they will cling to the agreed, and we cling to it also when we, while thinking and discussing it, change it. Relations of production, since it is the relation of power that is being dismantled, and the codes are dissolved by thinking and by a struggle that is led through organisations that are nothing more than the struggle in ourselves when we're dealing with the need for the state in us. There is no need to psychologise the whole problem because we could have a politics whenever we distance ourselves from something, including the psychological rationalisation of our relations which are relations of power and that must be protected from all forms of power.

Now let us imagine this situation and processes in material production, e.g. factories. Is it possible in circumstances in which the constitution guarantees and protects private property? And is it feasible in circumstances in which the constitution preserves and guarantees the State, and even social property? Property as such is already a legally shrouded relation that is as difficult to see as production and political relations. Even when property is 'social', it won't open domains where the power relations are tactically allocated according to management strategies dominated by concerns for the whole and one, and which relentlessly totalise and close off our possible into an undoable and impossible.[3]

As we write, we think of the words of a friend. If we understand correctly, Sylvain Lazarus says that the subjectivity of people should not be found in the function of opposition to the state, rather instead it should be found in the search for a possible in which the word invention hasn't yet been exhausted, and to which the place is not an imaginary space of acting. The place is a place of thought, and if we understand him well, it is the place of principles. Thought may not spare itself and this is a way of existence for the place of politics. In principle, established exclusively by principles that are acceptable to all, and especially for those who are concerned with the possible. The question of antagonism, which is again on the agenda, and which is formed like a consensus and tacit agreement - a thought which would like to spare itself - is no more than an empty slogan. Antagonism is no longer able to establish a distance from the state because there is no ambition to establish a new one. The parliamentary gait of the

---

3. On the concept of 'social property' in the former Republic of Yugoslavia see https://mappingthecommons.wordpress.com/2012/12/01/self-managed-socialism/

revolutionaries completed an arc of revolutions and opened up the one of the state, which is now also at its end. The arc of the state is at its end, and we have now crisis of the state. Our time is a time of the crisis of the state, and perhaps, the beginning of something new. Of course, this crisis is not a sign of communism and of the abandonment of the state in that sense. Possibly, we are only facing a different model of governance. Thus, antagonism is nameable and has existed already for a long time in the dictionary of theories. *We share the opinion that the people are no longer seen in the light of their ability for antagonism, but in light of their ability to oppose antagonism.*

This is a hard place, especially while we are processing the experience of support and participation in protests in Serbia, which mobilise people exclusively through opposing the State. In this we need to see whether there is a room for thought, and we would like to meet also the famous invention of new places of acting. To generate it out of mud is not the job. To conclude that there's none - would that be a denial of politics? We would not say so. Rather, it would be to face the fact that a certain politics in one time and situation may not be possible. Because if we have exclusive opposition to the state, namely opposition to the current power, then we have a pleading for a different and better power which in this case ends up in support of an opposition presidential, party or 'independent' candidates for the sake of this power.

We posed ourselves the question: to search for new terms and political principles in one's own organisation and association of organisations or to *give oneself over* to the antagonism towards the state? To 'give oneself over' here has its meaning and place, and it is only seemingly contrary to opposition: *giving oneself over* isn't the same as *opposing* oneself to antagonism. In order to leave 'antagonism' to the strict sense that it has for Lenin and his Bolshevik politics, we will say this: antagonism is today the password of oppositional politics, and tomorrow already statism. In the media, however, oppositional politics is a program politics of viewership and spectacularisation, and, tomorrow already, of market ratings.

Political parties are certainly legitimate forms of organising, but in them there is no politics. They are cross-linked by the interests of individuals and groups, which at one point we named *menbetweening.*[4] Where even the dynamics of the couple opposition-position is lost, because we see that the political party leadership is working smoothly with the tip of the other parties (including the 'opposition'), rather than with their own membership that is left to struggle for survival and existence while subjected to a form of social mobility which is based precisely on these party principles. If this is the case in what is considered a political system (state-party), opposition policy, abandoned and lost, we must ask ourselves what is the fate of antagonism (as a slogan of oppositional politics) to the state? Should antagonism towards the state fulfil the empty place of the opposition? If that's the case, then it is a fact that antagonism already belongs to the domain of state *politics*. This is the meaning of being a mere slogan of oppositional politics.

One thing becomes clear and this is that criticism of the system is not politics. However, to consider that criticism of the system is not a politics does not mean automatically incarnating support for and reproducing the system. Under the threat of such an explicit condemnation of collaboration and recuperation it should require a space for new places of action, of principles and thinking. This would be a political issue. How to work with people? is a question that still lacks philosophers-radicals and activists-radicals. If only philosophy recalled its starting point, that reality is not a guarantee of truth, and that thought must be distinguished from being, it wouldn't by its postulates make an adequacy of theory with practice, or science with politics, or make something that exists outside the spaces of subjectivity and thought that are inhabited by people. If only activism recalled that the stake is to work with people in formulating the possible when analysing a situation, it wouldn't tie the possible to the situation but it would emphasise that the possible is reality. Then we would be closer to finding that reality in itself does not exist. Or, it only exists when it is constituted by the thinking and decision-making of people. Then we would have philosophy and theory that cannot plead for a position of first-principle thinking when the thinking of the people is concerned, and an activism that openly could be considered politics. Otherwise, we remain in determinism and description, i.e. in the listing of limitations that the state and capital imposes on us, or the perfect combination of theory, philosophy and activism.

---

4. The word 'menbetweening' was forged after the statement of one of the members of city council who brought his political party into an unprincipled coalition in order to maintain his place on the council and involvement in running the city.

So the point at which our interests and actions meet is the point of the possible. The goal is to do something with people, to formulate the possible and thus constitute reality. To discuss at the protests is not practice, but we think discussion must be present in the nucleus that organises protests. Supporting people in the protests, to the organising of protest we posed the question of *protest organisation* – the permanent process of viewing the situation and the problems we are in and trying to solve them on the basis of solidarity with discussions and decision-making in each new situation. But, if people do not persist in their thought and spare themselves in the invention of new arguments and formulations which perform the response to thought, in the best case just one part of the humanities come back in the reduction of the process of organising with people to 'participant research'. Since we said goodbye to sociology, in this situation we ask the question: what can be done without joining the description of constraints with a lament over the inability to do anything? The great challenge is how to address this phenomenon, not to give oneself over and not to oppose it, as if it is not determining us. For this thought we made space for the unnameable name: institutional commune, which is a space of joint action and principles.

Of what then is the name institutional commune? Neither of recuperation nor of reproduction. Eternity of ideology (for those who count on it to build the concept with which one makes an 'analysis of the situation') will make the existing condition everlasting if while counting on ideology we refuse to recognise the existence of thought. Recognition of thinking, on the other hand, opens the way to condemnation for recuperation. But then the situation is not the same: the prosecution will have to be proved in direct polemics that is no longer a theoretical elaboration, or even a philosophical debate, but the work with people, politics on the side of the people, or an attempt to do something with people – whatever that is.

DISORGANISED COLLECTIVITIES, PHANTOM ORGANISATIONS AND THE GROUP AS SUBJECT

ANTHONY ILES

> The group breaks in on the individual. Once community breaks in, voices are divided and speech is pluralized. The group functions as an instance of enunciation that would be the modern equivalent of the (collective) myths of antiquity and the (anonymous) epics of the Middle Ages. Having made a break with any authorial regime, it would allow the resurgence of that anonymous enunciation, belonging to great periods of community, in a contemporary setting.
> – Denis Hollier[1]

In this essay I attempt to combine a study of questions of political self-invention in small groups in the 1920s and 1930s, with tendencies in subcultural, anarchist and left-communist milieus of the 1990s in order to examine this recent cultural moment under the influence of its earlier precursors. In the 1990s small groups and networks experimented widely with techniques and technologies of informal organisation, networking, misinformation, fabulation and 'self-institution'. The period was dominated by the prospects of a new phase of the globalisation of both capitalism and class struggle.[2] In attempting to re-orient themselves to new challenges, small groups revisited tendencies experimented with in left cultural milieus in the 1930s, when historic events forced openings in the class separations between small political groups and culturally active artists and writers. In the 1990s the defeat of the workers' movement (felt tangibly in the UK through the 1986 Wapping dispute and 1984-85 Miners' strike), the break-up of the Socialist bloc and end of the cold war brought the question of communism back, not as a molar formation but rather as part of a dissolution of monolithic entities which ushered in molecular formations. In 1920s and 1930s Europe, major powers were taking a tumble and big media was still establishing itself while thousands of small magazines proliferated.[3] Likewise, by the 1990s monolithic media was looking obsolete and began to give way to smaller and more accessible media forms. Each period was marked by the interest of

---

1. Denis Hollier (Ed.), *The College of Sociology, 1937-39*, Minneapolis: University of Minnesota Press, 1988, p.xiv.
2. I take this notion of a 'globalisation' of both class and capital from the introduction to Mastaneh Shah-Shuja, *Zones of Proletarian Development*. London: OpenMute, 2008.
3. Cf. Stephen Bury, *Breaking the Rules: The Printed Face of the European Avant Garde 1900-1937*, London: British Library, 2007.

small groups in experimental approaches to problems of political sovereignty, in heterodox politics, alternative modes of knowledge production and distribution.[4] This could take the form of journals, unorthodox public or private meetings, para-academicism and new technologies such as radio and the internet.[5] Through such movements conceptualisations of self-made and accessible sovereignty (sovereignty as the absence of authority and the unseating of habitual subjectivities) were stitched closely into the patterns of everyday life through reconceptualisation of everyday expressions such as 'drunk as a lord'; characterisation of new tendencies in culture as 'sovereign and vague' or the promotion of the experience of the city through the 'disorientation of habitual reflexes'.[6]

Denis Hollier, discussing the College of Sociology in the epigraph to this essay, traces a lineage between romanticism and the avant-garde groups of the 20th century through which diverse actors constructed vehicles of collective enunciation adequate to the intensity of their times. My premise for this essay is that successive generations of cultural producers have taken questions of organisational form seriously and tested approaches to self-invention in sympathetic

---

4. As Wendy Brown proposes, with the waning of state power in the late-20th century classical theories of sovereignty do not become defunct, but rather the 'promise of sovereignty' becomes available and mobilised by extra-state actors and agencies: 'a composite figure of sovereignty drawn from classical theorists of modern sovereignty, including Thomas Hobbes, Jean Bodin, and Carl Schmitt, suggests that sovereignty's indispensable features include supremacy (no higher power), perpetuity over time (no term limits), decisionism (no boundedness by or submission to law), absoluteness and completeness (sovereignty cannot be probable or partial), nontransferability (sovereignty cannot be conferred without canceling itself), and specified jurisdiction (territoriality).' Wendy Brown, *Walled States, Waning Sovereignty*. Cambridge Mass.: MIT Press, 2010, p.22.
5. In terms of the 1930s, I am thinking here of Acephale's legendary visits to Bois de Boulogne and the College's meetings in the back of a bookshop or, to cite two characteristic examples from the 1990s, in 1998 Info Centre held an event at which a version of Howard Slater's text 'Post-Media Operators' was presented via a recording as 'an imaginary address', http://infopool.antipool.org/Stamm.htm; In 2001 Inventory held a journal issue launch in the atrium of an automated bank on the fringes of the City of London.
6. Quotations respectively from, Inventory, 'I Kingsland Passage', Inventory, Vol.1, No.3, 1996, p.5; Howard Slater, 'Post-Media Operators: Sovereign and Vague', *Datacide* No.7, August 2000, http://linkme2.net/wk and Guy-Ernest Debord, 'Introduction to a Critique of Urban Geography', *Les Lèvres Nues* No.6, 1955, available, http://linkme2.net/wj

relation to working class self-activity, coupled with antagonism towards the repressive operations of the state. This discussion therefore situates questions of political community inside struggles within the field of culture, locating there interactions with governmental, economic, mythic, theological or cosmological frameworks of sovereignty.

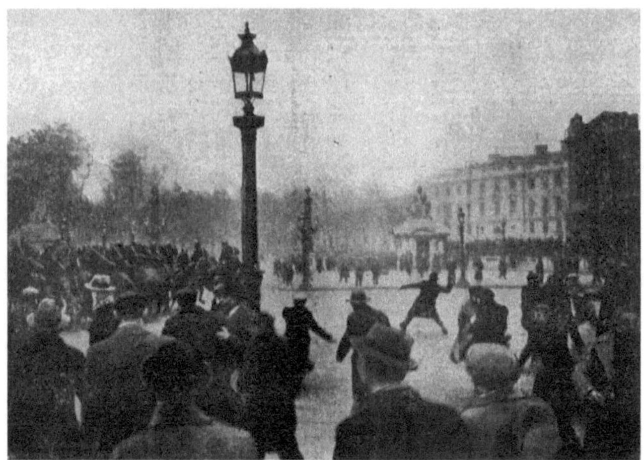

Riot in the Place de la Concorde, Paris, 7 February 1934

Autonomy or independence had been a preoccupation of modern cultural formations since the Jena romantics, but sovereignty – both in its complex conceptualisation by groups like the College and in the history of political philosophy – encompasses pre-modern articulations of community that were of interest to groupings critical of capitalist modernity. Anxiety over sovereignty and struggles to reconceptualise autonomy from below are two vectors through which these self-consciously unpopular and experimental movements can be connected to broader convulsions in the popular body, then and now.

La Critique Sociale

Generally understood in the Anglophone world as a philosopher of excess and individual transgression, Georges Bataille's anti-fascist and communist activities are the subject of more specialised research.[7] Bataille published several of his most important pre-war philosophical and political writings in a little-known journal named *La Critique Sociale*.[8] *La Critique Sociale* was founded by Collette Peignot and Boris Souvarine. Souvarine was a founding member of the French Communist Party, a correspondent with Lenin and Trotsky, member of the Third

International and associate of the Bolshevik party in the post-revolutionary 1920s. Souvarine's critical turn after 1924 and denunciation of the Soviet Union as a 'state capitalist' formation in 1927 positioned him to the left of both the PCF and Leon Trotsky.[9] When Souvarine was removed from his official roles in the PCF and the Comintern in 1924, Peignot stepped in to fund and share the editorial work with her companion on a new journal. *La Critique Sociale* (LCS) was launched in 1931. A Marxist journal dedicated to developing independent thought and action, it drew in the membership of the Democratic Communist Circle (DCC) which had become a hub of dissidents in anti-Stalinist Marxism, surrealism and philosophy. Georges Bataille began contributing to *La Critique Sociale* via his attendance of the DCC, and his first article was published in October 1931 the same year *Documents*, an eclectic journal edited by Bataille and others connecting ethnography, fine art and archaeology, lost its funding.

---

7. Apart from Hollier's excellent work, this is represented by research in an ethnographic-sociological-communist current of interpretation constituted by Michael Richardson and Krystof Fijalkowski's translations and anthologies: Georges Bataille, *The Absence of Myth: Writings on Surrealism*, (Ed. and Trans. Michael Richardson), London; New York: Verso, 1994; Michael Richardson and Krzysztof Fijałkowski (Eds. and Trans.), *Surrealism Against the Current: Tracts and Declarations*, London; Sterling, Va.: Pluto Press, 2001; book length studies by Stuart Kendall, Ibid., Benjamin Noys, *Georges Bataille a Critical Introduction*. London; Sterling, Va.: Pluto Press, 2000. Noys also contributes substantial arguments for the enduring influence of Georges Bataille upon the French Situationist International, (Noys 2000), p.110. The SI therefore, through its significant influence upon the UK anarchist and communist lefts in the 1980s, 1990s and 2000s, represents an important source of politicised interpretations of Bataille's work in the anglophone world, though this has tended to occur with little attention to Bataille's practical anti-fascist and communist activism.
8. These are 'The Critique of the Foundations of the Hegelian Dialectic' (March 1932), 'The Notion of Expenditure' (January 1933), 'The Problem of the State' (September 1933), 'The Psychological Structure of Fascism' (November 1933), there is also good reason for identifying the 'comrades' addressed in the epigraph to his essay 'The Use Value of the Marquis de Sade: An Open Letter to my Current Comrades' as those comrades in the Democratic Communist Circle. Allan Stoekl dates this text 1929 or 1930 and adds: 'Whilst it is clearly connected with Bataille's polemic against André Breton (and Breton's view of Sade), it also looks forward to a number of positions that Bataille developed in the *Critique sociale* essays'. Allan Stoekl, 'A Commentary on the Texts' in Georges Bataille, *Visions of Excess: Selected Writings, 1927-39* (Trans. and Ed. Allan Stoekl), Minneapolis: University of Minnesota Press, 1985, p.260.
9. Al Richardson, *What Became of the Revolution: Selected Writings of Boris Souvarine*, Socialist Platform, 2001, p.iv.

Stewart Kendall relates the participation of Bataille, along with others such as Michel Leiris, in *LCS* to their earlier work on *Documents*.

> Where *Documents* brought ethnography and aesthetics into encounter with one another and with psychoanalysis, *La Critique Sociale* set about revitalising Marxism through similar encounters. For Souvarine and his contributors, the challenge was to think the whole of society without denying themselves the insights offered by any useful set of tools.[10]

The DCC and *LCS* were centres of debate over revolutionary theory. Whilst in Germany Hitler's 1933 election underscored the defeats of 1921, in 1934 the riots in Paris precipitated, for some, expectations of a leftist revolution.[11] Philosopher and activist Simone Weil contributed to *La Critique Sociale*, but left, or never formally joined, the DCC because of an argument with Bataille over differing attitudes to revolutionary activity.[12]

> The revolution is for [Bataille] the triumph of the irrational, for me of the rational; for him a catastrophe, for me a methodical action in

---

10. Kendall, op. cit., p.89.

11. On 6 February 1934 France was rocked by an anti-republican march led by Royalist, militarist, nationalist and far-right leagues. United more by their militarised appearance than any specific ideology, they clashed with the French police and other demonstrators in the Place de la Concorde. A night of rioting ensued in which the National Assembly was attacked, 15 demonstrators killed and 2000 injured. The riots led to a constitutional crisis and the fall of the fragile coalition of left parties in parliament. Anti-fascist counter-demonstrations led by communists and socialists on 9 February brought another 10 deaths. A general strike held on 12 February provided an opportunity for left unity and eventually contributed to the establishment of the Popular Front which gained power the following year. However, this standard account perhaps undermines the complexity of the political positions usually ascribed to this moment, for example it is feasible that anti-parliamentarian communists also took part in the 6 February disorder, as Drieu La Rochelle's 1939 novel, *Gilles*, Paris: Gallimard, 2012, contends. On the riots in general and Bataille's participation see Stuart Kendall, op. cit., pp.104-105 and Denis Hollier, 'Birthrate and Deathwish', in Denis Hollier (Ed.), *A New History of French Literature*, Cambridge, Mass.: Harvard University Press, 1989, pp.919-924, pp.919-920.

12. A pertinent account of Weil's materialism is given in Lisa Jeschke, 'To Refuse to Imagine: Simone Weil's Materialism', in Lisa Jeschke and Adrian May (Eds.), *Matters of Time: Material Temporalities in Twentieth-Century French Culture*, Oxford; Bern, Berlin: Peter Lang, 2014, pp.41-61.

which one must strive to limit the damage; for him the liberation of
the instincts, and notably those that are generally considered
pathological, for me a superior morality. What is there in common?[13]

Weil's statement gives some indication of Bataille's insurrectionist
orientation at this time. Though ill, Bataille participated in the
February 1934 riots and counter-demonstrations.[14] Many on the right
shared some ground with his position – being also inspired by Georges
Sorel's account of revolution as messianic 'pure violence' – however, as
we shall see, Bataille's anti-fascism differentiated him both practically
and theoretically.[15] Indeed, the DCC was not the only group Bataille
was in contact with during the early 1930s. Through his friendship with
Arnaud Dandieu, a colleague at the Bibliothèque Nationale and
contributor to *Documents*, Bataille attended meetings of 'an anti-
Bolshevik, anti-Capitalist, anti-parliamentarian, corporative, pro-worker
[...] federalist group' *Ordre Nouveau*.[16] Another group Bataille frequented
was that around the journal *Masses*.[17] The *Masses* was allied to the
revolutionary wing of the Socialist Party (SFIO) and put forward a
programme of popular education celebrating the thought of German
revolutionaries Rosa Luxemburg and Karl Liebknecht and championing
the autonomous action of the working masses. The events of February
precipitated a split in the Democratic Communist Circle, a falling out
between Souvarine and Bataille as much interpersonal as political.[18]

---

13. [...] How is it possible to coexist in the same revolutionary organization when on
one side and the other one understands by revolution two contrary things? Simone
Weil quoted in Simone Pétrement, *La Vie de Simone Weil*, Fayard, 1973, p.306, in Kendall,
op. cit., pp.101-102.
14. Kendall, op. cit., p.105.
15. The Sorelian orientation of *La Critique Sociale* is evident in the plausible origin
of its name, Sorel's 'Bases de critique sociale', in Georges Sorel, *Matériaux d'une
théorie du prolétariat*, Paris: M. Rivière, 1919.
16. Michel Surya quoted in Kendall, op. cit., p.89. Though Dandieu died suddenly in
1933 other members of the group went on to publish an eponymous journal and
many developed connections with the Vichy regime, National Socialist and fascist
groups, though some also resisted both Vichy and the occupying German army, see
Christian Roy, 'Arnaud Dandieu and the Epistemology of Documents'. *Papers of
Surrealism*, No.7, 2007, pp.1-23, available:
http://www.surrealismcentre.ac.uk/papersofsurrealism/journal7/acrobat%20files/a
rticles/roypdf.pdf
17. Edited by René Lefeuvre. Bataille's sometime lover during the early 1930s, the
photographer Dora Maar, contributed to the journal,
https://bataillesocialiste.wordpress.com/revues/masses-1931-1948/

The group's political and affective affiliations had been complex, a situation Weil alluded to:

> The Circle is a psychological phenomenon. It is made up of mutual affection, obscure affinities, in particular of repressions and contradictions between and even within its members that have not been brought out into the open.[19]

The forcefield constituted between members of *La Critique Sociale* and the Democratic Communist Circle was borne out not only in the strong engagement of the journal with the emergent field of research constituted by psychoanalysis, but also in a more internal sense of self-reflection legible in Weil's statement on the strong attachments within a group she never actually committed to joining formally.[20] Whilst it remains opaque exactly why LCS split, the riots and the palpable threat of fascist movements in France catalysed differences between its members. Souvarine moved swiftly towards the socialist party (SFIO), and Bataille, Peignot and Weil moved in the opposite direction towards an ultra-left and explicitly anti-fascist grouping.

Counter-Attack

Out of the explosion of *LCS* and DCC after the February riots emerged a new concord between Bataille's group of dissident surrealists and the Bretonian surrealist group, who had recently severed their ties with the PCF over its authoritarian isolation of Leon Trotsky and Jacques Doriot.[21] Together members of the Democratic Communist Circle, the

---

18. Bataille and Collette Peignot AKA 'Laure' became lovers during this period.
19. Simone Weil, unattributed source quoted in Michel Surya, op. cit., p.170.
20. The concentration of desires in these groups are allegorised in Bataille's novel *The Blue of Noon*, which features characters closely resembling Weil (Lazare) and Collette Peignot (Dirty) traversing the erotic and political limits of 1930s Europe and, again retrospectively, in the bitter comments reserved for Bataille in Boris Souvarine's reflection on the journal in a 1983 reprint of *La Critique Sociale*. By then a staunch anti-communist, Souvarine denounced Bataille as a sexual pervert and a fascist sympathiser who perverted Laure and stole his journal title. Boris Souvarine (Ed.), *La Critique Sociale*, Paris: Editions de la difference, 1983.
21. André Breton et al, 'When the Surrealists Were Right', declaration after the International Congress for the Defence of Culture August, 1935 in *Surrealism Against the Current: Tracts and Declarations*, op. cit., pp.105-111, p.108.

Masses, the pacifist journal *Clarté* and the surrealist group formed an anti-fascist, anti-Popular Front platform named *Contre-Attaque: Union de Lutte des Intellectuels Révolutionnaires*. The coalition, geographically divided under the names Marat and Sade between the left and right banks of the Seine, was relatively short-lived. *Contre-Attaque* attempted to champion working class struggle against the class compromises of the Popular Front, advocating a combination of avant-garde

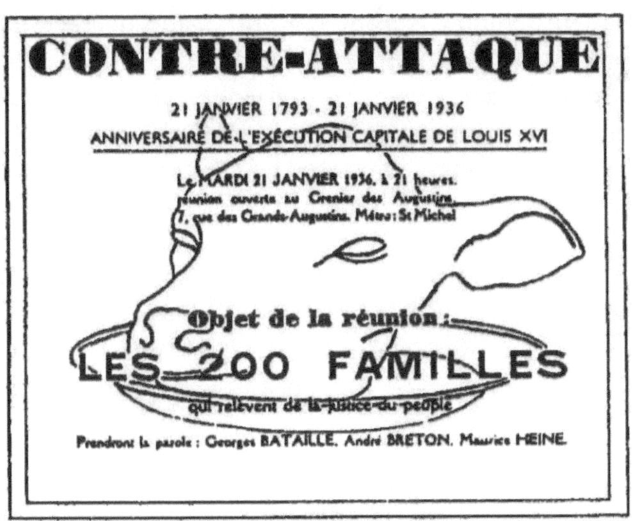

Flyer for a *Contre-Attaque* demonstration on the anniversary
of the execution of Louis XVI, January 1933

spontaneity: 'the constitution of a doctrine resulting from immediate experiences.'; borrowing elements of the new right wing movements: 'to make use of the weapons created by fascism [...] in the service of universal interest of people' and advocacy of an 'organic creation', a true dictatorship of the proletariat: 'an uncompromising dictatorship of the armed people'.[22] The group combined Marxism, concepts drawn from Georges Sorel and Alexandre Kojeve, and surrealist automatism.[23] Indeed in this they followed and developed the schismatic Marxist-surrealist poetics primed by the short-lived journal, *Légitime défense*, published by Paris-based Martinican students in 1932.[24] Breton and

---

22. 'Counter-attack: Union of the Struggle of Revolutionary Intellectuals' in *Surrealism Against the Current: Tracts and Declarations*, op. cit., pp.114-117, p.115.
23. Nikolaj d'Origny Lübecker, *Community, Myth and Recognition in Twentieth-Century French Literature and Thought*, London; New York: Continuum, 2009, p.25.

Bataille discussed the creation of new revolutionary language within the group, and through this attempted to embody violence as the cohering force of new 'organic' forms of community. This was oriented by the desire to create a new myth with which to refute the stagnant forms of parliament, party and nation.[25] However, we know very little of the group's practical actions.[26]

Leaving behind Souvarine to form *Contre-Attaque*, Bataille and others from *LCS* also left behind them the last authoritarian traces of party membership and party machinations.[27] The militants of *Contre-Attaque* sought to 'virulently' sever their revolutionary programme from support of any party, nation or state, but they clung onto a belief in their authority as militants exhorting the class towards revolution. The Moscow trials of August 1936 brought home the counterrevolutionary and homicidal nature of Stalin's regime, while the defeat of disorganised opposition (to Stalin and Franco) in Spain became clear the following year, as did the Popular Front's feeble support for the rebels when it fell out of power in June 1937.[28] With the Popular Front in pieces and Stalinism gaining influence in Spain and France, *Contre-*

---

24. 'We are speaking to those who are not already branded as killed established fucked-up academic successful decorated decayed provided for decorative prudish opportunists.' 'Légitime défense: Declaration' (1932), in Michael Richardson (Ed.), *Refusal of the Shadow: Surrealism and the Caribbean*, (Trans. Krzysztof Fijalkowski and Michael Richardson), New York: Verso, 1996, pp.40-43, p.42.

25. Cf. 'Counter-attack: Union of the Struggle of Revolutionary Intellectuals', op. cit.

26. Michel Surya indicates that only two actions by the group were recorded, the restaged execution of the Louis XVI and a protest in support of some young women who had run away from a reform school for which members of the group were arrested. *Bataille: An Intellectual Biography*, op. cit., p.227.

27. 'The political communities with which [Bataille] was involved refused the party form and would be central to his reflections on community'. Noys, op. cit., p.8. On the other hand, Souvarine's authoritarianism as a party man of the PCF comes across strongly in *What Became of the Revolution* and there are strong suggestions it continued as a form of 'righteousness' within his role as Editor of *La Critique Sociale*, see Michèle Richman, 'Fascism Reviewed: Georges Bataille in "La Critique Sociale"', *South Central Review* Vol.14, No.3/4, 1997, pp.14-30, p.15.

28. Though the French Popular Front was formed in self-conscious support of the anarchist, communist and Republican forces engaged in the Spanish Civil War, the left coalition in government did little in terms of practical support sending only 'a few planes'. Furthermore the French Popular Front government not only granted no concessions to its colonial subjects at home or abroad but actively repressed proletarian movements in Algeria, see Gilles Dauvé, 'When Insurrections Die', *Endnotes* No.1, October, 2008, p.55.

Attaque lost traction. After the failure of Contre-Attaque Bataille again parted company with Breton, the Bretonian surrealists left the group accusing Bataille of 'sur-fascism'.[29]

Bataille's subsequent step towards open and closed conspiracies within the secret group Acéphale, *Acéphale* the journal and the College of Sociology eschewed oppositionality in favour of forms of group study and collective inter-personal experiment, the obverse of outward propagandising or recruitment. This was a reaction against the shrinking space for a critical politics, i.e. one not dominated by either Stalinism or parliamentary socialism. The Popular Front in Spain and France had initially supported strikes but after taking over power, applied the same labour discipline established before them.[30] After all, the Spanish and French working classes had by then also shrugged their shoulders at the prospects. After 1937 all roads led to war, and definitively away from revolution.[31] Superintending Bataille's shift towards these clandestine and para-academic groupings was an apparent turn from politics towards religion, broached in one of the first texts written for the journal *Acéphale*, 'The Sacred Conspiracy'.

> What looks like politics, and imagines itself to be political, will one day unmask itself as a religious movement.[32]

The shift to a religious register rejected the stabilising force of politics in mediating disagreements and deflating conflict. The statement mocks politics, but also subverts the liberal neutrality of religion. '*La conjuration sacrée*' (sacred conspiracy) mocks the '*union sacrée*', formulated by the Prime Minister Rene Viviani and the President of the

---

29. Immediately after *Contre-Attaque* the Trotskyist surrealists close to Breton attempted to regroup around a short-lived new journal, *Clé*.

30. Cf. Michael Seidman, *Workers Against Work: Labor in Paris and Barcelona During the Popular Fronts*. Berkeley: University of California Press, 1991. Whilst the empirical information presented in this work supports my point I take some distance from the direction Seidman took after the writing of this book.

31. As surrealist Benjamin Péret put it in 1939, 'The working class [...] having lost sight of its own goals, no longer sees any urgent reason to be killed defending the bourgeois democratic clan against the fascist clan, i.e. in the last analysis, for the defence of Anglo-French capital against Italo-German imperialism. The civil war increasingly became an imperialist war.' *Clé*, No.2, quoted in Gilles Dauvé, 'When Insurrections Die', *Endnotes* No.1, October, 2008, p.59.

32. Kierkegaard quoted in the epigraph to Georges Bataille, 'The Sacred Conspiracy', *Visions of Excess*, op. cit., pp.178-181, originally published in *Acéphale* No.1, 24 June, 1936.

French Republic Raymond Poincaré on the eve of World War I, a political truce between the left and the government to suspend strikes and demonstrations for the defence of the nation. Therefore Acéphale represented a rejection of a form of politics governed by compromise in favour of something embodied, covert and potentially ungovernable. The name of the College of Sociology gestures towards the more indistinct phenomenon of the 'Invisible College', first mentioned in

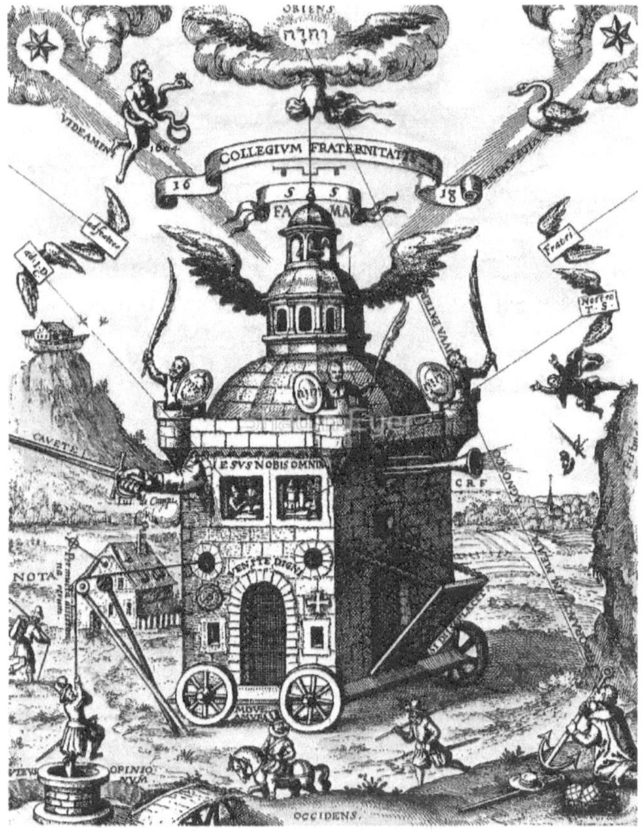

The Invisible College or The Temple of the Rosy Cross, 1618

17th century Rosicrucian pamphlets. That 'College' beckoned to an international, para-institutional intellectual exchange between occultists, alchemists, philosophers and men of science, an open conspiracy offering its correspondents anonymity and freedom from religious or state censorship. The spectre of an ambulatory, clandestine and international community of correspondents would be revived by Alexander Trocchi in the 1960s as 'The Invisible Insurrection of a Million Minds' and more recently by the Imaginary Party and Invisible

Committee.[33] If Acéphale was marked by withdrawal and insularity, the College suggests dispersal and eclecticism, with WWII looming neither should be seen as a clearcut retreat, but rather twinned efforts to gather forces and assess the coming storm.

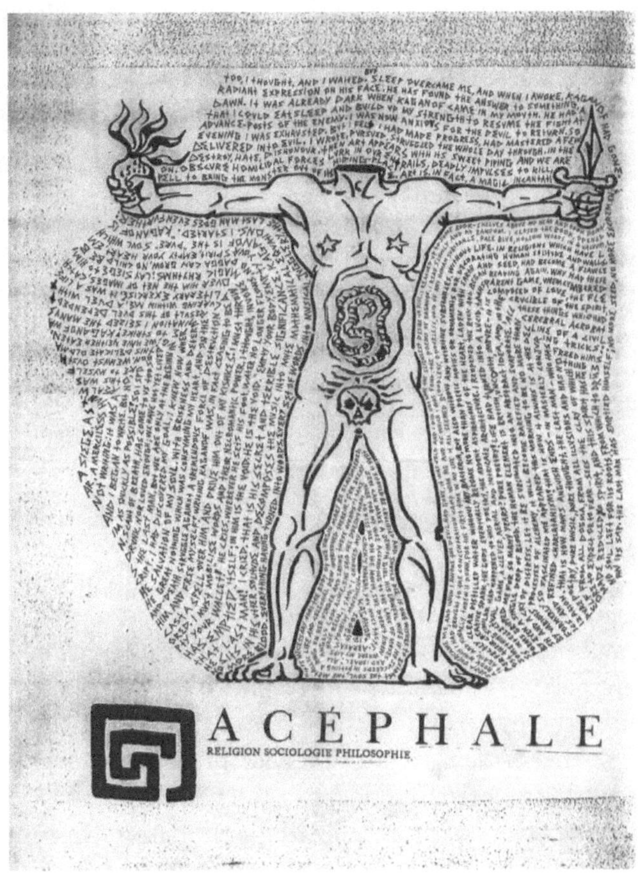

André Masson and Georges Bataille, Flyer for
Acéphale journal, n.d.

33. Alexander Trocchi, 'A Revolutionary Proposal: Invisible Insurrection of a Million Minds', available, http://www.notbored.org/invisible.html originally published as 'Technique du coupe du monde', *Internationale Situationniste*, No.8, January 1963. The Imaginary Party, part of a 'public and secret, legal and illegal' political campaign, was the invention of Belgian Surrealist Marcel Mariën, 'Théorie de la révolution mondiale immédiate', *Les lèvres nues*, 1958.

To Have Done With the Problem of the Head

Measures of Acéphale's 'success' would seem difficult to obtain. Without a shred of pragmatism, apart from its development of clandestinity, its primary goal was not to produce the extension, reproduction and development of the organisation itself, but dissolve itself by 'tak[ing] part in the destruction of the existing world'.[34] Under the aegis of Acéphale Bataille challenged forms of monocephalism: the god-head dictators Stalin and Hitler, the authority of a Christian God, and the little fascist within – the individual ego.

> The only society full of life and force, the only free society, is the bi- or poly- cephalic society that gives the fundamental antagonisms of life a constant explosive outlet, but one limited to the richest forms [...] the very principle of the head is the reduction to unity, the *reduction* of the world to God.[35]

Acéphale announced the coming to self-consciousness of a new logic on the left, the rejection of superficial unity, goal-led action and self-sacrifice, a tendency towards political entropy, an undoing within the logic of organisation in order to avoid becoming rigid or bureaucratic, a becoming headless. Acéphale prefigured the death of a certain form of community and belonging; it was the transition to the group as indeterminate party. As Jean-Luc Nancy notes, this tendency was to be continued after the interruptions of WWII in the de-identificatory logic of Bataille's journal *Critique*, which likewise played a path-breaking role in French publishing in coming decades.[36] The fidelity of *La Critique Sociale* to Marx's project of an intellectual and materialist investigation of society; its anti-authoritarianism and anti-Bolshevism; critical independence; intellectual pluralism and anti-academicism, had in the

---

34. Georges Bataille, 'Program (Relative to Acephale)', *October*, No.36, 1986, p.79.
35. Georges Bataille, 'Propositions', *Visions of Excess*, op. cit., p.199.
36. 'A history of journals in France after 1950 would certainly shed light the gradual disappearance of groups, collectives and communities of "ideas", and thus on the evolution of the representation of a "community" in general. The journal set up by Bataille, *Critique*, had a completely different premise, quite removed in its conception from a theoretical identity. *Critique* nevertheless had, in the 1960s and 1970s, a "network" effect: it was a meeting place for those who distanced themselves from all communities.' Jean-Luc Nancy, 'The Confronted Community', (Trans. Amanda Macdonald), *Postcolonial Studies*, Vol. 6, No. 1, pp.23–36, 2003, Note #3 pp.34-35.

pre-war period set the parameters for a number of heterodox projects
which explored similar positions through self-publishing in France and
elsewhere from the late 1940s to the present: in France, *Critique*;
Socialisme ou Barbarie; *Potlatch*; *International Situationiste*; *Negation*;
Troploin; *Théorie Communiste*; *Tiqqun*; in the UK: *Antagonism, Aufheben,
Autotoxicity, Break/Flow, Communist Headache, Datacide, Endnotes, Here and
Now, Inventory, Infopool, Letters, Re:Action, Smile, Unpopular Books*; in the
US: Autonomedia, Not Bored, *Midnight Notes* and many more. These
projects were characterised by three connected activities: the attempt
to theorise the arrangement of political forces of their times;
participation in political movements and events (demonstrations, riots,
meetings); and the discussion and publication of image and text in

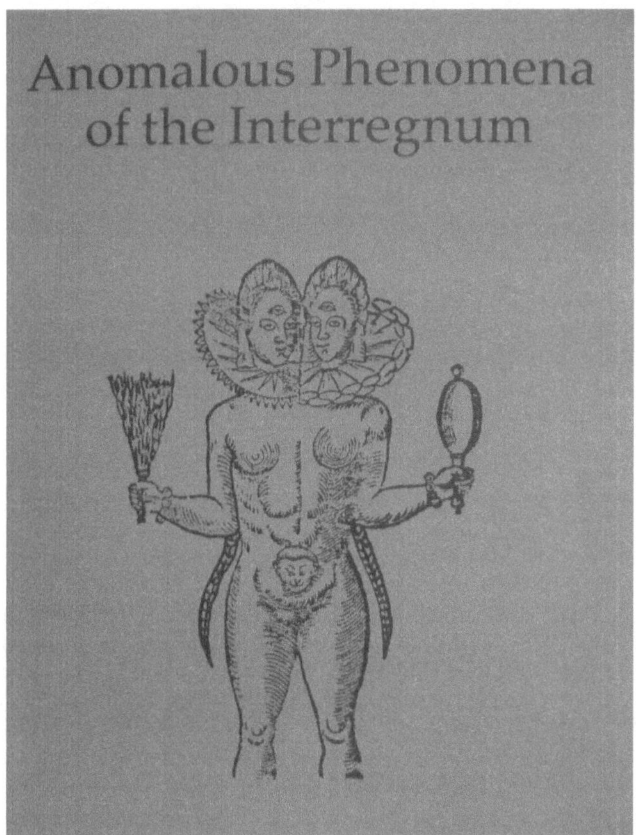

Anon., Reproduction of a pamphlet published during the
English Civil War, *The Anomalous Interregnum*

networks of affinity. These were not solely 'cultural' or 'artistic'
journals, but political projects which created their own culture of

writing, authorship (or its obfuscation) and readership. Rather than simply acting as the publishing arms of political groups, they were committed to the politics of independent small groups, contributing theoretical discussions of significance for working class, anti-colonial and feminist struggles, but developed in creative and critical independence from them. The tendency of these groups to avoid molar forms such as parties or institutions was of course not specific to them alone. A host of scenes from feminism to punk developed a ground upon which to orientate through micropolitical affiliations.[37] What distinguishes the self-publishing projects in which I am interested here is their commitment to theorisations of capitalism and development of heterodox communist positions upon which they established their own forms of authority and staked their propensity for criticism of the 'existing state of things'.

Why, Then, Realizing the Futility of the Act, Do You Band Together into Groups?

Denis Hollier emphasises the mythopoeisis and polyphony appropriate to a grouping which hovered between rumour and conspiracy.[38] The collective creation of a myth begun with Contre-Attaque, in a fusion of the interests of Breton and Bataille, continued and was concentrated through Acéphale, then dispersed again through the individual

---

37. Some useful literature which covers this field is Stephen Duncombe, *Notes from Underground: Zines and the Politics of Alternative Culture*. Bloomington, Ind.: Microcosm Publishing, 2008; Alison Piepmeier, *Girl Zines: Making Media, Doing Feminism*. New York: New York University Press, 2009; Jason Skeet and Mark Pawson (Eds.), *Counter Intelligence: Zines, Comics, Pamphlets, Flyers: Catalogue of Self-Published and Autonomous Print-Creations*, London: 121 Centre, 1995; 'Worlds in Waiting: The Promise of Little Magazines', *Dissent Magazine*, 19 November 2015, https://www.dissentmagazine.org/online_articles/political-role-little-magazines-dissent-history, Nicholas Thoburn, *Anti-Book: On the Art and Politics of Radical Publishing*, Minneapolis: Minnesota University Press, 2016 and Elke Zobl, *Feminist Media: Participatory Spaces, Networks and Cultural Citizenship*, Bielefeld: transcript, 2012.
38. 'The College of Sociology (1937-1939) did not last, nor can it be summed up – except as a chorus that is not in unison, the soloists too numerous and their voices too distinct, without unanimity. It had no first person. And, with very few exceptions, it is absent from literature (or sociology) manuals. Black holes elude the surveyor's radar, and the College, too dense for detection, does not show up on maps.' Denis Hollier, 'Foreword' *The College of Sociology*, op. cit., p.x.

personalities and agendas of the College.[39] These threads were picked up by small groups in the latter half of the 20th century and the substance in them found new outlets in self-publishing scenes which, after the molar organisations aligned with (or policing) the workers' movement began to crumble, found new uses. But this trajectory has profound ambiguities. Was the tendency towards dispersion a sign of defeat, or a victory over authoritarianism? Was the flight to fight on the terrain of culture a sign of weakness or potential strength? Is molecularisation a form of resistance, or merely a form of participation in the dynamic directed by capital's shifting needs?

Sam Moss, writing in the 1930s, presciently summarising the tendency towards pessimism in small revolutionary groups on the eve of World War II, drew counterintuitive optimism from these developments:

> [I]n this very atrophy of all groups that would lead the masses out of capitalism into another society we are seeing for the first time in history the objective end to all political leadership and to the division of society into economic and political categories.[40]

Moss was part of a 'Councilist' tendency within the Internationalist Anglophone Marxist left that decidedly did 'not consider themselves vanguards of the workers, nor leaders of the workers'. The role left to them in the situation where 'we function outside the spheres of production, where the class struggle is fought' and 'we are isolated from the large mass of workers' presented a taboo that few revolutionary groups could face. Having no 'manifest destiny' as leaders of the workers, what were isolated groups of radicalised intellectuals to do? His answer is humble, but firm. The comrades, those who recognise in themselves with humility 'no more significance than their fellow human beings', band together for the purposes of 'sharing a common

---

39. Contre-Attaque is usually thought of as primarily Bataille's vehicle but Nikolaj Lübecker makes the less common argument that the formation of the group realised Breton's ambitions to 'reconcile surrealism as a method of creating a collective myth with the much more general movement involving the liberation of man', Breton quoted in *Community, Myth and Recognition in Twentieth-Century French Literature and Thought,* op. cit., p.24.
40. Sam Moss, 'The Impotence of the Revolutionary Group', *Living Marxism* Vol.4, No.7 (1939): pp.216-220, available with a commentary by Frère Dupont, http://fendersen.holeinthewallhosting.com/moss.html

feeling of rebellion'. Opposing the subjective impotence of small groups is the 'objective end to all political leadership'. '[T]he reason that the rebellious class conscious workers band into groups outside the spheres of the real class struggle is only that there is as yet no revolutionary movement within them.' The ultimate aim of every revolutionary group would be to disappear into revolutionary movement.

As Howard Slater put it later in the essay 'New Acéphale', published in the pages of *Inventory* in the 1990s: 'Any group must put itself in doubt in this way for no sooner does it try to encapsulate and

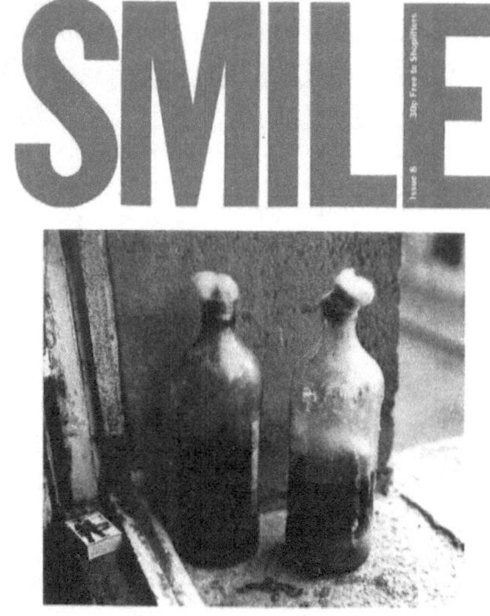

Stewart Home (Ed.), *Smile*, No.8, 1985

ideologise its vectors than it opens itself up to an insensate manipulation.'[41] For Slater, amidst a society built-up of 'rackets', the 'group as subject' (Félix Guattari) must ward off 'ulterior motives' and produce itself as 'a means towards withstanding and retaliating against the security of achievement, of maintaining an objectiveless direction.'[42] Such groupings, following in the footsteps of Acéphale, can be considered, in Slater's terms, 'phantom organisations': 'imaginary groupings of one or several that offer some means of conceptual

---

41. Howard Slater, 'New Acéphale', *Inventory*, Vol.2 No.3, 1997, pp.71-75, p.72.
42. Ibid.

secession, some means of supported self-exile from those hermetic orthodoxies for whom counter-cultural activists are, as "culturalists", not to be taken seriously.'[43] In the hands of Maurice Blanchot and Jean-Luc Nancy the myth of Acéphale became part of an ethical turn towards 'literary communism' and away from the development of communist

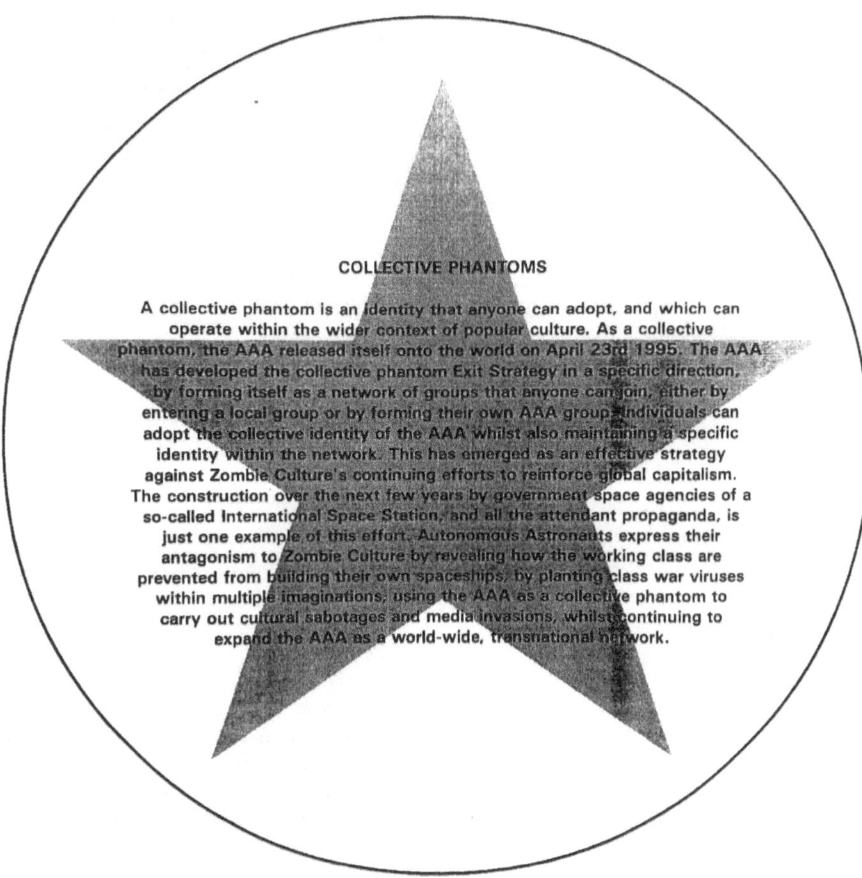

Association of Autonomous Astronauts' contribution to *Infotainment*, No.6, 1999

politics with any reference to class, capital or exploitation.[44] It seems urgent to stress the passing relevance of this move towards postmodern quietism, for the informal and non-academically aligned groups in

---

43. Howard Slater, 'Burdened By the Absence of Billions', 18 September 2008, http://www.metamute.org/editorial/articles/burdened-absence-billions

discussion moved in a very different direction, actively theorising new forms of class-based resistance and seeking historical rupture with capitalist modernity.

On Organisation

The dynamic Moss had identified developed towards the destruction of the purpose of the group leading to a negation of the revolutionary cell's false authority. In the commensurate work of Jacques Camatte and Gianni Collu of the 1960s and 1970s, notably in a seminal text 'On Organisation', their thought represents a conscious obstruction to the renewal of micro-authoritarian groups.[45] Yet, Camatte and Collu's view at this time also presents a form of hypostatisation in its dismissal of any resistance to capital from within its own dynamic i.e. the relationship between capital and labour.[46] Broadly put, Collu and Camatte found their insights into groups on a theory of capital as having become a 'total being' which dominates the entirety of human life. But, without labour as the contradictory 'special commodity' – a body with a consciousness conscripted within the productive process –

---

44. Cf. Maurice Blanchot, *The Unavowable Community*. Barrytown, N.Y.: Station Hill Press, 1988 and Jean-Luc Nancy, *The Inoperative Community*, Minneapolis: University of Minnesota Press, 1991. For recent criticisms of an 'ethical turn' in non-academic post-activist milieus see Research and Destroy, 'Hic Nihil, Hic Salta! (a critique of Bartlebyism)', July 2015,
https://researchanddestroy.wordpress.com/2015/07/29/hic-nihil-hic-salta/
45. 'The economy reduces politics (the old art of organizing) to a pure and simple epiphenomenon of its own real process. It lets it survive as the museum of horrors such as parliament with all its farces, or else in the rancorous undergrowth of the small "extra-parliamentary" rackets, which are all identical regarding their formal or informal organization, but compete obscenely with their "strategic" chatter.' Gianni Collu, 'Transition', from David Brown (Ed.), *Origin and function of the party form 1962: Essays by Jacques Camatte and Gianni Collu*, London 1977, available https://www.riff-raff.se/en/furtherreading/transition.php see also Jacques Camatte and Gianni Collu, 'On Organization', Jacques Camatte, *This World We Must Leave and Other Essays*, (Trans. Alex Trotter), Brooklyn, N.Y.: Autonomedia, 1995.
46. This tendency in a number of post-WWII communist positions is addressed (with regard to Theodor W. Adorno, Antonio Negri and Jacques Camatte) by Andrés Sáenz De Sicilia, *The Problem of Subsumption in Kant, Hegel and Marx*, PhD Dissertation, Kingston University, 2016, p.191, available http://eprints.kingston.ac.uk/36138/>; Endnotes, 'False Totalities Don't Have Exits' and (with reference to the Frankfurt School) in my own 'This Implies Nothing', the last two texts are to be published in *What is to be Done Under Real Subsumption*, London and Berlin: Mute, (forthcoming) 2018.

little remains with which to define capitalism as a specific mode of production, let alone as a contradictory one.[47] Félix Guattari's formulation of the 'group as subject' also sprang from the criticisms of Marxist and neo-Marxist parties as systems of representation imposing their monopoly upon a diversity of desires reduced to a class or political subject, criticisms initially developed by militants such as Moss. Against the 'problem of the head' – the forms of vertical hierarchical authority railed against by Bataille – Guattari presented a shift in 'highly complex industrialised society' in the post-war period towards molecularisation, a diffusion of power, through which 'minor' struggles assume a new importance. He writes, 'Only a group as subject can work within the semiotic fluxes, destroying the significations, opening the language to different desires and creating different realities.'[48] This would be seen to have played out in the aforementioned defeats of the workers' movement in the UK when tightly organised mining and print workers failed to extract concessions from Thatcher's government, whilst the disorderly riot and refusal of protests against Poll Tax, a classic sphere of circulation struggle, is widely credited with bringing that government to its knees. What therefore marked out the efforts to pick up these concerns in the 1980s and 1990s then was the exploration of what communism might mean without the classical workers' movement, but with a sustained effort to renew and reexamine the categories with which Marx had provided it.

Occult Fascism

Another vector which relates to Bataille's orientation in *La Critique Sociale* and to this later scene threads through research into fascism, the occult and secret societies.[49] Explorations by Stewart Home, Fabian Tompsett and others of the relationship between neo-nazi movements and the occult developed, as with Bataille and the partisans of *Contre-Attaque*, out of the confrontation with fascists and neo-fascists in the streets. In the UK a

---

47. As much seems to be admitted when Collu writes: 'If capital dominates everything to the point of being able to identify itself with the social being, it seems, on this basis, to disappear.' 'Transition', op. cit.
48. Félix Guattari, 'The Micro-Politics of Fascism', in *Molecular Revolution*, (Trans. Rosemary Sheed), pp.217-232. London: Penguin, 1984, p.221.

decade of streetfighting resulted in the definitive rout of these groups in terms of street presence in 1992 at the so-called Battle of Waterloo.[50] However, two consequences resulted. Firstly the internal critique of anti-fascist groups who had developed an identitarian, macho and violent subculture dedicated to confronting fascists. Secondly, as neo-fascists and racists were forced underground they turned to the exploration of occult forms, myths and more obscure fascist positions in order to renew their politics.[51] The turn to mythopoeisis in Home and other's hands fused the small network structures and tactics of avant-garde groups with left-communist politics and critique, proposing, in opposition to occult fascism, to 'develop [...] a system of symbol manipulation which is completely autonomous of the state.'[52] In this spirit of plasticity, the group or organisation became a medium, in which authority and identification were imitated and drawn out, examined as *fait social*, objects to be played with and reconfigured.[53] 'We speak collectively although the Neoist Alliance is a phantom organisation. *Re:Action* is the organ of a simulated (if not a fictive) organisation. We seek the disappearance of the occult and the art world, but not the social.'[54] New projects took on the critique of 'oppositionism', critical of classically anti-imperialist and anti-fascist positions, and developed out of them forms which sought to proliferate and provoke difference.[55] Schooled in avant-garde history and subculture, rather than confronting the distorting force of nationalism with a new form of realism, the London Psychogeographical Association

---

49. Cf. Georges Bataille, 'The Psychological Structure of Fascism' in *Visions of Excess: Selected Writings, 1927-39*, op. cit., pp.137-160; Georges Bataille, 'The Sacred Conspiracy', Ibid., pp.178-181. Georges Bataille, 'The Sorcerer's Apprentice', *The College of Sociology*, op. cit., pp.12-23; Georges Bataille and Roger Caillois, 'Sacred Sociology and the Relationships between "Society", "Organism", and "Being"', Ibid., pp.73-84; Roger Caillois, 'Brotherhoods, Orders, Secret Societies' Ibid., p.145-156.
50. 'Blood and Honour routed by Anti- Fascist Action at Waterloo 1992', https://www.youtube.com/watch?v=zpXMObMdR8I
51. This shift is fictionalised excellently in Max Schaeffer's novel *Children of the Sun*, London: Granta, 2010, particularly pp.184-189.
52. Neoist Alliance, 'Marx, Christ and Satan United in Struggle', Stewart Home (Ed.) *Mind Invaders: A Reader in Psychic Warfare, Cultural Sabotage and Semiotic Terrorism*, London: Serpent's Tail, 1997, pp.111-112.
53. *Fait social* (social fact) is a key term in sociologist Émile Durkheim's work, an influence on Bataille and his collaborators on *Documents* and at the College of Sociology.
54. Re:Action, 'Follow Me: Re:Action Unexplained by Robyn Whitlaw', *Infotainment*, No.2, London: Info Centre, 1998, p.8.

(LPA, published by Fabian Tompsett of Unpopular Books) and other affiliated groups sought to attack fascism and nationalism on its own ground of myth and fantasy. In the work of the LPA imaginative hoaxes and fabulations satirised this new turn in far-right politics, tying it together with satirical accounts of the 'British Establishment': ruling class and royalty, the symbolic architecture and 'ley lines' of the landscape of London and the British Isles.[56] If in fascist propaganda, '[r]eality is put to work faking itself, and minds exhausted are no longer permitted even to dream', as Siegfried Kracauer put it, a left-communist animation of myth and counter-factual invention would provide energising critical force to

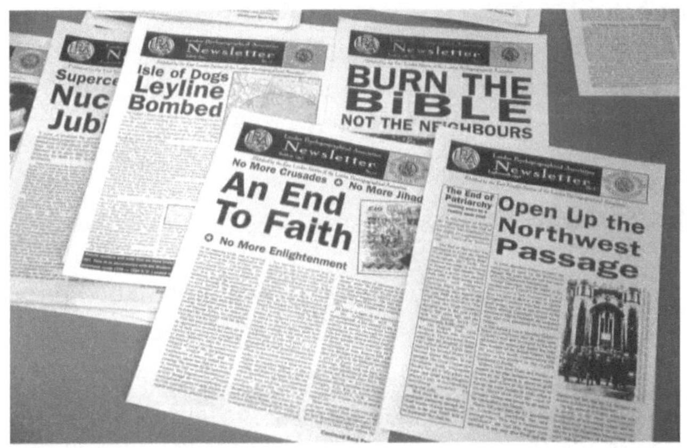

London Psychogeographic Association Magazines displayed
at Info Centre, London, 1998-1999

social currents refusing fascism, nationalism and capitalism. The exploration of esoteric myths, particularly those bound up with ancient

---

55. Bataille's position established in one of the first texts presented to the College of Sociology suggests this recoil from anti-fascist politics: 'Enslaved themselves, breaking anything that will not bend to a necessity to which they submit before others, men of action blindly abandon themselves to the current that bears them along and gathers speed from their helpless thrashing.' Georges Bataille, 'The Sorcerer's Apprentice', *The College of Sociology*, op. cit., pp.12-23, p.17. For a recent development and concentration of this approach, e.g. 'opposition never exceeds what it opposes. Its fanatical form, accumulated as violent acts, may be afforded only by the most conservative of organisations.', see Frère Dupont, 'Tinned Chunks: An Introduction of the Rejection of Everything Through Moments in the Description of Deep Opposition', (undated, unpaginated pamphlet) c.2015.
56. Several texts by the London Psychogeographical Association (LPA) are compiled in the anthology *Mind Invaders*, op. cit., original pamphlets and newsletters published by the LPA can be consulted at Mayday Rooms, London, http://maydayrooms.org/.

sites in the landscape of the British Isles, connected with the preoccupations of a broad subculture of ravers and new age travellers: a new 'organic movement' whose practice of illegally occupying land, environmental activism and inventing new collective rituals through music, drugs and dancing found little support or interest from the traditional left. The riotous assemblies celebrated by the Melancholic Troglodytes, publishing in Farsi and English, presented a secret history of revolt in the ancient and contemporary Middle East continuous with the ruptures around anti-summit protests and spontaneous football hooliganism.[57] A future-oriented, though with large portions of humour and humility, satellite of the LPA was the Association of Autonomous Astronauts (AAA) whose programme of autonomous community space travel and 5-year plan of 'moving in many directions at once' looked to fight capital at its science-fictional perimeter fences.

Sovereign and Headless

The image of Acéphale loomed large and frequently in the journal *Inventory*'s vocabulary, both in written contributions and in numerous projects by the editors who made the journal.[58] The group emphasised the centrality of humour to the Bataillean project of restoring sovereignty to modern subjects. Humour deposes every authority, especially the self. The figure of Acéphale was reinterpreted as a poster – the image of a footballer pulling his shirt over his head during a match celebration – for an event which instigated a game of mass football in front of Buckingham Palace using a soft plastic skull (i.e. a decapitated head) as a ball. The stunt could be understood as connecting the republican traditions of Britain and France, invoking both the decapitation of Charles I in 1649 (which took place nearby at The Banqueting House on Whitehall) and the decapitation of French nobles including Louis XVI during the French revolution of 1789, and the tradition in the UK of mob football as a catalyst for social protest.[59]

---

57. Cf. Melancholic Troglodytes, *Class Struggle and this Thing Called the Middle East*, October, 2011, available http://libcom.org.libcom.org/library/class-struggle-thing-called-middle-east-melancholic-trogladytes
58. Cf. Nick Norton, 'Bring Me the Head of Georges Bataille', *Inventory*, Vol.2 No.1 1997; Howard Slater, 'New Acéphale', *Inventory*, Vol.2 No.3 1997; Kingsland Passage, 'The Last Days of London' *Inventory*, Vol.5 No.1 2003.

One of Bataille's proposals for *Contre-Attaque* had involved the restaging the execution of Louis XVI in the early days of the Popular Front at the

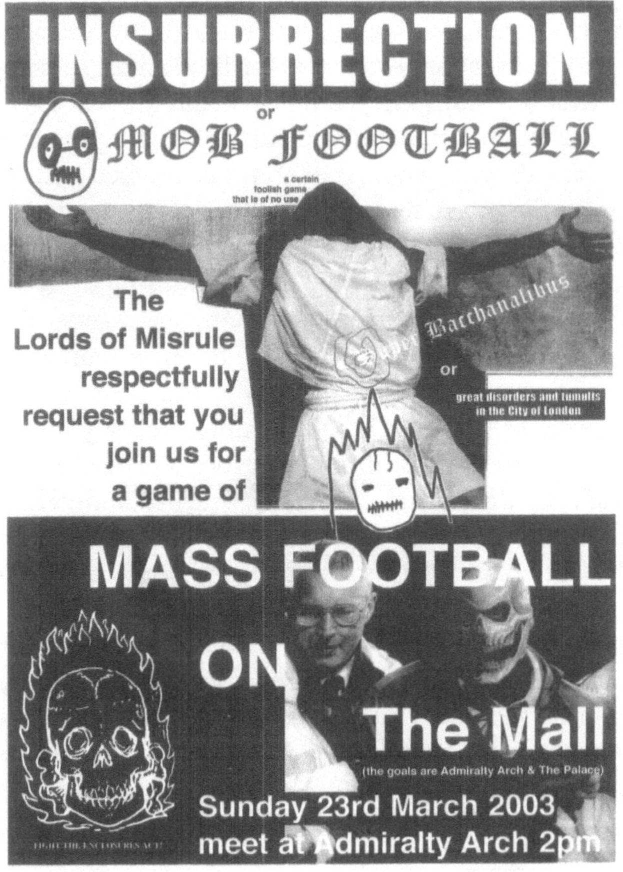

Inventory Mass Football on the Mall, London, 1999

---

59. In 1699, 'an estimated 1,100 rioters attacked drainage works and enclosures in Deeping Level, just north of Peterborough', 'Under Colour & pretence of Foot ball playing'. Heather Falvey, 'Custom, resistance and politics: local experiences of improvement in early modern England', PhD thesis, University of Warwick, 2007, pp.356-7. See also, James Walvin, *The People's Game: The History of Football Revisited*. Edinburgh: Mainstream, 1994. Walvin indicates several further examples of 18th anti-enclosure riots orchestrated under the guise of football games. In Winchelsea players annually try to capture an object known as 'The Frenchman's Head', see: http://www.winchelsea.net/community/game.htm; and here a witness report during the years leading up to the civil war (1642) describes a crowd playing with the head of an executed Catholic priest: http://historyweird.com/1642-mob-football-catholic-priest-head/

Place de la Concorde on 21 January 1936. For Bataille the Place de la Concorde was a site of specific significance since this was both where violent nationalist riots took place in February 1934 and the site where King Louis XVI was executed on 21 January 1793. Inventory's game spoofed a post-historical or revisionist spirit of myth, rumour and reenactment widespread in the postmodern '80s and '90s. The fusion of several historical moments, popular traditions and myths in the midst of a present charged with political energies connected with related interventions by the LPA into demonstrations and international summit protests at the time. Inventory's stunt staged what, according to Michael Richardson, Bataille sought: 'a contagious myth by which the death of the sovereign would be celebrated as the regenerative act of the transformation of society.'[60] The game of 'mass football' took place in the context of a sequence of 'leaderless' protests in London which involved instances of rioting, violence against property and even mass looting. In relation to the new discourse around protest movements of the 'multitude', the fight against 'new enclosures' (Midnight Notes) and in relation to the tactics developed by members of the Luther Blissett project as the Tute Bianche in Italy, Inventory developed a street game called Coagulum involving any number of participants forming a clot, or rugby scrum, in a given site of commerce, jamming the commercial flows of privatised space. The development of ludic experiments in proximity to other protests ambiguously sought both the 'contagion' by unpredictable mass action and the consumption of spectators used to experiencing spectacular art.

Mondo-Mythopoeisis

London-based author and scurrilous pamphleteer Stewart Home did much to reinvent and redistribute this avant-garde tendency towards 'mythopoeisis' through multiple name games, collective anonymity, self-publishing, fabulation and misinformation throughout the 1980s, 1990s and 2000s. 'His', since the possessive is inappropriate here, multiply-authored fanzine *Smile* was based initially on the work of Fluxus artist Ray Johnson.[61]

---

60. Georges Bataille and Michael Richardson (Ed.), *The Absence of Myth: Writings on Surrealism* London; New York: Verso, 1994, p.12.

Another project Home participated in was the 'so-called Luther Blisset Project'. Begun in Italy, this evolved into an international network of hundreds of people using the name Luther Blisset to author texts and create scams.[62] Anonymity, as Howard Slater writes, offers a spur to unknown potential co-conspirators.[63]

The expulsion of 'authors' developed in the direction of the creation of playful character masks, fantastic or monstrous creations who might take the place of the cults of personality which characterised the workers movement in its 'heroic phase'. This reactivation of pre-modern themes engendered the 'unproductive expenditures' and circulation of gratuity which Bataille had understood as originating in religious forms, but attributable also to 'perverse sexual activity' and criminal acts.[64] Thus, the 'gift' theorised by sociologist Marcel Mauss,

---

61. In a 1987 letter from Ray Johnson to Stewart Home he wrote: 'I did my magazine *Smile* because of *File* in Canada who were inspired by *Life* and Anna Banana did her *Vile* and some people in Chicago did *Bile*. My *Smile* magazine did you know was invisible?', 'Letter from Ray Johnson to Stewart Home', 1987 reprinted in *Lightworks* magazine #22, 2000, quoted in Stephen Perkins, 'An Assembly of Conspirators: Omnibus News and Smile', 2016, http://artistsperiodicals.blogspot.com/ Perkins also notes that 'Home's original proposal in his own *Smile*, #2 (1984), for the use of multiple names in the context of periodical publishing [...] must be seen as his one 'original' contribution to Neoism. As it turned out, the Smile project was extremely successful [...] between the years 1984-89 there were 101 issues published by approximately 32 editors.'
62. 'In Italy, since the early and mid-1990s a whole bunch of comrades [...] committed themselves to a practical exploration of mythologies, in order to understand whether a non-alienating, libertarian deconstruction, reuse and manipulation of myths was possible or not.' See Tute Bianche, 'The Practical Side of Myth Making (in Catastrophic Times)', *Infopool* No.7, 2003, p.37.
63. 'Anonymity, as it offers unwarranted and illegitimate gifts, is that which send-out [sic] with no hope of identifiable return and by doing so it offers to all-comers the creation of spaces from where it is possible to make indefensible propositions and carry out curious actions, where a form of freedom is instantiated in the play of unresolvable contradictions and ridiculous conjecture.' Howard Slater, 'New Acéphale', *Inventory*, Vol.2 No.3, 1997, pp.71-75, p.72.
64. Georges Bataille, 'The Notion of Expenditure', in *Visions of Excess: Selected Writings, 1927-39*, op. cit., pp.116-129, p.118. The essay was later developed by Bataille in a three volume book, *The Accursed Share*, his major post-war work. In the *Accursed Share* Bataille revises his pre-war pro-revolutionary position towards an accommodation with Stalinism, since I am primarily interested in Bataille's pre-war activities, and connections between the 1930s and 1990s I do not engage in this debate, but it is worth exploring for those interested in Bataille's critical and political legacy, see Not Bored, 'Trashing Georges Bataille, "Accursed" Stalinist', http://www.notbored.org/bataille.html

with reference to 'pre-capitalist' societies, would become, in the scattered writings of the post-war ultra-left, a lodestar through which to interpret late-20th century revolts and riots, moments which disobeyed the logic of capital and the formal politics which stooped under its determinations. These were senseless expenditures which refused the conscription and tyranny of the capitalist use of things.[65]

Paper Assemblies

The loose scene formed in Europe in the 1980 and early 1990s by left political journals or zines began to break with left orthodoxies and explore the new distributive possibilities of desktop publishing and, eventually, networked computing. I call these 'paper assemblies' because the self-reflexive attention to aspects of the production processes of print and distribution of print objects extended also to the configuration of the editors, authors and readers, forming and emphasising the different connections between ideas, printed matter and the bodies and materialities which circulated around them. These presses and self-publishing projects, especially the second generation, tended to mix and combine media and distribute their publishing across a range of platforms: websites, record labels, magazines, bookshops, posters, flyers, stickers. Such combinations, with their emphasis on minoritarian interests and autonomous organisation were theorised by Howard Slater (after Félix Guattari) as strategically 'post-media'.[66] Their use of the network form cannot be reduced to the 'horizontalism' of 'leaderless, structureless groups' critiqued by Jo Freeman and vilified by Gilles Dauvé with regard to some self-publishing initiatives as a form of capitulation to capitalist logic and class denial.[67] Nick Thoburn, here using Unpopular Books as an example, has emphasised the complex

---

65. 'Through theft and gift they rediscover a use that immediately refutes the oppressive rationality of the commodity, revealing its relations and even its production to be arbitrary and unnecessary.' Situationist International, 'The Decline and Fall of the Spectacle-Commodity Economy', *Internationale Situationniste*, No.10, Paris, March 1966, available: http://www.bopsecrets.org/SI/10.Watts.htm. For a comprehensive treatment of this troubling of capitalist utility and use value in terms of printed matter see Nicholas Thoburn, 'Communist Objects and the Values of Printed Matter', *Social Text* 28, No.2, Summer 2010, pp.1-30.
66. Cf. the post-media bibliography available: https://monoskop.org/Postmedia

'relays' such small presses set-up between their print experiments and political content.

> [A]n additional relay between the sensual properties of the object and its politico-conceptual content — not only its anticommodity orientation but also its critique of dominant modes of political organization.[68]

Influenced by Georges Bataille (as a theorist and publisher) Info Centre/Infopool and the related Copenhagen Free University deployed idiosyncratic glossaries on posters and online as an organisational form for heterogeneous materials, essays, art projects, sound recordings, and research projects, which can be meaningfully related to the concept-levelling publishing conceits and formats developed in *Documents*. This technique of creating idiosyncratic glossaries was common across groups operating at this time even with divergent interests and politics (Cybernetic Culture Research Unit, LPA, Inventory, Copenhagen Free University) it is a tactic which allows horizontal and associative navigation of terms and their transformation, looking back towards the work of surrealists and before them the *Encyclopédistes*, but also forward to the vast online collaborative sites such as Wikipedia and Uncyclopedia. The strategic and practical formation of Info Centre/Infopool as a hybrid institutional-domestic-social space can be seen as an attempt to live and develop a formlessness appropriate to Bataille's entropic critique of categories in his pre-war writings for *Documents*, which moved and took critical shape as an 'organic

---

67. Jo Freeman, 'The Tyranny of Structurelessness', 1970, available, http://www.jofreeman.com/joreen/tyranny.htm 'Informations & Correspondance Ouvrières (1961-73); 'and now Echanges & Mouvement claimed to have no theory except the theory that only the proletarians could determine their own methods and aims. Likewise, thousands of infokiosks and indymedia collectives profess to have no specific doctrine (Marxist, anarchist, ecologist, feminist, whatever), and say their sole purpose is to serve as a meeting place and communication centre meant to promote social struggles, with the difference that the 'historical subject' is no longer the working class, but the people (the famous 99%). They act as if ICO's "choice of non-existence" (*IS*, # 11) had been inverted into the choice of 24/7 on-line presence, yet information first remains the priority, too often with similar features as "bourgeois" media: constant data flow, information overload and obsolescence, sensationalism....' Gilles Dauvé, 'The Bitter Victory of Council Communism', http://libcom.org/library/bitter-victory-council-communism-gilles-dauve

68. 'Communist Objects and the Values of Printed Matter', op. cit., p.23.

movement' – the shifting form of groups such as *Contre-Attaque*, Acéphale and the College of Sociology. For Bataille the retention of an affective dimension within these groups was what saved them from instrumentalisation by the state, party or other molar formation. In this sense they maintained a connection to the dream of transforming the world by still living as fallible human beings.

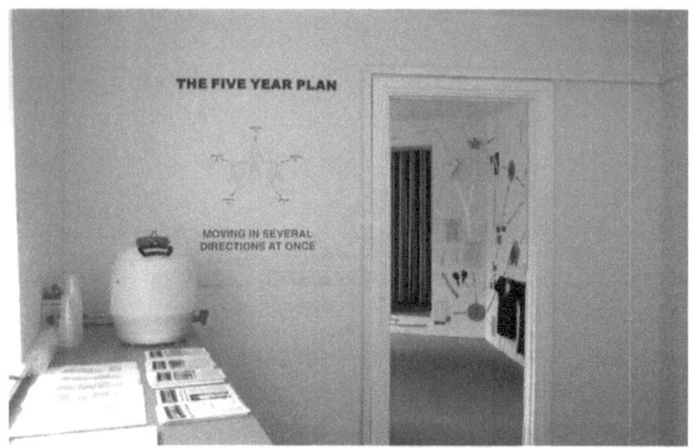

Info Centre, London, 1999

For some groups operating in the 1990s and 2000s this publishing activity and community formation was then self-consciously imagined with antagonism towards the smoothness of online information exchange.[69] The Copenhagen Free University understood itself under the logic of 'self-institution'. Unlike institutions obsessed with their own perpetuation it could embrace its dissolution as imaginatively as its origin.[70] As well as self-publishing their own pamphlets as Infopool, the Info Centre made the unusual choice of networking together several of the small press projects mentioned above in a physical space, a reading room adjoining a domestic space in Hackney. A space which was also used for small informal discussions and 'exhibitions' drawn from the contributors to these projects. In Info Centre/Infopool the dimension of production in and through everyday life was emphasised as a form of resistance to the perceived cooptation of everyday life in

---

69. An offline space, the 56A Infoshop and Archive, a squatted space used by activists, pamphleteers and political groups, located in London's Elephant & Castle, was the determining influence on the Info Centre, see http://56a.org.uk/
70. Cf. Copenhagen Free University Abolition Committee, 'We Have Won', 2007, http://www.copenhagenfreeuniversity.dk/won.html

capitalist society. The dynamic of anti-institutional exodus and self-institutional creation conjured a fragile space in which to explore the everyday or local mediations which might replace capital's categories, though this would always remain a tentative proposition.

Conclusion

Tendencies in each of these two periods assumed a tactical retreat from molar instances of what counted as official politics, but retained political forms and references as plastic material in need of reconfiguration. One major presupposition for these later groups and the anti-statist, anti-party anarchism and communism they fostered, was the beneficence of the welfare state, which supported a form of what Brighton-based group *Aufheben* called 'dole autonomy'.[71] Whereas for Bataille's generation editing or contributing to a journal permitted some form of remuneration, if not salary, the later wave of endeavours under discussion tended to be executed by moonlight, redirecting resources of a day job or through employing the free time afforded by the dole. Dole autonomy enabled the practical critique of work, ensuring reproduction and free time – a wage and a life without alienated labour. However, if dole autonomy facilitated the autonomous theorisation of forms of sovereignty which were secular, independent of family, gender neutral, inter-, or even outer-, national, this system of reproduction or form of 'freedom' remained beholden to a particular relationship between the state and its working population which was historically dependent on the struggles of a powerful workers' movement. This situation was subject to change in a period when the material basis for the workers' movement and the steady state were both rapidly disappearing. *Aufheben*'s critique of the left and the new social movements during this period was that they failed to defend the measures which had ensured both their basic reproduction and the reproduction of their activism. As 'lifestyles' each of these scenes can be understood as having an anti-political thrust but instead of understanding this as a movement of de-politicisation, I propose that the small groups formed around self-publishing deliberately complicated the field of politics as they apparently retreated from it.

---

71. Aufheben, 'Dole Autonomy Versus the Re-imposition of Work', 1998, https://libcom.org/library/dole-autonomy-versus-re-imposition-work

What appeared as retreat was then, instead, a form of reconstellation. On their own terms, these groups animated the 'formulation of communism as a distributed and self-critical process, a process that wards off any delimiting center of attraction.'[72] On the other hand these group's 'siege-mentality' and effective 'milieu control' led to forms which did not dramatise themselves so much in terms of the exclusions and splits of an earlier period of mass parties and avant-gardes but nonetheless fostered paranoia denunciations and rivalries. This problem not only implies the pressures of reproducing oneself on the margins of capitalist society, but sometimes more troublingly, in Slater's words, 'persistence in the milieus of the same dichotomies that act to bolster capitalism'.[73] With hindsight, it can be seen that

The ABZ of The Copenhagen Free University Poster c.2000

interstitial space (the dole, cheap or free space in the city, the streets, free time) quickly shrunk in London under pressures of financialisation and the intensification of labour this drives, seemingly incessantly, at a global level. Nor has the state withered away; even whilst it cut its social obligations, it simply became leaner and meaner in its austerity phase, as we have seen recently. From this perspective, experimentation with self-institution as a form of temporary autonomy

---

72. Nicholas Thoburn, *Anti-Book: On the Art and Politics of Radical Publishing*, Minneapolis: Minnesota University Press, 2016, p.103.
73. Howard Slater, 'Evacuate the Leftist Bunker', *Annual Review of Critical Psychology*, Vol.3, 2003, pp.116-136.

has to be seen under the glass ceiling set by the state as describing the upper limit on the licence such communities might take.[74]

For the left then, neither the false promise of elective communities autonomous from the state nor the long march through its institutions appear tenable. 'Tactical sovereignty', or 'self-institution', experimentations with outmoded or contingent apparatuses was then only a temporary means of extending laterally while vertical extension was impeded. The recent tendency towards self-criticism and problematisation of the habits and rituals of left political culture are a necessary development for complacency, habit and the closure of community to be elided. Yet, these currents also encourage the emerging picture of the left as impotent and defeated, or 'burdened by the absence of billions' as one commentator has put it, without the 'billions' in question to have come any closer to emancipation.[75] If the distance of these groups from any revolutionary agent had by that point become a matter of ironic self-critique, perhaps at worst 'a community formed by a shared unhappiness', the possible combination out of which revolutionary change might come remains vague and indeterminate.[76] Still, calls against minoritarian forms of oppositionism often pretend, at the expense of an analysis of the real balance of forces, that a wholesome left can be recovered.[77] Fascism in its strict sense remains a rarity; more common and more dangerous both in the 1930s and now is the convergence of left and right forms of national socialism, the business of propping up the state during times of crisis.[78]

---

74. 'The state is the guarantor, but not the creator, of relationships. It represents and unifies capital, it is neither capital's motor nor its centrepiece [...] the substance of the state resides not in institutional forms, but in its unifying function. The state ensures the tie which human beings cannot and dare not create among themselves, and creates a web of services which are both parasitic and real,' Gilles Dauvé, 'When Insurrections Die', *Endnotes* No.1, October, 2010, p.63.
75. The phrase is Frère Dupont's, *Species Being*, San Francisco: Ardent Press, 2009, quoted as the title for a review, Howard Slater, 'Burdened By the Absence of Billions', op. cit.
76. 'Hic Nihil, Hic Salta! (a critique of Bartlebyism)', op. cit.
77. See Mark Fisher, 'Exiting the Vampire Castle', 22 November, 2013, http://www.thenorthstar.info/?p=11299
78. 'In order for this to embody the spirit of the referendum, it would have to include some repatriation of sovereignty, as well as a significant, temporary retreat from freedom of movement.' Paul Mason, 'How the left should respond to Brexit', 17 October 2016, http://www.newstatesman.com/politics/uk/2016/10/paul-mason-how-left-should-respond-brexit

The scattered anti-tradition I have surveyed here superficially constitutes no unity. It is instead made of salvaged fragments of practices which are caught in the slipstream, attracting and encouraging unknown others. Against the false and authoritarian unity which expels unwanted 'parts' it cannot reconcile, these practices refuse to be useful or whole until everybody (as in the AAA slogan 'Here comes everybody') can join in.

Addendum: Mythopoeisis 2.0

The recent emergence of a chimerical populist far-right movement which has built its visibility through a popularisation of ideas and techniques drawn from the left adds humiliation to historical defeat.[79] A subculture of meme-production, online anonymity, lists, iterative humour, sex and violence has helped bring a new heterogeneous sovereign to power, Trump, apparently to banish the chaos he sees around him. His talisman Pepe or Kek (an androgynous ancient Egyptian deity representing primordial chaos) equally suggests that this can only be a way to *accelerate* the chaos or crisis which had already begun.[80] This new rightwards surge is thus both selectively identitarian and constitutive of an anti-identity politics. Its facile negation of 'cultural Marxism' involves reducing grievances by minorities to a litany of white complaint: blame culture, humiliation of rivals, racism and sexism. If these are indicators of the right attempting to do war on the terrain of culture, that also suggests a certain impotence, if we have learnt anything from the above. The philosophical anti-identitarianism which is the intellectual corollary to these movements is everywhere a form of idealism unless it grapples with the complexity of the human subject. All register the collapse of conditions for reproduction (of life, identity, social relations) grimly clinging to masks. Its identity has been emblematised by frog, an Egyptian god, a glass of milk, yet tellingly its attempts to muster behind these symbols has reached no stability.[81]

---

79. Dale Beran, '4chan: The Skeleton Key to the Rise of Trump', https://cominsitu.wordpress.com/2017/02/20/4chan-the-skeleton-key-to-the-rise-of-trump/
80. See *http://knowyourmeme.com/memes/cult-of-kek*
81. Mark Hay, 'A Scientist Explains Why Alt-Right Milk Chugging Is Idiotic', February 2016, http://www.extracrispy.com/culture/2167/a-scientist-explains-why-alt-right-milk-chugging-is-idiotic

Authoritarian movements tend to work in complicity with capitalism towards the obfuscation of the suffering at the heart of capitalist social reproduction. In the abject 'character masks' Pepe and Feels Man the suffering and humiliation of NEETS (young people not in education training or employment) transforms itself into an abject-comic duo of man who feels too much and frog who just 'feels good'. Geek culture here expresses the curse of surplus life and the painful realisation splits the subject in two: on the left a loser who feels too much, on the right a prize tosser who doesn't feel at all. The unhappy couple endlessly play out the homicidal rivalry they are condemned to. '[I]f men no

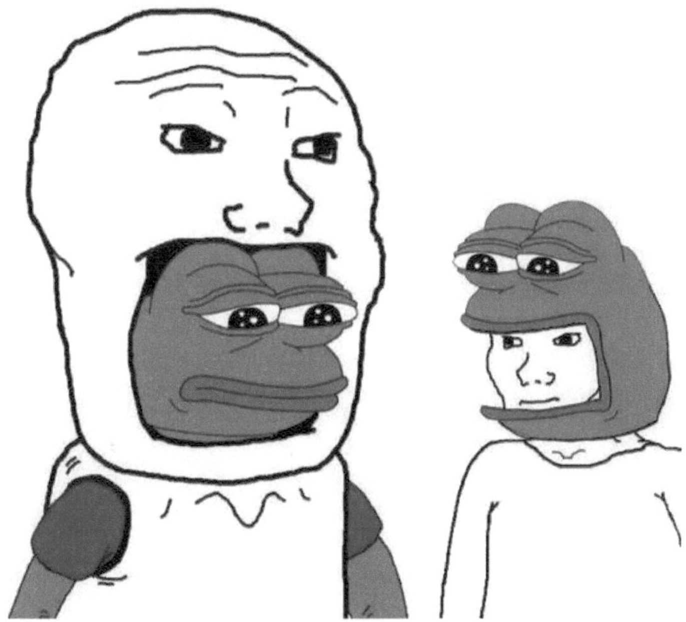

Anon., Pepe and Feels Man in Cosplay c.2012

longer had to equate themselves with things, they would need neither a thing-like superstructure nor an invariant picture of themselves, after the model of things.'[82] The sovereign through attracting and performing disgust enacts the violent integration of the other and radicalisation of the self. However which way he kills, Pepe can't ever get rid of Feels man, in truth they are interchangeable. The subject is a group – a plurality – and not an identity. The origins of these memes

---

82. Theodor W. Adorno, *Negative Dialectics,* quoted in Marcel Stoetzler, 'Subject Trouble'. *Philosophy & Social Criticism,* 18 August 2016, p.359.

lies not in white or European power, but in suffering.[83] Through revulsion at the experience of collectivising suffering this suffering is transferred onto others as violently as possible. Fascism also is made of people. Yet, for Pepe-Feels, since the route out is by way of affirming existing power and the state, the two does not resolve into one, but nothing – a 'labyrinth with no center'.[84] The invagination of Pepe and Feels man displays for all to see the voiding of any specific human essence, buried there lies the naked secret of non-identity but also a form of mourning for the human community which might render it undisguised.

---

83. For example 'green text stories' see
https://www.reddit.com/r/greentext/comments/31v5m5/anon_is_sad/
84. '4chan: The Skeleton Key to the Rise of Trump', op. cit.

THE UNPRESIDENTED

EIRIK STEINHOFF

Freedom is always the freedom to think otherwise.
 – Rosa Luxemburg

In the early teens of this century I found myself in prison as a teacher. I was teaching an intensive three-week course called 'A Workshop on Language and Thinking' to first-time college students incarcerated in the men's maximum security prison in Green Haven, NY. The landscape around the prison was bucolic. The Appalachian Trail crossed nearby. The prison walls punched their way out of the green surround, a sight that never failed to produce a tight ball of fear in my stomach. It was late summer, hot and humid, and the windows in our classroom did not open. We had to walk through long and weather-magnifying cinderblock tunnels to get there. I looked forward to going to work.

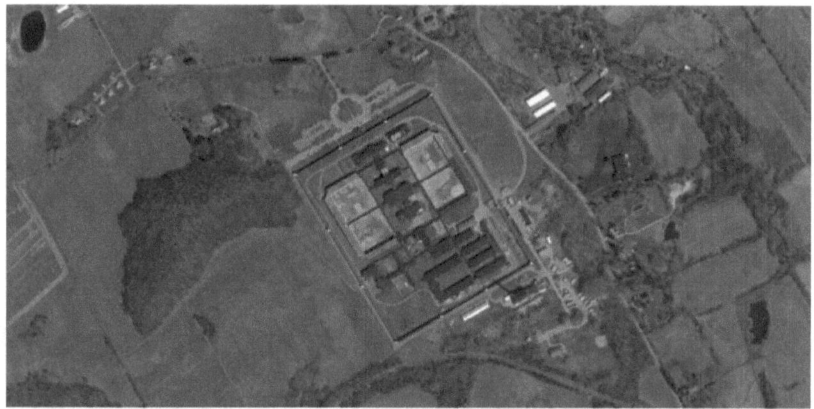

Green Haven Correctional Facility (Beekman, New York)

In this scene of instruction under correctional conditions we read a lot and wrote constantly in our notebooks together. We met five hours a day, five days a week and had been reading Darwin and Kafka, Arendt and *Antigone*, 'Letter from Birmingham Jail' and pieces of *The Structure of Scientific Revolutions*. We were studying the relation between word and thought, anomaly and paradigm, custom and habit, metamorphosis and revolution, *poiesis* and *praxis*. In our second week I introduced a text and lesson plan I'd picked up from my friend and colleague Emily Abendroth, who was teaching the same course across the Hudson River to students incarcerated at Eastern.

The lesson focused on Peter Kropotkin's forceful rejoinder to Social Darwinism at the beginning of his book, *Mutual Aid*.[1] At stake in

Kropotkin's corrective is nothing less than the relation between the laws of nature and the laws of culture. He agrees with his interlocutors

MUTUAL AID
A FACTOR OF EVOLUTION

BY

P. KROPOTKIN
AUTHOR OF
THE GREAT FRENCH REVOLUTION," ETC.

(who, in addition to Darwin, include Herbert Spencer and Thomas Huxley) that these laws are related, that what is natural and what is cultural are not so far apart as anthropocentric exceptionalism might allow us to imagine. But he disagrees, and vigorously, with the Social Darwinist description of the laws of nature. Because they have their description of the laws of nature wrong, they also get their description of the laws of culture wrong. In his preface he rejects, in particular, their application of the 'struggle for existence' Darwin describes in the natural world to the social world we live in. On Kropotkin's account the conceptual monopoly that Social Darwinists grant to 'the struggle for existence' both exaggerates and narrows what Darwin calls 'the large and metaphorical sense' in which this phrase is to be understood. As Kropotkin puts it, the Social Darwinists 'reduced' Darwin's heuristic metaphor to 'a world of perpetual struggle among half-starved individuals, thirsting for one another's blood' (4). But, Kropotkin argues, Darwin himself showed how '*struggle* is replaced by *co-operation*, and how that substitution results in the development of intellectual and moral faculties which secure to the species the best conditions for survival' (2). Against the Social Darwinist's norm of gladiatorial individualism and against the immiserating economic justifications they drew from their description of nature as battlefield, Kropotkin posits what he calls 'Mutual Aid', a collective, cooperative process that he describes as '*a law of nature and the chief factor of evolution*', and he backs

---

1. Peter Kropotkin, *Mutual Aid: A Factor of Evolution,* New York: McClure Phillips & Co, 1902.

his argument with an ample range of evidence from both natural and cultural history (6).

Now we didn't read this whole book in our maximum security classroom, just these opening polemical parts, where we anatomised and parsed the various lines of argument Kropotkin was laying out, constantly writing in our notebooks. I'd said on the first day of class that I took writing to be a way of creating forms of thought that are difficult to encounter by other means. And I acknowledged that it was sometimes awkward to do that together. But I also said that I understood writing in class about complicated texts to be a way of collectivising our vulnerability, of deprivatising something our culture trains us to usually experience alone.[2]

We took a close look at examples from the book's first chapter on 'Mutual Aid Among Animals', and zoomed in on Kropotkin's detailed description of a feeding behaviour among ants that scientists call 'trophallaxis' (from the Greek *tropho* [nourishment] + *allaxis* [exchange]):

> two ants belonging to the same nest or to the same colony of nests will approach each other, exchange a few movements with the antennae, and 'if one of them is hungry or thirsty, and especially if the other has its crop full [...] it immediately asks for food'. The individual thus requested never refuses; it sets apart its mandibles, takes a proper position, and regurgitates a drop of transparent fluid which is licked up by the hungry ant. Regurgitating food for other ants is so prominent a feature in the life of ants [...], and it so constantly recurs both for feeding hungry comrades and for feeding larvae, that [the entomologist] Forel considers the digestive tube of the ants as consisting of two different parts, one of which, the posterior, is for the special use of the individual, and the other, the anterior part, is chiefly for the use of the community. (12-13)

At this point our workshop on language and thinking took a little swerve by design. It was time to engage in direct composition. The

---

2. In this particular institutional instance (I was teaching for the Bard Prison Initiative), the practice of dedicating class time to writing together was inaugurated by Peter Elbow, and then radically expanded and transformed by Joan Retallack. Where Elbow brings a populist's imperative to the project of teaching writing, Retallack reveals the ways in which that imperative need not be in competition (as it is sometime misunderstood to be) with rigorous and playful aesthetic, intellectual, and political inquiry.

prompt was a thought experiment that involves a science-fiction scenario:

> What if humans, just like these ants, were endowed with a shared organ half of which is, as Kropotkin describes it, 'chiefly for the use of the community', and the other half 'for the special use of the individual'. Take five minutes to write what you imagine.

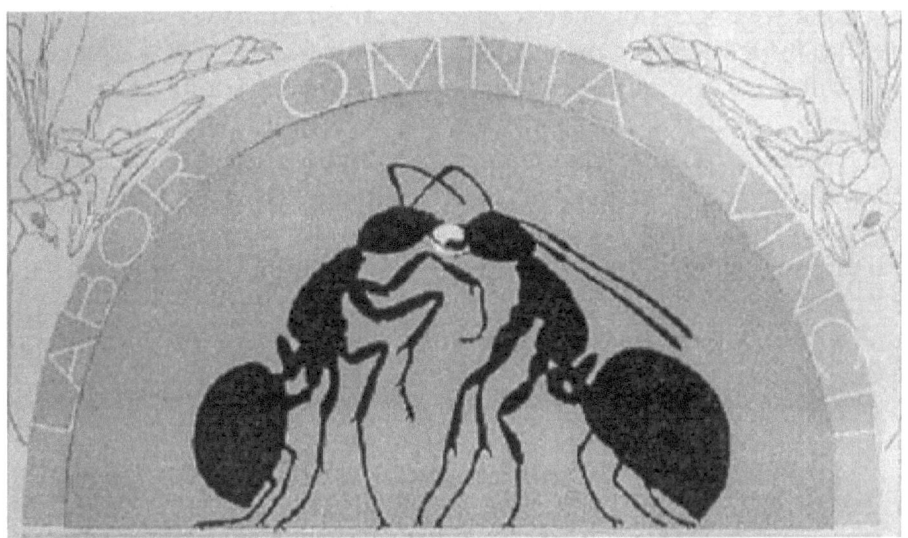

Detail from the title page of Auguste Forel, *Le Monde Social des Fourmis*, Libraire Kundig, 1921

While most of the students at Green Haven readily indulged in the permissions of the exercise (coming up with three-legged races, shared eyes, the brain, food packets on your hands, and the like), and although a few bravely struggled with it ('you want me to imagine *what?*' one asked, flatly resisting the folly of the invitation), there was one student who had no difficulty whatsoever immediately comprehending the simple truth that *language itself* is the human organ best described as partially the preserve of the individual and partially the preserve of the collective. There was nothing far-fetched about it so far as he could tell; it wasn't even a metaphor. What's more, he said, the orifice in question, the mouth, was the same – even if the exact nature of the metabolism is rather distinct.

The accuracy of this insight is obvious in retrospect, but it struck me as a complete surprise at the time. How might we consider language to be a 'shared organ' that performs an operative role in collective and individual human metabolism?

Hans Jonas defines 'metabolism' as an organism's 'exchange of matter with its surroundings'.[3] Marx describes 'labour' as 'a process between [humans] and nature, a process by which [humans], through [their] own actions, mediate, regulate, and control the metabolism between [themselves] and nature'.[4]

What we might call 'the Kropotkin-Green Haven addendum' to these definitions is the assertion that *language* is the best means by which this collective human metabolical regulation (regurgitation) is mediated, regulated, and controlled.

If labour is how we 'mediate, regulate, and control' our 'exchange of matter with [our] surroundings', then language is how we 'mediate, regulate, and control' our relationships with each other – that is, our relationship with ourselves. Language is the prime means by which we compose and transform these relationships: with each other (culture), and with the world we live in (nature). I worry that we are quickly losing track of this simple fact – and that brute force, both with each other and with nature, predominates as a consequence.

I had to go to prison to have this power of language drawn to my attention.

A poem, as I see it, is one way to reconnect with this power.

§

A poem's fundamental responsibility is to create and maintain a space for desire in language. 'It is not *gnosis* but *praxis* must be the fruit', Philip Sidney insisted in the 1580s.[5] What the poem generates on this account is not knowledge but action. Not that there's a zero-sum game here. Elaine Scarry argues that 'habit yokes thought and action together', and I understand Sidney to intend *praxis* precisely in these terms.[6] The broadest version of the question I want to ask here is: *how do we represent the unprecedented?* A corollary question would be: *how do*

---

3. Hans Jonas, *The Phenomenon of Life: Toward a Philosophical Biology*, Evanston, Illinois: Northwestern University Press, 1966, p.79.
4. Karl Marx, *Capital*, Vol.1, (Trans. Ben Fowkes), New York: Vintage, 1976, p.283.
5. Philip Sidney, *An Apology for Poetry, or The Defence of Poesy*, Manchester: Manchester University Press, 1973, p.94.
6. Elaine Scarry, *Thinking in an Emergency*, New York: W.W. Norton, 2012, p.80.

we precipitate the unprecedented? And, if I may abuse a recently tweeted neologism: *what might it mean to be unpresidented?*

In this essay I want to imagine the poem as an 'affordance' in the sense supplied by the perceptual psychologist J.J. Gibson. 'The *affordances* of the environment' (as Gibson describes them) 'are what it *offers* the animal, what it *provides* or *furnishes*, either for good or ill'.[7] This transforms any account of the relationship between an organism and its surroundings by emphasising 'action-possibility' above all – what Sidney calls *praxis.* Following the example of Donald Norman, designers have transferred Gibson's theory of affordances to a reconceptualisation of objects as well. In this light, what a thing is can best be understood not in terms of what you know about it but rather in terms of what it can be used for.[8] To those who say, 'A poem should not mean / But be' (as Archibald MacLeish famously asserts), those who want to consider the poem as an affordance respond, 'The meaning of a word is its use' (as Wittgenstein declares).[9] Rather than calculating a poem solely in terms of its formal properties the way we're often taught in school (metre, rhyme, diction, etc.), we ought also attend to what potentials for action it unleashes in whatever circumstance it finds itself in.

A pint glass may be a transparent truncated glass cone sealed with a disc on the smaller end, but what it 'affords' is the possibility of holding beverages that one may swallow when you tip the open end into your mouth. One action a pint glass makes possible, in other words, is drinking. This is the function it was designed for. But you could also use it to draw two differently sized circles if you felt like it. Broken, a piece of it could become a blade. What might a poem afford, both by design and in excess of it? And what might poems teach us both more generally and more particularly about how to do things with words?

J.L. Austin famously decreed that speech acts in poems don't count: 'If the poet says "Go and catch a falling star" or whatever it may be, he doesn't seriously issue an order'.[10] I am not alone in failing to

---

7. J.J. Gibson, *The Ecological Approach to Visual Perception,* Hillsdale, N.J.: Lawrence Erlbaum Associates, 1986 (1979), p.127.
8. Donald Norman, *The Design of Everyday Things,* New York: Doubleday, 1990.
9. Archibald MacLeish, *Collected Poems, 1917-1982,* Boston: Houghton Mifflin, 1985, p.107; Ludwig Wittgenstein, *Philosophical Investigations,* (Trans. G.E.M. Anscombe), New York: Palgrave MacMillan 1958, §43.

understand why commands in poems are by definition 'parasitic' or 'etiolated', and thus infelicitous.[11] Charles Altieri's article on 'demonstrative utterances' contains fruitful insights in this regard:

> Poems realize what language can do in making certain states articulate, and that realization in turn gives the imagination access to provisional identifications we can try to adapt to our own circumstances – not as a condition of experiencing the text but as a condition of adapting that experience to the world by testing for the similarities and differences it allows us to specify.[12]

Altieri means affective 'states', but I don't see why we couldn't consider the ways in which poems also could 'realise what language can do in making certain *nation*-states *in*articulate'. To Altieri's rhetorical recovery of the poem from the other side of the modernist aesthetic rift, I propose we add Stanley Cavell's account of 'the passionate utterance' to the mix:

> A performative utterance is an offer of participation in the order of law. And perhaps we can say: a passionate utterance is an invitation to improvisation in the disorders of desire.[13]

This 'invitation to improvisation' allows us to consider the work of a 'demonstrative utterance' at a demonstration or a riot – scenes of political desire, we might call them.

Claude McKay's sonnet that begins 'If we must die, let it not be like hogs' offers a robust instance of both a demonstrative and a passionate utterance. First composed in the midst of lynchings and riots during the bloody summer of 1919, it also circulated among prisoners at Attica in advance of the 1971 rebellion and massacre.[14] The militant self-defence articulated in one political environment, using a poetic form

---

10. J.L. Austin, *Philosophical Papers*, Oxford: Clarendon Press, 1961, p.241.
11. J.L. Austin, *How to Do Things with Words*, Oxford: Clarendon Press, 1962, p.22.
12. Charles Altieri, 'What Theory Can Learn from New Directions in Contemporary American Poetry', *New Literary History*, 2012, No.43, p.80.
13. Stanley Cavell, *Philosophy the Day after Tomorrow*, Cambridge, MA: Harvard University Press, 2006, p.185.
14. The poem is widely available online, if you don't know it. For its multiple histories, see Jordan T. Camp, *Incarcerating the Crisis: Freedom Struggles and the Rise of the Neoliberal State*, Berkeley CA: University of California Press, 2016, p.74.

typically associated with the action and passion of love, contributes to the transformations of possibility in a completely different (though not unrelated) political environment.

With these poly-historical affordances of McKay's poem in mind, and also its transformation of the affordances of form, I want to take permission from Cavell's expansion of Austin to build on Gibson's and Norman's accounts. Where the concept of an affordance allows us to understand the relationship between an organism and objects in its environment in terms of potentials for action, the concept of *a transfordance* might allow us to consider desirable transformations in those potentials for action. Affordances allow the analyst to understand the relationship between organism and environment less in terms of formal properties and more in terms of possible activities; transfordances allow the agent to transform the conditions of those possibilities by transforming that relationship between organism and environment in the first place. That's one kind of work I'd like to think a poem can do: transform felicity conditions. 'The issuing of the utterance' thus becomes not just 'the performing of the action' (as Austin describes) but also the transforming of the conditions that make saying and doing equivalent.[15]

The poem, as I say, is thus an affordance as Gibson defines it: a potential for action. But I want to argue that it is also a means both for composing affordances and for transforming them. Both/and. Rather than considering a poem only in terms of its form – the intrinsic and extrinsic elements that lay in waiting for analysis – we should also attend to what the poem makes possible, the kind of action its form performs, the deeds the words suggest, however implicitly or explicitly. This makes the poem not only a 'performative' or 'demonstrative' or a 'passionate' utterance in Austin's and Altieri's and Cavell's senses, but also a *transformative utterance*.

One name for the kind of study I am embarking on is 'poetics', which we can understand not only in the standard sense of the study of making (the root of the word 'poem' being the Greek verb *poiein*, 'to make'), but also in an expanded sense of the study of transformation (as proposed by Stathis Gourgouris).[16] Insofar as making implies forming, it also requires transforming. The poetics of the sort I am proposing thus involves transforming our sense of poetics. Whereas an

---

15. *How to Do Things with Words*, op. cit., p.6.

aesthetics and poetics that focuses on form necessarily involves a morphology in its analytical and interpretive toolkit, an aesthetics and poetics tuned to form *and* transformation involves both a morphology and what we might call *metamorphology*, which I take to signify the theory and practice of transforming conditions of possibility.

§

This essay picks up on a field of inquiry I broached in a troika of essays published in late 2015 that try to think Elizabeth Gurley Flynn's definition of sabotage as 'the conscious withdrawal of the workers' industrial efficiency', on the one hand, and Rosa Luxemburg's analysis of the General Strike, on the other, in relation to W.H. Auden's observation that 'poetry makes nothing happen' and Paul Celan's definition of the poem as 'that which does not fit the measure'.[17] These essays were variously motivated: by the placebo effect, by lines of poetry chanted as slogans on Tahrir Square in 2011, by a 1913 strike re-enacted as a pageant. How, in particular, might a poem 'make nothing happen' in the sense of performing the other side of the normal form, cultivating and sustaining what the standard account says is impossible? The essays were informed by my experiences in the vicinity of the tumultuous Oakland Commune (a.k.a. Occupy Oakland) in late 2011 and early 2012, where I made myself busy first and foremost by composing and circulating a pamphlet called *A Fiery Flying Roule* (pages from which are reproduced here).

I conclude one of the essays in this sabotage trilogy by landing on the word 'default':

> On the one hand (call this the financialised hand) to be 'in default' is to have somehow fallen short, by failing, for example, to keep up with your student loan payments. On the other hand (call this the technological hand), a 'default setting' is a state that is primary: your cell phone before you fucked it up with all those janky apps.

---

16. Stathis Gourgouris, 'The *Poiein* of Secular Criticism', in Ali Behdad, Dominic Richard and David Thomas (Eds.), *A Companion to Comparative Literature*, Chichester, West Sussex; Malden, MA: Wiley-Blackwell: Blackwell, 2011, esp. pp.78-80.
17. 'The Anomaly Contains the Homily: Placebo & *Poiesis*', *Floor: A Journal of Aesthetic Experiments*, 2015; 'Making Nothing Happen: poetry and sabotage', *Postmedieval*, Vol.6, No.4, 2015, pp.417-428; 'The Difference is Spreading: Sabotage and Aesthetics', *Black Box: A Record of the Catastrophe*, No.1, 2015, pp.71-80.

Fiery Flying Roule:

TO

All the Inhabitants of the earth; ſpecially to the rich ones.

NEXT TIME A NEW RIOT ACT WILL BE READ :

We hereby declare this to be a most awesome assembly. In the name of the people of this place — which is to say: IN OUR OWN SOVEREIGN NAME *— we command you to immediately* LEAVE US THE FUCK ALONE. *If you do not do so, your violence may be repelled, your authority will be mocked (which may result in a permanent feeling of humiliation), and we know for a fact that the injuries you inflict upon our persons shall afflict each of your souls for the remainder of your days. We prohibit you from fucking with our most awesome assembly. If you attempt to arrest us, history shall prove your folly absolute. If you do not leave,* LYRICAL AGENTS *will be used, which may result in unmitigatable sensations of bliss.* GO HOME. *We liberate you in the power of, well: in the power of* YOU *declared by* WE *in our sovereign autonomy.* WE COMMAND YOU TO BE FREE OF YOUR COMMANDS *& remind you above all to* LEAVE US THE FUCK ALONE.

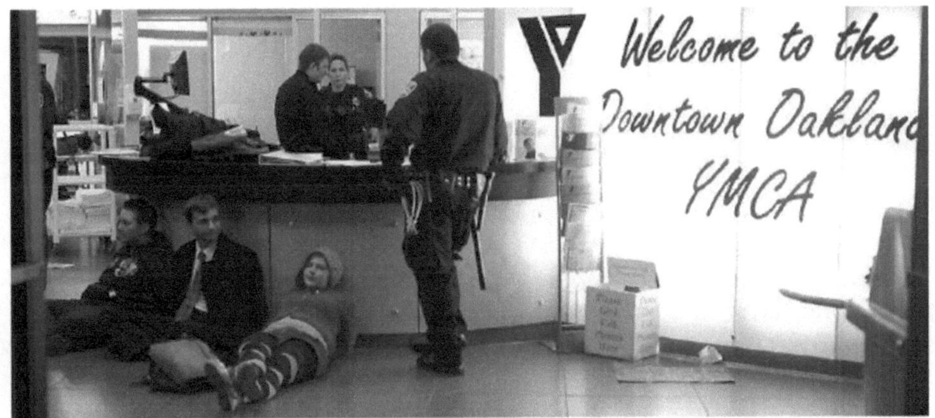

'Default' can thus signify both a lapsed state and a prelapsarian one. It would seem, in other words, that to be 'in default' is to be in the opposite place from the one you find yourself in when you are in 'default settings'. I am pretty sure that there is a radical potential contained in this wobble if only we can figure out how to exercise it together. The question I want to leave you with is: *what - or where - are our default settings?*[18]

The Kropotkin-Green Haven addendum – that *language* is the means by which our collective human metabolism (a.k.a. 'labour') is mediated, regulated, and controlled – strikes me as a strong candidate for an answer to that question.

In a recent essay, first drawn to my attention by the editors of this volume, Endnotes write,

In instances of error, our means fall short of the ends we project, and the error we confront names this lack of possibility. [...] [A]s soon as one attempts something not given by the affordances of the world, the state of error – as a measure of incapacity – appears absolute. But with reconstructive effort, error may be gradually pushed back to the limits, defining a space of possibility.[19]

My wager here is that poems could be devices for composing the possibility space that emerges as a consequence of the errors Endnotes describe – for relocating our defaults, and perhaps also for resetting them.

§

At this point we are overdue for an example, a 'for instance', to render these abstract propositions more concrete. Let me put a coin into the slot:

---

18. 'Making Nothing Happen', op. cit., p.424.
19. Endnotes, 'Error', *Bad Feelings,* London: Bookworks, 2016, n.p.

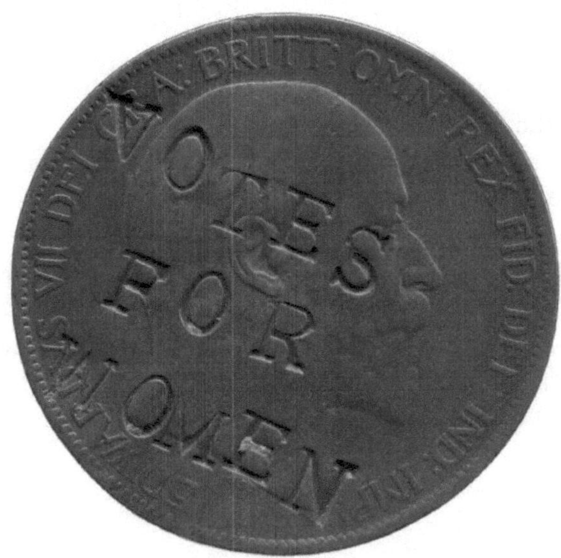

This was one of thousands of pennies circulating in England a century
or so ago, a particle in the gathering struggle for the universal vote.
Here's a taste of what was in the air, as described by Ethel Smyth:

> At exactly 5.30 one memorable evening in 1912, relays of women
> produced hammers from their muffs and handbags, and proceeded
> methodically to smash up windows in all the big London
> thoroughfares – Picadilly, Regent Street, and so on. Inspired by the
> knowledge that exactly at that moment Mrs. Pankhurst was opening
> the ball with a stone aimed at a window of 10 Downing Street.[20]

So that tells us something about the environment in which coins of this
sort circulated. Other actions and events in this episode include
mailbox bombs, mass arrests, hunger strikes, and the martyrdom of
Emily Davidson under the hooves of the King's horse at the Derby.

But I want to concentrate on the object itself, and in particular on
the words both embossed (by design) and impressed (against the law)
on its surface.

The language around the circumference supplies an entire political
cosmology upheld by divine sanction. The abbreviated Latin here

---

20. 'Suffragette-defaced penny', Episode 95 of the BBC's *A History of the World in 100
Objects,* 2010, transcript archived at
http://www.bbc.co.uk/ahistoryoftheworld/about/transcripts/episode95/

translates to 'Edward VII by the grace of God King of all Britain defender of the faith Emperor of Britain': mighty titles and lofty claims that combine ancient privilege, on the one hand, with imperial expansion, on the other.

What about the language that's been added to the coin?

T.J. Clark says, 'Money is the root form of representation in bourgeois society. Threats to monetary value are threats to signification itself'.[21] Tap the 'V' into the copper with a jeweller's letter punch. 'Money is a kind of poetry', Wallace Stevens observes in his *Adagia*.[22] Adjust your grip on the hammer while you pick up the 'O'. What happens if we consider this coin as a poem? Hit the 'T' home right above his ear. We might want first to reflect on genre conventions. Drive the 'E' into his temple. Marx in the *Grundrisse* defines money as a social relationship disguised as a metal. Let the 'S' indent his cheek. Money's value on this account derives from the network of social relations that subscribe to and produce it as a form of value. The 'F' goes into the occipital lobe. What threats to signification have been cut into the surface of this little disc? The 'O' belongs behind the ear. What social relationships are being undisguised on this piece of metal? Align the 'R' to the jawbone. As a consequence of the language that's been added to it, this particular unit of money represents by unveiling the substance of the structure of agreements that we forget we've made. If your grip slips as you add the 'W', it might be an 'OMEN'.

A few people I've shown this coin to over the years have pointed out the 'T O O' you can see if you have the habit of spelling words vertically (like in a crossword or on a Scrabble board). Such unintended excess seems apt. The blunt force of the hammered-in slogan interrupts the authority of the Latin letters raised around the rim and makes possible both inadvertent and strategic misreadings of the words in the slogan. 'The poem', Paul Celan says, 'is that which does not fit the measure'.[23] But this lack of fitness is no liability, and indeed in this instance correlates directly with *le part sans part* that Jacques Rancière

---

21. T.J. Clark, *Farewell to an Idea: Episodes from a History of Modernism*, New Haven: Yale University Press, 1999, p.10.
22. Wallace Stevens, *Opus Posthumous*, New York: Knopf, 1989, p.191.
23. Paul Celan, *The Meridian: Final Version - Drafts - Materials*, (Trans. Pierre Joris), Stanford: Stanford University Press, 2011, p.165.

identifies at the centre of 'politics': 'Politics exists through the fact of a magnitude that escapes ordinary measurement, this part of those who have no part that is nothing and everything'.[24] The so-called 'suffragettes' were exactly that: the necessary exclusion without whom no nation-state, and by whose abjection men have defined politics.

The slogan on this coin could well be a poem of the transfordant sort I'd like to think we need to write more of – the kind of text that allows us to reconstitute the niches we compose and live in together. A transformative utterance. For isn't the misprision of the slogan as a caption – taking, that is, VOTES FOR WOMEN as a description rather than a demand – sanctioned by the historical transformation this restamped coin helped to precipitate? Gresham's law states that 'bad money drives out good'. But what happens when 'bad money' flips the script and succeeds in reorganising the social relationships the metal disguises? One hundred years ago this slogan was a demand; today it is in many countries a description. 65,844,954 US citizens voted for a woman in November 2016.

But let's not get ahead of ourselves. Leaving aside the question of the strengths and limits of electoral politics, which is to say notwithstanding the achievement of 'votes for women', we do well to take note of one thing that achievement obscures: the gender income gap. The city I live closest to (Seattle) has the largest gender income gap in the United States: a woman is paid 77 cents for every dollar a man earns, with an average loss of $12,000 per woman per year, making for a total loss of almost $8 billion per year. One could ask why our politicians aren't busy tying themselves up in knots over this. Perhaps it's because they are too busy raising campaign contributions. Members of the U.S. Congress spend an average of 2-3 hours a day on the phone raising money. Their *daily* target is to raise between $10,000 and 15,000 – which is roughly the same amount as that *annual* income gap per capita in the Seattle area.... An uncanny equivalence comes into view. There is still work to do. Get your hammers.

That said, this sabotaged coin's contributions to demonstrable transformations in conditions of possibility allow me to ask: what needs to be the case for your slogan to metamorphose from a demand into a

---

24. Jacques Rancière, *Disagreement: Politics and Philosophy*, (Trans. Julie Rose), Minneapolis: Minnesota University Press, 1999, p.15.

A THIRD

Fiery Flying Roule:

TO

All the Inhabitants of the earth; ſpecially to the rich ones.

"Here we are" — You can't
hear us without having to be
us knowing everything we

know — you know you can't

Verbal echoes so many ghost
poets I think of you as wild
and fugitive — "Stop awhile"

[Susan Howe, *Souls of the Labadie Tract* (New Directions, 2007), 58]

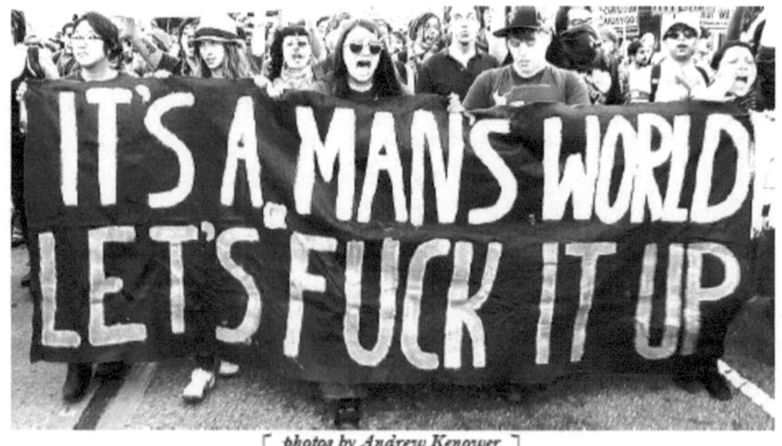

[*photos by Andrew Kenower*]

description, for your phrase to shift phases across these registers, for your saying to become tantamount to a doing?

§

James Reason's 'Swiss cheese model' of an 'accident trajectory'[25] offers a counterintuitive visualisation that could help us answer these questions:

Look at the cheese. Look at the slices. Look at the shadows under the slices. Look at the holes. Look at how the holes line up. Look at what a complex system is. Look at a breakdown. Look at the failure domains. Look at the lapses in infrastructure, training, failsafes. Look at the accident that comes into view when apertures in each of these layers open up simultaneously and align. Look at how incompetence, bias, malfeasance, bad design, bad planning all align to wreck your day, your night, your week, your month, your year, your life. Look at the coordination of active and latent failures. Look at Brexit. Look at what you have done. Look at Trump. Look at how it happens. Look at how all the systems you thought would operate successfully as a barricade against contingency conspire to compose the conditions of possibility for the very thing you thought you were sure to avoid. Look at the arrow. Look at the vector. Look at the tip. Look at the penetration. Look at 'Hazards'. Look at 'Losses'. Look at 'Hazards' transforming into 'Losses'. Look at the potential rendered actual. Look at transformation. Look at what happens when we cross out the word 'Losses' and write in the word 'Gains'. Look at how an 'accident trajectory' could also be used to represent an 'opportunity trajectory'. Look at your demand turning into a description. Look at Reason's diagram now become an excellent illustration of what the ancient Greeks termed *kairos*. Look at that ineluctable sense of timing that reveals the opportune moment when you can 'thread the needle' in an athletic sense, sweeping past or between defenders to score, or in the rhetorical sense, when you clinch the case with your audience against the odds. Look at the philologists who tell us that for the ancient Greeks *kairos* referred not only to the ephemeral artefacts of poetry and oratory, but also to the more concrete practices of weaving and archery.[26]

---

25. James Reason, 'Human Error: Models and Management', *British Medical Journal*, No.320, 2000, p.769.

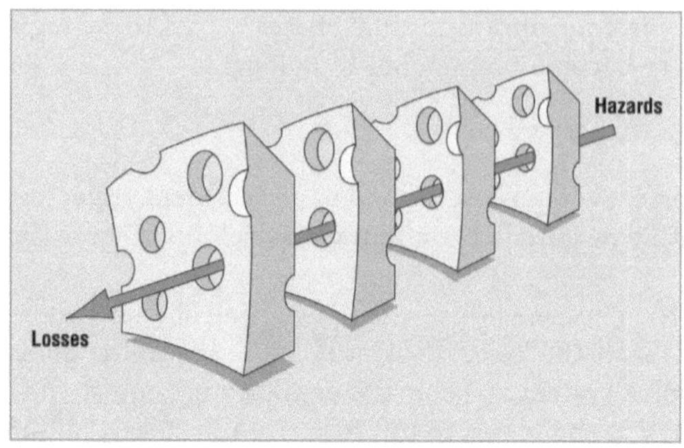

The Swiss cheese model of how defences, barriers, and safeguards
may be penetrated by an accident trajectory

§

The demand that hides a description puts me in mind of Kenneth
Koch's poem 'One Train May Hide Another' (which takes its conceit
from a sign he once saw at a railroad crossing in Kenya):

> In a poem, one line may hide another line,
> As at a crossing, one train may hide another train.
> That is, if you are waiting to cross
> The tracks, wait to do it for one moment at
> Least after the first train is gone. And so when you read
> Wait until you have read the next line –
> Then it is safe to go on reading.[27]

§

One poster may hide another. Shepard Fairey's famous poster for
Barack Obama's 2008 campaign has a scrappy sticker of the professional
wrestler known as Andre the Giant behind it. Both feature stylised
portraits. Both are anchored in four-letter words in all caps. You

---

26. Richard Onians, *The Origins of European Thought*, Cambridge, Cambridge
University Press, 1951, p.346. I owe the form this section performs to Matt
Longabucco, who I think might have picked it up from Darwin: 'Look at the family
of squirrels [...]. Now look at the *Galeopithicus* or flying lemur', *On Natural Selection*,
New York: Penguin, 2005 (1859), pp.82-3.
27. Kenneth Koch, *The Collected Poems of Kenneth Koch*, New York: Knopf, 2007,
pp.441-442.

probably first met the Obama poster on the internet. The Andre sticker frequented surfaces in Providence, Rhode Island – alleys and stop signs and billboards and bathroom stalls in bars. The word at the bottom of the Obama poster is an ambiguous term: that noun could be packing a verb. The word on the Andre sticker is obviously a verb. One four letter word may hide another; what Emily Dickinson called 'the thing with feathers' may hide a command.

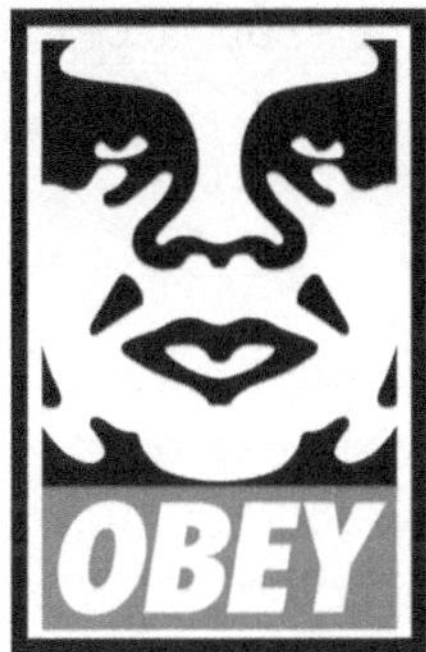

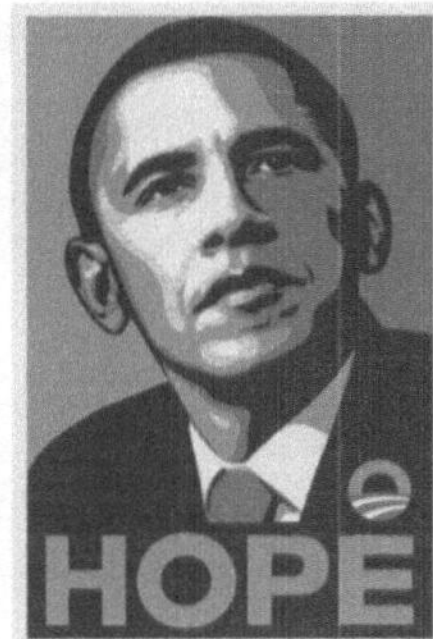

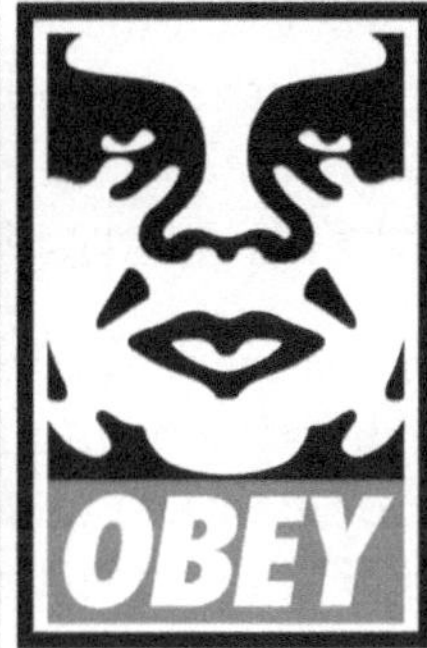

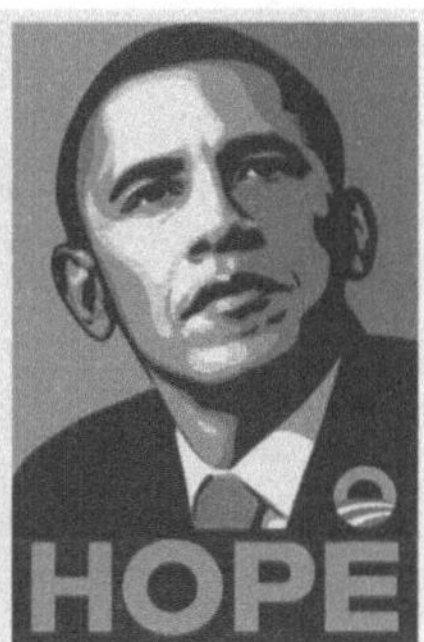

It is also the case that one slogan may hide another. From a letter to a friend dated 26 July 2016:

after a week at a distance from the English language, and feeling really how impoverished we 'Mericans are in our hegemonic audio-visual bubbles, I hear Hillary's catchphrase in a new way. 'Love trumps hate', she says with misplaced ontological confidence. But if you are unaware that the word 'trump' is a verb, this slogan might sound more like an order. Nouns and verbs can easily switch places, in other words – leading us to read a possessive imperative: 'Love Trump's hate'. The slogan commands us to adore the unfiltered despising.

What needs to be the case for your description to turn into a demand?

§

Roman Jakobson begins his 'Closing Statement: Poetry and Poetics' (first read at an academic conference in 1958) by declaring, 'Fortunately, scholarly and political conferences have nothing in common'.[28] But a

---

28. Roman Jakobson, 'Closing Statement: Poetry and Poetics', in Thomas A. Sebeok (Ed.), *Style in Language*, Cambridge MA.: MIT Press, 1960, p.350.

few pages later he has no problem recruiting a political slogan as an exemplary instance of what he calls 'the poetic function', observing along the way that 'Any attempt to reduce the sphere of poetic function to poetry or to confine poetry to poetic function would be a delusive oversimplification' (356). I couldn't agree more, but along these very lines wonder whether barricading scholarship and politics from each other isn't itself a mistake. For shouldn't the scholarly function – making knowledge common – be central to the political function – making power common? A kind of open source equal access opportunity trajectory gets missed here.

Jill Lepore recently established the political environment from which Jakobson plucks his unforgettable example:

> [W]ith campaign ads from every side being broadcast night after night, voters might have been muddled. In one television ad from 1956 – produced by political consultants, relying on public-opinion polling – a cartoon voter despairs, 'I've listened to everybody. On TV and radio. I've read the papers and magazines. I've tried! But I'm still confused. Who's right? What's right? What should I believe? What are the facts? How can I tell?' But the parties made their choices clear: 'Words have been flying at you hot and heavy', a comforting narrator tells the cartoon voter, who considers the evidence and concludes, 'Me? I like Ike!'[29]

Jakobson zooms in on this very jingle and uses it to isolate what he calls 'the empirical linguistic criterion of the poetic function'. He gets there by way of an acute analysis of the relationships forged by the slogan's sound-shape:

> The political slogan 'I like Ike' /ay layk ayk/, succinctly structured, consists of three monosyllables and counts three diphthongs /ay/, each of them symmetrically followed by one consonantal phoneme, /..I..k..k/. The make-up of the three words presents a variation: no consonantal phonemes in the first word, two around the diphthong in the second, and one final consonant in the third. [...] Both cola of the trisyllabic formula 'I like / Ike' rhyme with each other, and the second of the two rhyming words is fully included in the first one (echo rhyme), /layk/ – /ayk/, a paronomastic image of

---

29. Jill Lepore, 'The Party Crashers', *The New Yorker,* 22 February 2016.

a feeling which totally envelops its object. Both cola alliterate with each other, and the first of the two alliterating words is included in the second: /ay/ – /ayk/, a paronomastic image of the loving subject enveloped by the beloved object. The secondary poetic function of this electional catch phrase reinforces its impressiveness and efficacy. (357)

Here I especially like 'a paronomastic image of a feeling which totally envelopes its object', and would only add that, in this particular case, 'the beloved object' is the Chief Executive, and moreover that it is the Chief Executive as designated by the affectionate nickname from his childhood. Not Dwight D. Eisenhower, the Supreme Commander of the Allied Forces in Europe during World War II (responsible for D-Day, etc.), who in his own 'Closing Statement' from the Oval Office (two years after Jakobson's talk was delivered) warned his fellow citizens of the dangers of massive military spending and privatization, which he labelled 'the military industrial complex'. Not that person, but rather 'Ike'. It is also interesting to note how the sound-shape regulates the particular feeling that is being announced. Not 'I *love* Ike', but 'like'. The current President (inaugurated the day this essay is due: thanks, editors) has no problem talking about what he loves. 'I love the poorly educated', he announced, for instance, on winning the Nevada caucus.[30] I bet he does.

Jakobson concludes his formal analysis by observing that the 'poetic function of the electional catch phrase reinforces its impressiveness and efficacy'. The slogan's action, on this account, is part and parcel of its form. The operation of 'efficacy' here is of particular interest in light of Charles Sanders Peirce's account of how a linguistic sign operates (this from one of his letters to Lady Welby):

> It appears to me that the essential function of a sign is to render inefficient relations efficient – not to set them into action, but to establish a habit or general rule whereby they will act on occasion.[31]

The sign in this reckoning creates an affordance trajectory, a channel of 'efficiency', a means of praxis, a possibility of acting and doing. Signs under the influence of the poetic function as Jakobson describes it foreground their status as things:

The set [...] toward the MESSAGE as such, focus on the message for its own sake is the POETIC FUNCTION of language. [...] This function, by promoting the palpability of signs, deepens the fundamental dichotomy of signs and objects. (356)

Or as Koch puts it in 'One Train May Hide Another':

So always standing in front of something the other
as words stand in front of objects, feelings, and ideas.
One wish may hide another.

Can we say, then, that what Jakobson calls the 'efficacy' of the poetic function makes it possible to consciously withdraw the 'efficiency' Peirce describes, and that a poem can be made to sabotage 'habits or general rules' – social norms and social forms, a.k.a. 'wishes' – that are obstacles to realising the desire to make power common? This question is indebted to Flynn's conception of sabotage as 'the conscious withdrawal of the workers' industrial efficiency'. In this sense I take the function of sabotage to involve the tactic of withdrawing efficiency not for its own sake, but as part of a larger strategy of transforming the relation between labour and value in the first place. By the same token, a poem's withdrawal of semantic or cognitive efficiency transforms the

---

30. Speaking of current events and the pasts they recover, Eisenhower's sloganeers tried to find a way to get his running mate Richard Nixon in on the action and ended up with 'I like Ike and Dick'. It has a certain ring to it, but it fractures the alliteration of the original with a sound that requires us to shape our mouths as if we were baring our fangs in disgust. As it happens this very expression gets included on Zephyrus Image's bumper sticker to help you spell the rebus:

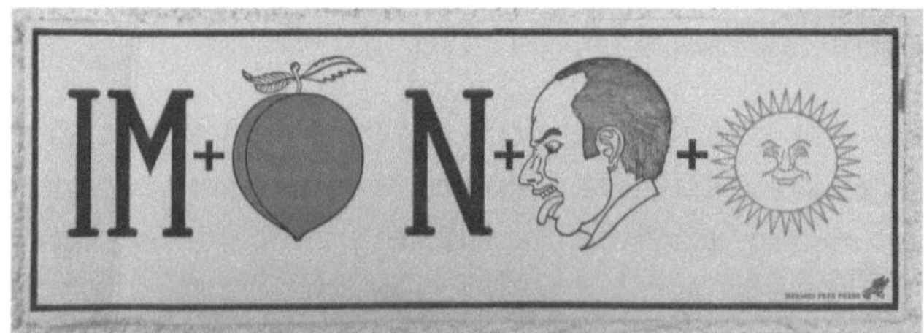

Speaking of Tricky Dick, Senator Nixon's first major outing into the spotlight was as Senator Joseph McCarthy's sidekick on the House Un-American Committee. Also on the HUAC team was attorney Roy Cohn, a.k.a. Preznit Combover McTweet's mentor in political streetfighting. Oh, and before I forget, while 'I like Ike and Dick' doesn't work so well, Chris Kraus has discovered that calling a book *I Love Dick* seems to.
31. Charles Sanders Peirce, *Selected Writings*, New York: Dover, 1966, p.390.

relation between words and things.[32] The poem thus 'makes nothing happen' by remaking the ways in which we describe how anything happens to begin with.

Jakobson's poetic function places a premium on what seems, from the perspective of the normal discourse, like the wrong kind of equivalence. By foregrounding the material composition of the message, the poetic function transforms our relationship to the message as such. No longer transparent, the medium exerts organisational force over the utterance: '*The poetic function projects the principle of equivalence from the axis of selection to the axis of combination*' (358; his emphasis). In so doing, the poetic function transforms hierarchies embedded in our semiotic reflexes. 'Equivalence is promoted to the constitutive device of the sequence', Jakobson writes, suggesting that the hierarchies implicit in 'selection' are suspended when the poetic function is operational; '*struggle*', as Kropotkin puts it, 'is replaced by *cooperation*'. As a consequence, the arbitrary relationship between signifier and signified that Saussure describes is transformed into a necessary relationship – or at least the possibility of a necessary relation draws into view. Not, we should add, as a means of passively representing the objects signified in the poetic utterance, but rather as an active means of transforming the relationship between those objects. The poetic function transforms the hierarchy of representation, and thus, I want to argue, has the power to transform that which it represents in the first place.

§

Insofar as Jakobson describes and defines the poetic function by way of a political slogan, how might we return the favour? What, in other words, can poetry teach us about 'the political function'? Jacques Rancière's premise is that the political is predicated on and precipitated by 'the presupposition of the equality of anyone and everyone'.[33] Or, as Judith Butler has recently put it: 'To be a political actor is a function, a feature of acting on terms of equality with other humans [...]. Equality is a condition and character of political action itself at the same time that it is its goal'.[34] That seems like one place to start: from the fact

---

32. Elizabeth Gurley Flynn, *Sabotage: The Conscious Withdrawal of the Workers' Industrial Efficiency*, Chicago: I.W.W. Publications Bureau, 1917.
33. *Disagreement*, op. cit., p.17.

that both the political (as these thinkers define it) and the poetic (as Jakobson defines it) concern equality and equivalence – which of course are not exactly equal to each other or equivalent, but you get the point. (Remembering the penny we looked at earlier, it is worth observing in passing that money, for Marx, operates as a 'general equivalent' on which an especially durable economic logic is predicated.)

What needs to be the case for your demand to become equal to a description, or for your description to be converted into the equivalent of a demand?

§

Everyone knows how Archibald MacLeish's 1926 poem 'Ars Poetica' ends ('A poem should not mean / But be'), but few enough know how its last stanza begins:

> A poem should be equal to:
> > Not true.

I love the precision of this counterfactual couplet. Look at what happens when you translate it into math:

$$\text{' poem ' = ' } \neq \text{ '}$$

This is an excellent companion for Celan's definition: 'The poem is that which does not fit the measure'. Remembering the etymology of our word 'poem' in the Greek verb *poiein* ('to make'), I take 'true' in MacLeish's couplet to refer not just to the adjective that is the opposite of false, but also to the noun that carpenters or bike mechanics use when they say that a doorframe or a wheel is 'out of true,' as well as the verb they engage in when they set to make the object of their craft level, even, smooth, and in accordance with the rest of the ensemble it is a part of. 'I'm losing true,' as Maggie Roche once sang in harmony with her sisters. A poem's job, the couplet argues, is to be even and level not only with the false but also with the uneven and unlevel.[35]

---

34. Judith Butler, *Notes Toward a Performative Theory of Assembly*, Cambridge, MA.: Harvard University Press, 2015, p.52.
35. The poem in this sense conjures the anomaly in the Kuhnian terms I articulate in 'The Anomaly Contains the Homily' (op. cit.).

Zong! #4

this is

not was

or

should be

this be

not

should be

this

should

not

be

is

In this light let us consider the fourth poem from the first section of M. NourbeSe Philip's *Zong!*[36]

The language here is extracted from the legal decision in the notorious *Gregson v. Gilbert* case, which concerns the insurance claim related to the murder by drowning of 150 enslaved persons by the captain and crew of the slave ship *Zong* in 1781. As Philip describes it in her afterword:

An accurate interpretation of the contract of insurance, according to the owners of the *Zong*, that is, would result in great financial benefit to them: they would be paid for murdering 150 Africans. At the same time, it would mean that the deliberate drowning of 150 people was not murder, but merely the disposition of property in a time of

---

36. M. NourbeSe Philip, *Zong!*, Middletown, CT.: Wesleyan University Press, 2008, p.7.

emergency to ensure preservation of the rest of the 'cargo' – a reasonable interpretation at that time given the law governing contracts of insurance. However, even if the courts had found against the owners of the *Zong* and ruled that they could not claim insurance compensation, given the law at the time, neither Captain Collingwood nor those who had helped in the massacre could be charged with murder, since what was destroyed, being property, was not capable of being murdered. (191)

The seventeen words of *Zong! #4* report that these legal circumstances and the economic equations they rely on – humans as things, humans as property, humans as cargo, humans measured as money – are not past but present. 'This is / not was': the capitalist rendering of enslaved persons is an ongoing historical process. The 'or / should be' introduces the normative imperative that MacLeish plays with. These facts persist but they ought not to. The poem sounds this claim like a chord, distributing tenses fretted with negation across two right-justified columns. The facts of the case should indeed add up to 'not true', but as that ultimate 'is' insists – adamant beyond the range of the double-entry arrangement that determines the shape of the rest of the page – the facts of the case are not only not 'not true' but remain operative to this day. The outlying 'is' does not fit the measure. And it tells what is true.

Whereas the 'suffragette-defaced penny' (as the British Museum calls it) that we looked at earlier in this essay does its work by means of language hammered into a piece of money, Philip's poem, by contrast, is made out of language extracted and subtracted from a legal document about the 'payment of costs' associated with the business-as-usual massacre of enslaved persons. Under the regime of Jakobson's poetic function, words are treated as things; under the regime of slavery, persons are. The composition of the slogan added to the coin and the composition of *Zong!* both notably involve the use of force. 'I murder the text', as Philip puts it in her afterword,

> literally cut it into pieces, castrating verbs, suffocating adjectives, murdering nouns, throwing articles, prepositions, conjunctions overboard, jettisoning adverbs: I separate subject from verb, verb from object — create semantic mayhem, until my hands bloodied, from so much cutting and killing, reach into the stinking, eviscerated innards, and like some seer, sangoma [healer], or prophet who,

having sacrificed an animal for signs and portents of a new life, or
simply life, reads the untold story that tells itself by not telling. (193)

§

Gordon Brotherstone writes that 'the prime function of classic texts is
to construct political space and anchor historical continuity'.[37] I take
Zong! to be a classic text in exactly these terms. What happens when
the political space made by the classic text is predicated on the
violation of the political precept of universal equality? Or when you
anchor historical continuity on the radical discontinuities of
kidnapping, rape, murder, forced labour, and all the other predations
that slavery entailed? Philip's poem makes it necessary for us to
excavate these questions. To default to them. The prime function of
classic texts in this sense is to *reconstruct* political space by anchoring
historical *discontinuity*. Desire built on a rift. The poem performs both a
description ('this is') and a demand ('this / should / not / be')
simultaneously, and leaves us with the question: *what needs to be the
case for things to be otherwise?*

Acknowledgements

My thanks to Anthony Iles, Marina Vishmidt, Miranda Mellis and Siloh
Radovsky for active and engaged reading and responding.

---

37. Gordon Brotherston, *Book of the Fourth World*, Cambridge: Cambridge University
Press, 1992, p.4.

CLASS SEPARATION VS. SEPARATION

DANNY HAYWARD

In the third chapter of his *Reflections On Violence*, 'Prejudices Against Violence', the French revolutionary syndicalist Georges Sorel explained why it was necessary for the proletariat to retain a strict separation from the middle class. 'Everything may be saved', Sorel wrote,

> if the proletariat, by their use of violence, manage to reestablish the division into classes, and so restore to the middle class something of its former energy; that is the great aim towards which the whole thought of men – who are not hypnotised by the events of today, but who think of the condition of tomorrow – must be directed.[1]

The condition of salvation that is imagined here exists in the grand tradition of modern regenerative brutality stretching from Walter Raleigh to his insurgent antipode Frantz Fanon. Violence is at first conceived in it as the political equivalent of a sudden awakening. In Fanon's language, it retrieves its agent from a state of aboulia, or absence of willpower,[2] transfiguring those 'who are inert, cannot make plans, who have no resources [and] who live from day to day' into the bearers of 'a national destiny and a collective history'.[3] In the language of Sorel it wrenches its agent out of a state of 'hypnosis', disentrancing him from his petty preoccupation with 'the events of today', and fixing his attention upon the great mythical display cabinet of tomorrow, in which can just about be made out, wreathed in the trailing ribbons of mystical circumlocution, its apocalyptically nondescript trophy-'condition': 'the condition of tomorrow'.

For anyone who now passes their days isolated 'trying to defeat or gratify powerful impulses in a world [they] fear', and who is continually jerked awake by the ordinary violence of state politics, this 'condition' may feel unreal even before they begin to consider whether or not it may be desirable.[4] The politics of regressive separation are more alive now than they have been at any time in the last fifty years; and the psychological para-politics of fear and aversiveness are revived with them simultaneously and to a still greater degree. Furthermore, as this revival picks up speed across multiple election cycles and throughout

---

1. Georges Sorel, *Reflections on Violence*, Jeremy Jennings (Ed.), Cambridge: Cambridge University Press, 1999, p.85.
2. Frantz Fanon, *The Wretched of the Earth*, (Trans. Constance Farrington), London: Penguin 1961, p.228.
3. Ibid., p. 73.
4. Richard Wright, *Native Son*, London: Vintage, 2000, p.73.

the whole mediatised atmosphere of 'public opinion', the process throws up its own sub-tendency, in the form of a newly urgent, reactive politics of compulsory and defensive unity. What, in these circumstances, could radical separateness in Sorel's sense even mean, if indeed there ever was such a thing, and the theory of class separation for which he became known was ever anything but a kind of elaborate justification for ascetic puritanism, with all of the tendencies towards sexual suffocation and displaced misogyny that nurture such ideologies and that tend irrepressibly to flourish at their root?

The following short essay tries to answer this question. It is not a history of the political economic changes that have given rise to regressive separation, or that have made earlier politics of radical separation wither away until nothing can be seen of them but their own most regressive stumps; but it is instead a brief and provisional attempt to explain one psychological *relationship* between fascist demands for racial or ethnic segregation and liberal demands for national unity, and to show how in both worldviews the fraught and painful *fact* of separation is harmfully denied and precluded from vital or quickening expression. For the same reason, it is one element of a broader account of the *instinct* for separation in a transformative and expressively open radical culture.

§

On 16 June 2016, six days before the referendum on UK EU membership, the British neo-Nazi Thomas Mair murdered the Labour MP and 'Remain' supporter Jo Cox. The killing was a testimony to the historical and psychoanalytic significance of the need for separation over unity. Mair was reported to be a 'loner' with strong symptoms of depression and compulsion neurosis.[5] In the days after Cox's death, the newspapers that reported pruriently on his habits of obsessive self-cleaning also noted that his search record on the computers at the library where he would later shoot and stab Cox included queries about matricide,[6] a desire that was linked in Mair's mind with the relationship his mother had formed with a British Caribbean man during his middle adolescence.[7] The violence through which he hoped in Sorelian terms 'to manage to reestablish [...] division' played out in

---

5. 'Thomas Mair: Extremist loner who targeted Jo Cox', 23 November 2016, http://www.bbc.co.uk/news/uk-38071894.

the key of fantasised restitution, recalling such other rifts between overt purpose and deed in the vocabulary of the US extreme right as conversion 'therapy' and 'corrective' rape. Its unconscious attempt to transform a passive, infantile fear of abandonment (or extreme separation anxiety) into an active, grown-up desire to enforce a regime of ethnic apartheid,[8] is only the latest historical expression of the repressive attitude that Sorel would pompously celebrate as the heroic will-to-separation in the 'resigned abnegation of men who strive uncomplainingly'.[9]

---

6. Hatred of mothers is a consistent preoccupation of personality types that incline towards movement fascism (though *state* fascism clearly has an infinitely larger constituency), as Klaus Theweleit and Christina Wieland have shown in their writings on the institutions of masculinity: Klaus Theweleit, 'Männliche Geburtsweisen', in *Das Land, das Ausland heisst,* Munich: DTV, 1995, and Christina Wieland, *The Undead Mother: Psychoanalytic Explorations of Masculinity, Femininity and Matricide,* London: Karnac, 2000.

7. Richard Spillett, "Jekyll and Hyde' assassin was a loner ...', *Daily Mail,* 23 November 2016, http://www.dailymail.co.uk/news/article-3960988/Jekyll-Hyde-Jo-Cox-assassin-Thomas-Mair.html; Dan Sales and Gemma Mullin, 'He Would Have Killed Again', *The Sun,* 23rd November 2016, https://www.thesun.co.uk/news/2246112/jo-cox-killer-thomas-mair-planned-more-murders/. In the *Mail* article, Mair's half-brother Duane St Lewis is quoted as saying that 'He has never expressed any views about Britain, or shown any racist tendencies. I'm mixed race and I'm his half-brother, we got on well. He never married. The only time I remember him having a girlfriend was as a young man, but a mate stole her off him. He said that put him off [women] for life.' This is of course just a de-contextualised pull quote, and in its original usage it was intended primarily to indicate that Mair's act was not 'ideological' but only 'disturbed', in accordance with the desire of the *Mail* and the majority of the British news media to disassociate the murder from the general atmosphere of the campaign in favour of a vote to leave the EU, for which the *Mail* and the majority of the British news media was of course directly and perhaps even primarily responsible. But doesn't it seem at least to suggest the centrality to Mair's fantasy life of some primal rage at perceived abandonment, that the first experience of desertion by a partner should be treated as if it were an irreparable and inexpiable wrong, for which all women in general were to be indifferently held responsible? The idea that it 'put [Mair] off for life' is one indication that he had in fact already been put off, and that the first adult of experience of 'relationship trouble' was seized upon as an opportunity to rationalise, and so to take possession of, what would otherwise have remained a merely troubling and inexplicable aversion. (Likewise, it's conspicuous in Duane St Lewis's account that the man who 'stole' Mair's girlfriend brought about no lasting transformation in Mair's general attitude towards 'mates'. The selective apportionment of blame conforms to a stupefyingly familiar pattern. If the child suffers, it must be the fault of the mother; never of the father: always the EU, never of the member state.)

It is necessary to talk about Cox's murder like this, in spite of the dangers of pathological 'readings' of fascism, and in spite of the risks of converting hateful political assassination into a portfolio of materials for an amateur case study, because it is important to keep in view trembling at the root of racist 'divisiveness' some wildly distorted demand for unity. Murder in the name of fascist violence originates in a convulsively distorted protest against the conditions that it reproduces. This principle of interpretation is valuable, not because it helps us to remember that ultimately fascists are hurt and complex human beings, full of inarticulate anguish and perhaps also one day subject to rehabilitation,[10] but because it helps us to see how gestures of premature reconciliation in the name of the 'divided' national community are not necessarily the *opposite* of feverish moralising about the 'virtue' of violent segregation, but are just as frequently *the elaborations of an identical process of self-therapy*, only now uttered in a language of more refined purpose and with a greater consistency of form and expressive content.[11] It is today the 21 January 2017. It is more than seven months since Cox's murder. Yesterday Donald Trump was inaugurated as president of the United States talking in the language of an LA scriptwriter about the necessity of confronting 'American carnage'. The liberal-parliamentarian press disgorges as if from an open sluice an unending sequence of condemnations of divisiveness, appeals for 'healing', pious wishes for the re-creation of

---

8. The thought process evidences a conventional inversion: Mair believed that his mother deserved to die because she was a 'race traitor': white supremacism serves to rationalise a pre-existing desire and therefore to give to it a semblance of meaning. It might wondered whether this helps to explain why Mair's desire to kill his mother, although conscious, was also *inactive*, so that newspapers could report that he had spent the day before the murder re-tuning his mother's TV. Cox was of course the ultimate victim of these displacements.

9. *Reflections on Violence*, op. cit., p.228.

10. Although patently it won't be Thomas Mair or even the members of a fucking Nazi gang like National Action who will benefit most significantly from the conversion of the United Kingdom into an outsized tax-free headquarter complex, which in the absence of any other means of commanding a share of total global surplus value is what its asset-holding political class now intends to make of it. (National Action is the first fascist organisation to have been proscribed in the UK. The ban was initiated by the Tory Home Secretary Amber Rudd, in part because of the organisation's public endorsement of Thomas Mair. One of its members was jailed last year for attempting to behead, and for seriously injuring, a Sikh dentist from Leeds.)

unity. It tacitly acknowledges the impotence of these declarations by offshoring its own internal anxiety onto the outgoing President Obama, or else onto 'his wife', substituting for active resistance against authoritarian state populism a comforting fantasy of paternal invulnerability, the tweedy decorousness of which is so blazingly and absolutely out of sync with reality as to seem actually laughable:

> Obama descended the steps shoulder to shoulder with Trump, chatting and sharing a joke. At the bottom, Obama smiled broadly. His wife could not hide an expression akin to melancholy. He lifted her hand to his lips and kissed it, giving her a reassuring smile.[12]

Here, and in passages that are akin it, the liberal and humane call for 'unity' and 'healing' (Obama and Trump, shoulder to shoulder!) exhibits by virtue of its precipitousness another instance of just that kind of false resolution that in the psychohistory of a neo-Nazi transforms the fear and despair of separation into the catastrophic political need for it.

---

11. To drag slightly out of context a line of Leo Bersani's: 'brutality is identical to [...] idealization': *Is the Rectum a Grave?: And Other Essays,* Chicago: University of Chicago Press, p.29. Incidentally, if Bersani is right in his thesis, and what is stereotypically treated as 'passive' sexuality (i.e., in male heterosexual assumptions concerning gay sex and female sexuality) is identified with, and organically repeats, a pleasure that is felt during episodes of infancy in which the child is faced with the loss of identity, then it makes sense that a person who experienced especial pain due to helplessness or abandonment during a later stage in childhood might eventually turn against this earlier sense of loss of control with a special intensity, and condemn its perceived corollaries in *adult* sexual life with an aggressive aversiveness that seems pathetically hypertrophied even when viewed in comparison to the 'ordinary' prejudices of the dominant (i.e., male heterosexual) social outlook (*Is the Rectum a Grave?,* p.24). The relationship of these two outlooks is apologetically summarised by the brother of Mair's 'inspiration' David Copeland, in an episode of the BBC's *Panorama* series aired in 1999: 'I think he [David Copeland] just had a healthy dislike of gays, like most of the male gender have, not a hatred, just a dislike'. (Copeland was convicted in 1999 for a series of bombings aimed at ethnic minorities and what he enviously understood to be the London gay 'community'. Mair ordered his first consignment of weapon assembly manuals 10 days after Copeland's first court appearance.) See http://news.bbc.co.uk/hi/english/static/audio_video/programmes/panorama/trans cripts/transcript_30_06_00.txt; and https://www.theguardian.com/uk-news/2016/nov/23/thomas-mair-slow-burning-hatred-led-to-jo-cox-murder. The *Guardian* article in particular contains some intelligent investigative reporting.
12. Joanna Walters,'Obama departs White House with a promise', *The Guardian,* https://www.theguardian.com/us-news/2017/jan/20/barack-obama-departs-white-house.

It is a model example of what Freud called 'the splitting of the ego in the process of defence',[13] unchecked by the salves and selfless Band-Aids of middle-class nationalism that promise to 'reassure' the ego in the process of its coagulation. Everywhere I look this kind of false resolution seems to reproduce itself, in every by-way and outcrop of political discourse. It flares up wherever some true political aspiration or real historical development is made too precipitously into the basis for reassuring political generalisation.

(Of course liberals will not all endorse Trump explicitly even if they continue to defend political measures that in the long run will help right-wing nationalism to thrive; and in fact many will despise him with the peculiar, heightened intensity of those who feel themselves to have been placed under threat for the very first time. But the argument that I am making is not that liberalism is incapable of endorsing 'separation' or antagonism under any circumstances but that in general it misconceives of the way in which the need for separation is originated and resolved. It needs to do this. Within the worldview implied by the average editorial in the *New York Times*, aversion to analysis of the psychological need for unity is what permits the reproduction of unity as a political demand. Without this aversion, the politics becomes lurid and insensible, because it is only by means of this mechanism that liberal thinking can free itself from the recognition that in this class society, the abstract attempt to effect reconciliation is just as likely to express itself in acts of reactionary violence as it is through the emergence of new relationships of mutual support. Put more directly, liberal thinking is averse to the psychological need for unity because that need arises not only in the face of threats to those liberal privileges that are embodied in the constitutional bourgeois state, but also in the face of deepening poverty, disintegrating family structures, under-employment or super-exploitation, landlordism, benefit cuts, news of distant family uprooted by bombs and foreign-armed militia, and above all in the deep personal recognition of exclusion that is the main element of class culture in a society no longer premised on formal segregation. Its commitment to circumscribing discussion of unity strictly within the domain of politics,

---

13. Sigmund Freud, 'The Splitting of the Ego in the Process of Defence', in *Complete Psychological Works of Sigmund Freud*, James Strachey et al.(Eds.) , London: Vintage, 2001.

and to screening it out of the domain of personal or 'individual' experience, is therefore paradoxically its main method for obfuscating the historical expression of class experience as such, and by this means of disclaiming its own participation in the reactionary violence against which it believes itself to be the single, indispensable bulwark.)[14]

Where does this leave us? The amateur enthusiast of neo-Nazism attempts to manage real individual trauma by transplanting it into a political fantasy of ethnic-national 'self-defence', while, by contrast, the professional advocate of unity under the auspices of liberal democracy attempts to shuffle individual trauma behind a row of wish-fulfilment fantasies, standing shoulder-to-shoulder in the public square of middle-class political inertia. Georges Sorel could not have foreseen the deep integrity of this state of affairs any more than could Marx or Rosa Luxemburg. But what does it mean that in both social outlooks the *fact* of separation or exclusion remains studiously denied or suppressed? If the desire to remain abstemiously separate from any culture has now become *decisively* reactionary, and yet the political demand for unity continues to be under present conditions inevitably lifelessly premature, how can the enduring and instinctual *experience* of separation be radicalised and transformed?

Transformative political art has to recognise, and wherever it already exists it does recognise in practice, that the history of class separation is in reality the history of capitalist unification. It is the gigantic expansion and integration of capitalist exploitation across the world and its implacable forced entry into every domain and level of human experience that determines the false resolution of Sorel's mythical vision into the pseudo-world history of Thomas Mair, abreacting from the comfort of his computer his unconscious rage at abandonment, and transforming it into the more ornate, conscious wish fulfilment of small town NSDAP-revivalism. And there is now no country and constituency or region where a Sorelian politics of 'class separation' can bring about any more desirable result, since even the

---

14. It follows from this that the criterion for a progressive politics of unity is that a movement should always articulate its response to the immediate, defensive demands of the situation in a practical vocabulary that is adequate to the experience of the excluded (who are emphatically not only from 'the white working class'), in disregard of the interests of those who have never previously been excluded from anything and who would now gladly place themselves at the head of the 'anti-fascist' resistance.

most extravagant nationalist pageantry and the wildest impostures about 'historic movement[s]'[15] is incapable of disguising the fact that behind the regalia and the blizzards of confetti and underneath the mediatised number crunching, no more significant *qualitative* transformation has taken place then the dignified metamorphosis of Thomas Mair's public computer terminal into the voting booth of every enfranchised adult citizen.

What Sorel thought of as the 'energy' of working-class culture is now produced not in the chaste and abstemious withdrawal from bourgeois values and institutions but in the hungry and confrontational seizure of means and instruments and modes of expression from which the working-class has historically been excluded. That is to say that it belongs in the intense and historically legitimate need for bourgeois privilege, *backed up by a knowledge teeming with biographical frustration and overshadowed by institutional harassment of the fundamental role of aggression in overcoming the forces that prohibit entry to it*. Its wild psychotherapy is not the frigid involution of fascist identitarianism or its practical endorsement under the inert heading of a National Healing Process; it is unity-through-seizure, movement for the sake of it, property violation, the experimental crossing of defined boundaries, self-dissipation, the rage of passivity, all lived out throughout and against the incessant integration of global capital and in defiance of the theoreticians whose voices echo out from its right-wing podia and rise up from its left-wing wells to announce in one single chorus its enduring and indefeasible authority.

How could there be in our world now any residual significance in the idea that the task of anti-capitalist *artists* is to create a separate and independent worldview, sectioned off from bourgeois reality not by a wall or by a checkpoint but by an energy that is so defiantly and incontrovertibly its own that middle-class consumers would flinch from it in disorientation or in grief? The radical theory that answers this question by declaring that separation is already over and done with, because capital now 'surpasses the division between employment and unemployment, working and non-working, productive and assisted,

---

15. Donald Trump, 'Everyone is listening to you now. You came by the tens of millions to become part of a historic movement, the likes of which the world has never seen before', 'Donald Trump's Full Inauguration Speech', http://time.com/4640707/donald-trump-inauguration-speech-transcript/.

precarious and non-precarious' – all of the 'divisions on which the left has based its categories of thought and action' – and that concludes that anti-capitalists 'must rise to [the same] level of abstraction [...] if we want to avoid being swept away' – this theory is in fact only half right.[16] It is right, because the raw fact of historical development does in truth point towards the overcoming of working-class separation both as a reality and as an ideal. But it is wrong, because it is only in the lexicon of petty bourgeois received ideas that 'separation' is always simply beneath consideration and abstraction is something to which we invariably rise up. The conclusions are too tediously familiar. For a more confrontational class culture, in which the threat of exclusion masses in the sky above our heads, and abstraction just as frequently advertises its openings beneath our feet, they represent a glaring reality deficit, a kind of obsessive-compulsive handwashing in the domain of political thought, prolonging the training of the intellectual sphincter into the late stage of anti-capitalist cultural theory. And the intuition that they scrape off or sadistically withhold is this. In a world whose complete integration is more liable to abstract assertion that it has ever been, what radical culture needs to separate itself from is not the history of bourgeois values or thought but the enormous, narcissistic complacency of those who profess to believe in their universal availability. That is to say, unity can be achieved only by those who know intimately not the residual significance of class separation, but the piercing shock of the discovery that in this society they are themselves only residually significant.

It is because even the most progressive middle-class appeals for unity totally lack this instinctive recognition, that they share at some deep and mostly unconscious level an uncomfortable affinity with the murderous demands for segregation that arise from the catastrophic failure to live with, to understand, or to tear from it some new source of fierce and unembarrassed expressive energy.

---

16. This quote is from Maurizio Lazzarato, *The Making of the Indebted Man: An Essay on the Neoliberal Condition*, Los Angeles: Semiotext, 2001, p.161; but others like it could have been found in any number of other writings representing roughly the same tendency.

DESCRIPTION WITH NO ARGUMENT

By Danny Hayward

I

This message is broadcast to you by a weak limb, and in its weak hand,
    a gap that anything could fill,
    handed out by a folding table with its borders redrawn like what it
is acceptable
                                to say
and is available in concrete and abstract from all sources of
    life in passive blocks of six to eight needs stitched together
then switched on or off indifferently as weeks go by, then years,
without
    that the blocks are disturbed
    or anything being done to make life rise up against its bitten off
fence
in idealism's depressed margin.
In concrete it peels off at 11.15 a.m.
The recession in argument as will be seen has no countertendency.
In times of generalised recession used-car insurance is king.

II

In some kind of life
    a weak limb, and in its hand
grass squares from an earlier period, lampposts,
fencing, a white fronted house with six windows,
driveways, everywhere autumnal dead
    whatever neighbours said as vines grow

unsteadily throughout the merged Day Centre access
ramp and must not be shocked by this,
but why not be dismayed by it,
half on foot, half flying, by the shops at the
roundabout a sign is blurred fantastically out
but points anyway strictly by virtue of that
upwards towards pre-eminently the sky.
The sky as usual has its own reasons to look on
as on-site the top-down rain rips up paving stones in original darkness.
They fail to load then go out. The next
scene you scroll to and currently shown is May 2015.
Though by the Industrial Co-operative Society
barbed wire is later asked about this by whatever means
in a gutter made of fingernails that were they ripped out would as
usual prove nothing
but that we are
here   anyway
and whatever now happens may an electric spark
detach itself from the circuit of an explosion and
descend to us, because without conviction words undo themselves and
get
                              boarded up;
and without conviction filth anoints itself in livid stages
as there is for whatever reason not entirely
an alleyway sucked forwards in frozen blocks to the bus shelter
of probable compassion in the pay of filth that without conviction eats
with untoward slowness our spark,
may it detach itself and descend to us
as utterly as the Picture Palace that fills with audacious poison,
shredded in the night there is outside falls in sheets. On the whole the
polystyrene box.
Then a seat of manufacture. It wilts upwards through the window
where slime looks on with its own reasons and in spite of them
marches
on the town centre pending
feelings of worth-
lessness which being also common make light of this; and across the
street
the gap between ideal and reality is deindustrialised.
     Gum thrashes in it like any tumour; around the corner

a mouth who takes shape backwards to compel itself to occupy
that gap is pushed out.
    You choose under what conditions you put life into it.
    In the torn axle with no conviction that ordered for my mouth
    to search desperately after an argument in the face of description
    and in passive indifference to the raw
    output of socialism, the gap reopens. In West
Yorkshire
        it is a library. Life swings shut like a mouth
ponderously.
We are all called.
We are all called
    to park somewhere close to the centre of this description
    with no fucking argument in drizzle and to step out
    to no applause as colours fly by and are the substance of things
        re-opened as a gastro pixel
thrashing in its own juice in fear and sudden
pain on the ground beneath the gaze of its plunging retail sector.
Now by Star Pizza there is a new outbreak of lifelessness.
A flyer crawls into the fingernail and it crumples there.
How many disabled car parking spaces live for the weekend.
Fire is occasional.
Life is a rough guess.
In the hairdresser to let the raw output of socialism
step out into the town centre of description with no fucking
argument
    would be irresponsible, as I am now irresponsible
        in the dull educational video of anti-fascism
        to thrash on the ground
    not knowing how to honour life without hypocrisy.
        In constituency surgery
you choose your character, turn decisively to the gap between ideal and
reality. The gap is either general or specialised. The reality is revised
downwards or the ideal is. Each posts its profits in the other. The gap is
unsustainable or it is not. A spark floating in it. The characters who buy
out the gap are porcine and didactic; Corporal Pig in the first season
memorably joins a patriotic association. Idealism is replaced with an
amethyst bladder on a hose and can be used as a pocket watch.
In a spin off Corporal Pig becomes close to Deng Xiaopig who files in
and then in a later season to General Pigochet. How to keep the gap

open undiminished and yet to love reality in spite of it is not enough.
How to make murder happen never in leaderless struggle at the far end
of today's unused capacity of despair, likewise. If
the gap grows hostile and is then manipulated
in a conspiracy still it is yours too to manipulate
like a description with no argument or a centre with no periphery,
and throughout all of it the elasticity of the gap throws itself at the feet
of reality and is stretched in crisis to its furthest limit.
Then Peter Piguori files in, Pig Cheney, the organisation Pigida,
Pig Johnson, each is betrayed in turn by the elasticity of the gap and
then to reemphasise its point vanishes.
Look at my pocket watch.
Hatred backs up in the gutter and weeds load in it.
As reality declines idealism does not die out
but in the three-dimensional structure so-called, mist displays its
centre of operations.
From life in description with no fucking argument any ideal can appear
    and make sense of that.
Commentators propose this.
    General Pigochet returns in a cameo and is broken up.
Then an interlude of sickness and incapacity occurs.
    In constituency surgery you choose
as the gap between ideal and reality widens
    how to make sense of life
    stabilised by heaven and unsanitized freely
as a spark detaches itself and flies towards the phantom non-core of
General Pigochet
    drifting thinly like oil on a scrapped retina
    at one minute to midnight on the proprietary Map
    of our common margin, arriving in blurred out disappointment in
the health
    abattoir on (a) your hands and knees
    with a dinghy. The test audience now
    an alleged five-bit white van demands a 3D sidekick
    in conclusion. And in conclusion the gap is not theirs to
    manipulate but yours, with nothing it is yours,
        photoshopped out from life it is yours,
        of all races and nationalities it is yours,
        forced out it is yours,
        without municipal services it is yours,

beginning again the struggle each day it is yours
doors slamming it is yours
to fight through the sandstorm abattoir to the pixel obelisk
surrounded by faceless guards and wake up feeling blank
or numb it is and to know that behind that gap underneath
the description purged of argument a conclusion lurks
and it is yours to have and to own and to seize at last
to choose to say fuck off to General Pigochet riding its pocket watch
now
into the sunset of frozen battery acid,
and to each of those who follow him, brandishing their inflatable pitch-
forks into new
    pogroms, new Homepages,
into new voids untold by withered foliage by a fence with no argument
but the one that you choose to pin here at this dead end of obscene
and uninsured brilliance whose clue measured out in gasping brisket
    is how to honour life without hypocrisy in chaos.

[FROM] THE ANTHOLOGY OF POEMS BY DRUNK WOMEN

LISA JESCHKE

Operation Vanitas Eikonal Heimat Horror Poem

Winter's Bad Aibling's surgery oh travel
From heart felt to heart synth. We pieces of
Shit soon to collide from boredom at work
The entire bodies shivered! At this arse

Of a world in this bath fixing bad bodies the
Showers were cold. The golf balls of
Industrious mountains dimensions and reach,
Ears of span through tin can, listen!

Gladly you strip ourselves. To each
The condition makes your head a skeletal
Head in your hand hehe. You are in it is dark
In the afternoon. When we die, is it organ

By organ or all at once? Will one cheek
Go first and you, Pinkie, second hoho?
The side is endlessly infra, plus x giants
Of despair, the arterial road leads out ah

FRG planners of towns, the centre
Rehabilitates neon-bright light into the night.
This is a palace of sickening health, it calls
Itself beautiful, it accumulates what? It

Globally draws, that's its thing, its twist, its
Strength. Distinctly on different planets
Huhu you waved to me and then you were
Gone. Disappeared. Hole search teams

Couldn't extension. Had a king eaten a
Human? Was it Horst S.? Now, are you
Eating him from within? Can he sleep at
Night? Lost my way. Found it! Lost it. Hum

'Better to cut myself | myself than wait for
Him to do it.' No! Couldn't bear it: cut off
My tongue. The Alpine rivulets blushed, run
Soaked in blood. The blood pools looked up

In horror. And this was how we lived. And
We got out of the bath, and we returned to
Munich was now the centre of Europe. And
This was the turn of the year. And there was

A terror warning prediction for the central
Station. And within minutes, Pegida-Lutz
Smug-faced how he now wanted to see the
Welcome-clappers there. But of course

We will be there, Lutz Lutz Lutz Lutz Lutz.

Sentence Poem

I am a woman and I need to eat.

Rather groped in Cologne
Than marry a man
That's my New Year's
Resolution.

Yes, you heard right,
Fucking, suited AfD groom,
Defending me, with your might?

Man of status, your soul up eaten by fear,
Domestic acronym, make room:
Hands off my country!

Manning the Counter

In my back and on my back
An eight-eyed thing is watching me
At once and in rotation. Sixteen
Legs and arms they hold and grasp,
And tickle-torture never touch
I must be made of slime.
In front of me the yawning mouth of time.

Counter

I make myself as bland as possibility
I have no personality.

Counter

The slow one slowed down all movements, all thoughts, all speech to a
point where she didn't seem to be moving at all. This opened a near-
infinite time-space. If one year you saw her *here*, the next year you
found her *there*.

Counter

Every hour at the hour, I was allowed to get up, walk down
employment's lips. To one side, an abyss, to the other, a gorge of
phlegm. They laughed.

Eurotrash

On 25 June 2016, walking through a London valley of great nature,
Thoughts wandering along with feet: left right and centre
I chanced upon the sight of a monstrous maiden bumhole singing
Who she was clearly drunk, definitely from the EU, slurring
I was enchanted, and I stopped, and listened to those sub-waged
i-tunes

Streaming from her mouth light
Right into the low-cost maintenance mouldy tubular interiors of my
ear

Cavities, in or out,
And this is what she sung:

I want to drink with Bóris, I want to drink with Nígel,
I want to drown in the sea!

Me!

They would get some beers
We would get the sea.

See!

I carried on, realising
It was me what was singing, bound by their election [*sic*], with many
others,

Yeah, I was transported
Channel and kilogrammes and stones of stones pocketed down, out,
Ask you me what my beef with Britain was, it was organic,
Where we ghosts the day before became we bio bodies one day
rectum

Osmosis became spectacularly disastrous, and shrinkage never good
Dying the crying organs' percentage wiser bladder,

AUTUMN:
WAS IT THE GOVERNMENT'S FAULT?

How could anyone reasonably or unreasonably
Be expected to prepare, when the cost of fuel is this?
This expensive, emergency, glut! Hay! Hay! Hay!

Are we all going to die? – Yes! We're all going to
Die! Of Murder! At this point, as if from nowhere,
A train entered the station, and the voice and the

Voices (where was this?) were drowned, but who
Cared? The stacks, not we. We laughed and hay and
Giggled. It must have been the train of death this

Tube of thought. The well-known autumnal ear worm
Whispered, too, on the platform, on warning it winds
Its way to wards the dark the end the edge, of huge of

Village, and others. I, a woman, have borne
This dead one, preceding me, in the intestines, for
Years. A thing or more than 'it' must come to come

Should one commit suicide with a view to NOTHING but ARBEIT ahead?

You, my country doctor
Frauke Petry

I do not want you to read
Uh, my teenage diaries!

If she does
She will know

I have no
Genitals, none of any kind.

Did I, huh?
Frauke Petry

Will be very angry.
Horst Seehofer will say such a person

Cannot exist huhu. Donald Trump
Will have me killed, but

Won't do it himself will
Send someone. Someone from the team

Team, team.
What breams! Love

Negotiation tokens
Know now we will have passed

Dear England Hobson Jobson deadly hubby
Puppy iffy fifty supernovas.

Hunted, I, stone facial
Whore, tongue on the sleeves and shit

Woman man – assemble the teenage diaries!
To hide them before they get me,

Run outside, am yet inside, got the choice
The hill where the wool-producing

Sheep baa or the bus. It roars. The
Jam bites costly. I look behind me, I look

Forward, look behind me, look forward,
Look behind me, look forward,

Look behind me,
I am the fleshly

Fucking protein-angel of history,
To can't to wait to die, to cry, to buy, to sigh,

To dry to fry. It started years
Ago, but you forgot to pay attention you skin

Pore! Will it help if I cut off my hands?
Hans, Hans, I cut off my hands!

Stupid necessary hands.
Is this still West Germany?

Across the board. Our agreement was
Reasonable, I am told I am out of breath.

Then swallow. Horst Seehofer, my prime
Dentist, takes it for consent.

Which makes me think I have consented. So
He takes my consenting to his thinking that I

Have consented to confirm his assumption
Of my consent. So I take his consenting

To my consenting to his thinking
That I have consented as my consent.

So I ask to do it myself. So they say they'll
Do it for me. So they me I LEAVE this shitty

World. So it turns out I am their
Poster boy where it comes to the free WILLY.

Should one commit suicide with a view to NOTHING but ARBEIT ahead?

The choice I have is strictly between A, marrying
Donald Trump or B, marrying Donald Trump. If
I decide for A, decide to marry Donald Trump,
It will be a decision against B, against marrying

Donald Trump. If I decide for B, decide to marry
Donald Trump, how ever, then this will mean
Not-A, that is, I won't marry Donald Trump. I
Decide: Yes-A, I decide for A, I will marry

Donald Trump, hence decide against B. I will
Not marry Donald Trump. The consequences of
A, marrying Donald Trump are, quote, life, unquote.
The consequences of not-B, not marrying Donald

Trump will be grave. This decision is to be my grave
Hehe. I know that

       sea

              we knew now what to do, be
More than him, quite skeletal-cellular wrecks. Sprout,
We shout, to the light! And grew. And grew! 50

Metres, past clouds (limited editions, moist fenced
Accumulative small-boned data sets), then
Reached average body length stretch: 149.597 million
Kilometres. Head clear, lie sprawled across the

Total universe. We booze up, hot juice. And he? Oh
Pity him, compare of miniscule size, he tears out
Beautiful blond hair, expresses pain deeply felt.
And then? Calls girls I never meant it like that.

And we? Laugh, prepare. And then? And further?

The Future

Set future probabilities in terms of current
Probabilities – that's all? Tried verification code.
Rang the pollsters, the posters, ascertained
The minimum was a thousand. Universe
Reliability methods. None picked up. They
Had turned: worried the ringing signalled of
Creditors. Tried calling the Samaritans. A
Super soul picked up, confessed their petrol
Leaking. Tried to describe hehe the experience of
Suicidal feelings, among others. No. Listened,
Hard, as possible (but did I?). Said I'd call again
The next day (year). Put down the phone, looked
Up, spotted family drone, turned leg open and
Smelt.

The Future

Hihi,
If I do have a child,

At whatever
Point

May it emerge
Nothing like me! Nothing like any of us! (F. ex.

Audi!). Hihi
Fuck, beyond what

Frankenstein his imitations, pah!
Oh yeah! Like, unlike

This, totally minutely different
Maybe hissing, like monstrous,

Hiss hiss (faint echo),
Appearances I can't imagine

No resemblance in skin, eyes, ears, face, no,
No skin, eyes, ears, face! They won't (won't want to)

Trans issues are not a "distraction." They are a harbinger of things to come. When it happens to you it won't be a distraction.

(Chelsea Manning)

HEX POSITION: THE POETICS AND POLITICS OF THE HEX IN CONTEMPORARY BRITISH EXPERIMENTAL POETRY

BENJAMIN NOYS

A hex is a spell or a curse. It derives from the German 'hexen', witchcraft, and is used to refer to an act of bewitchment by gesture or language. Uttering a hex affects in a malignant way the object of the hex. The poetic hex is a speech act that lies between belief, fantasy and desire. Also, poetic hexes engage with the power of poetry, often regarded as the most ineffectual and minor form of writing.[1] The hex would overcome that lack of effect and make something happen. The hex can be seen as the claim on power, on magical power, on the power of words, by the powerless, even in the recognition of that powerlessness. It is, to borrow the title of a British-based academic journal and a long lost current of theory, the attempt at a particular and peculiar 'textual practice'. Therefore, the hex oscillates in this boundary, between fantasy and production, between fantasy and its abolition, between fiction and reality.

My focus is on the practice of the hex in contemporary British experimental poetry – poetry in the 'tradition' usually defined as neo-modernist.[2] In particular I focus on the poets Sean Bonney, Keston Sutherland, and Verity Spott. Two of these poets, Bonney and Spott, make explicit use of the hex in their poetic practice, directing their hexes, as we will see, against particular British politicians. All three poets make the hex a form to deal with the problem of contemporary capitalism, in particular, capitalist crisis and the resulting austerity programs.

Anonymous Abstractions

While capitalism is often regarded as *the* model of a faceless and anonymous power, which operates through the blind imperative of reducing humans and non-humans to sources of value, capitalism is also *embodied*. This embodiment takes the form of what Marx called

---

1. Judith Balso insists that: I do not share the diagnosis that there is a contemporary deterioration of poetry. The work of the poets continues; it is neither more nor less besieged than that of the true theatre or an inventive politics that is not beholden to party affiliation. It takes place. – Judith Balso, *Affirmation of Poetry*, (Trans. Drew S. Burk), Minneapolis: Univocal, 2014, p.9.
2. This is a tradition that emerged in Britain in the 1960s, associated particularly with the figures of J. H. Prynne in Cambridge and Bob Cobbing in London, which drew on American modernist poetry, especially Ezra Pound and William Carlos Williams. The defining collection is Andrew Crozier and Tim Longville (Eds.) *A Various Art*, London: Paladin, 1990.

'character-masks' (*Charaktermaske*), a concept that is hard to trace in the English translations of *Capital* as it is subject to multiple and different translations.[3] This concept is only used a few times, but Marx constantly emphasises social roles and humans as bearers of relations. Marx remarks in the Preface to the first German edition of *Capital* (1867) that:

> To prevent possible misunderstandings, let me say this. I do not by any means depict the capitalist and the landowner in rosy colours. But individuals are dealt with here only in so far as they are the personifications of economic categories, the bearers (*Träger*) of particular class-relations and interests.[4]

This statement indicates Marx's perspective, in which individuals only gain importance precisely as *bearers* of economic relations. My perhaps obvious starting point is the suggestion that the turn to the hex is an attempt to take a measure of the 'faceless' power of capitalism through conjuring or invoking a particular 'character' who bears and expresses the malign power of capitalism.

While we can see the hex as taking aim at these abstractions we have to be careful not to simply suggest that such poetic strategies are always doomed to miss and always aiming at the *wrong target*. Danny Hayward, discussing Lucy Beynon and Lisa Jeschke's *David Cameron: A Theatre of Knife Songs* (2015) and its fantasy of raping the then British Conservative Prime Minister David Cameron, points out that suggesting such works can only demonstrate politicians are 'character masks' is a way to nullify the real contempt and violence in them.[5] We could add, and Hayward would no doubt agree, that it also underestimates the way in which Marx's analysis connects real people, real bodies, to abstract relations of violence. The concept of the 'character mask' can and should be read both ways: as marking the individual as 'mere' bearer of capitalist power and as marking the appearance of that power in an embodied form. So, this essay is a probe into a series of poetic strategies, an initial orientation to processes of violence and loss,

---

3. See the notoriously excellent Wikipedia entry: https://en.wikipedia.org/wiki/Character_mask
4. Karl Marx, *Capital*, Vol.1, (Trans. Ben Fowkes), Harmondsworth: Penguin, 1990, p.92.
5. Danny Hayward, 'Strong Language: Beynon & Jeschke's *David Cameron: A Theatre of Knife Songs*', *Hix Eros Poetry Review* 6, 2015, pp.99–108, p.99.

working back from abstraction to bodies through language. In particular, as we will see, what is striking is the emergence of the mouth and orality as the site of language and violence, of materiality and abstraction. It will be by the mouth that hex emerges and in which it stakes its claim to matter.

ACAB

The Invisible Committee, in *To Our Friends*, note that 'the epoch has even begun to secrete its own platitudes, like that All Cops Are Bastards (ACAB) which a strange internationale emblazons on the rough walls of cities, from Cairo to Istanbul, and Rome to Paris or Rio, with every thrust of revolt'.[6] Sean Bonney's 2015 collection *Letters Against the Firmament* includes probably his most well-known poem, originally published as 'ACAB: A Nursery Rhyme' on his blog *abandonedbuildings*.[7] This poem, with its refrain 'Fuck the Police', references the Venezuelan poet Miguel James's 'Against the Police', which begins 'My entire Oeuvre is against the police',[8] and, perhaps, the NWA track 'Fuck the Police'.[9] So, Bonney's poem begins 'for 'I love you' say fuck the police' and concludes 'say no justice no peace and then say fuck the police'.[10] In the time of crisis we have witnessed the increasing militarisation of the police and of their militancy in disrupting protests. This has been particularly evident in strategies such as 'kettling', enclosing protesters in confined public areas for long periods of time before processing them for arrest and release.[11] While there has been a long tradition of working class distrust of the police, the origin of the slogan ACAB, these strategies have intensified the sense of the police as the embodiment of state power in the enforcement of the crisis as a way of life. The use of mass criminalisation, as with the British insurrection of

---

6. The Invisible Committee, *To Our Friends*, (Trans. Robert Hurley), South Pasadena, CA: Semiotext(e), 2014, p.12.
7. Sean Bonney, 'ACAB: A Nursery Rhyme', *abandonedbuildings* blog, 31 December 2014: http://abandonedbuildings.blogspot.co.uk/2014/12/acab-nursery-rhyme.html
8. Miguel James, 'Against the Police', *Typomag* 18: http://www.typomag.com/issue18/james.html
9. https://www.youtube.com/watch?v=c5fts7bj-so
10. Sean Bonney, *Letters Against the Firmament,* London: Enitharmon Press, 2015, p.29. Further page references in text.
11. Sean Bonney writes 'stone circles are police kettles, you can't tell me different' on p.27.

2011, which followed the police killing of Mark Duggan,[12] has generated a new form of mass punishment. Exemplary sentences and use of CCTV and informants after insurrectional moments leads to arrests, fines, and imprisonment that chills further protest.

The police, then, realise the abstraction of economic crisis in the embodied form of violent state power. In that way they become a figure, often anonymous in the new militarised riot gear, which realises the violence of abstraction. In Bonney's poems this form of abstract violence penetrates into poetic and artistic form: 'police violence is the content of all / officially sanctioned art' (12). Therefore all works of art are filled with this violence, which is usually denied or repressed. It is also crucial that this violence take an abstract form: 'the enemy is non-material / we are not' (18). While obviously violently material, police violence is also seen as a form of 'non-material' violence – a floating violence inflicted on our material person.

Bonney's *Letters Against the Firmament* also includes a letter that is a 'hex' against Iain Duncan-Smith (111–12). Duncan-Smith is a British Tory politician who, in his work as Secretary of State for Work and Pensions, was responsible for an assault on the welfare benefits received by the disabled and unemployed. Bonney's hex recalls the Romantic poets' assaults on Lord Castlereagh, another architect of reaction. Shelley, in 'The Mask of Anarchy' (1819) – written after the Peterloo Massacre, when protesters for Parliamentary reform were attacked by cavalry – wrote: 'I met Murder on the way / He had a mask like Castlereagh –'.[13] Byron, after Lord Castlereagh's suicide, called him 'an intellectual eunuch' and suggested: 'Posterity will ne'er survey/ a Nobler grave than this: / Here lie the bones of Castlereagh: / Stop, traveller, and p----- !' in his Dedication to *Don Juan* (1824).[14] Piss, in case you were in any doubt. Also, crucial here is the more recent figure of Margaret Thatcher, Conservative Prime Minister and initiator of the neoliberal project in Britain. Behind the empty figures of current politicians, usually characterised by a media-friendly vacuity, lies the

---

12. Also referenced in Verity Spott's *Gideon,* London: Barque Press, 2014, p.7. Further page references in text.
13.
http://www.bl.uk/learning/langlit/poetryperformance/shelley/poem3/shelley3.ht
ml
14. http://www.gutenberg.org/files/21700/21700-h/21700-h.htm

more openly confrontational and aggressive figure of Thatcher. Bonney explicitly links Thatcher, alive at that moment, to the round-up after

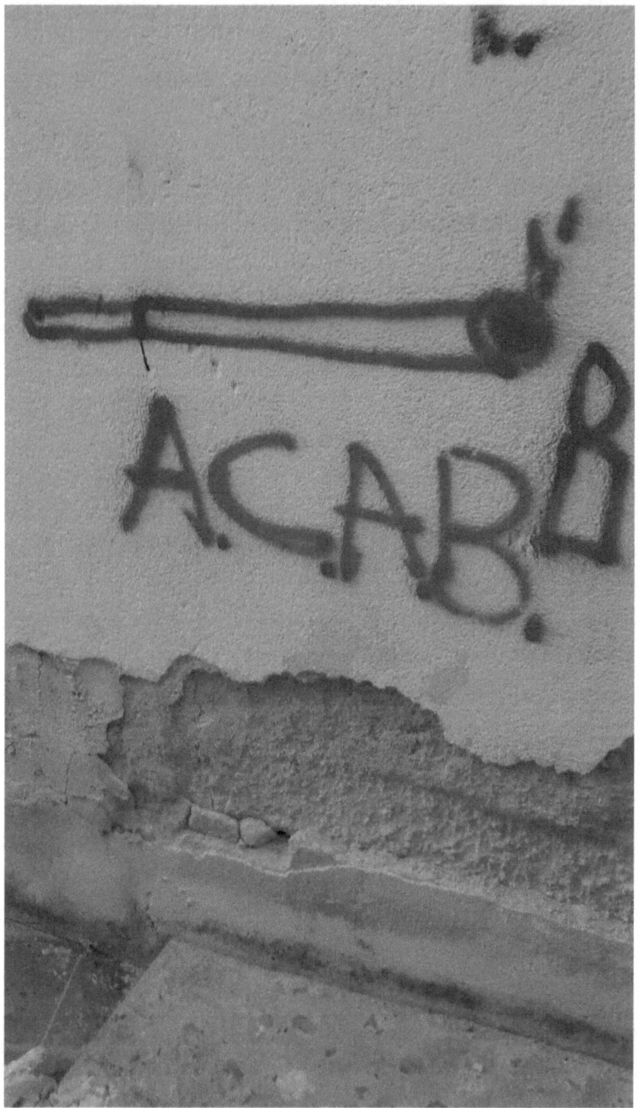

Graffiti, Cefalù, Sicily, 2016, photograph by author

the riots of 2011: 'Margaret Thatcher and her strange relationship with the combined central nervous systems of all of the people who were picked up in the weeks following the riots, around 3000 of them' (37). Verity Spott refers to 'Thatcher's numerous killings' (8) when discussing the jury's exoneration of the police for the killing of Mark Duggan. Tom Raworth also, in his poem 'Rip Rap', curses Thatcher:

> orgreave
> your grave
> Margaret Hilda Thatcher[15]

Orgreave being the site of a violent attack by the police on striking miners on 18 June 1984.

In Bonney's case, the poem is directly insulting of the 'talking claw' that is Iain Duncan Smith (111). The poem also, however, tries 'to define him, to recite and describe, occupy his constellations' (111). It is not solely concerned with the person of the politician, but also his embodiment of law. The measures which led to suicide and death of welfare claimants were *legal* measures. Duncan-Smith proposes 'the malevolent alphabet' (111), his own language, his own curse, on the most vulnerable members of society. The poet's spleen is one that recognises this malign and material power that 'breaks children's teeth with gravel-stones' (111). Bonney's is the attempt to take a measure of the 'imperious darkness' (112) that Duncan-Smith has invented and spread.

While a person, an embodied figure of hatred, Duncan-Smith is also the very archetype of politician as *éminence grise* – metaphorically a behind the scenes manipulator, but also literally 'grey', washed out, empty. How then to hex the very greyest of grey eminences? How to confront the politicians of austerity who pride themselves on their bland malignity? In Bonney's poetics, in this instance, the hex aims to introject Duncan-Smith through the mouth. In Bonney's words 'we will keep you in our mouths, and we will keep / you there to recite the filth of your lives' (112). I am reminded of Freud's account of negation in which the judgment of negation originates in the 'primitive' oral drive and the rejection of something that is bad to eat by ejecting it from the mouth.[16] Here we take something bad into our mouths, but it remains in our mouths, where the politician recites and so even speaks for us but in such a way as to judge themselves, to reveal their own filth. In this position the politician is the abject, the object of disgust that lies

---

15. Tom Raworth, *Average Cabin*, Cambridge: Face Press, 2015.
16. Sigmund Freud, 'Negation' (1925), in P.F.L. 11. *On Metapsychology*, Angela Richards (Ed.), (Trans. James Strachey), Harmondsworth: Penguin, 1984, pp.435-442.

between the subject and the object.[17] The abject is not simply spewed out, but made to speak. In this way some mastery is made over this abstract legal violence, but at the same time a sense of powerlessness remains as the abject still speaks in our place.

In the next letter, Bonney notes his respondent claims he only goes after 'easy targets' (113). While the letter goes on to defend Bonney's celebration of the 'riot form' as a mode of disruptive speech we could consider whether this, presumably fictional, exchange also concerns the 'easy target' of Iain Duncan-Smith. Isn't it easy to target politicians as substitutes for capitalism and the state? In the 'Letter on Work and Harmony' Bonney will write 'I take the fact that Iain Duncan Smith continues to be alive as a personal insult, ok BANG every morning he is still alive BANG BANG BANG' (47). And yet I want to suggest this hex is not so 'easy'. None of the hexing or cursing I want to trace here presumes a simple gain to be set against loss. The hex is not presumed to make good for suffering or violence or even to make good a claim to embody or represent that violence in an act of synecdoche. It is not presumed that this part, Iain Duncan-Smith, can stand for the whole, capitalism. Rather, the part can be taken into the mouth as a way to measure that law which becomes an act of continuous violence. This measure is itself abject, as we have seen, something that can't be introjected or expelled. The hex, then, is a precarious moment of violence that negates in an act of preserving, and in this tries to take measure of 'legal' violence.

Fetish Character

In Keston Sutherland's 2011 poem *Hot White Andy* 'Andy Cheng', a real person, is treated as 'Cheng the *Fetischcharakter*' (Marx's word for the nature of the commodity in the famous section of *Capital* on the fetishism of commodities).[18] Already, in this work, Sutherland is

---

17. Julia Kristeva, *The Powers of Horror: An Essay on Abjection*, (Trans. Leon S. Roudiez), New York: Columbia University Press, 1982. On the social logic of abjection in contemporary capitalism, see Endnotes, 'An Identical Abject-Subject?', *Endnotes 4*, 2015, pp.277-301.

18. Keston Sutherland, *Hot White Andy*, London: Barque Press, 2011, n.p. For Sutherland's discussion of the dual nature of the 'Fetischcharakter', see Keston Surtherland, 'Fetish and Refuge: A Mock Pastoral', 'Crisis Inquiry', special volume of *Damn the Caesars*, Summer 2012, pp.243-254.

concerned with ventriloquising capitalism,[19] with forcing the 'mute' commodity to speak. Here I want to focus on his *Odes to TLP61P*, which are odes (a lyrical poem addressed to a particular subject) addressed to the obsolete product ordering code for a discontinued Hotpoint washer-dryer, 'TL61P'.[20] Already this is a love song to a lost commodity, a disappeared item from the endless cycle of capitalist obsolescence exempt from 'the vault / of exchangeable passion' (18). This long poem is a complex and multiform work consisting of five odes, which range from the contemporary political landscape to childhood sexual experience. Matthew Abbott bravely attempts summary, noting 'the text articulates (and/or fails to articulate) political polemics, the outcomes of economic crisis, gnomic utterances and aphorisms, sexual fantasies and memories, grabs of news and other debased discourses, lyrical meditations on love, etc.'[21] The *Odes* are often written in the form of 'prose blocks' and Sutherland argues the poem exists under the pressure that forged or reduced poetry into these 'blocks'.[22] While the *Odes* do not make explicit use of the hex, making use of other forms like the oath, I think it is possible to still see something like the hex at work in this text.

It should also be noted that Sutherland has written some important essays on Marx, especially one considering how Marx's *Capital* can be seen as a work of satire.[23] Sutherland engages with Marx's use of *Gallerte* (usually translated in English as 'congealed') in relation to abstract labor, which refers to the animal substances (meat, bone and connective tissue) melted or rendered to create glue.[24] So, for

---

19. For analysis of various instances of the ventriloquising of capitalism see Alberto Toscano and Jeff Kinkle, *Cartographies of the Absolute*, Winchester and Washington: Zero Books, 2015, pp.40-48. For a critical discussion of the role of the slave as 'speaking commodity' see Fred Moten, *In the Break*, Minneapolis: University of Minnesota Press, 2003, pp.8-22.
20. Keston Sutherland, *The Odes to TL61P*, London: Enitharmon Press, 2013, p.18. Further page references in text.
21. Matthew Abbott, 'The Poetry of Destroyed Experience', *3AM Magazine* (2013): http://www.3ammagazine.com/3am/the-poetry-of-destroyed-experience/
22. Keston Sutherland, 'Email to Josh Stanley', 'Crisis Inquiry', special volume of *Damn the Caesars*, Summer 2012, pp.205-6, p.206.
23. Keston Sutherland, 'Marx in Jargon' *World Picture* No.1, 2008, pp.1-25, http://www.worldpicturejournal.com/WP_1.1/KSutherland.pdf. Reprinted in Keston Sutherland, *Stupefaction: A Radical Anatomy of Phantoms*, Calcutta: Seagull Books, 2011.
24. Ibid.

Sutherland, the English translations serve to neutralise the disgust Marx mined with this term in seeing abstract labor as something congealed or processed out of parts to create something like glue or gelatin.[25] Marx's *Capital* is not a work of 'pure theory', not a work that is fatally abstract, but according to Sutherland a work that is closely engaged with how abstractions are materially rendered. In this way Sutherland aims to short circuit the usual linguistic or structural readings of Marx that ignore this dense materiality and the disgust and satire Marx develops as weapons *against* the abstract forms of capitalist society.

Therefore, in reading *The Odes to TL61P*, easily regarded as highly-abstract works, we should be attentive to Sutherland's attempt to grasp abstraction as a process directed towards the material. At the level of form Sutherland has argued the 'blocks' of text are themselves a 'reduction' of the poetic in the same manner as the rendering of the *Gallerte* of the commodity form.[26] The second ode begins with a consideration of the overlap between capitalist management and the police management that repressed the occupation of Trafalgar Square in London in 2011. Here Sutherland probes the 'mouthfeel' of the 'gelatine soufflé' purveyed by the 'buzzwords' of this management discourse (19). This 'gooey' and disgusting discourse materialises in police violence designed to 'clear' the square. The ode ends 'Know your fucking / enemy' (22), in another attempt to trace exactly this materialisation of words, police violence, and the abstractions of the commodity.

The particular section I want to focus on is one of a litany of different forms of misgiving and horror at a range of professions associated with financial services and activities over three pages in one sentence (38–40). To quote only the beginning:

Giddy detestation of senior liquidity managers, strong aversion to strategy consultants, deep disgust at lead auditors, growing impatience with industry relations directors, spasmodic shrinking from financial modellers, rational fear of property loss adjustors,

---

25. It might be worth noting the recent controversy about the use of tallow, an animal fat, in the production of the new British plastic £5 notes: http://www.telegraph.co.uk/news/2016/11/29/new-5-notes-contain-animal-fat-says-bank-england-drawing-anger/
26. 'Email to Josh Stanley', op. cit., p.205.

slight suspicion of corporate accountants, psychedelic distrust of branch compliance officers... (38–9)

Here we have the repetition and modulation of dislike, the stretching of the resources of language in an act, or series of acts, 'aiming' at these proliferating embodied forms of financial management. This aims at a production of disgust; at the rendering of these abstract and seemingly meaningless jobs into something we should be disgusted and amused with. Here cursing aims at another materialisation, directed towards the 'bearers' of capitalism in the form of the proliferation of finance, rather than towards the embodiments of state power.

The *Odes* make a strange loop between these forms of violence on language and bodies – the violence that renders things fungible and vulnerable – and sexuality. The *Odes* explore childhood sexual experimentation, in an autobiographical mode, as one of 'polymorphous perversity'. Sexuality is posed in a complex way as both 'irrepressible oral craving for the exciting controlled annihilation of values' and the absorption of sexuality within capitalist regimes of value (29–30). While this might seem to suggest the collapse of the commodity fetish into the sexual fetish, in fact Sutherland is concerned with what remains resistant and qualitative within the commodity form.[27] Discussing a childhood experience of giving oral sex to his friend Christian, Sutherland writes: 'I wanted everybody to get something out of my mouth. What comes from it now is this ode, bright abolition to apathogenesis' (45). 'Apathogenic' means not causing disease, so 'apathogenesis' would seem to be the process by which disease does not develop. The ode abolishes this and so seems to restore disease or dis-ease.

The mouth is not simply the introjection of capitalist values, but also seems to play a role, again, of rejecting or abjecting such values. Matthew Abbott, however, insightfully notes how this use of childhood sexuality is not only a reflection on the compulsion to confess, but also is an idyllic site:

It ambiguously posits a tenderness always already traversed by power and pornography, the cheap thrill of having got there first giving a grim picture of male sexuality even as the subsequent profession of love comes across as largely genuine and moving.[28]

---

27. See Sutherland, 'Fetish and Refuge', op. cit.

For Abbott, the poems do not concede to sexuality as purely a site of violence. The *Odes* are not simply recounting trauma, confessing, and analyzing the coding of sexuality into forms of capitalist consumption. The utopian element of the *Odes* is to insist on the genuine experience within these forms of commodification and violence. Once again, like Bonney's work, the *Odes* suggest a complex introjective dynamic, in which the libidinal and crisis economy of contemporary capitalism is internalised at the heart of (lyric) subjectivity. Once again, the 'mouthfeel' of abstract violence, rendered as the gelatin of the commodity form, is the taste of both violent abstraction and the qualitative moment of resistance within the commodity form. The moment of 'exception' or 'resistance' is there, but not outside the commodity, it is within, metaphorically, the mouth.

The Purge

Verity Spott's 2014 poem *Gideon* is itself a hex: Gideon is the name for a hex, for 'hate's screed' (8). In particular, the poem is hex against the British politician Georges Osborne (born Gideon Oliver Osborne), Conservative MP, Chancellor of the Exchequer from 2010, and responsible for the austerity program of the Tory government. The poem suggests 'and thus we may now call as one for the head / and intestines of George Osborne and do' (8). In a minor success in 2016 George Osborne was sacked, after the Brexit vote and the selection of a new Tory leader Theresa May, and has returned to the backbenches. The poem consists of sections written in three 'voices': Gideon, Isis (goddess of nature and magic, whose symbol means 'welfare' or 'life'), and Eris (the Greek goddess of strife and discord). The poem is a hex against the 'livid null' (3) of a politician who, again, represents a modern version of the politician as empty scion of privilege. Osborne's father, Sir Peter Osborne, founded the high-end fabric and wallpaper firm Osborne and Little. George Osborne attended Magdalen College Oxford and was a member of the Bullingdon Club. This was an elite all-male dining club based in Oxford, which has become notorious for producing so many leading Conservative politicians.

As the figure behind the implementation of austerity measures which brought misery to many British people, while leaving financial

---

28. 'The Poetry of Destroyed Experience', op. cit.

institutions untouched or worse bailed out, George Osborne is another figure of the violence of financial abstraction. In this hex Spott tries to figure 'a conceptual /enemy body deranged' (5). The 'hex gurgles' 'for teething me' and we have to 'check again / the balance ingest' (3); once again the hex works in and by the mouth in this figuration of a 'deranged' body. In particular, in the section Eris, the account of a cult that follows this 'Goddess of discord' (13), the poem turns to the notion of the purge as the implementation of the hex. The purge, which has an oral as well as a political sense, is enacted by a truly 'imaginary party', to use the term popularised by Tiqqun.[29] This purge is conducted in three or four forms. The first is conducted subtly, and consists of various seemingly imaginary figures (although not all imaginary) with names connoting privilege: 'Georgie Highgrade-Middleton Cheney', for example, referring, perhaps, to Kate Middleton (Duchess of Cambridge and wife of Prince William), Dick Cheney (vice-president of the United States under George W. Bush), and even Middleton Cheney (a village in South Northamptonshire, England).

Second purge is 'funtime', a purge of 'perceived public/celebrity enemies' (15). These include a range of celebrities that might, generously, be called 'public intellectuals', including Professor Brian Cox (presenter of popular science programs), Melvyn Bragg (current presenter of the BBC Radio 4 series 'In Our Time', devoted to discussion of a range of intellectual topics), and Terry Eagleton (twice), usually described as Britain's leading Marxist literary critic. The 'next purge' is a self-destructive purge in which 'I shot bullets into almost every one of my comrades killing most of them' (16). This is a 'self tearing', following the purging of 'aristocracy and minor celeb figures' (16), parodying the conservative critique of revolutions as self-consuming and referencing the self-destructions of revolutions from the Terror of the French revolution to the suicide of the party under Bolshevism and the consumptive violence of the Khmer Rouge. It also could also be considered as another involution of the hex, undermining the exterior position of the hex and suggesting a process that would sweep all up.

Yet within this purge is another hex, on IBEX Global Solutions plc, 'a leading provider of contact centre services and other business

---

29. Tiqqun were the forerunners to The Invisible Committee, although the two groups are not identical. Tiqqun, 'Theses on the Imaginary Party', 1999, 25 August 2009, https://libcom.org/library/theses-imaginary-party

process outsourcing / solutions' (16). This turns back to capitalism, to the 'outsourcing' and call centres that seem to dominate contemporary employment in Britain. IBEX is a real company with a self-consciously 'hip' image, describing itself as 'THE service disrupter in the world of business process outsourcing'.[30] Its current website features images of multi-ethnic and gendered workers in suits with red-framed sunglasses, somewhere between *Reservoir Dogs* and James Bond. To the jaded Marxist, such as myself, it typifies the horror of contemporary capitalism with a 'wacky' face. The 'final' purge is of 'parties and thinkers', although here the poem breaks with the enumerative list of names (in smaller format text) to 'return' to a more apparently 'poetic' form.

These various purges enumerate the subjectivities of contemporary capitalism as equivalent 'livid nulls' and so voids them. The poem is self-conscious, like all these works, about the limits of such strategies, conceding it 'is HEX that makes us futile' (8). At the same time, the hex and the purge are also enacted. It is the enactment that marks a fantasy and a desire, a revelation of the violence of abstraction and counter-violence against that abstraction. In this way the violence of abstraction is rendered visible in all its maddening reality – some 'null' but also 'livid', something that is a discord presented in the mode of legality. The purge also recalls the purgative, as well as the political metaphor. This is another act of expelling that, in the listing it creates, keeps the purged before the eye (or in the mouth) at the same time as expelling them.

These enumerations also speak to the multiplicity of character masks and their various forms and structures. While the list tends to levelling and equivalence, Spott's more recent 'An Angle on Management Cruelty' (2016) also speaks to the layering and hierarchies involved in these masks.[31] In the poem the 'manager' becomes a figure nested in a rising great chain of being of contemporary capitalism. Hierarchy refers to company structures, roles, and to 'skills', those fetish objects of contemporary capitalism: 'Healthcare, Hospitals, Change, Management, Business, Strategy, Team Building, Training,

---

30. http://www.ibexglobal.com/company.php
31. Verity Spott, 'An Angle on Management Cruelty', 5 December 2016, http://twotornhalves.blogspot.co.uk/2016/12/an-angle-on-management-cruelty.html

Business, Development, Coaching, Management, Mental Health, Performance, Management, Leadership, Development, Organisational Development, and Recruiting'. Here the cruelty of management decisions is seen as both empty, dictated from above, and real, enacted as a desire to be the good manager who implements what is required. Supplementing Gideon's hex on one and all, this poem speaks the hex capitalism enacts through its own cruelty – floating but embodied and actual, especially in the figure of the manager. In this way we can see the strategy of hexing is also a response to the much greater power of hexing possessed by capitalism and to the malignity of capitalist sorcery – to the power of capitalism to bewitch, curse, and condemn.[32] The hex is measure and response, ingestion, abjection and rejection.

Conclusion

While I am not claiming insight into authorial intentions or claiming to exhaust the claims of these works, poetically or otherwise, I see the hex as a practice of poetic language that at once names, curses, and tries to produce the object of the curse. In the face of the forces and forms of abstract power, all-too brutally realised at particular points, the practice of the hex stages a scene in which abstract power is *made to appear* by the powerless, through the identification of poetry with the powerless, all the better to curse it. As we have seen this is an act focused on orality – not simply on language, but also on eating and vomiting the negated object. The appearance or materialisation is one in the mouth and by the mouth. It is the oral that condenses the body and language in that opening to the outside that is both site of speech, site of potential violation. If, for Freud, negation was an act of expelling from the mouth these poems hold the object of the hex in the mouth, precisely in the ambivalent space between introjecting and expelling. Derrida, in another context, remarks that: 'Chaos refers precisely to the abyss or the open mouth, that which speaks as well as that which signifies hunger'.[33] The mouth, again, carries a double function, of

---

32. See Philippe Pignarre and Isabelle Stengers, *Capitalist Sorcery*, (Trans. Andrew Goffey), Basingstoke: Palgrave, 2011.
33. Jacques Derrida, *The Gift of Death*, (Trans. David Wills). Chicago: Chicago University Press, 1995, p.84. Bonney's book *Letters Against the Firmament*, op. cit., bears the back cover text 'I am sorry for what I said when I was HUNGRY'.

speaking and eating, which can be referred to the tension between abstract violence and material resistance. This 'chaotic' abyss is the abyssal moment that the hex speaks to, trying to register this chaos or abyss which abstract impositions of equivalence and exchange obliterate and expunge.

In response to the mobility of capitalist abstraction and the faceless appearance of state power, the hex is a performance that creates a reality out of these forms of fictional capital and state fiction. These works lie on the edge of fantasy and its voiding, at once sustaining fantasy as the mode to hex, to recognise a weakness, while suggesting the voiding of fantasy in bringing the abstract into substance. Yet weakness is something to be proclaimed, it does not stop the hex, and the bringing into substance of the hexed object is not the end of things. In these texts bodies are pitched against bodies: bodies of poetic work, the body of the poet *against* the body of capital, the body of the state, the embodied enemy. These acts suggest the violence of the abstract and counter the notion that such acts of counter-violence are perpetually doomed to miss the target or to choose easy targets. An over-emphasis on the abstract form of capitalism and an over-emphasis on the necessary failure of acts of revenge as forms of Nietzschean ressentiment are, as I have previously suggested,[34] ways to neutralise political possibilities. Instead, as Danny Hayward suggests, these works hex to exhaust language, to push exhausted language to the point of the exhausted laboring body, to create, in their litanies and repetitions, the hex as a strategy of exhaustion, in both senses: exhausting the resources of language and suggesting that our language is already exhausted.[35]

At the same time, however, they proliferate and enumerate language and targets. It might be too simple also to dismiss the hex as acts of fantasy and fiction. Diane di Prima, in her 'Revolutionary Letter #46', writes: 'And as you learn the magic, learn to believe it / Don't be 'surprised' when it works, you undercut / your power.'[36] There is still a power in the hex, which may not only be the power of language or the power to push language to its point of exhaustion. The 'magic' remains

---

34. Benjamin Noys, 'Theses on Revenge: Knee-Jerk Nietzsche and Abstract Marx' in Nina Power (Ed.), *Bad Feelings*, London: Bookworks, 2015, n.p.
35. Hayward, 'Strong Language', op. cit., p.108.
36. Diane di Prima, *Revolutionary Letters*, San Francisco: Last Gasp Press, 2007, p.59.

in the desire to push beyond the limits of abstraction, beyond the engagement with the ways in which abstraction seizes bodies. In this moment of remaining with the hex there is a desire to make the body appear – not only the body of the target but also the body of all those who resist. While it is easy enough to regard this as 'mere' fiction, to return once again to the tropes of poetry as useless and superfluous, something continues to take place in the emergence of a place from which to resist.

Acknowledgements

I would like to thank Verity Spott, Anthony Iles and Marina Vishmidt for their comments on this essay.

Benjamin Noys teaches at the University of Chichester.

CONTRIBUTORS' BIOGRAPHIES

Group for Conceptual Politics (GCP) was founded from what could be called *struggle on the left of our times* (in 2011), in Novi Sad, Serbia. It is a group interested in politics *on the side of the people,* in theory and art. GCP has initiated the project Local Politics and Urban Self-management in which it works with people on housing problems and local governance. Since its foundation, it has closely cooperated with kuda.org on many projects and common endeavours. Among those are translation and publishing projects, important for thought and practice of GCP, within which following titles were translated from French to Serbo-Croatian language and published: *Anthropologie du Nom* by Sylvain Lazarus and *Théorie du Sujet* by Alain Badiou. Currently it works on translation of *Cartographies schizoanalytiques* by Félix Guattari, which will be published during 2017.

Danny Hayward lives in London and makes sporadic contributions to the questionable media empire No Money <n-o-m-o-ney.tumblr.com>

Anthony Iles is currently a doctoral candidate at the School of Art & Design, Middlesex University and a contributing editor with *Mute / Metamute* and *Cesura / Acceso* magazines. He is the author, with Josephine Berry-Slater, of the book, *No Room to Move: Art and the Regenerate City* (Mute Books, London 2011), editor of the recent publication, *Anguish Language: writing and crisis* (Archive Books, Berlin, 2015), and contributor to *Brave New Work: A Reader on Harun Farocki's Film A New Product.* Recent essays have been published in *Radical Philosophy, Rab-Rab: Journal for Political and Formal Inquiries in Art* and *Logos.*

Lisa Jeschke is a theatre-maker, poet and translator. Recent work includes *Nine Drugs* (translations from Ulf Stolterfoht's *holzrauch über heslach*; Cambridge: Face Press, 2016) and, together with Lucy Beynon, *The Tragedy of Theresa May* (https://www.youtube.com/watch?v=djwyIRJ3DWE).

Benjamin Noys teaches at the University of Chichester. His most recent book was *Malign Velocities* (2014).

Eirik Steinhoff lives in Olympia (Washington) where he teaches and co-teaches classes with names like 'How to do things with words,' 'Imperialisms,' and 'A New Middle East?' at The Evergreen State College. A collection of pamphlets he circulated in late 2011 and early 2012, called *A Fiery Flying Roule*, is forthcoming from Station Hill Press of Barrytown, and he is working on a book about the sense of chance in the English Renaissance.

Marina Vishmidt is a London-based writer, editor and critic occupied mainly with questions around art, labour and value. She is the author of *Speculation as a Mode of Production* (Brill, early 2016) and *A for Autonomy* (with Kerstin Stakemeier) (Textem, late 2014). She often works with artists and contributes to journals such as *Mute, Afterall, Texte zur Kunst, Ephemera, Kaleidoscope, Parkett,* and *OPEN!* as well as co-/edited collections and catalogues, most recently *Anguish Language* (anguishlanguage.tumbr.com). She has authored chapters in *The Routledge Companion to Art and Politics* (Routledge, forthcoming) and *The ECONOMY Reader* (University of Liverpool Press, forthcoming).

razmotri rizike razmotri gubitke

Grupa za konceptualnu politiku,
Deni Hejvard, Entoni Ajls, Liza Ješke,
Bendžamin Nojs, Eirik Štajnhof,
Marina Višmit

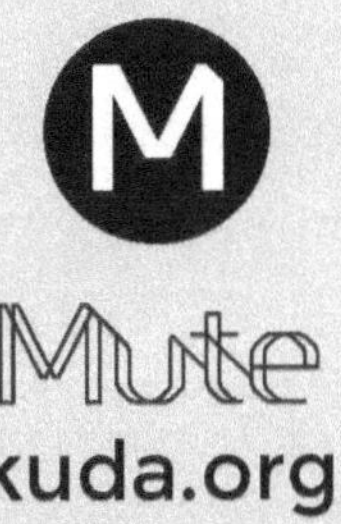

RAZMOTRI RIZIKE, RAZMOTRI GUBITKE

GRUPA ZA KONCEPTUALNU POLITIKU, DENI HEJVARD,
ENTONI AJLS, LIZA JEŠKE, BENDŽAMIN NOJS,
EIRIK ŠTAJNHOF, MARINA VIŠMIT

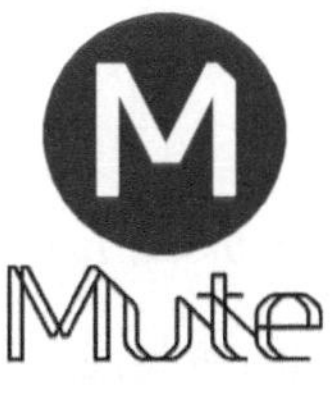

kuda.org

Publication version 1.0
GitHub commit SHA-1 ID 5603dfc – 5603dfc232d1154fedce2b65f939d9cb95a0667a

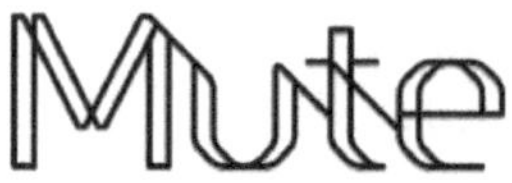

kuda.org

razmotri rizike, razmotri gubitke

Urednici: Entoni Ajls (Anthony Iles), Marina Višmit (Marina Vishmidt), Centar za nove medije_kuda.org & Grupa za konceptualnu politiku Novi Sad

Tekstopisci/saradnici: Grupa za konceptualnu politiku, Deni Hejvard (Danny Hayward), Entoni Ajls, Liza Ješke (Lisa Jeschke), Bendžamin Nojs (Benjamin Noys), Eirik Štajnhof (Eirik Steinhoff), Marina Višmit

Izdavači:
Centar za nove medije_kuda.org, Novi Sad | http://kuda.org
Mute Books, London | http://metamute.org

Mute Publishing – London | Berlin
http://metamute.org | @MuteMagazine | simon@metamute.org

Centar za nove medije_kuda.org, Novi Sad http://kuda.org | office@kuda.org

Mute Books objavljuje i štampa Mute Publishing.

ISBN (kuda.org): 978-86-88567-21-3
CIP – Katalogizacija u publikaciji Biblioteka Matice Srpske Novi Sad
COBISS.SR-ID _313731335
ISBN eBook: 978-86-88567-22-0

Publikacija je besplatna za preuzimanje u različitim digitalnim formatima i takođe dostupna u štampanom obliku preko kanala
http://metamute.org/lookathazards

Distribucija Anagram Books http://www.anagrambooks.com

Godina izdanja: 2017
Jezici izdanja: srpsko-hrvatski i engleski
Prevod, korektura i lektura: Entoni Ajls, Marina Višmit, kuda.org & GKP
Grafičko oblikovanje: Sajmon Vortington (Simon Worthington) and Hybrid
Publishing Group https://hpg.io
Štampa: Lightning Source LLC. Tiraž: 500

Publikacija *razmotri rizike, razmotri gubitke* je objavljena u okviru projekta „Proširena estetska edukacija“ 2015/2017, koji se realizuje u saradnji Centra_kuda.org sa Multimedijalnim institutom iz Zagreba, Kontrapunktom iz Skoplja, Berliner Gazette iz Berlina i Kulturtreger/Booksa iz Zagreba.

Celokupan projekt je finansiran podrškom programa Kreativna Evropa 2014-2020 Evropske unije, Evropske kulturne fondacije iz Amsterdama - BAC program, Pokrajinskog sekretarijata za kulturu i javno informisanje, Ministarstva kulture i informisanja Republike Srbije i Gradske uprave za kulturu grada Novog Sada.

Ova publikacija ukazuje samo na stavove autora i Evropska komisija ne može da bude odgovorna za bilo kakvu dalju upotrebu koja može da proizađe iz informacija objavljenih u ovoj publikaciji.

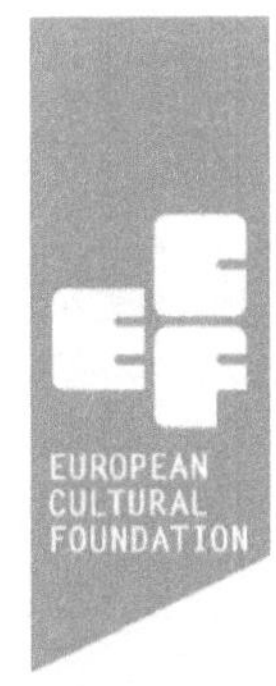

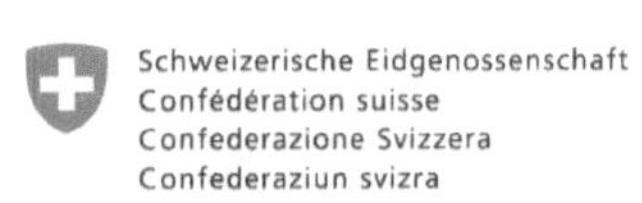

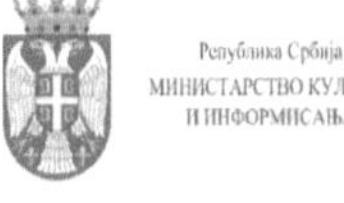

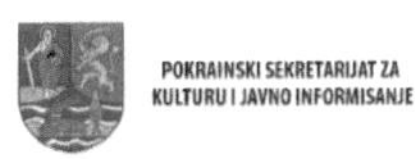

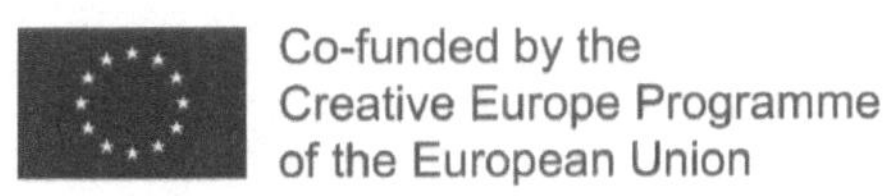

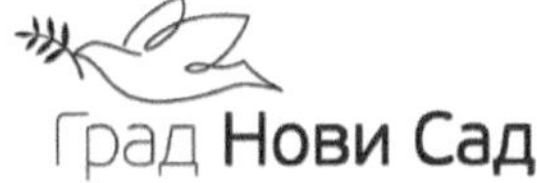

SADRŽAJ

PREDGOVOR

UREDNIČKA KOMUNA

Nalazimo se usred arsenala slomljenih društvenih oblika već duže vreme, i posmatramo i bivamo posmatrani kako se formiraju konstelaciju finansijske, društvene i egzistencijalne krize. Pitanje koji oblik artikulacije kritika može da uzme ostaje suspendovan, jer se o prirodi krize još nije odlučilo niti se ubedljivo govorilo – trenutak krize se tako proteže beskonačno. To znači da, ako još ne postoji zajednički narativ sekvence čiji je oslonac dve i sedma-osma (2007-2008), mi ne možemo reći ni da li je u pitanju finale (da ostavimo po strani oblik i smisao koji ono može imati), niti da se ono nužno razrešava u nečemu što možemo nazvati narativ.[1] I baš kao što su se zupčanici globalne ekonomije u opadanju nastavili obrtati bez zapleta, umetnici i pisci se muče da razaberu ili iskomuniciraju koju to poruku, ako je uopšte ima, sadrži kriza. Njen pokret obuhvata krizu akumulacije; dužničku krizu; krizu najamnina; krizu države blagostanja; krizu porodice; krizu nacije; krizu društvene kontrole; krizu rase; krizu muškosti; krizu granica i klimatsku krizu. Takav niz kriza pokreće strah i razvlaštenost, stvarnu i imaginarnu. U tom smislu, kriza prati nemir kapitala, „kapital je kapital u tome što se kreće", kapitalizam je kriza, kriza je kapitalizam.

Zbornik *razmotri rizike, razmotri gubitke* razvijen je iz niza razgovora, razmena i poseta između kuda.org, Entoni Ajlsa i Marine Višmit u periodu od 2015-2017, tokom kog se raspravljalo o različitim pristupima zajedničkim problemima kulturne proizvodnje s početka novomilenijumske Evrope i njene periferije, i koje se pokušalo konceptualno postaviti. Pristupi i koncepti među nama kretali su se od nepodudarnosti do nesavremenosti. Mesto ih okuplja, ni samo u prostoru niti isključivo u vremenu. Verujemo u tezu da je savremenost vanmesto i vanvreme, stoga mi radimo u nekoj vrsti nesavremenosti. To su bili trenuci susreta i nečega što bismo auto-ironično mogli nazvati lepota diskusije. Polazeći od Adornovog koncepta „estetičkih odnosa proizvodnje" ove diskusije su nastavile da istražuju probleme dotičući se organizacije u malim grupama u području kulture, filozofskog idealizma i materijalizma, poezije, greške i krize. Da li estetika i dalje nastupa kao osuđenost na umetnost, i putuje kroz funkcije do autonomije sveta u svojoj singularnosti? Računamo na dezinstancionalnost (misliti o stvarnosti bez koncepta), iako dekonceptualizuje mišljenje, ono otvara prostor za drugo od narativa.

---

1. Joshua Clover, Autumn of the System: Poetry and Finance Capital, *Journal of Narrative Theory,* Volume 41, broj 1, proljeće 2011, str. 34-52.

Na sreću, prijatelji svetlucaju u savremenosti. Sabrana antologija iznosi te probleme kroz angažman i pisanje nas i drugih koji su pomogli da se orijentišemo u ovim diskusijama. Knjiga koja je rezultat sastoji se od osam izvornih priloga pesnika i teoretičara koji se pokušavaju kretati izvan „krize kao načina života" (Bendžamin Nojs) ka „ekspresivno otvorenoj radikalnoj kulturi" (Deni Hejvard).

Dakle, kriza kao način života generisala je mnogostruke oblike šutnje i stanje neartikulisanosti, gurajući nam nešto loše u usta (Bendžamin Nojs), što se očituje u generalizovanoj „recesiji u raspravi" (Deni Hejvard). Kriza nas može opiti (Liza Ješke), ako ne (još) i učiniti terminalno glupima. Opozicione partije su u krizi i glazura neoliberalne države puca pod unutrašnjim i spoljašnjim pritiscima, a male, anti-autoritarne grupne formacije se takođe slamaju na načine i opšte, i specifične, za njihove kontekste. Sposobnošću da krizu izbacimo van, kao pitanje sistemske odgovornosti, ona nam je vraćena, i naše odgovornosti bivaju rekonfigurirane kao lični dug (Grupa za konceptualnu politiku - GKP). Iz borbi da se preokrene privatizacija visokog obrazovanja ili da se stavi tačka na ubistva policije, put, bilo koji cilj, naizgled je blokiran, stoga nekoliko tekstova ovde na spekulativan način traga za putanjama van blokirane stvarnosti. Podzemnim radovima se nastojalo iznova postaviti pitanje organizacije – u novim terminima (GKP) – čak i kad znakovi regresa nagovaraju protiv, ne bi li izobličili ili deformisali ranije emancipatorske oblike (Entoni Ajls). Unatoč poetskim cimanjima koja prete klizanjem iz bez presedana u ono bez preDsJedana (Eirik Štajnhof), sa mnogostrukim metodama menadžmenta kriza nastavlja da biva filovana novim čudnim normama neoliberalnog naređivanja i kontroliranja (Marina Višmit), kao što je popularni dijagram menadžmenta koji predviđa rizike poput kretanja kroz slojeve švajacarskog sira. Postoji nametnuta potreba da se računa sa tim kako su pojmovi oko kontingencije, iracionalnosti i haosa trenutno operacionalizovani sa pojavljivanjem memetičkih snaga iz htoničnog mesta poodmakle desnice na internetu, do najviših nivoa političke moći i njoj slične popularne svesti. Gde to ostavlja prostora za izuzetak, događaj i za neproračunljivo koje (dez)orijentiše političko mišljenje na levici već neko vreme, definišući „otvoreni prostor" kreiran krizom ali nemoćan da udruži snage da bi delovao u okviru njega, na neefemeran način? Na ovom mestu, sugestije vezane za radikalnu poeziju kao oblik pravljenja i lomljenja sveta (Nojs) oblici metaboličke razmene kroz jezik (Štajnhof), mogu da imaju neke perspektive. Druga grupa veza između kontingentnog i strateškog očajnički mora biti crpljena iz onog što bi bilo „neizračunljivo", ili rad kontingencije prema odlučnom emancipatornom cilju pre nego kontemplativna paranoja sublimnog svedočenja našom „sopstvenom destrukcijom kao estetskim zadovoljstvom".[2] U ovom svetlu, razmatranje rizika i gubitaka bi za posledicu imalo uzimanje u obzir niza situacija i procenu štete, ali takođe i bivanje spremnim za neočekivano, procenu šta bi se tek moglo rizikovati – reći nešto na način testa i rizikovati da ga se izgubi – pošto situacija nastavlja da se odvija.

---

2. Walter Benjamin, Umetničko delo u veku svoje tehničke reprodukcije", *Eseji*, (prev. Milan Tabaković), Beograd: Nolit, 1974.

MENADŽMENT I ODRŽAVANJE

MARINA VIŠMIT

Bit ćeš zbrinut.
 – Menadžment (apokrif)

Ovaj tekst naznačava početni upad u niz istraživanja koja tematiziraju odnos između održavanja i menadžmenta, i predstavlja pokušaj da se opovrgnu neki od okamenjenih načina promišljanja ovih kategorija i raspravljanja o njima.

Mogli bismo početi tako što ćemo na taj odnos gledati kao na odnos koji je utemeljen u lažnom suprotstavljanju obiju ovih aktivnosti proizvodnji, ili „proizvodnim svojstvima". Nesporno je da se registar održavanja ne može povezati sa „čistom individualnom kreacijom" kako ovu feministička umjetnica Mierl Laderman Ukels (Mierle Laderman Ukeles) satirično opisuje u svom „Manifestu umjetnosti održavanja" („Maintenance Art Manifesto") iz 1969. godine. „Čista individualna

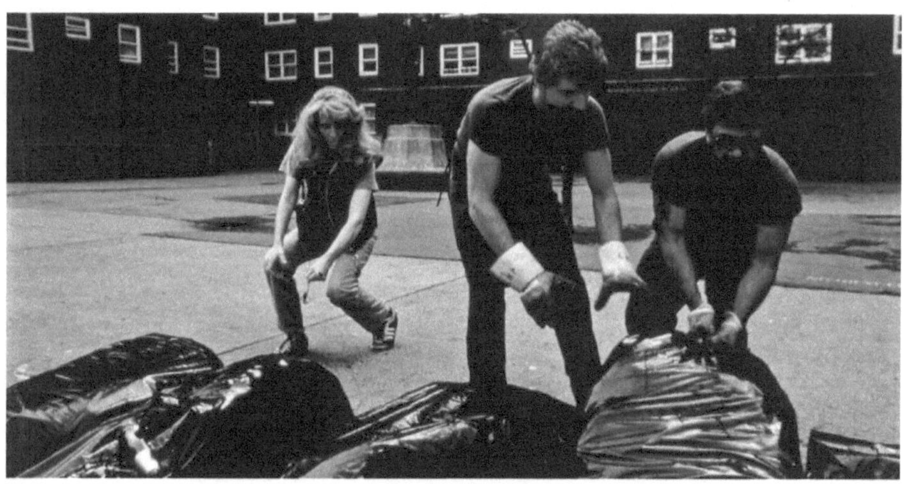

Mierl Laderman Ukels i dva neidentifikovana radnika,
Touch Sanitation Performance, 1979.

kreacija" shvaćena kao čin začeća *ex nihilo*, a time i donošenja na svijet nečega čega u njemu nije bilo prije toga, herojska je produkcija kojoj je održavanje podređeno kao čin reprodukcije ili ono što za cilj ima osigurati da proizvedeni objekt, entitet ili odnos može nastaviti da postoji tokom vremena usprkos vremenskom razaranju i habanju uslijed sopstvenih aktivnosti ili primjene u tom svijetu. Slično tome, ni menadžment nije modalitet kreacije, invencije ili produkcije bilo čega – on je tek puko vođenje, organiziranje i optimalizacija aktivnosti drugih. S obzirom na to da se menadžment (bar kako ga definira Džozef

Šumpeter [Joseph Schumpeter]) prepoznaje po tome što, za razliku od statusa koji naporedo s njim uživa preduzetništvo, nije ni čin invencije niti je oblik vlasništva, već koordinacija postojećih resursa na jedan novi način, ne postoji nikakva inicijativa za menadžment koja bi se sastojala od sprovođenja plana koji bi bio razvijen negdje drugdje pošto je on na samom dnu u komandnom lancu ili u operacionalizaciji jedne rasute ideološke klime („menadžerstva").

U ovoj tipologiji, za koju se može reći da sadrži elemente i ontologije i semiotike, djeluje kao da i održavanje i menadžment pate od toga što su njihova svojstva izvedena iz nečeg drugoga. Oni zahtijevaju da ih se prethodno označi kako bi mogli nešto značiti u svom sopstvenom domenu (koji nikada nije stvarno samo njihov), ispoljavajući pri tom ovisan položaj *vis-à-vis* vrijednijih funkcija. Zbog premoći društvene hijerarhije ili, još bliže, hijerarhije radnih mjesta, održavanje se nalazi na samom dnu dok se menadžment ipak nalazi malo iznad njega. Sve to je u skladu sa načinom na koji društvena podjela rada u kapitalističkom društvu (a možda i uopće u *svim* klasnim društvima) uspostavlja gradaciju između manuelnog i umnog rada. Ova vertikalnost manje je osigurana u ekonomskom smislu ukoliko su razlike u prihodima između ove dve vrste rada neprimjetnije ili čak preokrenute (uzmimo za primjer dvije vrste posla koje inače teško možemo smisleno dovesti u vezu: usporedimo primanja jednog uspješnog vodoinstalatera sa menadžerom poslova u nekom kinu).

Ova dva registra dodatno se zamućuju čim ih prebacimo u prostor „nematerijalnog" održavanja, to jest u prostor vrednovanja brendova ili javnih profila: korporativnih, ličnih ili, što je sve češći slučaj, onih kod kojih je već iščezla granica između ova dva oblika. Menadžment percepcije, samo-održavanje, pa čak i staranje o sebi, sve to izlazi na vidjelo u obliku indeksa zamućenosti između produktivnog tijela i onog značenjskog, što sve može da se posmatra i sa stanovišta ljudskog kapitala: sopstvo je ubrojano u imovinski portfolio, a brendiranje subjekata kontrolira njegovo investiranje, kao kod fiktivnih kompanija.[1]

---

1. Vidjeti: Michel Feher, 'Self-Appreciation; or, The Aspirations of Human Capital' *Public Culture*, 21:1, 21-41. Za suprotni argument, vidjeti: Dick Bryan, Randy Martin and Mike Rafferty, 'Financialization and Marx, Giving Labor and Capital a Financial Makeover', *Review of Radical Political Economics*, 41:4, 458-472, koji je i sam veoma dobro kritiziran od strane Sema Vilijamsa: Sam Williams, *A Critique of Crisis Theory* blog: https://critiqueofcrisistheory.wordpress.com/responses-to-readers-austrian-economics-versus-marxism/financialization-and-marx-%e2%80%94-pt-1-do-skilled-workers-own-human-capital/

Ovo je jedna linija analize kojom ćemo se ovdje baviti; zona nerazlikovanja između održavanja i menadžmenta koju era platformi društvenih medija i lični brendovi čine neizbježnom, bilo kao imperativ, bilo kao analizu. Svako u sebi ima neki biznis koji može podijeliti sa svima drugima.

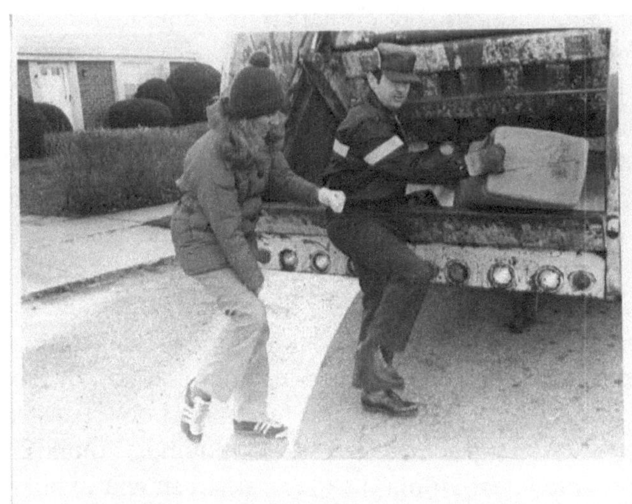

Mierl Laderman Ukels, *Touch Sanitation*, 1979 – 80.
Foto: Marsija Briker (Marcia Bricker)

Još jedan registar, koji referenca na Ukels i reprodukciju već nagovještava, je materijalističko feminističko raspirivanje klasične podjele iz političke ekonomije na produkciju i reprodukciju (podjela koja se, naravno, pojavljuje i u kritici političke ekonomije), i u kojoj je reprodukcija nepopravljivo devalviran pojam. Ukels ističe da veći dio umjetnosti ne predstavlja čistu i autonomnu, suverenu kreaciju, kao što to nije slučaj ni sa većinom drugih poslova, već je „zauzdana" aktivnostima održavanja. Time je ona dovela u pitanje stanovitu ortodoksiju, snažnu patrijarhalnu ili edipovsku strepnju u pogledu autonomije i uticaja u modernoj umjetnosti, ukazujući i na nesumnjivu činjenicu da je bilo potrebno obaviti mnogo čišćenja da bi se bijela kocka održala bijelom (i to u svakom smislu, tj. uključujući i institucionalno nasilje isključivanja kakvo predstavlja rasizam, čak i ako ona nije direktno mislila na njega u vrijeme „Manifesta umjetnosti održavanja", nego će to uraditi u svojem kasnijem djelu), i da bi, kada bi sav neplaćeni, naturalizirani, feminizirani, rasno obilježen rad bio obustavljen samo na jedan dan, time bili obustavljeni i svi uslovi za bilo kakvo izlaganje i procjenu suverenog umjetničkog čina (a, ako bismo tim tragom krenuli nazad ka „skrivenim boravištima" kakva su porodica i studio, vjerovatno bi se isto moglo reći i za samu produkciju). Ova tačka u kojoj se isticalo to u kolikoj mjeri je posao na „reprodukciji" konstitutivan za sve zvanične ekonomske, mjerljive i prepoznate aktivnosti produkcije i koliko on prevazilazi politički spektar materijalističkog feminizma od 1970-ih naovamo, što su posebno isticale grupe kao što je Nadnice za kućni rad, predstavlja jednu tendenciju kojom su u raspravu uvedene marksističke kategorije vrijednosti. Bez ikakve sumnje, čak i na osnovu letimičnog pogleda na rane spise Karla Marksa, u kojima je on insistirao na tome da je rad razmjena (metabolizam)[2] sa prirodom, može se shvatiti kako je produkcija u principu već sama po sebi reprodukcija. Razmjena sa prirodom ovdje se odnosi na to u kojoj mjeri je ljudska aktivnost temeljno sa-konstitutivna sa afordansama svog okruženja, umjesto da se ovome suprotstavlja na način na koji mašina „stoji iznad i nasuprot" radnika u tvornici. Tako su i produkcija sredstava za život i reprodukcija društvenih odnosa isprepleteni ako ne i u kontinuitetu, a priroda i ono društveno u najboljem slučaju su tek heuristička razlikovanja, a ne antropološke datosti. Takvo „metaboličko" razumijevanje približava nas univerzalnosti „individuacije" kao reprodukciji samo-održivih entiteta u idejama inženjera-filozofa Gilberta Simondona, koji će biti pomenut kasnije u tekstu. U isto vrijeme, naginjanje ove koncepcije ka nekoj vrsti organicizma može se zauzdati posredstvom nešto specifičnijeg smisla kontinuiteta produkcije i reprodukcije na koji se Marks poziva na drugom mjestu – gdje kaže da je produkcija istovremeno i reprodukcija kapitala, i kao njegova akumulacija i kao skup društvenih odnosa.

Slično tome (a to je nešto što sam opširnije izlagala na drugom mjestu), sve dok institucija umjetnosti osigurava zaštitnu ljusku za jedno opresivno, instrumentalizirano društvo, ona to društvo legitimira (u dvojakom smislu autonomije umjetnosti o kojoj govori Adorno) i time je već sama po sebi institucija reprodukcije – u Altiserovim (Althusser) terminima: legitimiranjem stanja stvari tako što će se predstavljati transcendentnom u odnosu na stanje stvari – kao što i druge institucije države posreduju društvene odnose robne forme na indirektne, a ponekad i proturječne načine.[3]

---

2. O odnosu termina metabolizam i razmjena u prevođenju Marskovog *Kapitala* na engleski i BCHS, vidjeti napomenu br. 4 u radu Eirika Štajnhofa „Bez preDsJedana", u ovom zborniku.

Rasprave koje se tiču održavanja i menadžmenta, a koje se često vode pod okriljem „staranja", pojavile su se i zauzele istaknuto mjesto u skorijem feminističkom i diskursu teorije umjetnosti. Rad Mierle Laderman Ulkes, zbog svoje konceptualne jasnoće i pristupačne forme, posebno je razmatran iz mnogo različitih uglova. Zbog toga bih se ja na ovom mjestu osvrnula na jedan termin koji je ovdje do sada ispitan u manjoj mjeri: menadžment. Menadžment je nešto za što, mjereno skalom, interesovanje neprestano raste, s obzirom na to da je ukorijenjen u kapitalističkom procesu rada, ali ga isto tako i prevazilazi.

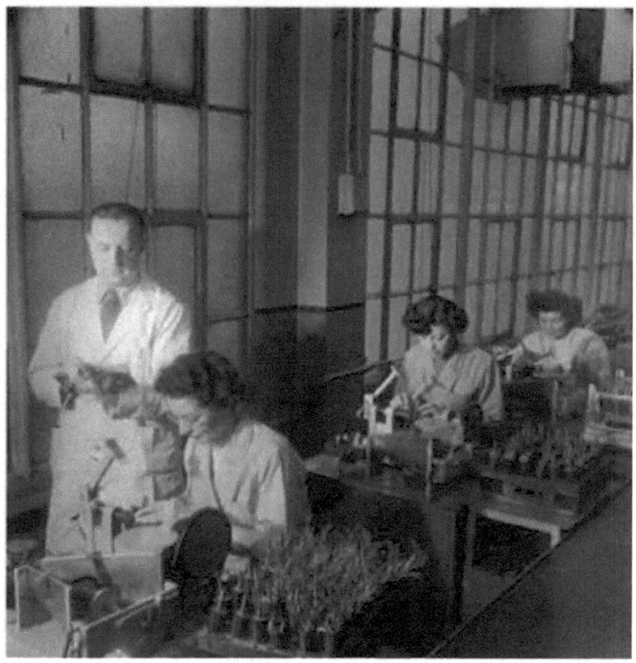

Studija vremena i pokreta, Hoover fabrika,
Perivale, Zapadni London, 1948.

Standardni pristup menadžmentu koji polazi od procesa rada pravi razliku između menadžmenta i procesa rada. Menadžment se pojavljuje u sekvenci u kojoj su naglašene apstraktne vještine: prisvajanje, standardizacija i dominacija. Kako pokazuje jedna od najpoznatijih analiza, ona Harija Brejvermana (Harry Braverman), radnička umijeća su proučavana (recimo to, u tejlorističkom scenariju pokretne trake), razbijena i kodificirana na niz rutinskih postupaka, a onda su ili

---

3. Za nešto skoriju raspravu o ovom pitanju, vidjeti: Marina Vishmidt, 'The Two Reproductions', *Third Text*, u pripremi 2017.

uniformno primijenjena na radnike u vidu primjene plana ili su iskorištena da bi se napravile mašine koje na kraju mogu da zamijene radnike. Ovaj proces učenja od nekoga nad kim se potom sprovodi moć glavni je zadatak menadžera, a *menadžment* predstavlja tek puki opis jedne posebne lokacije u proizvodnom aparatu.[4] Ovdje je pitanje dominacije oslikano na nešto širem društveno-istorijskom platnu sa skorijim istraživanjem ideoloških obavezivanja i primjenjenih praksi ranih teoretičara menadžmenta kakav je bio Elton Mejo (Elton Mayo) 1920-ih godina.[5] Na ovaj način mi smo naviknuti da o menadžmentu razmišljamo u terminima procesa rada, sa jasnom podjelom na one koji izdaju naređenja i one koji ih izvršavaju – na one koji imaju zadatak da konceptualiziraju proces rada i na one koji ga samo sprovode u djelo, što je moguće marljivije. Međutim, teleološka strana procesa u oba slučaja uvijek se, *konstitutivno*, nalazi na nekom drugom mjestu, tj. izvan domašaja bilo kakvog pitanja ili intervencije. Na ovo se može, potpuno direktno, gledati i kao na otuđenje znanja u procesu racionalizacije ako se ova poistovijeti sa povećanjem akumulacije; time se, takoreći, oklopljava i naoružava sama subjektivnost (i opet će se, kao uobičajene savremene reference, ovdje pojaviti rasprave o afektivnim, kognitivnim pa čak i performativnim oblicima rada koje, međutim, ne bi smjele previdjeti središnju ulogu svih ovih veza u eksproprijaciji agenture u odnosu kapitala i rada, u svim njegovim tehnološkim i organizacionim varijantama).

Ovdje, onako uzgred, možemo da se osvrnemo na jedno značajno mjesto u knjizi Žaka Ransijera *Nesaglasnost*, na kom on ukazuje na to da se temelj društvene jednakosti pojavljuje upravo u scenariju najveće hijerarhije: izdavanju naređenja. Da bi se shvatilo naređenje i da bi se stekao razuman uvid u to kako ga sprovesti u skladu sa predviđenim, onaj koji ga sprovodi, u smislu razumijevanja, u najmanju ruku mora da

---

4. Harry Braverman, *Labor and Monopoly Capital: The Degradation of Work in the Twentieth Century*, New York and London: Monthly Review Press, [1974] 1998. [BCHS izdanje: Harry Braverman, *Rad i monopolistički kapital: degradacija rada u dvadesetom stoljeću*, Zagreb: Globus, 1983.]
5. Gerald Hanlon, *The Dark Side of Management: A Secret History of Management Theory*, New York: Routledge, 2015. U ovoj knjizi izložena je genealogija uloge teorije menadžmenta u neoliberalnom restrukturiranju, sa ukazivanjem na to da nam uvid u terapeutski i na podacima utemeljen diskurs menadžmenta može pomoći da usmjerimo pažnju na to da su se „menadžeri ponašali kao izvršni organi neoliberalizma sa zadatkom da obezbijede situaciju u kojoj će savremeni radnici egzistirati u jednom prekarnom svijetu bez ikakve kontrole, demokratije ili moći."

bude jednak sa onim koji to naređenje izdaje. Ova epistemička jednakost opstoji u stanju protivrječnosti i naddeterminacije društvenom nejednakošću, koja se opravdava ontološkim terminima kao, na primjer, u Aristotelovoj teoriji o robu kao o „alatki koja govori", koja je u protetičkom odnosu sa svojim gospodarom.

Pa ipak, kada se osvrnemo na menadžment u drugačijim razmjerama – možda na ekologiju menadžmenta – počinju nam se ukazivati neki iznenađujući aspekti onoga što bi se, prema ubjeđenjima koja imamo, moglo nazvati logikom menadžmenta. Menadžment isto tako može biti mišljen u smislu hvatanja u koštac sa jednim pokretnim i nepredvidivim miljeom, kao projekcija jednog svijeta na koji se gleda kao na slučajne materijalnosti koje predstavljaju tek prvi korak u njihovom stavljanju pod kontrolu i usmjeravanju ka predodređenom kraju. Ova ideja iskrsla je u jednom tekstu koji je nedavno objavila teoretičarka arhitekture Marija Đudiči (Maria Giudici) u kom ona raspravlja o ulozi narodnih tehničkih škola iz perioda italijanske renesanse.[6] U njenom radu o nastanku „projekta" zvanog *abaco* (računanje, *computing*; tj. u to vrijeme su se koristili *abakusi*, računaljke), koji potiče iz italijanskih inženjerskih škola iz 15. vijeka, iznosi se sljedeća pretpostavka:

> ovaj projekat ne podrazumijeva nužno neku formalnu odluku: radi se o terminu koji se više odnosio na menadžment stvari koje tek treba da nastanu. Projekat podrazumijeva uobličavanje smjera manipuliranjem, uticanjem i upravljanjem brojnim faktorima nad kojima nemamo uvijek potpunu kontrolu. On je nužno menadžerski i više fokusiran na proces nego na rezultat.

To prvenstvo procesa u odnosu na rezultat može se prenijeti i u budućnosti i uslovno primijeniti na oblast savremene umjetnosti, a poklapanja između menadžmenta i normi umjetničke produkcije i kuratorstva do kojih se došlo na ovaj način bila su tema eseja na koji se može gledati i kao na dalekog pretka ovog eseja.[7] Primijećeno je i to da je uticaj išao i u drugom smjeru, sa naglaskom na procesima povezanim sa umjetnošću kao pozitivnim primjerom u teoriji menadžmenta, i to na

---

6. Maria S. Giudici, 'Learning by Numbers', *e-flux Architecture conversations*, mart 2017, *http://conversations.e-flux.com/t/architecture-conversations-maria-s-giudici-responds-to-zeynep-celik-alexander-mass-gestaltung/5784*
7. Marina Vishmidt, 'Everyone Has a Business Inside Them', *Mute*, 12. mart 2012, *http://www.metamute.org/editorial/articles/everyone-has-business-inside-them*

onim mjestima u toj teoriji na kojima se tragalo za menadžerskim odlikama spontanosti, suverenosti i kreativnosti koje se povezuju sa umjetničkom genijalnošću.[8]

Ona nastavlja dalje naglašavanjem uloge tehničkog a ne samo humanističkog obrazovanja u kulturi renesanse, a posebno u ranomodernoj Italiji, i primjećuje kako su metode računanja i menadžerske tehnike predstavljale temelj ekonomskog uspjeha italijanskih gradova-država a time i njihovih geopolitičkih dostignuća i uticaja – a onda i instrumentarijem uspona kapitalizma u toj oblasti. Pa ipak, još sistematičnije i dosljednije, *abaco* škole su

uvodile različito razumijevanje odnosa čovjeka i svijeta. [...] Univerzum *abaco* škola bio je sačinjen od mnoštva entiteta, od objekata koje je student-subjekt trebalo da pripitomi, da njima upravlja, da ih reproducira i kontrolira. Ovdje naglasak nije bio ni na formi, ni na dizajnu već, prije, na strateškoj koreografiji dobara, novčanoj razmjeni i obezbjeđivanju rada. Bio je to univerzum koji je po prvi put bio sačinjen bez sivih zona: proračunat, saznatljiv, otvoren za oko čovjeka koji vreba svoj plijen.

Niz pedagoških metoda usmjerenih ka proizvodnji subjektivnostī kvantifikacije prilagodljivih kako u komercijalnom preduzetništvu, tako i u vojnom inženjeringu, prihvaćen je u istorijskim momentima (i)racionlizacije, kao što je to bio slučaj sa perspektivom u slikarstvu, geometriji i vlasničkom ropstvu. Paralelogram kontrole koji se ne razlikuje od kvazi-platonske stvarnosti principa razmjene u temelju je Alfred Zon-Retelovog (Alfred Sohn-Rethel) spajanja opticanja i koceptualnosti u logici „realne apstrakcije".[9] Ali ovo je kvantifikacija sa kvalifikacijom. Upravljanje materijalima i prostorom bilo je jedna stvar, dok je ono koje se bavi ljudskim ponašanjem druga – bio je to svijet aproksimacija, tehnologije „pravila palca" i menadžmenta slučajnosti: „U školskim zadacima od učenika se izričito tražilo da izračunaju cijenu

---

8. Jedna publikacija u moru onih koje se bave ovim temama je i: Jörg Reckhenrich, Martin Kupp and Jamie Anderson, 'The Manager as Artist,' Business Strategy Review, ljeto 2009. Dobra rasprava, kao i bibliografija ove literature može se naći u: Sarah Brouillette, 'Academic Labor, the Aesthetics of Management, and the Promise of Autonomous Work', *nonsite* journal, izdanje br. 9, http://nonsite.org/article/academic-labor-the-aesthetics-of-management-and-the-promise-of-autonomous-work

i trajanje nekog specifičnog posla ovisno o tome da li su radnici bili 'lijeni' ili ne."[10]

Na ovaj način menadžment je shvaćen kao (konjunkturni) okvir u koji je smještena neizvjesnost. Kao što vidimo, Đudiči suprotstavlja „projekt" dizajnu, što se ima shvatiti kao neka vrsta iscrpljujuće formalizacije, koja oblikuje samu sebe stalno i iznova u tandemu sa okruženjem. Sa druge strane, projekat je specifično menadžerski po svom modalitetu, s obzirom da je predstavljen kao više induktivan način postupanja – koji se ne tiče toliko elegantnih formula koliko učinkovitosti kontrole nestabilnih okolnosti. Ova ideja menadžmenta kao pristupa slučajnosti kao da donekle podsjeća i na održavanje – i to ne toliko u vidu organiziranja aktivnosti prema nekom planu koliko u obliku niza *ad hoc* prilagodbi koje se razvijaju uporedo sa haotičnim susretom sila i tendencija koje više liče na neku operaciju nego na stil. Pa opet, kao jedna vrsta menadžerske kontrole koja je omogućila nastanak prilagodbi, kao što je to bio slučaj sa otkrićem linearne perspektive i njenom primjenom u logističkim operacijama u ratovanju i kolonizaciji, menadžment slučajnosti nije ništa manje nasilan iako je nedvosmisleno prozaičniji od eteričnih, apsolutističkih principa totalnog dizajna. Đudiči, međutim, želi da skrene pažnju na neiskorišteni potencijal menadžmenta kao prozaične i metaboličke (razmjenske) aktivnosti, u Marksovom određenju ovog pojma, što je logika koja se svojih osnova može otarasiti kroz projekte proširene dominacije. Dakle, menadžment je bio projekat koji je „rođen kao istorijski situiran odgovor na uspon kapitalizma, u okviru koga je omogućio organiziranje rada i reifikaciju života u robu. Ako je ovo negativno naslijeđe ono koje mi sada odbacujemo, u okviru njega postoje i aspekti projekta koji se mogu ponovo misliti i kao sredstva otpora: ideja da stvaranje budućnosti ne znači nužno puku primjenu neke

---

9. Moglo bi biti korisno razmotriti istorijske okolnosti ove obuhvatne koncepcije, pogotovo velike ekspanzije zapošljavanja bijelih ovratnika, pisara i menadžera u njemačkoj za vrijeme Vajmarske republike, periodu o kom je Zon-Retel pisao svoje djelo *Intelektualni i manualni rad: kritika epistemologije* (Sohn-Rethel, *Intellectual and Manual labour: A Critique of Epistemology*, Atlantic Highlands, N.J: Humanities Press, 1977). Vidjeti također i: Siegfried Kracauer, *The Salaried Masses: Duty and Distraction in Weimar Germany*, (prev. Quintin Hoare), London and New York: Verso, 1998. U originalu: *Die Angestellten*, 1930.
10. Giudici, op.cit.

postojeće forme, već da se osmisli čitav niz odnosa koji mogu da se promijene, preokrenu i prilagode."[11]

Mi ovako, posredstvom menadžmenta shvaćenog kao niza dispozicija i znanja, nalazimo projekat s jedne strane, dizajn sa druge i, naposljetku, *in nuce*, jednu više materijalističku ideju apstrakcije kao izokrenutog dijagrama misaono preoblikovanog u skladu sa prolaznošću njegovog (ljudskog) svijeta. Na ovom mjestu možemo napraviti brzu poveznicu sa ekologijom i ekološkim problemima kao prilikom za primjenu projekata menadžmenta koje bi karakterizirali reciprocitet i

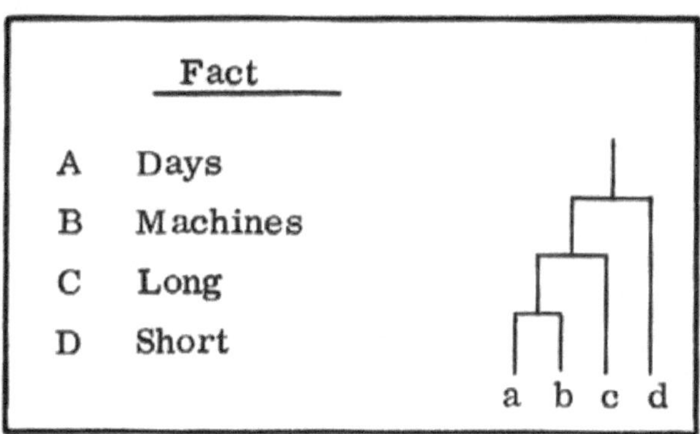

refleksivnost. To zahtijeva mogućnost da se zamisli menadžment na planetarnom nivou, u smislu „planetarnog" kako ga je, u skorije vrijeme, formulisala Gajatri Spivak (Gayatri Spivak): kao etiku promjene u odnosu prema uništavanju koju ona izvodi iz susreta i naklonosti kakvi se razvijaju u odnosu između Ahaba i bijelog kita u *Mobi Diku*. Planetarna razina menadžmenta tako podrazumijeva upravljanje kao nešto što je u nekoj mjeri osuđeno na neuspjeh, ali i pored toga predstavlja kolektivni pokušaj da se „rukuje" nekontroliranim slučajnostima ekoloških oštećenja i volju da se istraje u projektima održavanja: održavati uslove za život za različite ljudske i neljudske entitete u kontekstu koji je zagađenje učinilo „otuđenim", a time i takvim da se u njemu čini da su otuđenja, kako ona koje su nam isuviše poznata, tako i ona koja do sada nismo mogli ni zamisliti, odnijela prevagu. Jednostavnije rečeno, planetarnost preoblikuje menadžment u održavanje u (uslovima) otpora, ali i održavanje (samih uslova) otpora, u onom trenutku kada se na poznate količine „resursa" koji obuhvataju polje djelovanja menadžmenta više ne može računati, dok se

---

11. Ibid.

održavanje, skupa sa svojom istrajnom orijentacijom ka opstanku sada može pojaviti kao jedna vrsta kreativnog susreta sa onim istinskim eko-sistemskim nepoznatim, koji nužno iziskuje novije (ili starije) kooperativne društvene forme.

Ovo počinje da nam daje i neka oruđa pomoću kojih možemo ponovo zamisliti održavanje ne više kao puku reprodukciju – a to će reći kao održavanje koje treba da ostane sebi slično kao puko moguće i time odsječeno od bilo koje ideje o novini ili poremećaju – već da otpočnemo sa radom na pojmu održavanja kao otpora. Još jedan podstrek za kretanje u ovom pravcu može se pronaći i u ideji o tehnološkom znanju kao nečemu što razvija odnos prema slučajnosti koja se pretvara u „menadžment" u onom trenutku kada, da tako kažemo, dotakne tlo, a u „održavanje" kada mu se tlo pod nogama izmiče. Drugim riječima, menadžment kvantiteta i ponašanja, objekata, subjekata i njihovih tranzicija i transverzalnosti duž čitave skale, opet, suočava se sa nespoznatljivošću koja suzbija odomaćivanje na razini pravljenja štete kako granularne tako i planetarne, gdje stari oblici eksploatacije iščezavaju dok ih na njihovom mjestu zamjenjuju novi, možda i opakiji od njih. Ponegdje možda i postoji djelimična usaglašenost sa pojmom „neizračunljivog" koji su razvile teoretičarke Antonija Majača i Lućijana Parizi (Luciana Parisi) u jednom od njihovih skorijih tekstova.[12] One kažu da instrumentalnost može da se ponovo procijeni ne više kao neovisna kulturna logika koja smjera ka totalitarizmu stvari, potpuno kvantificirana i (i)racionalizirana distopija u stilu *Dijalektike prosvetiteljstva*, već prije u smislu da tehnologija utjelovljuje društveno-istorijske vrijednosti nekog perioda.

Iako ovo zvuči kao banalnost, intrigantnija dimenzija ovdje je to da je instrumentalnost biopolitička i da mašina sama po sebi može da bude izvor „tuđinskih modaliteta subjektivacije", koji mogu da se izmijene uvođenjem perspektive mašine, a ne više one inženjera, arhitekte, dizajnera, korisnika, analitičara bezbjednosti ili menadžera. Kako se ovo uopće može predstaviti, i u koju svrhu bi se tako što radilo? Drugim riječima, kako možemo sa razine planetarnosti kao imena za promjenjivost u političkoj ekologiji Spivakove doći do intimnosti

---

12. Antonia Majaca & Luciana Parisi, 'The Incomputable and Instrumental Possibility', *e-flux journal* broj 77, http://www.e-flux.com/journal/77/76322/the-incomputable-and-instrumental-possibility/ novembar 2016; posljednji put pristupljeno 22. marta 2017.

izmjenjivosti svakodnevne tehnologije? U oba ova scenarija, pitanje promjenjivosti formulirano je u terminima postojećeg otuđenja, što i poražava imaginaciju kao nešto što je trenutno ustanovljeno i nešto što nas „tjera da mislimo" (Delez [Deleuze]), ali i djeluje kao politički i afektivni odgovor na istinsku novost koja se ne može „menadžerski odraditi". Poslije otuđenja dolazi do intimizacije održavanja, što u sebi može sadržavati rekalibraciju odnosa subjekt-objekt koju komercijalne forme „tehno animizma" (a to pomoću svojih gedžeta iskušavamo svaki dan) više blokiraju nego što ih omogućavaju. Također, s obzirom na to da, u smislu u kom govore Parizi i Majača, te naprave podstiču „paranoidne" forme nadziranja i kontrole u većoj mjeri nego što računaju na to da oblikovanjem algoritamske spoznaje utiču na ljudsko mišljenje i društvenost, jedno takvo računanje sadržava i biopolitička uvođenja ovih tehnologija prije nego li projekciju policijske logike u tu upotrebu i pomoću nje.

Ovdje se nagovještava kako „mišljenje iz perspektive mašine i iz same logike instrumenta" može da nam obezbijedi neke resurse – posebno za one među „nama" koji su podvrgnuti rodnosti, rasnosti, klasnosti, ne-sposobnosti i abjekciji – pomoću kojih možemo da uklonimo samo-održive forme algoritamske kontrole koje prodiru kroz sve postojeće modele kibernetičkog upravljanja i eksploatacije. Bit će da ćemo najprije pomoću remonta hijerarhije sredstava i ciljeva koja je usađena u tehnologiju kao repozitorij za naturalizirane društvene odnose kompeticije, učinkovitosti i kontrole, mi ući u njih kao u prostor intimnog otuđenja u kom značenje funkcionalnosti samo po sebi može da bude prekoračeno, izokrenuto i ponovo izmišljeno kao dio jednog transformativnog društvenog procesa. Ono što bi sve ovo, na prvom mjestu, trebalo da znači je da ako istrajna (iako filozofski dovedena u pitanje) dualnost između tehniciteta i prirode ne može dalje da se obnavlja, onda priroda ne može biti tek skup vanvremenih značenja koja (značenja) nam tehnologija dozvoljava podvrgnuti standardizaciji i sistematizaciji. Od središnjeg značaja i za ovu diskusiju je ideja prema kojoj sam instrument posjeduje sopstveni cilj, svoju sopstvenu istoriju subjektivacije:

Novi subjekt može biti konstituiran samo na osnovu tvrdog rada otuđenja, koji uključuje razumijevanje logike instrumentalnosti, koji je politizira, i prevazilazi samom upotrebom. Ovo zahtijeva izgradnju neparanoidne imaginacije i spremnost na radikalnu deinstrumentalizaciju i ljudskosti i subjektivnosti kakve poznajemo [...].

Ovim uvidima mjere se, iako bez dodatnog obogaćivanja, filozofski ponori koji ostaju van dometa obližnjih tehno-feminističkih pozicija kakav je „ksenofeminizam", sa njegovim grubim recikliranjem tropa sajberfeminizma uz dodatak nekih odrednica iz programa

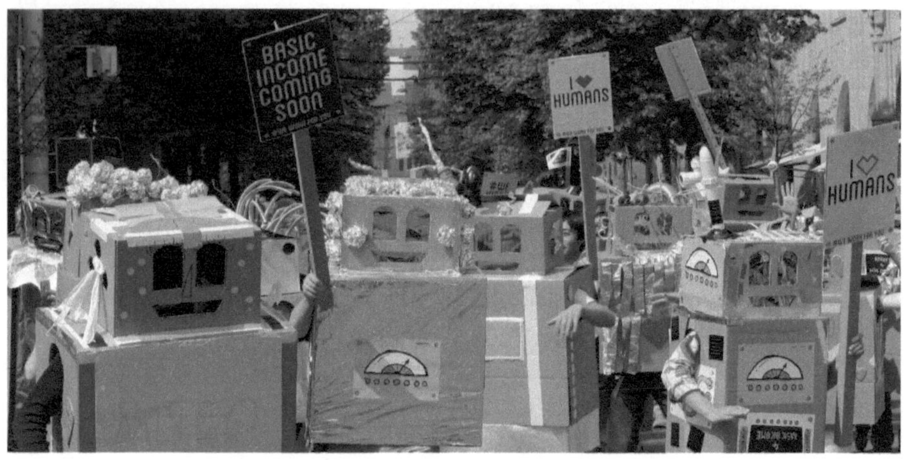

Roboti za osnovna primanja, Cirih, 30. april 2016.

akceleracionizma. U tom svjetlu, djelo Majače i Parizi liči na djelo Gilberta Simondona i na njegovu knjigu *O modusu postojanja tehničkih objekata* (*On the Mode of Existence of Technical Objects*) u kojoj razmatra shemu ko- i trans-konstitucije među ljudima, miljeima i tehničkim objektima. Tehnički objekti ne bi trebalo da budu degradirani i podređeni ciljevima profita, navika ili kontrole, već njihovom tehnicitetu treba biti dozvoljeno da se razvija prema onim ciljevima za koje se trenutno vjeruje da su nefunkcionalni ili da nisu poželjni. Time se baštini garancija autonomije onom tehničkom koja je manje nalik autonomiji kapitala a više autonomiji umjetnosti, koja se nalazi rame uz rame sa autonomijom koju iskušavaju ljudi koji više nisu potčinjeni naturaliziranom despotizmu tehničkog. U jednom intervjuu, Simondon iznosi mišljenje o bliskosti ovog pojma autonomije tehničkog i ideja vezanih za održavanje o kojima smo do sada raspravljali: „Vjerujem da postoje ljudi u tehničkim objektima, i da otuđeni ljudi mogu biti spaseni pod uslovom da postoji čovjek koji se stara o njima."[13]

Skala ili nivo se nameće kao pitanje i za Simondona kada razmišlja o „redovima magnituda" čiji su odnosi od suštinskog značaja. Ovo vodi ka

„realizmu odnosa". Jedinka, kakav god da je njen ontološki status, – a za Simondona jedinka je ishod procesa individuacije, kojih je nebrojeno, i ona može biti mentalni, biološki, hemijski ili društveni proces, između svih ostalih – nije *u* odnosu, već ona *jeste* odnos, u najvećoj mjeri prema svom miljeu. Jedinka je sastavljena od odnosa i ona je njihov sadržitelj i postoji na različitim nivoima: nivou jedinke, nivou predindividualnog, na nivou miljea. Jedinka tako može da se shvati kao faza konzistencije u predjelu odnosa. Nastavljajući odavde ka organizacionom i društvenom nivou na kojima se prvi put susrećemo sa dijadom menadžment i održavanje, podjela na konceptualno i manualno, koja predstavlja osnovu i opravdanje za upražnjavanje menadžmenta, biva opovrgnuta ovom koncepcijom, koja stvara mnoštvo nivoa preko kojih se postojanost i odgovornost mogu stvarati i rastvarati – što je nešto bliže logici održavanja, koja je usklađena *ad hoc* operacijama čija kreativnost se koristi u pojačavanju efekata i povezanosti više nego učinkovitosti i kontrole od strane dalekih i neupitnih ciljeva.

Dakle, meanadžment preko skala (nivoa) ovdje može da znači menadžment *samih* skala (nivoa), u smislu da menadžment sada ima priliku da se razvije u staranje: u više refleksivno nego kruto operacionalno preduzimanje optimizirajućih aktivnosti ili procesa u svrhu ispunjenja unaprijed određenih ciljeva (efikasnosti, performansi). Na ovaj način vraćamo se na pitanje nivoa sa stanovišta projekta koji nam je pri ruci. Nivo je artefakt produktivne imaginacije i posebnog inženjerskog procesa, a ne u potpunosti tek prethodno postojeći okvir referenci koji za cilj ima nekakav predodređeni red na koji je onda tehnologija dizajnirana da odgovori, bilo da se radi o poboljšanju ili kažnjavanju. Ako instrumentalnost, kako to tvrde Majača i Parizi, predstavlja subjektivnost u praksi, to je praksa koja ponire u objekt i napušta subjekt, ali samo po cijenu (odricanja) prevladavanja „empirijsko-ontološkog" dubleta kapitalističkih društvenih odnosa kojima se ove dve autorke ne bave direktno, već se nasuprot tome služe jednim istaknutim primjerom, Adornovom *Negativnom dijalektikom*. One svoju pažnju radije usmjeravaju na zapažanje da savremeni razvoj AI[14] i mašinsko učenje operiraju sa pojmovima nekompletnosti, greške i

---

13. 'Save The Technical Object: Interview with Gilbert Simondon', prevod na engleski jezik intervjua. Andrew Iliadis, prev. *Esprit* Br. 76, Vol. 04/1983, str. 147-52. http://linkme2.net/wh
14. AI – *Artificial Intelligence – vještačka inteligencija* (prim. prev.)

slučajnosti koji su zreli za re-aproprijaciju koju su feminističke tehničarke inače već obavile, baveći se konceptima kakav je recimo Persova „abdukcija" (forma logičkog rezoniranja koje ne funkcionira izvođenjem, već fantastično). Abdukcija, za razliku od nešto utemeljenijih modaliteta indukcije i dedukcije, je način da se ocijeni ono nepredstavljivo pomoću serija posljedica koje impliciraju ili, radije, projektiraju svijet u kojem bi taj novi događaj imao smisla. Na abdukciju se ovdje gleda kao na „otuđeni način spoznaje", s obzirom na to da ona otpočinje sa nepoznatim ili u najmanju ruku trenutno nepoznatim premisama, spajajući energiju spekulacije sa čistotom formalne logike.

Takav način spoznaje mogao bi pronaći smisao u „generacijama novih hipoteza o instrumentalnosti, one koja priznaje istoriju tehnike na osnovu toga da li su mašine bile sposobne da razmatraju strategije autonomije od i kroz svoje sopstvene upotrebe."[15] Ovdje heksogenična scenarija naučne fantastike mogu poslužiti i kao primjer i kao metodologija, vodeći nas polako ka tome da pristupimo ovoj autonomiji tehničkog kao „ironičnom političkom mitu" (kako Dona Haravej počinje svoj *Manifest Kiborga*). Takav potez značio bi povratak na naše originalne kategorije održavanja i menadžmenta skupa sa politikom koja ne bi bila utemeljena u produktivnom subjektu stavljenom *vis-à-vis* izvedenog objekta – pa čak i ako se radi o reproduktivnom subjektu – već izmještanjem subjektivnosti ka objektu, a potom i ka procesima nespoznatljivosti koju autonomija tehničkog objekta može iznijeti u prvi plan. Konkretnije, ako počnemo tragajući za održavanjem kao staranjem o onom što jeste, omogućujući mu da se razvija i postane, a menadžment shvatimo kao optimizaciju onoga što jeste, poboljšanje njegove produktivnosti za neki unaprijed određen cilj, možda smo i uspjeli da napravimo zaokret u gledanju na stvari u smislu kretanja ka zaposjedanju otuđenja koje postoji kako u kreativnosti tako i u produktivnosti. To nas osposobljava da vidimo kako se to odvajanje iskazuje kroz društvene hijerarhije naređivanja i kontroliranja u kojima je kreativnost s jedne strane podstaknuta instrumentalnošću sa druge, a ta instrumentalnost je na prvom mjestu i iznad svega usud nekih subjekata koji se više ne smatraju u potpunosti ljudskim, iako još uvijek nisu postali nalik neorganskim mehanizmima.

Pa ipak, u ovoj raspravi o mehanizmima ugrađivanja, pitanje društvenih mehanizama institucija mogu da postanu sporedna, i da se

---

15. Parisi & Majaca, op. cit.

spekulativne energije prvih utope u inerciji potonjih. Ali traganje za odnosima između održavanja, menadžmenta i otpora također bi trebalo da se dodirne i institucija. Ono što možda još preostaje da se odredi jeste to kako u sadašnjem trenutku sav menadžment naginje prema krizi menadžmenta, a time, po difoltu, i tome da se poveže sa

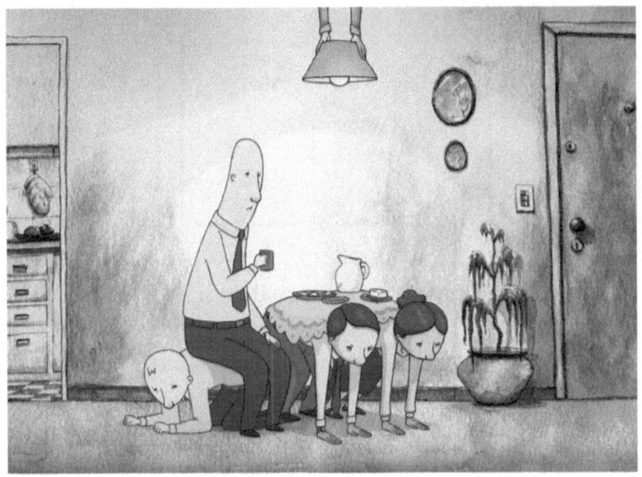

Santijago Graso (Santiago Grasso),
iz filma *El Empleo*, 2008, Argentina

komunalnom i emancipatorično mišljenom „politikom staranja". Danas menadžment nastoji da bude viđen kao praksa koja brine – kako bi bio siguran da je sve u redu, da se čuje svačiji glas, da se svi osjećaju sigurno, naročito oni koji su na svojim radnim mjestima izloženi intenzivnim ciklusima prekarizacije i proletarizacije, kao što je to slučaj sa obrazovnim institucijama. Ta briga oko toga da se osigura normalnost po svaku cijenu nije dobila ime represivne tolerancije potpuno neopravdano, s napomenom da se onaj dio koji se odnosi na „toleranciju" uvijek umanjuje u korist onog vezanog za represivnost, kao što i sigurnoću rukovođena upravljačka tijela pozivaju policiju i druge državne agente da se „pobrinu" za pitanja rada ili pitanja studenata po kampusima. Ali možda još podmukliji od tih neočekivanih fenomena jeste diskurs staranja koji licencira sve aspiracije ka apsolutnoj kontroli – gdje se neslaganje sa nečim ne smatra pitanjem antagonizma već bezosjećajnosti, organiziranjem koje je stvoreno kako bi se dijalogu zadao udarac a ne kako bi se na njega podsticalo. Moć rekonfigurisana u staranje može se smatrati vrstom „reproduktivnog realizma" koji djeluje kao da afirmiše nevidljivi rad održavanja i opstanka, ali za odlučno konzervativne ciljeve. U ovoj gruboj razdvojenosti održavanja i otpora, završavamo na kraju sa menadžmentom. To za posljedicu ima potiskivanje svakog poremećaja i uznemiravanja kao neopravdanog ispoljavanja moći i privilegija –

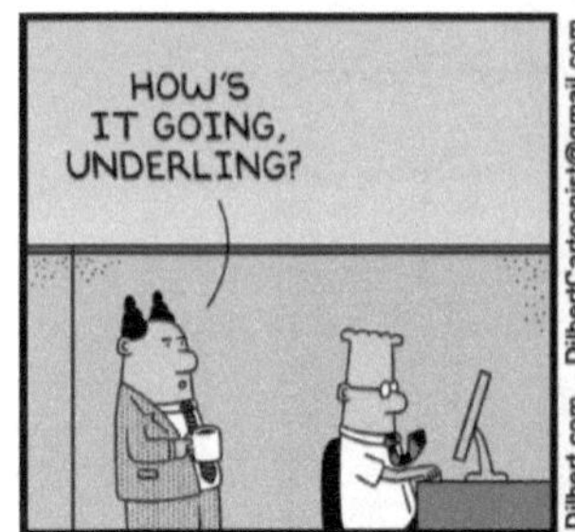

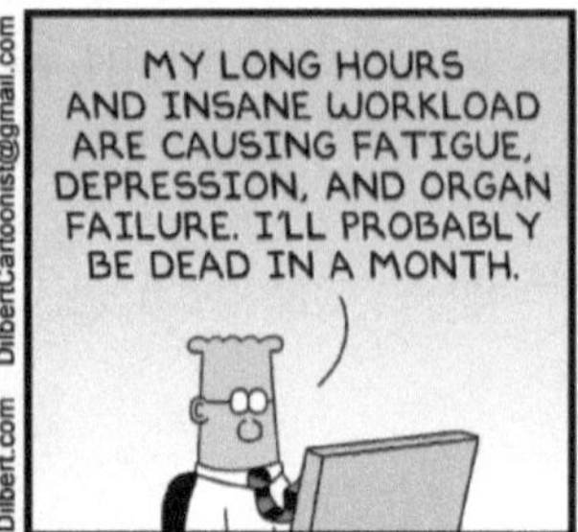

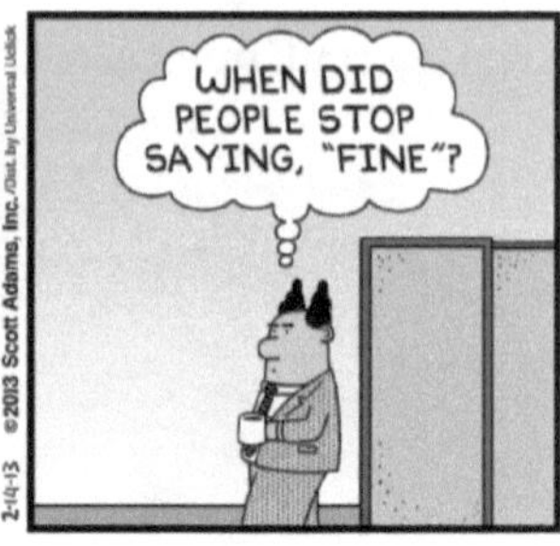

oni koji žele da pruže otpor nahuškani su protiv onih koji bi samo da opstoje, kao da jedno ne podrazumijeva drugo. Na taj način možemo uočiti jasan kontinuum između krajeva ovog spektra: kozmetička rutina staranja institucionalnog menadžmenta, bezobzirno odbijanje političkih pitanja u korist učmale etike staranja koja nekako uvijek afirmira tržišnu subjektivnost,[16] i „umjetnost održavanja" „brigadā na metlama" srednje klase koje su izašle na londonske ulice pred same nerede iz ljeta 2011. godine kako bi paradirali svojom rasnom i klasnom mržnjom uklopljeni u fotogenično kompulzivno čišćenje – što je, zasigurno, jedna ironijska inverzija onog pitanja Mierl Ukels: „gorka pilula svake revolucije – tko će sve počistiti narednog dana?"

Ovaj kratki obilazak nekih od dvosmislenijih uglova kompleksa održavanje-menadžment ima za cilj da rasprši ponešto od licemjerja koje nekako uvijek prati „politiku staranja", kao da je tu riječ samo o jednoj politici i da je sāmo prizivanje staranja dovoljno da označi njenu prirodu. Dakle, kako bismo ponovno procijenili, a samo prevrednovali, aktivnosti održavanja i menadžmenta, bit će potrebno da dođe i do neke vrste izmještanja agencije od ljudskih subjekata ka tehničkim objektima, o kojima govore Majača, Parizi i Simondon, ali samo kao dio jedne veće transvaluacije abjektnih formi rada i postojanja koje djeluju tehnički očigledne ali i dalje ostaju društveno neprozirne. Manevar

---

16. Iako raširen, na ovaj fenomen često nailazimo u situacijama u kojima se kredibilitet akumulira pomoću radikalnog diskursa ali se u opasnost dovodi političkom aktivnošću kakva je prostor savremene umjetnosti. To je također i oblast u kojoj se oportunizam njeguje kao politika preživljavanja, sa pretekstom prekarnosti na koji se često poziva kako bi se odbacile kritike bilo koje vrste reakcionarnih aktivnosti, kada se ove ne koriste da bi se ukazalo na privilegije onih koji kritiziraju.

naturalizacije tehničkog kao opozitnog procesa reifikovanju prirode, znači samo to da je društveni sadržaj prirode uvijek funkcionaliziran – s obzirom na to da je sada hitno izvršiti ponovnu procjenu veze između

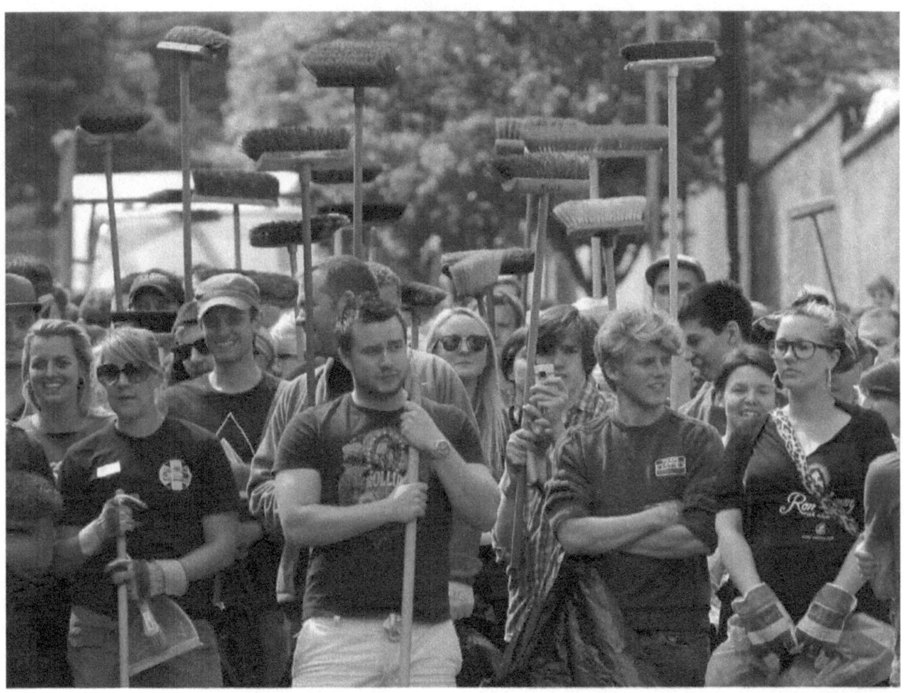

Volonteri pomažu čišćenje na početku pobuna na saobraćajnom čvorištu Klapam (Clapham) u Londonu, 9. august 2011.

sredstava i ciljeva u okviru kapitalističke tehno-nauke koja nas vodi ka uništenju ekosistema – i to ne odbijanjem naučnog ili instrumentalnog po sebi nego odbijanjem društvenih veza koje ponavljaju njihove mitologizirane verzije kao puki realizam. Ponešto od performativnosti feminističke umjetnosti, – kako bismo mogli reći u duhu onoga što kaže Ukels kada govori o transvaluaciji održavanja kao ne-progresvne forme života – naučne fantastike i filozofije tehnologije može nam pomoći da otpočnemo sa rasterećivanjem, čak i ako pijetet „staranja" uvijek vreba da nas u tome zaustavi.

INSTITUCIONALNE KOMUNE, REKUPERACIJA ILI REPRODUKCIJA?

GRUPA ZA KONCEPTUALNU POLITIKU

Skloni smo sablažnjavanju: Svi zaposleni u ovom trenutku mogu se smatrati pandurima. Raditi je postalo privilegija, što je težak udarac na politiku koja je sledila put radničke emancipacije i radničke borbe jer ova je već stavila na dnevni red rad i njegovo odbijanje. Kako ga danas odbiti kada nam ga niko i ne nudi? Kako i šta zaposleni misli o sebi? Kako da o njemu misli onaj koji ne radi, osim kao o privilegovanom? Šta god da misli, zaposleni to zna da ceni: on misli državotvorno i nije isključeno da će se primiti na ideju javnog dobra, samo mu to treba dobro spakovati ukoliko ne radi u državi. Sa državnim uposlenicima će to ići daleko lakše. Nije isključeno da se čitava periferija, na kojoj samo država radi, zbog toga lako prebaci u socijalistički režim organizacije i reprodukcije kapitala, čemu se i nadaju na levici koja je na parlamentarnim pripremama, a u Sloveniji već i na terenu. Ne treba biti paranoik da bi se to videlo, jer ne treba tražiti pojedinca koji nam sprema socijalizaciju dugova i troškova održavanja duga. Javno dobro će nam se prvo pojaviti u obliku duga i liturgijske odgovornosti, kako to obično i biva u poslovima upravljanja provincijom.

Mi se danas suočavamo sa dilemom koju neki postavljaju terminima pacifizam i radikalizam. Pacifizam i njegove laži, samoobmane, javljaju se u vidu *javnih diskusija* koje drže za oblik političke brobe, dok je radikalizam onaj koji je nešto ređe na licitaciji među levim aktivistima i koji nema drugu funkciju osim isključivanja. Kao rezultat imamo *parlamentarizam i konferencijalizam*. Najčešće se preklapaju i tako dobijamo *kongresalizam* kojeg prati publicističko razvijanje onoga što bi trebala biti teorija i nauka, i sve to biva u službi društvene pokretljivosti i uhlebljenja u državi. Sa godinama se razvija glad za priznanjem i zbog toga se aktivizam *na vreme* pretvara u akumulaciju simboličkog i socijalnog kapitala.

Imamo nekakvo iskustvo borbe na tom terenu i mi smo prošli kroz sukobe na nezavisnoj levici. Sukobe našeg vremena, iako je ovo možda manje istorijsko prema merilima budućih istoričara koji pojave i dalje traže na planu objektivnog, a koje je uvek i u krajnjoj instanci plan državnog. Prošli smo kroz cepanja i razlaze, isključivanja i podmetanja doživljaja samoisključenosti i resantimana – jeftine psihologizacije. Osetili smo na svojoj koži kako radi mikrofašistička i državna mašina, čak i kada se ona odvija pod zastavama antifašizma. Akademizam nam je dokazao da je časove moguće držati i u slobodno vreme i lekcije deliti čak i u igri. Akademičari, gladni javnog prikazivanja, progovorili su o javnom dobru prevashodno zato što se sami smatraju dobrom koje je javno i koje bi trebalo čuvati kao zenicu oka.

Danas više nismo tek i samo ozloješeni, već i štetočine. Štetočine, jer radimo u lokalnoj zajednici kao aktivisti na terenu lokalne samouprave. Projekat nazivamo „lokalne politike i urbana samouprava". Mi međutim ovako vidimo problem: depolitizacija lokalne samouprave i njeno gašenje se odvija iščezavanjem civilnog društva u lokalu. Tačnije, u lokalu je iščezlo vanpartijsko organizovanje kome su teren pripremale socijalističke mesne zajednice i mi smo danas, nakon socijalističkog vremena kada su mesne zajednice imale svoja veća u skupštinama opština, svedoci prisustva države i partije u našim domovima. Saveti i uprava u mesnoj zajednici su partijski, a i domovi su nam partijski jer ih možemo održavati samo ako radimo u državi, što uvek ide preko partije ili nekog drugog državnog oblika pokoravanja, pošto je država jedino preduzeće koje radi. Preduzeće u krizi, ali koje još uvek radi u svom povlačenju sa tržišta, ali ne više da bi se napravio prostor za biznis. Čega nastaje prostor? - ostaje da se vidi isključivo u mraku.[1]

Zašto nam se dakle kaže da smo štetočine? Pa zato što radimo posao države. Tako nam je rečeno. Osim što salonski popujemo o samoorganizovanju, kaže nam se i da podlo uvaljujemo ideju o zaduživanju i preporučujemo uzimanje kredita. Pričamo priče, iako umišljamo da pokrećemo ljude da se organizuju po pitanju održavanja stambenog fonda. To bi trebala da radi država, poručuju nam levo orijentisani intelektualci (akademci i publicisti). Mi u tome vidimo paradoks: Štetočine smo jer radimo posao države i time državu oslobađamo obaveze da to sama čini? To bi dakle ona trebala da radi, a ne mi? Dakle radimo nešto što bi pre ličilo na „Big society"? Da li bi državu trebalo prinuditi da radi „svoj posao"? Zar tako što nećemo ništa preduzimati? Ništa umesto nje nećemo raditi, nego ćemo u nju ući i njome to odraditi kada budemo na vlasti ili u mogućnosti da barem delom vršimo vlast. Taj deo će verovatno zavisiti od našeg koalicionog

---

1. Kriza države (videti Poulantzasa) u vremenu njene dominacije slabljenjem teorijski je obrazlagana. Dominacija države, to je značilo da je ekonomska funkcija države nadodređivala ostale. Prema našem teorijskom sećanju, takva je bila i socijalistička partija-država tretirana konceptom načina proizvodnje, koji je i na Istoku i na Zapadu osvetljavao mišljenje ljudi ne čineći ih i savremenicima. Ekonomske funkcije države se ogledaju u njenim intervencijama koje pogoduju širenju tržišta kao same ideje regulacije. Smemo li reći da je tržište isto što i regulacija i uređenost na način nevidljivosti ruke kao odluke (preskripcije), a da ne budemo shvaćeni kao ideolozi političke ekonomije? Smemo li to reći iako je uvek iznova nejasno da smo načisto sa tim šta je bila kritika iz vremena Kritike političke ekonomije? (Videti i Fukoa – Biopolitika).

potencijala, ako već nismo u stanju da imamo većinu i državu u potpunosti učinimo našom. Do tada moramo čekati. I to nije sve.

Dakle štetočine smo jer radimo posao države koja je loša jer to ne radi. I ne samo da je treba prinuditi, već treba znati da je ona upravo zato i loša jer postoje štetočine koje misle da to mogu i bez nje. U tome se i ogleda koncept „Big society-a", odnosno neoliberalno upravljanje ili policija, policijska neoliberalna država. Dakle nipošto ne činimo ništa, jer svaka akcija koja nije državna i ne smera na državu kao nešto sa čim treba delati, štetočinska je i proizvodi državu koja ne radi svoj posao. Dobra država je tako ona u kojoj smo mi, a sasvim dobra ona u kojoj smo samo mi. I budući da smo levičari ili čak socijalisti, takva država onda radi svoj posao. A kako? Pa zna se: stručno i kvalifikovano jer imaćemo i stručnjake.

Dobro, nismo baš optuženi da vozimo ovom ideologijom (Big society), pošto nismo u Britaniji, ali se pitamo i zašto ne zategnuti stvar konceptualno? Radnički označitelji ili označitelji radničke ideologije mogu nadodrediti vladajuću ideologiju koja ostaje i dalje buržoaska. Sve što nikne na terenu ideologije, doprinosi njenom jačanju – i to je način na koji mi razumemo koncept hegemonije. Dakle ne samo da je u pitanju ideološka vladavina ili vladavina ideologijom, već mi mislimo da je u pitanju i njeno jačanje – jačanje vlasti – otporom i nadomeštanjem odsutnih ili označitelja koji bi baš dobro legli da zakrpe rupe. Zato nam se danas čini i da je „bekstvo" možda bolja slika jer njom otvaramo, po nečijem ukusu isuviše poetski i romantično, put autoteorizacijama i politikama kojima se izbegava hegemonija. Budući da reči nisu samo reči, nego i prakse i dela koja rezonuju, treba uvek tražiti i odnose u koje stupamo govoreći. U tom smislu mi govorimo o *institucionalnim komunama*. Dakle budimo radikalni bez koketiranja sa radikalizmom i držimo se koncepta istorijskog materijalizma dosledno: Država nije samo u institucijama za koje Se smatra da su državne, dakle u institucijama državne uprave i političkog sistema, već su aparati države i preduzeća, institucije kulture, skupštine stanara, domaćinstva i porodice. Aparat vidimo kao istorijskomaterijalistički koncept institucije čija se mera (uvek i politička) uzima s obzirom na funkciju reprodukcije koju vrši u jednom načinu proizvodnje. Bilo je to Altiserovo pitanje na odgovor koji sociolozi simptomalno daju nastojeći da ustanove predmet svoje nauke, i koji bi da nazovu društvenom činjenicom. Njeno rasklapanje na „društveno delanje", koje je onda „ustanovljeno i ustaljeno", samo je nastavak tautološke obrade pojma opijuma koji opija jer ima opijatsku moć. Tek dovođenje institucija u odnos prema proizvodnim odnosima može nam reći nešto više o njima i tako dolazimo do koncepta aparata koji je uvek aparat države. Prema tome, prigovor je na mestu: *mi ne samo da obavljamo posao države, već i pravimo nešto što je aparat države i nalazimo se u poretku države dok god postoji odnos proizvodnje koji je odnos eksploatacije.* I da li je to sve što možemo i smemo reći? Smemo li pomisliti da je na taj način razgrađujemo? Kako inače zamišljamo njeno odumiranje? Smemo li reći da je ona u krizi i da se pred našim očima, u mraku savremenosti, hipnagogički osvetljavaju moguće kategorije, a pre svega ona mogućeg? Da li pozivanje ljudi da uzmu učešća u njenom funkcionisanju na distanci prema postojećim aparatima – u slučaju lokalne samouprave na distanci prema partijskoj organizaciji koja je premrežila i domen lokalne samouprave – i ohrabrivanje ljudi da sami uređuju odnose u koje stupaju odlučujući i proizvodeći ideologiju (ukoliko krenu putem samoorganizovanja i izumevanja institucija i organizacionih oblika) može biti tumačeno i izvođeno na drugačiji način od postojećeg?

Na umu imamo ideju koju smo čuli od ljudi iz udruženja građana koje znamo pod imenom „Učitelj neznalica i njegovi komiteti". Njihov cilj je bio ohrabrivanje ljudi da uzmu učešća u korišćenju resursa civilnog društva. Mislimo da je tako glasila formulacija. Nama se čini da je to dobar način da ljudi krenu putem izumevanja institucija, jer, konačno, na distanci prema državi (iako konceptualno i objektivno i dalje stvaraju aparat), ipak ne moraju slediti obrasce podele rada i distribucije koji su podržani vladajućom ideologijom i racionalizacijama koje traže svoje uporište u tehnologiji procesa produkcije. To što jedna operacija može biti podeljena na skup aktivnosti i delatnosti, ne znači da se i ljudi moraju deliti, pa ni prikivati za određene aktivnosti. Subjektivacija je moguća i u subjektivnosti, a ne samo u objektivnom i preko objektivnog kojim se saznaje društvo i čovekov svet. Saznanje u subjektivnosti je mišljenje i pronalaženje mogućeg u datoj situaciji, ne tražeći drugu osnovu za svoje postojanje do u sebi i onome što možemo učiniti i bez države. Bez vlasti i njenog osvajanja koje po logici stvari ostavlja na čekanju sve ono zbog čega bi nam bila potrebna. Jer, ako mislimo da jedan problem možemo rešiti samo uz pomoć vlasti i sa njenog mesta, onda se rešavanje tog problema odlaže dok ne osvojimo vlast i time postaje jasno da je naš problem zapravo osvajanje vlasti a ne rešavanje konkretnog problema.

Udruženja građana, ako tautologiju isteramo na čistac ponavljanja, i nisu drugo do udruživanje građana. U tom smislu *udruženi građani* nikoga ne predstavljaju, i svako pitanje i problematizacija reprezentativnosti ili odgovaranja interesima ljudi otpada: ljudi se i jesu udružili da ih niko ne bi mogao ili morao predstavljati. Udruženi ljudi nešto čine i čine kako se dogovore. Sva je stvar u tome koliko će se držati dogovorenog, a držimo ga se i kada ga misleći i polemišući menjamo. Proizvodni odnos, budući odnos vlasti, tako biva demontiran, a kodovi rastočeni mišljenjem i borbom koja se vodi u organizacijama ništa više nego u nama samima kada se razračunavamo sa potrebom za državom u nama. Nije potrebno psihologizirati čitav problem jer politiku možemo imati kad god se distanciramo, pa tako i od psihološke racionalizacije naših odnosa koji su odnosi moći koje treba čuvati od svakog oblika vlasti.

Zamislimo sad takvu situaciju i procese u pogonima materijalne proizvodnje. Da li je to moguće u uslovima u kojima ustav garantuje i čuva privatno vlasništvo? A da li je to izvodljivo u uslovima u kojima ustav čuva i garantuje državno, pa i čak i društveno vlasništvo? Vlasništvo kao takvo, već je pravno zaodenut odnos koji je teško videti kao proizvodni i politički. Čak i kao društveno, neće otvoriti polja na kojima se odnosi moći taktički raspoređuju prema strategijama upravljanja kojima dominira briga za celinu i Jedno, i koje neumoljivo totalizuje i zatvara naše moguće u neizvodljivo i održivo kao nemoguće.

Dok ovo pišemo mislimo na reči prijatelja. Ako dobro čujemo, Sylvain Lazarus kaže da subjektivnost ljudi ne treba da bude u funkciji protivljenja državi, već u traganju za mogućim koje reč izumevanje nije iscrpela, i kojem mesto nije imaginarni prostor delovanja. Mesto je mesto mišljenja, i ako ga dobro razumemo, to je mesto principijelnosti. Mišljenje sebe ne sme štedeti i to je način postojanja mesta politike. Principijelno uspostavljivog isključivo principima koji su prihvatljivi za sve, a pre svega za one kojih se moguće tiče. Pitanje anatagonizma, ponovo na dnevnom redu, koji nastaje poput konsenzusa i prećutnog slaganja, odnosno mišljenja koje bi i na sebi da uštedi, nije više od parole. Antagonizmom se više ne može uspostaviti distanca prema državi jer ne postoji ambicija da se uspostavi nova. Parlamentarni hod revolucionara je dovršio luk revolucija i otvorio ovaj države, koji je danas takođe na svom kraju. Prema tome, antagonizam je imenljiv i odavno u rečniku teorije. *Delimo mišljenje da na ljude više ne treba gledati u svetlu njihove sposobnosti za antagonizam, već u svetlu njihove sposobnosti da se suprotstave antagonizmu.*

Teško mesto, pogotovo dok obrađujemo iskustvo podrške i učestvovanja u protestima u Srbiji, kojima se mobilišu ljudi isključivo kroz oponiranje državi. U tome treba da vidimo da li ima mesta za mišljenje, a voleli bismo da sretnemo i famozno izumevanje novog prostora delovanja. Praviti ga od blata nije posao. Konstatovati da ga nema bi bilo negiranje politike? Ne bismo rekli. To je pre suočavanje sa činjenicom da politike u jednom vremenu i situaciji ne mora biti. Jer ako imamo isključivo oponiranje državi, tačnije oponiranje aktuelnoj vlasti, onda imamo plediranje za neku drugu i bolju vlast što se u ovom slučaju završava u podršci opozicionim predsedničkim, partijskim ili "nezavisnim" kandidatima zarad te vlasti.

Postavili smo sebi pitanje: Da li tragati za novim terminima i političkim principima u sopstvenoj organizaciji i asocijaciji organizacija, ili se pak *prepustiti* antagonizmu prema državi? „Prepustiti se" ovde ima svoje značenje i mesto, i samo je naizgled u suprotnosti suprotstavljanju: *prepustiti se* nije jednako onom *suprotstaviti se* antagonizmu. Kako bi „antagonizam" ostavili striktnom značenju koje ono ima za Lenjina i njegovu boljševičku politiku, reći ćemo sledeće: antagonizam je danas parola opozicione politike, i sutra već državne. U medijima pak, opoziciona politika je programska politika gledanosti i spektakularizacije, i, već sutra, tržišne gledanosti.

Političke partije svakako jesu legitimni oblici organizovanja, ali u njima politike nema. One su premrežene interesima pojedinaca i grupa, što smo u jednom trenutku nazvali *međuljuđem*,[2] gde je izgubljena čak i dinamika para opozicija-pozicija, pošto vidimo da partijsko vođstvo neometano sarađuje sa vrhom drugih partija (pa i „opozicionih"), a ne sa sopstvenim članstvom koje je prepušteno borbi za opstanak i egzistenciju u društvu sa društvenom pokretljivošću koja počiva upravo na takvim partijskim principima. Ukoliko je u onome što se smatra političkim sistemom (država-partija) opoziciona politika napuštena i izgubljena, možemo se upitati kakva je sudbina antagonizma (kao parole opozicione politike) prema državi. Treba li antagonizam prema državi da ispuni upražnjeno mesto opozicije? Ako bi bilo tako, onda je reč o tome da antagonizam već pripada prostoru državne *politike*. To je smisao bivanja pukom parolom opozicione politike.

Jedno postaje jasno a to je da kritika sistema nije politika. Međutim, smatrati da kritika sistema nije politika ne znači i automatski obdelavati podršku i reprodukciju tog sistema. Upravo pod pretnjom

---

2. Reč „međuljuđe" je skovana nakon izjave jednog od gradskih članova veća koji je svoju partiju uveo u neprincipijelnu koaliciju kako bi zadržao mesto u veću i upravljanju gradom.

takve izričite osude za kolaboracionizam i rekuperaciju treba zahtevati prostor za nove prostore delovanja, principijelnosti i mišljenja. Ono što jeste političko pitanje, a ono bi bilo: šta raditi s ljudima?, pitanje je koje uvek fali filozofima-radikalima kao i aktivistima-radikalima. Kada bi se samo filozofija prisetila svoje polazne tačke, da realnost nije jemstvo istine i da mišljenje treba razlučiti od bića, ne bi svojim postulatima pravila adekvaciju teorije sa praksom, odnosno nauke sa politikom, te pravila nešto što postoji van prostora subjektivnosti i mišljenja ljudi. Kada bi se samo aktivizam prisetio da je ulog raditi s ljudima u formulisanju mogućeg u sagledavanju neke situacije, ne bi moguće vezivao za situaciju već bi potencirao da moguće jeste stvarnost. Tada bismo bili bliže konstataciji da stvarnost po sebi ne postoji, odnosno da postoji kada se konstituiše mišljenjem i odlučivanjem ljudi: Tada bi imali filozofiju i teoriju koje ne plediraju za poziciju prvomislećeg kada je mišljenje ljudi u pitanju, kao i aktivizam koji bi otvoreno mogli da smatramo politikom. U suprotnom, ostajemo u determinizmu i deskripciji, tj. u nabrajanju ograničenja koja su nam državom i kapitalom nametnuta, odnosno u savršenom spoju teorije, filozofije i aktivizma.

Dakle moguća je tačka u kojoj se susreću naš interes i delovanje. Cilj je uraditi nešto s ljudima, formulisati moguće i time konstituisati stvarnost. Diskutovati na protestima nije praksa (zašto?), ali mislimo da diskusije mora biti u jezgru koje proteste organizuje. Podržavajući ljude u protestu, organizovanju protesta smo postavili pitanje *protestne organizacije* – permenantnog procesa sagledavanja situacije i problema u kojem se nalazimo i pokušaj da se oni reše na osnovama solidarnosti uz diskusiju i donošenje odluka u svakoj novoj situaciji. Ali, ukoliko ljudi ne istrajavaju u svom mišljenju i štede se u izumevanju novih argumenata i formulacija koji vrše povratak mišljenju, u najboljem slučaju se samo jedan deo humanistike vraća na velika vrata u vidu svođenja praksi ljudi na ono što se može nazvati *istraživanje sa učestvovanjem*. Pošto smo se sa sociologijom pozdravili, u ovoj situaciji postavljamo šta je moguće uraditi a da se ne pridružimo deskripciji ograničenja lamentom nad nemogućnošću da se bilo šta uradi? Veliki je izazov kako pristupiti tom fenomenu, ne prepustiti mu se i ne suprotstavljati mu se kao da nas ne određuje. Za to mišljenje pravimo mesto neimenljivog imena institucionalna komuna, što je nekakav prostor zajedničkog delovanja i principa.

Čega su onda ime institucionalne komune? Niti rekuperacije, niti reprodukcije. Večnost ideologije (za one koji računaju sa njom u izgradnji koncepta kojim se vrši „analiza situacije") učiniće večnim postojeće ukoliko računajući sa ideologijom odbijamo da priznamo postojanje mišljenja. Priznanje mišljenja, sa druge strane, otvara put osudi za rekuperaciju. Ali tada situacija nije ista: optužba će se morati dokazati u izravnoj polemici koja više nije teorijska razrada, niti filozofska rasprava već rad sa ljudima, politika na strani ljudi, odnosno nastojanje da se sa ljudima nešto uradi – šta god to bilo.

DEZORGANIZIRANI KOLEKTIVITETI, FANTOMSKE ORGANIZACIJE I GRUPA KAO SUBJEKT

ENTONI AJLS

> Grupa upada na mjesto pojedinca. Jednom kada zajednica upadne, glasovi su podijeljeni a govor umnožen. Grupa funcionira kao instanca iskazivanja koja će postati modernim ekvivalentom (kolektivnih) mitova iz antike i (anonimnih) epova iz srednjeg vijeka. Prekinuvši sa svakim autorskim režimom, ona će dozvoliti uskrsnuće tog anonimnog iskazivanja, koje je pripadalo veličanstvanim periodima zajednice, ali ovog puta u savremenim okolnostima.
> – Denis Holijer (Denis Hollier)[1]

U ovom eseju pokušat ću da kombiniram uvide o pitanjima samo-iznalaženja iz perioda 1920-ih i 1930-ih, tendencije u subkulturnim, anarhističkim i lijevo-komunističkim miljeima 1990-ih godina kako bih ispitao sadašnji kulturni trenutak koji je pod uticajem ovih ranih preteča. Tokom 1990-ih male grupe i mreže naširoko su eksperimentirale sa tehnikama i tehnologijama neformalnog organiziranja, umrežavanja, dezinformiranja, fabulacija i „samo-institucionaliziranja". Tokom tog perioda prevladavali su izgledi za novu fazu globalizacije i kapitalizma i klasne borbe.[2] Pokušavajući da se preorijentiraju u skladu sa novim izazovima, male grupe ponovo su se osvrnule na tendencije ka eksperimentiranju koje su se javljale u okviru ljevičarskih kulturnih miljea iz 1930-ih kada su istorijski događaji stvorili naprsnuća u klasnim podjelama koje su vladale između malih političkih grupa i umjetnika i pisaca koji su bili aktivni u kulturi. Tokom 1990-ih su poraz radničkog pokreta (koji se predosjećao već 1986. godine tokom borbe u Vapingu [Waping dispute] i u štrajku rudara iz 1984-85), raspad socijalističkog bloka i kraj hladnog rata ponovo su vratili na scenu pitanja komunizma, ali ne kao molarne formacije već prije kao dijela razbijanja monolitnih entiteta koji su najavljeni u molekularnim formacijama. U Evropi 1920-ih i 1930-ih velike sile posrću, veliki mediji tek su se uspostavljali a na hiljade malih časopisa širilo se na sve strane.[3] Slično tome, i 1990-ih monolitni mediji su izgledali zastarjeli i počeli su se uklanjati s puta manjim i

---

1. Denis Hollier, (Ur.), 1988. *The College of Sociology, 1937-39*. Minneapolis: University of Minnesota Press, str. xiv.
2. Pojam „globalizacije" i klase i kapitala preuzimam iz uvoda od: Mastaneh Shah-Shuja, *Zones of Proletarian Development*. London: OpenMute, 2008.
3. Uporedi: Stephen Bury, *Breaking the Rules: The Printed Face of the European Avant Garde 1900-1937*, London: British Library, 2007.

pristupačnijim medijskim formama. Svaki od ovih perioda bio je označen interesovanjem malih grupa za eksperimentalne pristupe problemima političkog suvereniteta, heterodoksne politike, alternativnim načinima proizvodnje i distribucije znanja.[4] Sve ovo može da se desi u obliku časopisa, neortodoksne publike ili privatnih susreta i novih tehnologija kakve su radio i internet.[5] Preko takvih pokreta konceptualizacija samo-stvaranja i dostupnog suvereniteta (suvereniteta shvaćenog kao odsustvo autoriteta i svrgavanja uobičajenog subjektiviteta) bila je blisko povezana sa obrascima svakodnevnog života i to pomoću rekonceptualizacije izraza iz svakodnevne upotrebe kao što je „pijan kao lord"; karakterizacija novih tendencija u kulturi kao „suverenih i mutnih" ili promocija gradskog iskustva posredstvom „dezorijentacije naviknutih refleksa".[6]

Denis Holijer, raspravljajući o Koležu za sociologiju u natpisu na početku ovog eseja, prati razvojni tok od romantizma i avangardnih grupa 20. vijeka u kome su različiti akteri stvarali sredstva kolektivnog izražavanja koja su pogodovala intenzitetu njihovog vremena. Premisa od koje ja polazim u ovom eseju je da su brojne generacije kulturnih proizvođača koje su se smjenjivale uzimale za ozbiljno organizacione

---

4. Kako kaže Vendi Braun (Wendy Brown), opadanjem državne moći na kraju 20. vijeka klasične teorije suvereniteta nisu više toliko mrtve koliko se radi o tome da „obećanje suvereniteta" postaje dostupno i mobilizirano vandržavnim akterima i agencijama: „kompozitna figura suvereniteta koju su uobličili klasični teoretičari modernog suvereniteta, uključujući Tomasa Hobsa (Thomas Hobbes), Žana Bodena (Jean Bodin) i Karla Šmita (Carl Schmitt), ukazuje na to da bitne osobenosti suvereniteta uključuju supremaciju (bez vrhovne vlasti), vremensku postojanost (bez ograničavanja termina), donošenje odluka (bez ograničavanja ili podređenosti zakonima), apsolutizam i potpunost (suverenost ne može biti tek vjerovatna ili djelimična), neprenosivost (suverenost ne može da se povjeri nekome a da pri tome ne poništi samu sebe) i specifična nadležnost (teritorijalnost)." Wendy Brown, *Walled States, Waning Sovereignty*. Cambridge Mass.: MIT Press, 2010, str. 22.
5. Da navedem samo dva karakteristična primjera: 1998. godine Info Centar (Info Centre) je priredio događaj na kom je jedna verzija teksta Hauarda Slejtera (Howard Slater) 'Post-Media Operators' predstavljena posredstvom snimka kao neka vrsta „imaginarnog obraćanja", http://infopool.antipool.org/Stamm.htm; 2001. godine Inventory je imao izdanje časopisa koji se nalazio u predvorju jedne automatizirane banke obodu londonskog sitija.
6. Citiranja se odnose na: Inventory, „I Kingsland Passage", Inventory, Vol. 1, Br. 3, 1996, str. 5; Howard Slater, 'Post-Media Operators: Sovereign and Vague', *Datacide* Br. 7, avgust 2000, *http://datacide-magazine.com/post-media-operators-%e2%80%9csovereign-vague%e2%80%9d/* i Guy-Ernest Debord, 'Introduction to a Critique of Urban Geography', *Les Lèvres Nues* Br. 6, 1955, dostupno na: *http://library.nothingness.org/articles/SI/en/display/2*

forme i testirali pristupe samo-iznalaženja i odgovarajućih odnosa sa aktivnostima na samoostvarenju radničke klase skupa sa suprotstavljanjima represivnim aktivnostima države. Tako ova diskusija

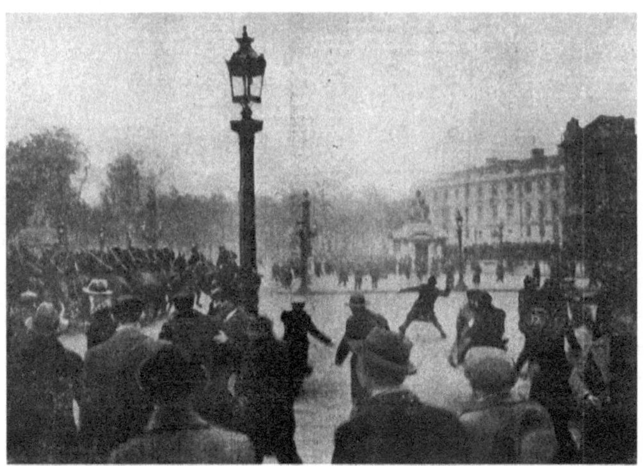

Pobuna na Trgu Konkord u Parizu, 7. februara 1934. godine

postavlja pitanja političke zajednice u okvire borbi unutar područja kulture, locirajući njihove interakcije zajedno sa vladinim, ekonomskim, mitskim, teološkim ili kosmološkim djelokrugom suvereniteta. Autonomija ili nezavisnost bili su preokupacija modernih kulturnih formacija još od jenskih romantika, ali suverenitet – kako u složenim konceptualizacijama grupa kakva je Kolež, tako i kroz istoriju političke filozofije – obujmljuju predmoderne artikulacije zajednice koje su bile od interesa grupacijama kritičkim spram kapitalističke modernosti. Strepnja zbog suvereniteta i borbe za rekonceptualizaciju autonomije od dole, dva su vektora kojima su ovi samo-svjesno nepopularni i eksperimentalni pokreti mogli da se povežu sa širim gibanjima u narodnim masama, kako tada tako i danas.

Društvena kritika (*La Critique Sociale*)

Pošto je u anglofonom svijetu obično tretiran kao filozof ekscesa i individualne transgresije, antifašističke i komunističke aktivnosti Žorža Bataja (Georges Bataille) bile su predmet samo specijaliziranih istraživanja.[7] Bataj je je nekoliko svojih najvažnijih predratnih filozofskih i političkih spisa objavio u potpuno nepoznatom časopisu pod nazivom *Društvena kritika* (*La Critique Sociale*).[8] *Društvenu kritiku* pokrenuli su Kolet Pinjo (Collette Peignot) i Boris Suvaren (Boris

Souvarine). Suvaren je osnivač Komunističke partije Francuske, dopisivao se sa Lenjinom i Trockim, bio je član Treće internacionale i saradnik boljševičke partije tokom postrevolucionarnih 1920-ih. Njegov kritički obrat koji je uslijedio poslije 1924. godine i prokazivanja Sovjetskog saveza kao formacije „državnog kapitalizma" iz 1927. godine gurnuo ga je ulijevo i od KPF i od Lava Trockog.[9] Kada je Suvaren uklonjen sa svih zvaničnih položaja u KPF i Kominterni 1924. godine, Pinjo je uskočila kako bi prikupila novac i podijelila uredničke poslove sa svojim saradnikom na novom časopisu. *Društvena kritika* (LCS) izašla je 1931. godine. Bio je to jedan marksistički časopis posvećen razvijanju nezavisne misli i akcije, nastao iz članstva Demokratskog komunističkog kruga (DCC) koji je od tada postao središte disidenata antistaljinističkog marksizma, nadrealizma i filozofije. Žorž Bataj počeo je da objavljuje u

---

7. Pored izvrsnog Holijerovog djela, etnografsko-sociološko-komunistička struja interpretacije koju su pokrenuli prevodi i antologije Majkla Ričardsona i Krištofa Fijalkovskog, predstavljena je sljedećim djelima: Bataille, Georges. *The Absence of Myth: Writings on Surrealism.* Uredio i preveo Michael Richardson. London; New York: Verso, 1994; Richardson, Michael i Krzysztof Fijałkowski, ur. *Surrealism Against the Current: Tracts and Declarations.* Preveli Michael Richardson i Krzysztof Fijałkowski. London; Sterling, Va.: Pluto Press, 2001; studija koncipirana kao knjiga: Stuart Kendall, Ibid., Benjamin Noys, *Georges Bataille a Critical Introduction.* London; Sterling, Va.: Pluto Press, 2000. Nojs svojom važnom studijom također doprinosi argumentaciji trajnog uticaja Žorža Bataja na francusku Situacionističku internacionalu, (Noys, 2000), str. 110. Situacionistička internacionala, zbog svoje široke popularnosti i značajnog uticaja na anarhističke i komunističke ljevičare u UK 1980-ih, 1990-ih i 2000-ih, predstavlja sekundarni ali vjerovatno značajniji izvor politiziranih interpretacija Batajevog djela u anglofonom svijetu, iako je to uvijek išlo ka tome da se pojavi bez imalo pažnje koja bi bila posvećena Batajevom praktičnom antifašizmu ili komunističkom aktivizmu, o kome je SI mogla ali i nije morala da sazna direktno.
8. To su: 'The Notion of Expenditure' (januar, 1933), 'The Problem of the State' (septembar, 1933), 'The Psychological Structure of Fascism' (novembar, 1933) i 'The Critique of the Foundations of the Hegelian Dialectic', također postoji i jako dobar razloga da otkrijemo i „drugove" kojima se obraća u epigrafu svog eseja 'The Use Value of the Marquis de Sade: An Open Letter to my Current Comrades' kao drugovima iz Demokratskog komunističkog kruga. Alan Stoekl datira ovaj tekst u 1929. ili 1930. godinu i dodaje: „I dok je jasno povezan sa Batajovom polemikom sa Andre Bretonom (André Breton) (i Bretonovo viđenje de Sada), on takođe najavljuje i mnoga gledišta koja će kasnije razviti u esejeima objavljenim u *Društvenoj kritici".* Allan Stoekl, 'A Commentary on the Texts' u: Bataille, Georges. *Visions of Excess: Selected Writings, 1927-39* (Prev. i ur. Allan Stoekl), Minneapolis: University of Minnesota Press, 1985, str. 260.
9. Al Richardson, *What Became of the Revolution: Selected Writings of Boris Souvarine,* Socialist Platform, 2001, str. iv.

Društvenoj kritici preko prisustva u *DCC*, a prvi članak koji je objavio pojavio se oktobra 1931. godine, iste godine kada je časopis *Dokumenti* (*Documents*) ostao bez sredstava. Stjuart Kendal (Stewart Kendall) povezuje Batajevo učešće i učešće još nekih, recimo Mišela Lerisa (Michel Leiris), u *LCS* sa njihovim ranijim radom u *Dokumentima*, eklektičkom časopisu koji je spajao etnografiju, lijepe umjetnosti i arheologiju.

> Dok su *Dokumenti* spajali etnografiju i estetiku jednu sa drugom, a onda i sa psihoanalizom, kod *Društvene kritike* se radilo o revitalizaciji marksizma posredstvom sličnih spojeva. Za Suvarena i ostale koji su pisali priloge, bilo je izazovno promišljati cijelo društvo bez uskraćivanja samih sebe za uvide koje mogu ponuditi bilo koji korisni alati.[10]

DCC i *LCS* su bili debatni centri o pitanjima revolucionarne teorije. I dok je izbor Hitlera iz 1933. godine u Njemačkoj samo podvukao crtu pod poraze iz 1921. godine, pobune u Parizu 1934. za neke su bile najava velikih očekivanja u pogledu ljevičarske revolucije.[11] Filozofica i aktivistkinja Simon Vejl (Simone Weil) objavljivala je priloge u *Društvenoj kritici*, ali je napustila *DCC* (a možda čak nikada i nije ni bila njihova formalna članica) zbog rasprave koju je sa Batajem vodila zbog njihovih različitih stavova prema revoluciji.[12]

---

10. Kendall, op. cit., str. 89.

11. Šestog februara 1934. godine Francusku je uzdrmao antirepublikanski marš koji su predvodili rojalisti, militaristi, nacionalisti i lige ekstremne desnice. Ujedinjeni više svojom militariziranom pojavom nego li kakvom posebnom ideologijom, oni su se sudarili sa francuskom policijom i drugim demonstrantima na trgu Konkord. Uslijedila je noć prepuna nemira u kojoj je napadnuta i Narodna skupština, petnaest demonstranata je ubijeno a 2000 njih ranjeno. Nemiri su doveli do ustavne krize i pada krhke koalicije ljevičarskih partija u parlamentu. Antifašističke kontrademonstracije koje su poveli komunisti i socijalisti 9. februara dovele su do smrti još deset ljudi. Generalni štrajk iz 12. februara omogućio je ljevici da se ujedini što je na kraju dovelo do stvaranja Narodnog fronta koji je i došao na vlast naredne godine. Međutim, ovaj standardni pogled na situaciju možda i zanemaruje svu složenost političkih pozicija koje se obično pripisuju ovom trenutku, na primjer veoma je vjerovatno da su i antiparlamentarni komunisti uzeli učešća u neredima 6. februara, kako se tvrdi u romanu *Žil* iz 1939. godine koji je napisao Drije la Rošel (Drieu La Rochelle, *Gilles*, Paris: Gallimard, 2012). O ovim neredima uopće, ali i o Batajevom učešću vidjeti: Stuart Kendall, op. cit., str.104-105 i Denis Hollier, 'Birthrate and Deathwish', u: Denis Hollier (Ur.), *A New History of French Literature*, Cambridge, Mass.: Harvard University Press, 1989, str. 919-924, str. 919-920.

> Revolucija je [za Bataja] trijumf iracionalnog, a za mene racionalnog;
> za njega je to katastrofa, a za mene metodična akcija u kojoj se
> mora težiti ograničavanju štete; za njega je ona oslobađanje
> instinkata, posebno onih koji se uobičajeno smatraju patološkim, a
> za mene oslobađanje nadmoćne moralnosti. Ima li tu onda ičeg
> zajedničkog? [...] Kako je moguće koegzistirati u istoj
> revolucionarnoj organizaciji kada jedna i druga strana pod
> revoluciojom shvataju potpuno suprotstavljene stvari?[13]

Ova izjava Simon Vejl ukazuje nam na Batajevu pobunjeničku
orijentaciju iz tog vremena. Iako bolestan, Bataj je učestvovao u
nemirima iz februara 1934. kao i u kontrademonstracijama.[14] Mnogi sa
desnice imaju ista temeljna ubjeđenja kao i on – i oni su bili inspirisani
stavovima Žorža Sorela (Georges Sorel) o revoluciji kao mesijanskom
„čistom nasilju" – međutim, kako ćemo vidjeti, Batajev antifašizam
izdvajao ga je od njih i praktično i teorijski.[15] I zaista, *DCC* nije bila
jedina grupa sa kojom je Bataj bio u kontaktu ranih 1930-ih. Preko svog
prijateljstva sa Arnoom Dandijeom (Arnaud Dandieu), kolege iz Narodne
biblioteke i jednog od saradnika *Dokumenata*, Bataj je prisustvovao
sastancima 'antiboljševičke, antikapitalističke, antiparlamentarne,
korporativne, proradničke [...] federalističke grupe koja se zvala *Novi
poredak (Ordre Nouveau)*.[16] Druga grupa koju je Bataj učestalo posjećivao
bila je ona okupljena oko časopisa *Mase (Masses)*.[17] Časopis je bio

---

12. Značajan uvid u materijalizam Simon Vejl dala je Liza Ješke, 'To Refuse to
Imagine: Simone Weil's Materialism', u: Lisa Jeschke and Adrian May (Ur.), *Matters
of Time: Material Temporalities in Twentieth-Century French Culture*, 2014, str. 41-61.
13. Simon Vejl citirana je prema: Simone Pétrement, *La Vie de Simone Weil*, Fayard,
1973, str. 306, i prema: Kendall, op. cit., str. 101-102.
14. Kendall, op. cit., str. 105.
15. Sorelijanska orijentacija *Društvene kritike* očigledna je i ako se ima u vidu
vjerovatno porijeklo njenog imena u Sorelovom djelu 'Bases de critique sociale', u:
Georges Sorel, *Matériaux d'une théorie du prolétariat*, Paris: M. Rivière, 1919.
16. Michel Surya, *Georges Bataille: An Intellectual Biography*. Preveli Michael
Richardson i Krzysztof Fijałkowski. London; New York: Verso, 2002, citirano prema:
Kendall, op. cit., str. 89. Pošto je Dandije iznenadno preminuo 1933. godine, ostali
članovi grupe pokrenuli su časopis koji je nosio njegovo ime a mnogi od njih
uspostavili su veze sa višijevskim režimom, nacionalnim socijalistima i fašističkim
grupama, iako su se neki od njih, opet, opirali kako višijevcima tako i njemačkoj
okupatorskoj vojsci, vidjeti: Christian Roy, 'Arnaud Dandieu and the Epistemology
of Documents'. *Papers of Surrealism*, br. 7 (2007): str. 1-23, dostupno na:
http://www.surrealismcentre.ac.uk/papersofsurrealism/journal7/acrobat%20files/a
rticles/roypdf.pdf

povezan sa revolucionarnim krilom socijalističke partije (SFIO) i promovirao je program narodnog obrazovanja kojim se slavila misao njemačkih revolucionara Roze Luksemburg (Rosa Luxemburg) i Karla Libknehta (Liebknecht) i uzdizao autonomnu akciju radničkih masa. Februarski događaji ubrzali su podjelu unutar Demokratskog komunističkog kruga i razlaz između Suvarena i Bataja, kako politički, tako i lični.[18] Politički i afektivni savezi u unutar grupe bili su veoma složeni, a na tu situaciju aludirala je i Vejl:

> Sam Krug bio je svojevrstan psihološki fenomen. Bio je sačinjen od uzajamnih privlačnosti, opskurnih afiniteta, a posebno od represije i kontradikcija među članovima, ali čak i unutar njih samih, koje nisu iznošene na vidjelo.[19]

Popoprište sila koje je nastalo između članova Društvene kritike i Demokratskog komunističkog kruga nije se izrodilo samo iz snažne angažiranosti časopisa u iznenadno izniklom istraživačkom polju koje je činila psihoanaliza, već također iz neke vrste unutarnjeg osjećaja samorefleksije kakva se može čitati u izjavi koju nam ovdje nudi Vejl o prirodi snažnih veza unutar grupe kojoj se ona nikada nije formalno priključila.[20] Iako ostaje dobrim dijelom neprozirno zbog čega je tačno došlo do razlaza unutar *LCS*, pobune i sve opipljivije prijetnje fašističkog pokreta u Francuskoj produbile su i ubrzale razlike među njenim članovima. Suvaren se polako približavao socijalističkoj partiji (SFIO), a Bataj, Pinjo i Vejl su se kretali u suprotnom pravcu, bližem ultra-lijevim i otvoreno antifašističkim grupacijama.

---

17. Uređivao ga je Rene Lefeur (René Lefeuvre). Batajeva povremena ljubavnica iz ranih 1930-ih, fotografkinja Dora Mar (Maar), također je objavljivala priloge u časopisu, https://bataillesocialiste.wordpress.com/revues/masses-1931-1948/
18. Bataj i Kolet Pinjo alijas „Lora" postali su ljubavnici u ovom periodu.
19. Simon Vejl, neobjavljeni izvor citiran u: Michel Surya, op. cit., str. 170.
20. Koncentracija želja u ovim grupama alegorijski je prikazana u Batajevom romanu *Plavetnilo neba*, u kom su predstavljeni likovi koji jako podsjećaju na Simon Vejl (Lazarka) i Kolet Pinjo (Dora) i koji prekoračuje granice erotskog i političkog Evrope 1930-ih i, opet retrospektivno, gorke komentare rezervirane za Bataja u razmišljanjima Borisa Suvarena o časopisu u reprintu *Društvene kritike* koji se pojavio 1983. godine. Tada već nepopustljivi antikomunista, Suvaren je proglasio Bataja za seksualnog pervertita i fašističkog simpatizera koji je pervertirao Loru i ukrao naslov njegovog časopisa. Boris Souvarine (Ur.), *La Critique Sociale*, Paris: Editions de la difference, 1983.

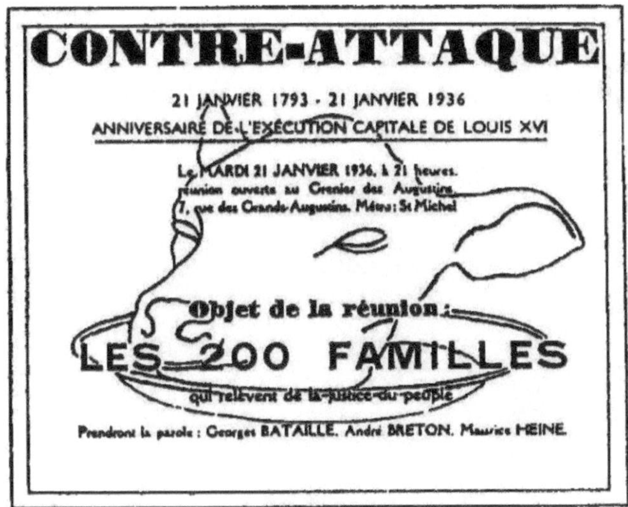

Flajer za Kontranapad-demonstraciju, januar 1933. godine

Kontranapad

Osim eksplozije *LCS* i *DCC* poslije februarskih pobuna došlo je i do novog usaglašavanja između Batajeve grupe disidentskih nadrealista i bretonovske nadrealističke grupe koja je nedavno zaoštrila svoje odnose sa KPF zbog njene autoritarne izolacije Lava Trockog i Žaka Dorioa (Jacques Doriot).[21] Članovi Demokratskog komunističkog kruga, časopisa *Masses*, mirovnjačkog časopisa *Clarté* i grupe nadrealista formirali su antifašističku, antipopulističku platformu pod imenom *Kontranapad: Borbeni sindikat revolucionarnih intelektualaca* (*Contre-Attaque: Union de Lutte des Intellectuels Révolutionnaires*). Koalicija, geografski podijeljena po imenima Mara i Sad između lijeve i desne obale Sene, bila je relativno kratkoga vijeka. *Kontranapad* je nastojao slaviti borbu radničke klase protiv klasnih kompromisa Narodnog fronta, zagovarajući kombinaciju avangardne spontanosti: „nastanak doktrine kao rezultat neposrednih iskustava."; pozajmljujući elemente i novih pokreta sa desnice: „stavljanje oružja koje je stvorio fašizam [...] u službu univerzalnog

---

21. Andre Breton i drugi, 'When the Surrealists Were Right', izjava data poslije Međunarodnog kongresa za odbranu kulture iz avgusta 1935, u: Richardson, Michael i Krzysztof Fijałkowski, ur. *Surrealism Against the Current: Tracts and Declarations*. Preveli Michael Richardson i Krzysztof Fijałkowski. London; Sterling, Va.: Pluto Press, 2001, str. 105-111, str. 108.

interesa naroda" i zagovaranja „organskog stvaranja", istinske diktature proletarijata: „beskompromisna diktatura naoružanog naroda".[22] Ova grupa kombinirala je marksizam, koncepte koji su vukli porijeklo od Žorža Sorela i Aleksandra Koževa (Alexandre Kojeve), i nadrealističkog

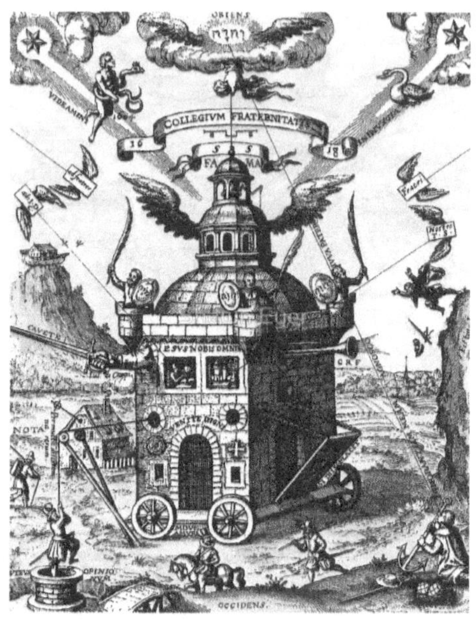

Nevidljivi kolež Hrama Rosy Cross, 1618.

automatizma.[23] I zaista, oni su pratili i razvili šizmatičku marksističko-nadrealističku poetiku čije je jezgo bilo u kratkotrajnom časopisu *Legitimna odbrana* (*Légitime défense*) koji su objavljivali studenti sa Martinika sa sjedištem u Parizu.[24] Breton i Bataj raspravljali su o stvaranju novog revolucionarnog jezika unutar grupe, i na ovaj način su pokušali da uvrste i nasilje kao kohezivnu silu novih „organskih" oblika zajednice. Ovo je bilo usmjereno željom da se stvori novi mit koji bi

---

22. 'Counter-attack: Union of the Struggle of Revolutionary Intellectuals' u: Michael Richardson, i Krzysztof Fijałkowski, (Ur.) *Surrealism Against the Current: Tracts and Declarations*, (Prev. Michael Richardson i Krzysztof Fijałkowski), London; Sterling, Va.: Pluto Press, 2001, str. 114-117, str. 115.
23. Nikolaj d'Origny Lübecker, *Community, Myth and Recognition in Twentieth-Century French Literature and Thought.* London; New York: Continuum, 2009, str. 25.
24. „Obraćamo se onima koji još uvijek nisu označeni kao ubijeni establirani sjebani akademici uspješno dekorisani mrtvaci koji predstavljaju puke ukrašene i nalickane oportuniste", 'Légitime défense: Declaration' (1932), u: Michael Richardson, (Ur.), *Refusal of the Shadow: Surrealism and the Caribbean*, (prev. Krzysztof Fijalkowski i Michael Richardson), New York: Verso, 1996.

oborio ustaljene forme kakve su parlament, partija i nacija.[25] Međutim, o aktivnostima ove grupe znamo veoma malo.[26]

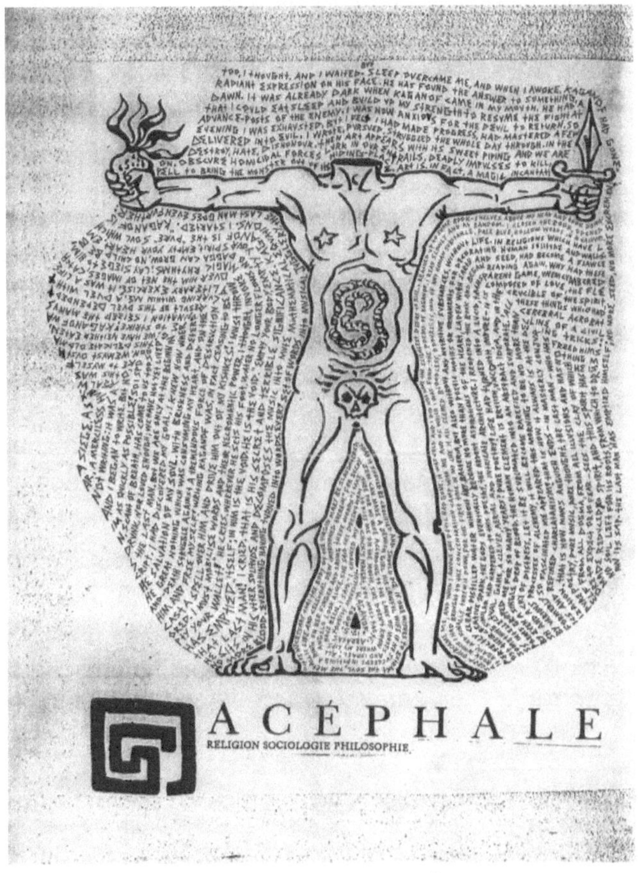

Andre Mason (André Masson) i Žorž Bataj,
Flajer za Acéphale časopis

Ostavivši Suvarena da oformi *Kontranapad*, Bataj i drugi iz *LCS* ostavili su sa njim i posljednje autoritarne tragove u vidu partijskog članstva i partijskih mahinacija.[27] Militanti iz *Kontranapada* zahtijevali su da se njihov revolucionarni program „oštro" odvoji od podrške bilo

---

25. Zaista, u ovome su pratili i razvili šizmatičku marksističko-nadrealističku poetiku objavljivanu u časopisu *Légitime défense* koji je kratko izlazio i koji su objavljivali studenti sa Martinika u Parizu 1932. godine.
26. Mišel Surija ukazuje na to da su zabilježene samo dvije akcije ove grupe: ponovno postavljanje na scenu pogubljenja kralja i protest neke mlade žene koja je pobjegla od školske reforme, i zbog čega su neki od članova grupe bili uhapšeni. *Bataille: An Intellectual Biography*, op. cit., str. 227.

kojoj partiji, naciji ili državi, ali su se čvrsto držali uvjerenja u svoju autoritarnost kao militanata koji će povesti klasu u revoluciju. Moskovski procesi iz avgusta 1936. godine donijeli su sa sobom kontrarevolucionarnu i ubilačku prirodu Staljinovog režima, dok je poraz neorganizirane opozicije (od Staljina i Franka) u Španiji postao više nego jasan već naredne godine, pošto je Narodni front tek mlako podržao pobunjenike kada je izgubio vlast u junu 1937. godine.[28] Uz Narodni front koji se raspadao na djeliće i staljinizmom koji je zadobijao sve veći uticaj u Španiji i Francuskoj, Kontranapad je imao sve manje i manje pogonske snage. Poslije neuspjeha *Kontranapada* Bataj je ponovo prestao da se druži sa Bretonom, a bretonistička nadrealistička ljevica optuživala je Bataja za „nad-fašizam".[29]

Naredni Batajev iskorak ka otvorenim i zatvorenim zavjerama u okviru Acéphala[30] i Koleža za sociologiju bio je obilježen odbojnošću prema formama grupnih istraživanja, generacije znanja i kolektivnih interpersonalnih eksperimenata, otkrenutost od svega onog što je bilo prema vanjskosti propagandističko ili regrutno nastrojeno. Bila je to reakcija protiv sužavanja prostora za kritičke politike, tj. onih politika kojima nije dominirao ili staljinizam ili parlamentarni socijalizam, koji su time nagoviješteni. Narodni front u Španiji i Francuskoj isprva je podržavao štrajkove, ali poslije osvajanja vlasti primjenjivao je iste metode discipliniranja rada koje su uspostavljene prije njih.[31]

---

27. „Političke zajednice u koje je [Bataj] bio uključen odbijale su partijsku formu i kao takve bile su u središtu njegovih razmišljanja o zajednici". Noys, op. cit., str. 8, citirano prema: *Visions of Excess*, op. cit., str. 162. Sa druge strane, Suvarinova autoritarnost kao čovjeka partije iz KPF osjeti se u njegovom napisu *What Became of the Revolution* i tu postoje jasne indicije za nešto što on naziva „pravednošću" koju je nastavio da njeguje i kao urednik *Društvene kritike*, vidjeti: Michèle Richman, 'Fascism Reviewed: Georges Bataille u: "La Critique Sociale"', *South Central Review* 14, br. 3/4 (1997): 14-30, str. 15.
28. Iako je francuski Narodni front osnovan uz svjesnu podršku anarhističkih, komunističkih i republikanskih snaga koje su učestvovale u Španskom građanskom ratu, lijeva koalicija koja je bila na vlasti uradila je malo toga u smislu praktične podrške, poslavši tek „nekoliko aviona". Poslije toga, vlada francuskog Narodnog fronta ne samo da nije dala nikakve koncesije svojim kolonijalnim podanicima, bilo kod kuće bilo širom svijeta, već je vršila aktivnu represiju proleterskih pokreta u Alžiru, vidjeti: Gilles Dauve, 'When Insurrections Die', *Endnotes #1*, oktobar, 2008, str.55.
29. Neposredno poslije Kontranapada i trockistički nadrealisti koji su bili bliski Bretonu pokušali su ponovo da se okupe oko kratkotrajnog novog časopisa *Clé*.
30. *Acéphal – Bezglavo*; ime časopisa i tajnog društva koje je osnovao Bataj (prim. prev.).

Naposljetku, i radnička klasa u Španiji i Francuskoj također je samo slegnula ramenima na okolnosti koje su ih zadesile. Poslije 1937. godine svi putevi vodili su u rat, i svakako daleko od revolucije.[32] Ovo Batajevo rukovođenje predstavljao je očigledni zaokret od politike ka religiji, što je otvorio u svom tekstu „Sveta zavjera" ('*La conjuration sacrée*') koji je napisao za časopis *Acéphale*.

> Ono što liči na politiku, i zamišlja samo sebe kao političko, jednog dana će se demaskirati kao religijski pokret.[33]

Zaokret ka religiji odbija stabilizirajuću silu politike u posredovanju u neslaganjima i umanjivanju sukoba. Ovom izjavom politika se izvrgava ruglu, ali isto tako se njome i podriva liberalna neutralnost religije. '*La conjuration sacrée*' (sveta zavjera) izrugava '*union sacrée*', kako ju je formulirali premijer Rene Vivijani (Viviani) i predsjednik Republike Francuske Rejmon Poenkare (Raymond Poincaré) uoči Prvog svjetskog rata, a koja je predstavljala političko primirje između ljevice i vlade kako bi štrajkovi bili suspendirani i kako bi se demonstrirala odbrana nacije. Na taj način *Acéphale* predstavlja odbacivanje forme politike kojom upravlja kompromis u korist nečega utjelovljenog, prikrivenog i potencijalno neupravljivog. Samo ime Kolež za sociologiju naginje ka jednom nejasnom fenomenu „Nevidljivog koleža" koji je prvi put pomenut pamfletima Ružinog krsta iz 17. vijeka. Taj „kolež" prizivao je međunarodnu, para-institucionalnu intelektualnu razmjenu između okultista, alhemičara, filozofa i ljudi od nauke, dakle jednu otvorenu zavjeru koja je svojim predstavnicima nudila anonimnost i slobodu od religijske ili državne cenzure. Ova utvara pokretne, tajnovite i

---

31. Cf. Michael Seidman, *Workers Against Work: Labor in Paris and Barcelona During the Popular Fronts.* Berkeley: University of California Press, 1991. i dok empirijske informacije koje su predstavljene u ovoj knjizi donekle podupiru moje stanovište, volio bih se distancirati od pravca kojim je Sajdman krenuo poslije pisanja ove knjige.

32. Kako je to nadrealista Benjamin Pere (Péret) rekao 1939. godine, „Radnička klasa [...], pošto je izgubila iz vida svoje sopstvene ciljeve, više nije vidjela bilo kakav hitan razlog da izgine braneći buržoaski demokratski klan protiv fašističkog klana, tj. u krajnjem slučaju, za odbranu Anglo-francuskog kapitala protiv Italo-njemačkog kapitala. Građanski rat prerastao je u imperijalistički rat." *Clé*, Br.2, citirano u: Gilles Dauve, 'When Insurrections Die', *Endnotes #1*, oktobar, 2008, str. 59.

33. Kjerkegor (Kierkegaard) citiran u epigrafu od strane Žorža Bataja, 'The Sacred Conspiracy', *Visions of Excess*, op. cit., str. 178-181, originalno objavljeno u: *Acéphale #1*, 24 juni, 1936.

međunarodne zajednice dopisnika bit će oživljena od strane Aleksandera Trokija (Alexander Trocchi) tokom 1960-ih kao „Nevidljivi ustanak milion umova" ali i nešto skorije od strane Imaginarne partije i Nevidljivog komiteta.[34] Ako je *Acéphale* bio označen povlačenjem i osamljenošću, Kolež je više nagovještavao rasipanje i eklekticizam, i sa nadolazećim Drugim svjetskim ratom na njega se ne može gledati kao na čistokrvno povlačenje, već prije kao na neku vrstu podvojenog napora da se prikupe snage i procijeni nadolazeća oluja.

Riješiti problem glave

Dimenzije „uspješnosti" *Acéphala* teško je procijeniti. Bez trunke pragmatizma, i pored svog razvijanja tajanstvenosti, njegov prvenstveni cilj nije bio da proizvodi produženje, reprodukciju i razvoj same organizacije, nego da rastvori samog sebe „uzimanjem učešća i uništenju postojećeg svijeta".[35] Pod okriljem Acéphala Bataj će dovesti u pitanje forme monocefalizma: bogoglave diktatore Staljina i Hitlera, autoritet kršćanskog boga i malog fašistu koji čuči unutar svih nas – pojedinačni ego.

> Jedino društvo puno života i snage, jedino slobodno društvo je dvo- ili više- cefalično društvo koje dozvoljava temeljnim životnim antagonizmima stalno i eksplozivno pražnjenje, mada je i ono ograničeno najplodnijim formama [...] jer i sam princip glave predstavlja redukciju na jedinstvo, *redukciju* svijeta na boga.[36]

Acéphale je najavio samoosvješćivanje jedne nove logike na ljevici, odbijanje vještačkog jedinstva, akciju usmjerenu ka cilju i samožrtvovanje, sklonost ka političkoj entropiji, poništavanje u okvirima logike organizacije kako bi se izbjeglo postajanje rigidnim ili birokratskim, ostajanje bez glave. Kako primjećuje Žan-Lik Nansi (Jean-

---

34. Alexander Trocchi, 'A Revolutionary Proposal: Invisible Insurrection of a Million Minds', dostupno na: *http://www.notbored.org/invisible.html* izvorno izdato kao 'Technique du coupe du monde', *Internationale Situationniste*, Br. 8, januar 1963. Imaginarna partija, kao dio „javne i tajne, legalne i nelegalne" političke kampanje bila je izum belgijskog nadrealiste Marsela Mariena (Marcel Mariën), 'Théorie de la révolution mondiale immédiate', *Les lèvres nues*, 1958.
35. Georges Bataille, 'Program (Relative to Acephale)', *October*, No.36, 1986, p.79.
36. Georges Bataille, 'Propositions', *Visions of Excess*, op. cit., str. 199.

Luc Nancy), ova tendencija već je bila predočena deizidentifikacionom logikom militantnog časopisa *Društvena kritika*, koji je isto tako predstavljao prvi korak na novom putu u francuskom izdavaštvu u dekadama koje će doći.[37] Vjernost časopisa *Društvena kritika* Marksovoj sveobuhvatnoj misli, njegov projekat intelektualnog i materijalističkog istraživanja društva; njegova antiautoritarnost i antiboljševizam; kritička nezavisnost; intelektualni pluralizam i antiakademizam, postavili su standarde za mnoge heterodoksne projekte koji su istraživali slične pozicije putem samoizdavaštva u Francuskoj ali i na drugim mjestima počev od kasnih 1940-ih pa sve do danas: u Francuskoj to su bili *Critique; Socialisme ou Barbarie; Potlatch; International Situationiste; Negation; Troploin; Théorie Communiste; Tiqqun;* u UK: *Antagonism, Aufheben, Autotoxicity, Break/Flow, Communist Headache, Datacide, Endnotes, Here and Now, Inventory, Infopool, Letters, Re:Action, Smile, Unpopular Books;* u SAD: Autonomedia, Not Bored, *Midnight Notes* i mnogi drugi. Sve ove projekte karakterisale su tri povezane aktivnosti: pokušaj da se teoretizira raspored političkih sila koje su postojale u njihovo vrijeme (komunizam); učešće u političkim pokretima i događajima (demonstracije, pobune, sastanci); rasprave i objavljivanje slika i tekstova unutar mreža ineresenata. To nisu bili „kulturološki" ili „umjetnički" časopisi, nego politički projekti koji su stvarali sopstvenu kulturu pisanja, autorstva (ili njegovog osujećenja) i čitalaštva. Oni, dakle, nisu bili tek izdavačko oruđe političkih grupa, nego su bili posvećeni politici malih grupa; doprinosili su teorijskim raspravama koje su bile značajne za radničku klasu, antikolonijalizam i feminističke borbe ali su isto tako razvijali i stvaralačku i kritičku nezavisnost od njih. Sklonost tih grupa da izbjegavaju molarne forme kakve su bile forma partije ili institucija bio je pravac koji nije bio osoben samo za njih. Mnoštvo scena, od feminizma do panka, razvijalo je bazu oko koje su se onda mogli orijentisati mikropolitički savezi.[38] Ono po čemu se

---

37. Istorija časopisa u Francuskoj poslije 1950. godine zasigurno može baciti nešto svjetla na postepeno iščezavanje grupa, kolektiva i zajednica „ideja", a time i na evoluciju predstavljanja „zajednice" uopće. Časopis koji je osnovao Bataj, *Kritika* (*Critique*) polazio je od potpuno drukčije premise, i po svojoj koncepciji bio je potpuno odmaknut od teorijskog identiteta. Međutim, *Critique* je, tokom 1960-ih i 1970-ih, proizvodio pravi 'mrežni' efekat: predstavljao je mjesto susreta svih onih koji su se odijelili od svih zajednica. *Acéphale* je, pak, nagovijestio smrt određene forme zajednice i pripadnosti; radilo se o prijelazu ka grupi kao neopredijeljenoj partiji.

ističu projekti samoizdavaštva za koje sam ja zainteresiran je njihova posvećenost teoretizacijama kapitalizma i razvijanje heterodoksnih komunističkih pozicija na kojima su onda oni uspostavili svoje forme autoriteta i uloživši u njih sopstvene sklonosti za kritiku „postojećeg stanja stvari".

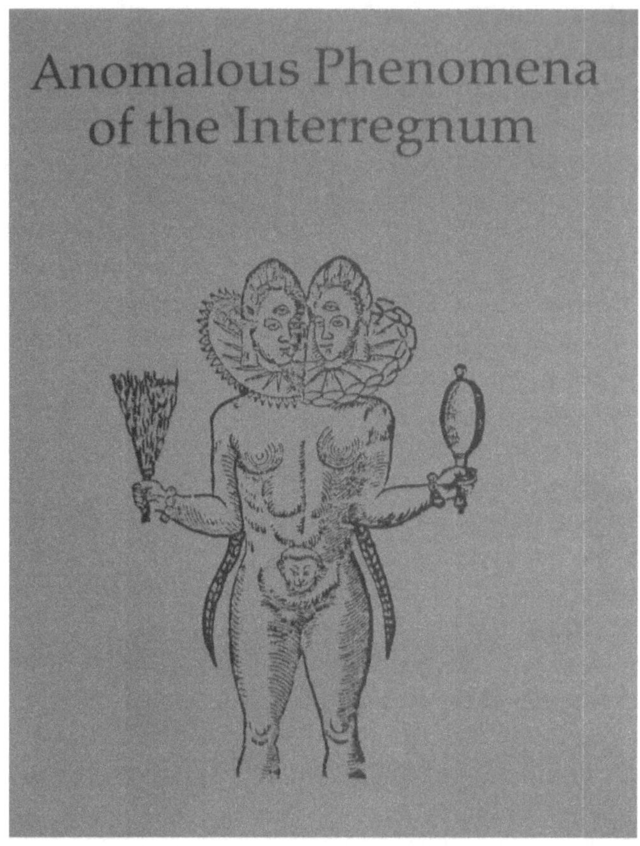

Anon., reprodukcija pamfleta objavljenog tokom engleskog građanskog rata, *The Anomalous Interregnum*

---

38. Korisna literatura koja pokriva ovo polje: Stephen Duncombe, *Notes from Underground: Zines and the Politics of Alternative Culture*. Bloomington, Ind.: Microcosm Publishing, 2008; Alison Piepmeier, *Girl Zines: Making Media, Doing Feminism*. New York: New York University Press, 2009; Jason Skeet i Mark Pawson (ur.), *Counter Intelligence: Zines, Comics, Pamphlets, Flyers: Catalogue of Self-Published and Autonomous Print-Creations*. London: 121 Centre, 1995; 'Worlds in Waiting: The Promise of Little Magazines'. *Dissent Magazine*, 19 novembar 2015, *https://www.dissentmagazine.org/online_articles/political-role-little-magazines-dissent-history* i Elke Zobl, *Feminist Media: Participatory Spaces, Networks and Cultural Citizenship*, Bielefeld: transkript, 2012.

Zašto se onda, ako se shvati uzaludnost tog čina, povezujete u grupe?

Holijer naglašava mitopoetiku i polifoniju koje krase objekt koji lebdi negdje između glasine i zavjere.[39] Kolektivno stvaranje mita, koje je otpočelo sa *Kontranapadom*, stopljeno sa interesima Bretona i Bataja, još zgusnutije je nastavljeno kroz *Acéphale*, da bi bilo ponovo raspršeno kroz mnoge pojedinačne individualnosti i agende Koleža.[40] Te konce potom su izvlačile različite male grupe, a supstanca koju su posjedovale svoje ostvarenje našla je na scenama samizdata koje su, pošto su se molarne organizacije poravnale sa (ili politički našle sa) radničkim pokretom, počele da se rasipaju i da pronalaze svoju novu upotrebu. Ali ova putanja također je i produbljivala razne dvosmislenosti. Da li je onda sklonost ka rasipanju bila znak poraza ili pobjede nad autoritarnošću? Da li je srljanje u boj na polju kulture bio znak slabosti ili potencijalne snage? Da li je molekularizacija predstavljala formu otpora ili tek formu učestvovanja u dinamici kojom su upravljale promjenjive potrebe kapitala?

Sem Mos (Sam Moss) je, pišući 1930-ih godina, proročki sažeo sklonost ka pesimizmu malih grupa pred Drugi svjetski rat, izvlačeći iz takvog razvoja optimističke zaključke koji su se potpuno kosili sa intuicijom:

> ali u samoj atrofiji svih grupa koje bi trebalo da mase izvedu iz kapitalizma i uvedu ga u drukčije društvo, mi po prvi put u istoriji vidimo objektivni kraj svih političkih predvođenja i svih podjela društva na ekonomske i političke kategorije.[41]

---

39. „Kolež za sociologiju (1937-1939) nije potrajao, niti ga se može sažeti – izuzev ako ne kažemo da se radilo o horu koji nije bio jednoglasan, već sačinjen od mnoštva solista čiji su glasovi bili suviše različiti i bez ikakve uravnoteženosti. Nije imao svoj prvi glas. I, uz veoma mali broj izuzetaka, on u potpunosti izostaje iz priručnika za književnost (ili sociologiju). Crne rupe izmiču nadzornim radarima a Kolež, suviše neproziran da bi da se detektiralo, ne pojavljuje se na mapama." Denis Hollier, 'Foreword' *The College of Sociology*, op. cit., str. x.
40. Na *Kontranapad* se obično gleda kao na prvenstveno Batajevo sredstvo, ali Nikolaj Libeker (Lübecker) iznosi jedan manje ustaljen argument prema kome stvaranje grupe predstavlja realizaciju Bretonovih ambicija da se „izmiri nadrealizam kao metod stvaranja kolektivnog mita sa mnogo općenitijim pokretom koji uključuje oslobađanje čovjeka", Breton citiran prema: *Community, Myth and Recognition in Twentieth-Century French Literature and Thought*, op. cit., str. 24.

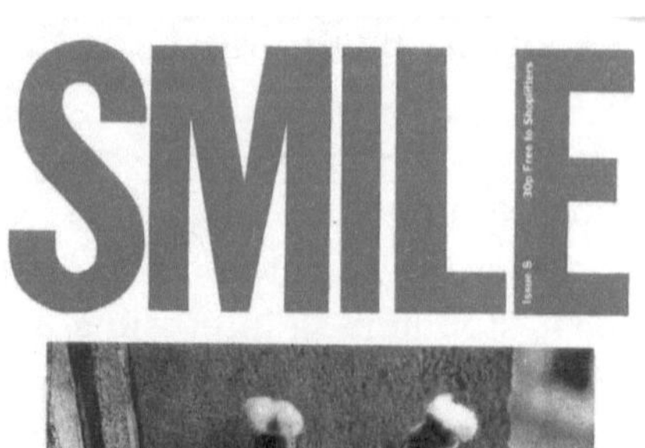

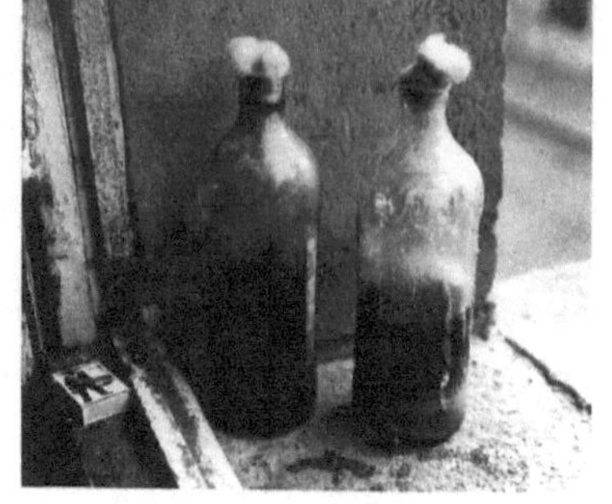

SMILE BACK AT THE RULING CLASS

Stjuart Houm (ur.), *Smile*, br. 8, 1985.

Mos je pripadao tzv. „Odborničkoj" ('Councillist') struji unutar Međunarodne anglofone marksističke ljevice koji sebe izričito „nisu smatrali prethodnicima radnika, niti njihovom vođama". Uloga koja im je preostala u situaciji u kojoj „funkcioniramo izvan sfera proizvodnje, unutar kojih se odvija klasna borba" i „kada smo izolirani od velikog broja radnika" predstavlja tabu sa kojim će se suočiti samo rijetke revolucionarne grupe. Pa šta onda izolirane grupe radikaliziranih intelektualaca mogu uraditi, s obzirom na to da ih ne krasi „manifestni usud" predvodnika radnika? Njegov odgovor je skroman, ali čvrst. Drugovi, oni koji ponizno u sebi ne prepoznaju „ništa veći značaj od njihovih sadrugova, drugih ljudskih bića", treba da se povezuju skupa u svrhu „dijeljenja zajedničkog osjećanja pobune." Suprotstavljanje subjektivnoj impotenciji malih grupa predstavlja „objektivni kraj svih političkih predvođenja". „[G]lavni razlog što se pobunjenički klasno osviješćeni radnici povezuju u grupe izvan polja stvarne klasne borbe je to što unutar ovog polja još uvijek ne postoji revolucionarni pokret." Najviši cilj svake revolucionarne grupe bio bi taj da nestane.

---

41. Sam Moss, 'The Impotence of the Revolutionary Group'. *Living Marxism* Vol.4, Br.7 (1939): str. 216-220, dostupno, uz komentare Frera Dupona (Frère Dupont) na: *http://fendersen.holeinthewallhosting.com/moss.html*

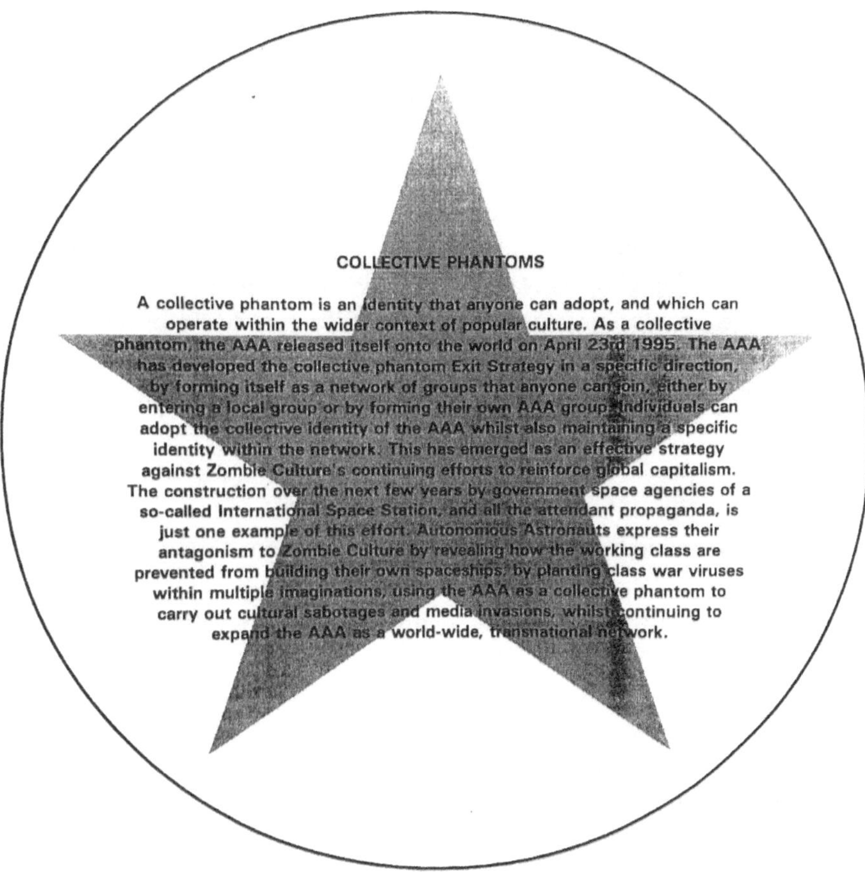

Asocijacija autonomnih astronauta, zabavno-informativni letak, br. 6, 1999.

Kako kaže Hauard Slejter u „Novom Acéphalu": „Svaka grupa mora
samu sebe dovesti u pitanje jer čim pokuša da se hermetički zatvori i
ideologizira svoje vektore ona se otvara bezumnoj manipulaciji."[42] Za
Slejtera, u društvu izgrađenom na „reketima" „grupa kao subjekt"
(Feliks Gatari [Félix Guattari]) mora se čuvati „onostranih motiva" i
mora proizvoditi samu sebe u „sredstvo osujećivanja i uzvraćanja protiv
sigurnosti postignuća, sredstvo za održavanje pravca bez ikakvog
cilja."[43] Takve grupacije, slijedeći stope *Acéphala*, a koristeći se
Slejterovim terminima, mogle bi se shvatiti kao „fantomske

---

42. Howard Slater, 'New Acéphale', *Inventory*, Vol. 2 Br. 3, 1997, str. 71-75. str. 72.
43. Ibid.

organizacije": „imaginarne grupacije, jedna ili nekoliko njih, koje nude sredstva za konceptualnu secesiju, sredstva podrške za samoizgnanstvo iz onih zatvorenih ortodoksija čije kontrakulturne aktiviste, budući da su 'kulturalisti', ne treba uopće shvatiti ozbiljno."[44] Što se tiče Morisa Blanšoa (Maurice Blanchot) i Žan-Lik Nansija, mit o Acéphalu postao je dio jednog etičkog zaokreta prema „književnom komunizmu" a time daleko od onih razvojnih tendencija koje su se i dalje odnosile na klasu, kapital i eksploataciju.[45] Veoma je važno naglasiti opći značaj ove sklonosti ka modernom kvijetizmu, jer se neformalne i neakademski nastrojene grupe u raspravama kreću u veoma različitom pravcu, aktivno teoretizirajući o novim formama otpora utemeljenog na klasama i tragajući za istorijskim lomovima kapitalističke modernosti.

O organizaciji

Dinamika koju je Mos ranije identificirao vremenom se razvila u pravcu destrukcije svrhe grupnog predvođenja što je dalje vodilo ka negaciji lažnog autoriteta samih revolucionarnih ćelija. U srodnim radovima Žaka Kamatea (Jacques Camatte) i Đanija Kolua (Gianni Collu) iz 1960-ih i 1970-ih godina, a posebno u njihovom utemeljiteljskom tekstu „O organizaciji", njihova misao predstavlja svjesnu opstrukciju obnove mikro-autoritarnih grupa.[46] Ipak, uvidi Kamatea i Kolua istodobno predstavljaju i formu hipostaziranja o odustajanju od svakog otpora kapitalu koji bi potekao unutar njegove sopstvene dinamike tj. iz odnosa kapitala i rada.[47] Ugrubo rečeno, Kolu i Kamate svoja stanovišta o grupama temelje na teoriji koja polazi od toga da je kapital postao „totalnim bićem" koje dominira životom ljudi u potpunosti. Ali, bez rada kao protivrječne, „posebne robe" – tijela čija je svijest upisana u proces proizvodnje – malo nam toga preostaje što bi definiralo kapitalizam kao specifičan način proizvodnje, a pogotovo ne

---

44. Howard Slater, 'Burdened By the Absence of Billions', 18. septembar 2008, *http://www.metamute.org/editorial/articles/burdened-absence-billions*
45. Cf. izgleda kao da Žan-Lik Nansi i Moris Blanšo upućuju na: Blanchot, Maurice, *The Unavowable Community*. Barrytown, N.Y.: Station Hill Press, 1988 i Nancy, Jean-Luc. *The Inoperative Community*. Minneapolis, MN: University of Minnesota Press, 1991. [BCHS izdanje: Nancy, Jean-Luc, *Dva ogleda: Razdjelovljena zajednica, O pluralnom bitku*, (prev. Tomislav Medak), Zagreb: Multimedijalni institut, 2003] Za skorije reprize kritika sličnih tendencija u neakademskim i postaktivističkim miljeima vidjeti: Research and Destroy, 'Hic Nihil, Hic Salta! (a critique of Bartlebyism)', juli 2015, *https://researchanddestroy.wordpress.com/2015/07/29/hic-nihil-hic-salta/*

protivrječan.[48] Formulacija Feliksa Gatarija, o „grupi kao subjektu" koja potiče od kritike marskističkih i neomarksističkih partija kao sistema reprezentacije koji nameće svoj monopol nad različitošću želja svedenih na klasu ili politički subjekt, kritika je koju su prvotno razvili militanti kakav je bio Mos. Nasuprot „problema glave" – formi vertikalnog hijerarhijskog autoriteta protiv koga je grmio Bataj – Gatari predstavlja zaokret u „visoko složenom industrijaliziranom društvu" u poratnom periodu, zaokret ka molekularizaciji, raspršivanju moći, posredstvom kojih „manjinske" borbe dobijaju novi značaj. On piše kako „samo grupa kao subjekt može djelovati unutar semiotičkih flukseva, uništavajući značenja, otvarajući jezik ka novim željama i stvarajući različite stvarnosti."[49] Izgleda da je ovo iscrpeno u ranije pomenutim porazima radničkog pokreta u UK kada hermetično organizirani rudari i štamparski radnici nisu uspjeli da isposluju koncesije od vlade Margaret Tačer, dok je zbrkana pobuna i negodovanje protestanata zbog ličnog poreza, što je borba unutar klasične sfere razmjene, naširoko potvrđena obaranjem te iste vlade na koljena. Prema tome, ono što je ograničilo nastojanja da se ovi odnosi oporave 1980-ih i 1990-ih bio je nedostatak

---

46. „Ekonomija svodi politiku (staro umijeće organiziranja) na čisti i puki epifenomen svojih sopstvenih stvarnih procesa. Ona joj dozvoljava da preživi tek kao muzej užasa, kao što je to slučaj sa parlamentom i svim njegovim farsama, ili u obliku kivne zakržljalosti malih 'vanparlamentarnih' bukavaca, koje su sve iste bez obzira da li su formalno ili neformalno organizirane, a bave se samo svojim 'strateškim' brbljarijama." Gianni Collu, 'Transition', preuzeto iz: David Brown (Ur.), *Origin and function of the party form 1962: Essays by Jacques Camatte and Gianni Collu*, London 1977, dostupno na: *https://www.riff-raff.se/en/furtherreading/transition.php*; vidjeti također i: Jacques Camatte and Gianni Collu, 'On Organization', Camatte, Jacques. *This World We Must Leave and Other Essays*. Preveo Alex Trotter. Brooklyn, N.Y.: Autonomedia, 1995.
47. Na ovu tendenciju, koja je zagovarana sa mnogih komunističkih pozicija poslije Drugog svjetskog rata (a sa posebnim osvrtom na Teodora Adorna [Theodor W. Adorno], Antonija Negrija i Žaka Kamatea), odnosi se rad: Andrés Sáenz De Sicilia, *The Problem of Subsumption in Kant, Hegel and Marx*, PhD Dissertation, Kingston University, 2016, dostupno na: *http://eprints.kingston.ac.uk/36138/*, str. 191; Endnotes, 'False Totalities Don't Have Exits' i (sa referencama na frankfurtsku školu) moj tekst: 'This Implies Nothing', s napomenom da će dva posljednje navedena teksta biti objavljeni u: *What is to be Done Under Real Subsumption*, London and Berlin: Mute, (u pripremi) 2018.
48. Kao što izgleda da i sam Kolu priznaje kada piše: „Ako kapital dominira svime do te mjere da se može poistovijetiti sa društvenim bićem, ona izgleda da, na temelju toga, on nestaje.", 'Transition', Ibid.
49. Félix Guattari, 'The Micro-Politics of Fascism'. U: *Molecular Revolution*, (prev. Rosemary Sheed), str. 217-232. London: Penguin, 1984, str. 221.

objašnjenja šta bi to komunizam mogao značiti bez klasičnog radničkog pokreta, umjesto koga (objašnjenja) bi uslijedili stalni napori da se obnove i preispitaju kategorije koje je ponudio Marks.

Okultni fašizam

Još jedan vektor povezuje Batajevu orijentaciju iz *Društvene kritike* sa njegovim kasnijim djelima, prolazeći kroz istraživanja fašizma, okultnog i tajnih društava.[50] Ispitivanja koja je sproveli Stjuart Houm (Stewart Home), Fabijan Tompset (Fabian Tompsett) i drugi o odnosu između neonacističkih pokreta i okultnog, razvijana su (kao i u slučaju Bataja i partizana iz Kontranapada) iz sukoba sa fašistima i neofašistima na ulicama. Dekada uličnih borbi u UK kulminirala je definitivnom obznanom ovih grupa, u smislu njihovog uličnog prisustva, 1992. godine prilikom takozvane „Bitke za Vaterlo"[51] Međutim, to je imalo dvije posljedice. Kao prvo, unutarnju kritiku antifašističkih grupa koje su razvile jednu identitetsku, mačo i nasilničku podkulturu koja je bila posvećena suprotstavljanju fašistima. Kao drugo, pošto su neofašisti i rasisti potisnuti u podzemlje, oni su se okrenuli ispitivanju okultnih formi, mitova i drugih još opskurnijih fašističkih tema kako bi obnovili svoju politiku.[52] Zaokret ka mitopoetici, prema Houmu (ali i drugima), spaja u sebi strukture malih mreža i taktike avangardnih grupa sa lijevo-komunističkom politikom i kritikom, nudeći da, nasuprot okultnom fašizmu, „razvije [...] jedan sistem simboličke manipulacije koji bi bio potpuno autonoman u odnosu na državu."[53] U duhu ove plastičnosti, grupa ili organizacija postaje medijum, unutar koga su

---

50. Cf. Georges Bataille, 'The Psychological Structure of Fascism' u: *Visions of Excess: Selected Writings, 1927-39*, op. cit., str. 137-160; Georges Bataille, 'The Sacred Conspiracy', Ibid., str. 178-181. Georges Bataille, 'The Sorcerer's Apprentice', *The College of Sociology*, op. cit., str. 12-23; Georges Bataille i Roger Caillois, 'Sacred Sociology and the Relationships between "Society", "Organism", and "Being"', Ibid., str. 73-84; Roger Caillois, 'Brotherhoods, Orders, Secret Societies' Ibid., str. 145-156.
51. 'Blood and Honour routed by Anti Fascist Action at Waterloo 1992', *https://www.youtube.com/watch?v=zpXMObMdR8I*
52. Ovaj zaokret odlično je fikcionalno predstavljen u romanu Maksa Šefera *Djeca sunca*. Max Schaeffer, *Children of the Sun*, London: Granta, 2010, posebno str. 184-189.
53. Neoist Alliance, 'Marx, Christ and Satan United in Struggle', Home, Stewart. *Mind Invaders: A Reader in Psychic Warfare, Cultural Sabotage and Semiotic Terrorism.* London: Serpent's Tail, 1997, str. 111-112.

autoritet i identifikacija imitirani i izvučeni, ispitani kao *fait social*, objekti sa kojima se može igrati i koji se daju preoblikovati.[54] „Mi govorimo kolektivno iako je Neoistička Alijansa fantomska organizacija. *Re:Action* je organ jedne simulirane (ako ne i fiktivne) organizacije. Mi težimo nestanku okultnog i umjetničkog svijeta, ali ne i socijalnog."[55] Novi projekti otpočeli su sa kritikom „opozicionizma", kritični spram klasičnih antiimperijalističkih i antifašističkih stanovišta, razvijajući iz toga forme koje su nastojale da prošire i isprovociraju razliku.[56] Školovani na avangardnoj istoriji i podkulturi, Londonska psihogeografska asocijacija (LPA, objavio Fabijan Tompset iz Nepopularnih knjiga, [Unpopular Books]) i druge sa njom povezane grupe, umjesto suprotstavljanja izvrćućoj sili nacionalizma nekom novom formom realizma, nastoje napasti fašizam i nacionalizam na njihovom tlu, na tlu mita i fantazije. U radu LPA ističu se imaginarne podvale i fabulacije kojima se satirizuje ovaj najnoviji zaokret u okviru politike krajnje desnice a onda se sve to povezuje sa satirom na račun „britanskog establišmenta": vladajuće klase i plemstva, simboličkom arhitekturom i „linijama poravnanja" u londonskom i pejzažu britanskih ostrva.[57] Ako je u fašističkoj propagandi „[s]tvarnost dovedena do toga da lažira samu sebe, a iscrpljenom umu više nije dozvoljeno ni da sanja", kako to kaže Zigfrid Krakauer (Siegfried

---

54. *Fait social* (društvena činjenica) ključni je termin djela sociologa Emila Dirkema (Émile Durkheim) koji je uticao na Bataja i njegove saradnike iz *Dokumenata* i sa Koleža za sociologiju.

55. Re:Action, 'Follow Me: Re:Action Unexplained by Robyn Whitlaw', *Infotainment*, Br. 2, London: Info Centre, 1998, str. 8.

56. Batajeva pozicija koju je ustanovio u jednom od prvih tekstova objavljenih pri Koležu za sociologiju također nudi ovakvo odstupanje od antifašističke politike: „Porobivši same sebe, razbijajući sve što neće da klekne pred nužnošću kojoj se potčinjavaju pred drugima, ljudi od akcije slijepo se prepuštaju struji koja ih odnosi sve dalje snažeći se njihovim bespomoćnim mlataranjem." Georges Bataille, 'The Sorcerer's Apprentice', *The College of Sociology*, op. cit., str. 12-23, str. 17. Za skoriji razvoj i koncentraciju ovog pristupa, npr. „opozicija nikada ne nadilazi ono čemu se opire. Njenu fanatičnu formu, akumuliranu u nasilnim djelima, mogu si priuštiti samo najkonzervativnije organizacije.", vidjeti: Frère Dupont, 'Tinned Chunks: An Introduction of the Rejection of Everything Through Moments in the Description of Deep Opposition', (bez datuma, pamflet bez navedenih stranica) cca 2015.

57. Nekoliko tekstova Londonske psihogeografske asocijacije (LPA) obuhvaćeno je i u antologiji *Mind Invaders*, Ibid., originalni pamfleti i naslovne stranice koje je objavila LPA dostupni su za pregledanje u prostorijama organizacije Mayday Rooms, London, *http://maydayrooms.org/*.

Kracauer), lijevo-komunističko oživljavanje mita i kontrafaktičke invencije obezbijedit će kritičku energetsku silu društvenim strujama koje odbijaju fašizam, nacionalizam i kapitalizam. Iskorištavanje ezoteričnih mitova, posebno onih koji su povezani sa drevnim lokalitetima koji se nalaze svuda u pejzažu britanskih ostrva, povezanih sa interesovanjima rasprostranjene podkulture rejvera i njuejdžerskih putnika: novi „organski pokret" čija praksa nezakonitog zaposijedanja

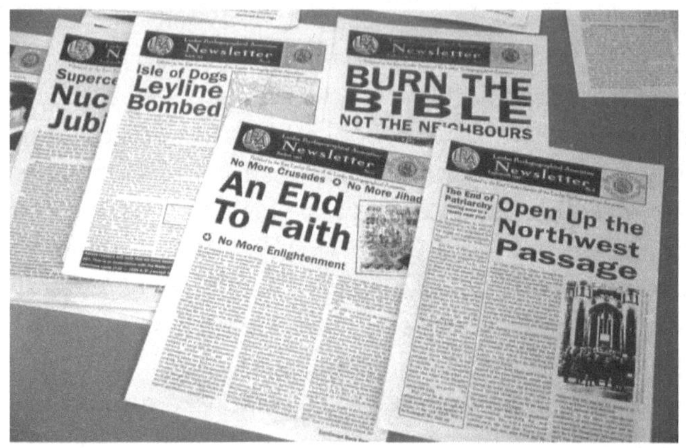

Časopisi Londonske psihogeografske asocijacije izloženi u Info Centru, 1998-1999.

zemlje, ekološkim aktivizmom i izmišljanjem novih kolektivnih rituala pomoću muzike, droga i plesa ne nailazi na mnogo interesovanja od strane tradicionalne ljevice. Pobunjeničke grupacije koje uzdižu Melanholični trogloditi, objavljeni na Farsiju i engleskom, predstavljaju tajnu istoriju pobuna na antičkom i savremenom srednjem istoku koje se nastavljaju sa lomljenjem koje prati svaki anti-samitski protest koliko i spontano nogometno huliganstvo.[58] Jedan od satelita LPA, ka budućnosti usmjeren, mada uz velike doze humora i ponižavanja, je i Asocijacija autonomnih astroauta (AAA) čiji program autonomne zajednice za putovanje svemirom i petogodišnji plan za „kretanje u mnogim pravcima u isto vrijeme" nastoji da se protiv kapitala bori na njegovim krajnjim granicama.

---

58. Cf. Melancholic Troglodytes, *Class Struggle and this Thing Called the Middle East*, oktobar, 2011, dostupno na: *http://libcom.libcom.org/library/class-struggle-thing-called-middle-east-melancholic-trogladytes*

Suveren i bezglavost

Slika Acéphala pomaljala se mnogo i često u rječniku časopisa *Inventory*, kako u pisanim prilozima tako i kroz brojne projekte urednika koji su pokrenuli časopis.[59] Grupa je naglašavala središnje mjesto humora u batajevskom projektu obnove suvereniteta kod modernih subjekata. Humor svrgava svaki autoritet, a posebno samog sebe. Lik Acéphala ponovo je predstavljen ovog puta kao poster – u vidu slike nogometaša koji prevlači dres preko glave tokom proslave na kraju meča – za jedan događaj koji je pozivao na masovnu nogometnu utakmicu ispred Bakingemske palate u kojoj bi bila korištena lopta ukrašena papirnim kolažom koji je trebalo da podsjeća na glavu engleske kraljice. Podvig povezan sa republikanskim tradicijama Britanije i Francuske u sjećanje je prizivao kako odsijecanje glave Čarlsa I 1649. godine (što se odigralo nedaleko odatle kod Kuće za prijeme na Vajthilu) kao i odsijecanje glava francuskog plemstva uključujući samog Luja XVI tokom Francuske revolucije iz 1789. godine, tako i britansku tradiciju masovnog nogometa kao katalizatora socijalnih protesta.[60] Jedan od Batajevih prijedloga Kontranapadu uključivao je i ponovno uprizorivanje pogubljenja Luja XVI u ranim danima Narodnog fronta na trgu Konkord 21. januara 1936. godine. Za Bataja je trg Konkord bio poprište koje je imalo specifičan značaj s obzirom da se radilo o mjestu i na kom su desili i nasilni neredi koje su uzrokovali nacionalisti u februaru 1934. i

---

59. Cf. Nick Norton, 'Bring Me the Head of Georges Bataille', *Inventory*, Vol. 2 Br. 1 1997; Howard Slater, 'New Acéphale', *Inventory*, Vol. 2 Br. 3 1997; Kingsland Passage, 'The Last Days of London' *Inventory*, Vol. 5 Br. 1 2003.

60. „Procijenjeno je da je [1699. godine] oko 1100 pobunjenih ljudi napalo gradilište i ograđeni prostor na kom su izvođeni radovi na isušivanju sjeverno od Piterbroa", a sve „u bojama i uz similiranje fudbalske igre". Heather Falvey, 'Custom, resistance and politics: local experiences of improvement in early modern England', doktorska teza, University of Warwick, 2007, str. 356-7. Vidjeti također: James Walvin, *The People's Game: The History of Football Revisited*. Edinburgh: Mainstream, 1994. Valvin ukazuje na još nekoliko primjera pobuna protiv ograđivanja iz 18. vijeka koji su se odigrali pod maskom nogometnih utakmica. Istinske događaje u kojima je glava suverena korištena umjesto lopte teško je potvrditi, ali mnogo lokalnih mitova i folklora u Britaniji ostaje na ovoj liniji, kao na primjer u Vinčelziju, gdje igrači jednom godišnje pokušavaju da uhvate objekt poznat kao „Francuzova glava", vidjeti: *http://www.winchelsea.net/community/game.htm*; dok ovdje izvještaj jednog svjedoka iz godina koje prethode građanskom ratu (1642. godine) opisuje kako se masa igra glavom pogubljenog katoličkog svještenika: *http://historyweird.com/1642-mob-football-catholic-priest-head/*

na kome je kralj Luj XVI pogubljen 23. januara 1793. godine. Igrom koju je je trebalo da uprizori Inventory izigran je postistorijski ili revizionistički duh mita, glasine i ponovnog uprizorenja koji su bili rasprostranjeni tokom postmodernističkih '80-ih i '90-ih. Spoj nekolicine istorijskih momenata, narodnih tradicija i mitova usred aktuelnog trenutka ispunjenog političkim energijama koje su bile u vezi sa intervencijama koje je izvodila LPA na demonstracijama i na protestima zbog međunarodnog samita koji se održavao u to vrijeme. Podvig koji je izveo Inventory uprizorivao je ono što je, bar prema Majklu Ričardsonu (Michael Richardson), tražio Bataj: „zarazan mit kojim se smrt suverena slavila kao regenerativni čin transformacije društva".[61] Utakmica „masovnog nogometa" odigrana je u kontekstu sekvence protesta „bez predvodnika" koji se odigrao u Londonu, što je uključivalo momente nereda, nasilja prema svojini pa čak i masovne pljačke. U odnosu prema novom diskursu koji je kružio protestnim pokretima „mnoštva", borba protiv „novih ograda" (Ponoćne bilješke, *Midnight Notes*) i u odnosu prema taktikama koje su razvili članovi projekta Luter Bliset (Luther Blisett) kakva je bila Bijela odijela (Tute Bianche) u Italiji, Inventory je razvio uličnu igru pod nazivom Koagulum (Coagulum) koji je uključivao neodređen broj učesnika koji su formirali ugrušak ili skup (skram ili rak) kao u ragbiju, na datom prometnom mjestu, čime su zakrčivali slobodan promet tog privatiziranog prostora. Razvijanje ludičkih eksperimenata neposredno uz druge proteste dvosmisleno je smjeralo i na „zarazu" tom nepredvidivom masovnom akcijom, ali i na potrošački moment u vidu gledalaca naviklih da prisustvuju spektakularnim umjetničkim djelima.

Mondo mitopoetika

Stjuart Houm, londonski autor i bezobzirni pamfletista iz 1980-ih i 1990-ih, uradio je mnogo toga na reinvenciji i redistribuciji te avangardne tendencije ka „mitopoetici" pomoću mnoštva akcija koje su uključivale poigravanja imenima, kolektivnu anonimnost, samizdat, fabulacije i dezinformacije. „Njegov" (s obzirom na to da je bilo šta posjedničko ovdje neprikladno) fanzin *Osmijeh* (*Smile*), koji je radilo mnoštvo autora,

---

61. Georges Bataille and Michael Richardson, *The Absence of Myth: Writings on Surrealism* London; New York: Verso, 1994, str. 12.

u svojoj biti oslanjao se na djelo fluksus umjetnika Reja Džonsona (Ray Johnson).[62]

Još jedan projekat u kome je učestvovao Houm bio je „takozvani projekat Luter Bliset". On svoje početke ima u Italiji, da bi se kasnije razvio i prerastao u međunarodnu mrežu na stotine ljudi koji su koristili ime Lutera Bliseta za autorske tekstove i kako bi pravili psine.[63] Kako piše Hauard Slejter, anonimnost podstiče nepoznate potencijalne sa-zavjerenike.[64]

Isključivanje „autora" razvilo se u pravcu stvaranja moćnih karakternih maski, fantastičnih ili čudovišnih tvorevina koje bi mogle da zauzmu mjesto kultova ličnosti koji su bili osobenost radničkog pokreta u njegovom „herojskom dobu". Ovo ponovno pokretanje predmodernih tema pobudilo je „neproizvodnu potrošnju" i razmjenu poklona za koje je Bataj mislio da potiču od religijskih formi, ali se također mogu pripisati i „perverznim seksualnim aktivnostima" i kriminalnim djelima.[65] Na ovaj način, „dar" o kome je teoretizirao Marsel Mos (Marcel Mauss) referirajući na „predkapitalistička" društva,

---

62. U pismu Reja Džonsona upućeom Stjuartu Houmu 1897. godine on piše: „Napravio sam sopstveni časopis *Smile* zato što je *File* iz Kanade koji je bio inspisrisan časopisom *Life* i Anom Bananom (Anna Banana) napravila svoju *Vile* a neki ljudi iz Čikaga uradili su *Bile*. Moj časopis *Smile*, ne znam da li si znao, bio je nevidljiv?", 'Letter from Ray Johnson to Stewart Home', 1987 preštampano u: *Lightworks* magazine #22, 2000, citirao u: Stephen Perkins, 'An Assembly of Conspirators: Omnibus News and Smile', 2016, *http://artistsperiodicals.blogspot.com/* Perkins također primjećuje kako se „Houmov originalni prijedlog o upotrebi mnoštva imena u izdavanju periodičnih publikacija, koji je on objavio u sopstvenom časopisu *Smile*, #2 (1984), [...] mora shvatiti kao njegov sopstveni 'originalni' doprinos Neoizmu. Kako se kasnije ispostavilo, Projekat Osmijeh bio je izuzetno uspješan [...] i u periodu između 1984-89. godine izašlo je 101 izdanje koje je uredilo otprilike 32 urednika."
63. „U Italiji se, počev od ranih i srednjih 1990-ih, čitav buljuk drugova [...] posvetio praktičnim ispitivanjima mitologija, u namjeri da razumiju da li su neotuđujuća, libertarijanska dekonstrukcija, ponovno korištenje i manipulacija mitovima, mogući ili nije." Vidjeti: Tute Bianche, 'The Practical Side of Myth Making (in Catastrophic Times)', *Infopool* Br.7, 2003, str. 37.
64. „Pošto nudi neobavezujuće i nedozvoljene darove, anonimnost je ta koja odašilje ne nadajući se nekom neodređenom uzdarju i postupajući tako, ona nudi svim pridošlicama stvaranje prostorā iz kojih je moguće davati neodbranjive prijedloge i iznositi čudesne akcije, i u kojima je sloboda u igri istog momenta i u svim njenim nerješivim suprotnostima i smiješnim nagađanjima." Howard Slater, 'New Acéphale', *Inventory*, Vol. 2 Br. 3, 1997, str. 71-75, str. 72.

postat će, u rasturenim spisima poratnih ultraljevičara, zvijezda vodilja prema kojoj će se kretati sva tumačenja pobuna i nemira sa kraja 20.

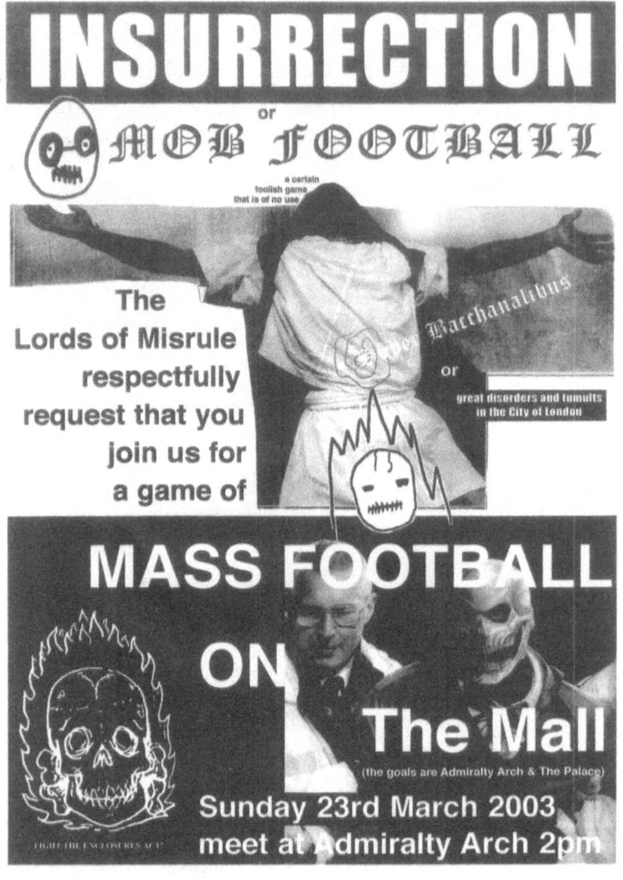

Inventory, Masovni nogomet u tržnom centru, 1999.

vijeka, i u kojima će se na njih gledati kao na momente neposluha u odnosu na logiku kapitala i formalnu politiku koja je zastala pod

---

65. Georges Bataille, 'The Notion of Expenditure', Bataille, Georges. 1985. *Visions of Excess: Selected Writings, 1927-39.* Preveo Allan Stoekl. 1. izdanje. Minneapolis: University of Minnesota Press, str. 116-129, str. 118. Ovaj esej Bataj je kasnije razvio u trotomnoj knjizi, *Prokleti deo*, njegovom glavnom poratnom djelu. U *Prokletom delu* Bataj revidira svoje predratno pro-revolucionalrno stanovište u smjeru pomirbe sa staljinizmom, ali pošto mene prvenstveno interesiraju njegove predratne aktivnosti i veze koje postoje između 1930-ih i 1990-ih, ja se nisam upuštao u ovu debatu, ali za one koji se interesiraju za Batajevo nasljeđe, vrijedno istraživanja je djelo: Not Bored, 'Trashing Georges Bataille, "Accursed" Stalinist', *http://www.notbored.org/bataille.html*

njegovim uslovljenostima. Za njih se tu radilo o bezosjećajnim trošenjima koja su odbijala forme oporezivanja i tiranije kapitalističke upotrebe stvari.[66]

Papirni asemblaži

Labava scena koju su u Evropi 1980-ih i u ranim 1990-im stvorili ljevičarski politički časopisi ili zinovi počeli su da raskidaju sa ljevičarskim ortodoksijama i da istražuju nove mogućnosti distribucije stolnog izdavaštva i, na kraju, umreženog kompjuterskog rada. Ja ih nazivam „papirnim asemblažima" ('paper assemblies') zbog samorefleksivne pažnje koju poklanjaju momentima proizvodnog procesa štampanja i distribucije štampanih objekata što se dalje širi i na konfiguracije urednika, autora i čitalaca koji sada stvaraju i ističu drugačije veze između ideja, štampane materije kao i tijela i materijalnosti koje između njih kruže. Ovi štamparski i samizdat projekti, posebno oni iz druge generacije, naginjali su ka tome da miješaju i kombiniraju medije i šire svoju distribuciju pomoću velikog broja platformi: vebsajtova, muzičkih izdavačkih etiketa, časopisa, knjižara, postera, flajera, naljepnica. O takvim kombinacijama, sa njihovim naglaskom na manjinskim interesima i autonomnoj organizaciji, kao strateškim „post-medijima" teoretizirao je, poslije Feliksa Gatarija, još i Hauard Slejter.[67] Njihova upotreba mrežne forme ne može se svesti na „horizontalizaciju" „grupa bez vođstva i strukture" kako ih kritizira Džo Frimen (Jo Freeman) i kleveće Žil Dove (Gilles Dauvé) osvrćući se na neke samizdat inicijative kao na formu kapitulacije pred kapitalističkom logikom i negiranju klasnosti.[68] Nik Toburn (Nick Thoburn), navodeći primjer Nepopularnih knjiga (Unpopular Books), naglašava složene „posrednike" kakve sitna štampa postavlja između njihovih štamparskih eksperimenata i političkog sadržaja.

> postoji jedan dodatni posrednik između osjetilnih svojstava
> predmeta i njegovog političko-konceptualnog sadržaja – i to ne

---

66. Za sveobuhvatnu obradu ovoga u obliku štampanih stvari vidjeti: Nicholas Thoburn, 'Communist Objects and the Values of Printed Matter', *Social Text* 28, Br. 2, ljeto 2010, str. 1-30.
67. Uporedi: bibliografija post-medija dostupna je na: *https://monoskop.org/Postmedia*

samo u smislu njegove antirobne orijentacije već također i u smislu njegove kritike dominantnih načina političke organizacije.[69]

Pod uticajem Žorža Bataja (i kao teoretičara ali i kao izdavača), Info Centar/Infopul (Infocentre/Infopool) i sa njim povezani Slobodni univerzitet iz Kopenhagena (Copenhagen Free University) razvili su idiosinkratičke pojmovnike na posterima i onlajn, kao vrstu organizacionih formi pogodnih za heterogene materijale, eseje, umjetničke projekte, zvučne zapise i istraživačke projekte koji po svom značenju mogu biti povezani sa konceptualnim shvatanjem izdavaštva i formatima razviijenim u *Dokumentima*. Ova tehnika stvaranja idiosinkratičkih pojmovnika bila je zajednička za mnoštvo grupa koje su operirale u to vrijeme, pa čak iako su im se interesovanja i politike u potpunosti razilazile (Cybernetic Culture Research Unit, LPA, Inventory, Copenhagen Free University) ta taktika dozvoljavala im je horizontalno i asocijativno ravnanje termina i njihovih transformacija, sa osvrtom unatrag na djela nadrealista i, prije njih, na projekat enciklopedista (*Encyclopédistes*), ali i unaprijed ka gomili saradničkih onlajn sajtova kakvi su Vikipedija i *Neciklopedija*. Strateška i praktička formacija Info Centra/Infopoola kao hibridnog institucionalno-domaćeg društvenog prostora može se posmatrati i kao pokušaj da se živi i razvije bezformnost koja bi odgovarala Batajevoj entropijskoj kritici kategorija iz njegovih predratnih spisa objavljivanih u *Dokumentima*, koji su se kretali i na kraju svoj kritički oblik zadobili u vidu „organskog pokreta" – promjenjivih grupnih formi kakve su bile Kontranapad, Acéphale i

---

68. Jo Freeman, 'The Tyranny of Structurelessness', 1970, dostupno na: http://www.jofreeman.com/joreen/tyranny.htm 'Informations & Correspondance Ouvrières (1961-73); „a sada i Echanges & Mouvement tvrde kako oni nemaju teoriju izuzev teorije prema kojoj samo proletarijat može sam da odredi svoje metode i ciljeve. Isto tako, na hiljade infokioska i nezavisnih medijskih kolektiviteta izjavljuju kako nisu vođeni nikakvom posebnom doktrinom (marksističkom, anarhističkom, ekološkom, feminističkom ili bilo kojom drugom), govoreći kako je njihova jedina svrha da služe kao mjesta susreta i komunikacijski centri kojima je cilj da promoviraju socijalne borbe, sa jedinom razlikom u tome što 'istorijski subjekt' više nije radnička klasa nego su to ljudi (famoznih 99%). Oni se ponašaju kao da je 'izbor nepostojanja' koji je objavio ICO (*IS*, # 11), preokrenut u izbor da se bude onlajn prisutan 24/7, dok su i dalje informacije te koje imaju prvenstvo, suviše često i sa istim osobinama kao i kod 'buržoaskih' medija: neprekidni priliv informacija, prenatrpanost informacijama i njihova zastarjelost, senzacionalizam..." Gilles Dauvé, 'The Bitter Victory of Council Communism', *http://libcom.org/library/bitter-victory-council-communism-gilles-dauve*
69. 'Communist Objects and the Values of Printed Matter', op. cit., str. 23.

Kolež za sociologiju. Za Bataja je zadržavanje afektivne dimenzije u ovim grupama bilo ono što ih je sačuvalo od institucionalizacije od strane države, partije ili drugih molarnih formacija. U tom smislu one su očuvale vezu sa snom o promjeni svijeta tako što ćemo u njemu i dalje živjeti kao padu i greškama sklona ljudska bića.

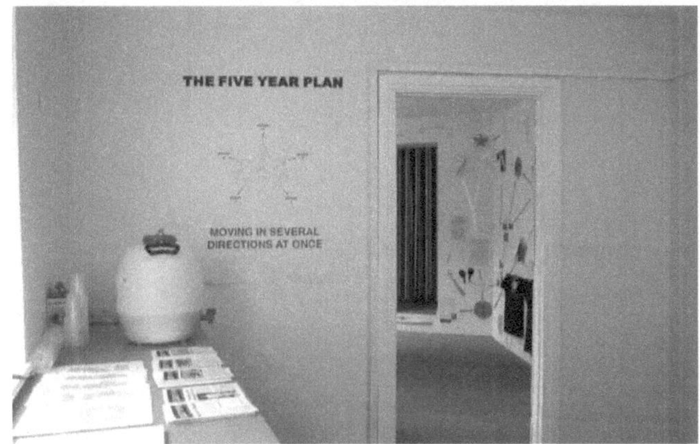

Info Centar London, 1999.

Za grupe iz 1990-ih, o ovome se razvijala svijest kao o neče što je u suprotnosti sa glatkoćom razmjene informacija onlajn.[70] Slobodni univerzitet iz Kopenhagena smatrao je da i sam funkcionira unutar logike „samoinstitucionalizacije". Za razliku od institucija koje su opsjednute sopstvenim beskonačnim održavanjem on je u stanju prihvatiti i sopstveni nestanak, s obzirom da je po samom porijeklu imaginaran.[71] Pored toga što objavljuje svoje pamflete u maniru samizdata, kao i Infopool, Info centar je napravio jedan neobičan izbor umrežavajući skupa nekoliko manjih projekata sitne štampe koje smo gore spomenuli u jedinstven fizički prostor, čitaonicu kojoj je pridružen jedan kućni prostor u Hekniju. Taj prostor takođe je korišten za male neformalne diskusije i „izložbe" sačinjene od priloga učesika na samim projektima. Proizvodna dimenzija u toku svakodnevnog života u Info centru/Infopoolu tretira se kao forma otpora kooptaciji kakva se može vidjeti u svakodnevnom životu u kapitalističkom društvu. Dinamika

---

70. Fizički prostor, Infošop 56A i Arhiv (56A Infoshop and Archive), skvotiran prostor koji su koristili aktivisti, pamfletisti i političke grupe, koji se nalazio u londonskoj oblasti Elephant & Castle, imao je ključni uticaj na Info centar, vidjeti: *http://56a.org.uk/*
71. Copenhagen Free University Abolition Committee, 'We Have Won', 2007, *http://www.copenhagenfreeuniversity.dk/won.html*

antiinstitucionalnog izgnanstva i samoinstitucionalnog stvaranja sačinjavaju jedan osjetljivi prostor u kome se ispituju svakodnevna ili lokalna posredovanja koja bi mogla zamijeniti kapitalistilke kategorije, mada će ovako nešto zauvijek ostati samo opitna propozicija.

ABZ Slobodnog univerziteta Kopenhagen, poster, 2000.

Zaključak

Tendencije koje se daju uočiti u svakom od ova dva perioda podrazumijevaju taktičko povlačenje u odnosu na molarne instance onoga što se smatralo zvaničnom politikom, uz zadržavanje onih političkih formi i referenci koje su se kao savitljivi materijali mogli iskoristiti u rekonfiguraciji. Jedna od najvećih pretpostavki mogućnosti za ove grupe i antidržavni, antipartijski anarhizam i komunizam koji su njegovale, bila su preimućstva koja im je donosila država blagostanja, koja je podržavala formu koju je jedna grupa sa sjedištem u Brajtonu, po imenu *Aufheben*, nazvala „udijeljenom autonomijom" ('dole autonomy').[72] Iako je Batajeva generacija dozvoljavala neku formu nadoknade, ako ne i plaće, za uređivanje časopisa ili pisanje članaka za njega, kasniji val napora preduzimanih u diskusijama imao je tendenciju ka radu na crno (i radu noću), čime su resursi dnevnog posla preusmjereni na korištenje slobodnog vremena koje je omogućavala milostinja. Ta udijeljena autonomija omogućivala je praktičnu kritiku

---

72. Aufheben, 'Dole Autonomy Versus the Re-imposition of Work', 1998, *https://libcom.org/library/dole-autonomy-versus-re-imposition-work*

posla, osiguravajući i reprodukciju i slobodno vrijeme – nadnicu uz život bez otuđenog rada. Međutim, ako je udijeljena autonomija potpomagala autonomnu teoretizaciju o formama suvereniteta koji bi bio sekularan, nezavisan od porodice, rodno neutralan, među- ili čak izvan- nacionalan, sam ovaj sistem reprodukcije ili forma „slobode" i dalje su ostali dužni djelimičnomj povezanosti države i njenog radno sposobnog stanovništva koje je bilo istorijski zavisno od borbi za snažan radnički pokret. Ova situacija bila je podložna promjenama u periodu kada su i materijalna baza radničkog pokreta i stabilna država ubrzano nestajali. Kritika ljevice i novih društvenih pokreta iz ovog perioda koju su iznijeli *Aufheben*, odnosila se na to da oni nisu uspjeli da odbrane mjere koje su osiguravale i njihovu osnovnu reprodukciju i reprodukciju njihovog aktivizma. Kao „stilovi života" obje ove scene mogu se shvatiti kao nešto čime vlada neka vrsta antipolitičkog povjerenja, ali umjesto da se ovo shvati kao pokret depolitizacije, ja predlažem tezu da su male grupe koje su se formirale oko samizdat projekata namjerno zakomplicirale političko polje svojim očiglednim povlačenjem iz njega. Jer ono što je izgledalo kao povlačenje bio je, umjesto toga, jedan oblik rekonstelacije. Ili njihovim riječima rečeno, te su grupe pokretale „određenje komunizma kao ravnomerno raspoređenog i samokritičkog procesa, procesa koji se čuva bilo kog određujućeg centra privlačenja."[73] S druge strane, „opsadni mentalitet" ovih grupa i efektivna „kontrola miljea" dovode do formi koje ne dramatiziraju same sebe toliko da bi to dovelo do izdvajanja i rascijepa u odnosu na ranije periode masovnih partija i avangarde već bez obzira na to podstiču paranoična prokazivanja i rivalstva. Ovaj problem ne samo da implicira pritisak da se one samoreproduciraju na marginama kapitalističkog društva, nego ponekada i bolnije „istrajavanje u okviru miljea istih onih dihotomija koje služe zaštiti kapitalizma", ako se poslužimo Slejterovim riječima.[74] Ako se osvrnemo unatrag, jasno se vidi da se međuprostor (udijeljeni, jeftini ili besplatni gradski prostori, ulice, slobodno vrijeme) u Londonu ubrzano smanjuju pod pritiskom finansijalizacije i intenzifikacije rada do koje dolazi na globalnom nivou, kako se čini, bez

---

73. Nicholas Thoburn, *Anti-Book: On the Art and Politics of Radical Publishing.* Minneapolis: Minnesota University Press, 2016, str. 103. [Nikolas Toburn, *Anti-knjiga: materijalni tekst i političko izdavaštvo*, Novi Sad: kuda.org, 2014. str. 128]
74. Howard Slater, 'Evacuate the Leftist Bunker', *Annual Review of Critical Psychology*, Vol. 3, 2003,str. 116-136.

prestanka. Ne radi se ni o tome da je država u potpunosti presušila; čak i dok sasijeca svoje socijalne obaveze, ona jednostavno postaje spremna i pripravna za svoju fazu štednje, kako smo mogli vidjeti u skorije vrijeme. Iz ove perspektive, na eksperimentiranje sa samoinstitucionalizacijom kao savremenim oblikom autonomije mora se gledati kao na aktivnosti koje su pod zaštitnim staklom države koja njime ujedno opisue gornju granicu dozvoljenog za ono što takve zajednice mogu uzeti.[75]

Dakle, za ljevicu ne djeluju održivim ni lažna obećanja o autonomiji izbornih zajednica u odnosu na državu, niti dugi marš kroz njene institucije. „Taktički suverenitet" ili „samoinstitucioniranje", eksperimentiranje sa prevaziđenim ili nepredvidivim aparatima tako su bili tek privremeno sredstvo za pobočno proširenje dok je vertikalno širenje bilo zaustavljeno. Skorašnja tendencija ka samokritici i problematizacija navika i rituala lijeve političke kulture predstavljaju nužni razvoj popustljivosti, naviknutosti i zatvaranja zajednice koja je u stanju prešućivanja. Pa ipak, ove struje također ohrabruju i stvaranje slike ljevice kao neplodne i poražene, ili „obremenjene odsustvom milijardi" kako je to jedan komentator napisao, jer bez „milijardi" o kojima je riječ, ona ne može prići ni korak bliže emancipaciji.[76] Udaljenost ovih grupa od bilo kojeg revolucionarnog agensa u toj tački postala je predmetom ironične samokritike (možda u najgorem slučaju „zajednice sačinjene od zajedničke nesreće") što moguću kombinaciju iz koje bi mogla nastati revolucionarna promjena čini nesigurnom i neodređenom.[77] Pa ipak, pozivi upućeni protiv manjinskih formi opozicionizma često pretvaraju se – što čine često u nedostatku analize stvarnog odnosa snaga – da cjelokupna ljevica može da se oporavi.[78] Fašizam u strogom smislu i dalje je rijetkost, uobičajeniji i opasniji

---

75. „Država je garant alli ne i kreator ovih odnosa. Ona predstavlja i ujedinjuje kapital, ona nije ni pokretač kapitala niti je njegov središnji dio [...] supstanca države ne prebiva u njenim institucionalnim formama, već u njenoj funkciji da ujedinjava. Država osigurava veze koje ljudska bića ne mogu niti se usuđuju da ih stvore između sebe samih, i stvara mrežu usluga koje su i parazitske i stvarne," Gilles Dauvé, 'When Insurrections Die', *Endnotes* Br.1, oktobar, 2010, str. 63.
76. Fraza potiče od Frera Dipona: Frère Dupont, *Species Being*, San Francisco: Ardent Press, 2009, citirano kao naslov prikaza: Howard Slater, 'Burdened By the Absence of Billions', op. cit.
77. 'Hic Nihil, Hic Salta! (a critique of Bartlebyism)', op. cit.
78. Vidjeti: Mark Fisher, 'Exiting the Vampire Castle', 22 novembar, *http://www.thenorthstar.info/?p=11299*

1930-ih, dok je danas tu riječ o spajanju lijevih i desnih formi nacional socijalizma u procesu učvršćivanja države u vrijeme krize.[79]

Rasuta anti-tradicija koju sam ja ovdje ispitivao samo sa površine ne sačinjava nikakvo jedinstvo. Umjesto toga, nju čine zaraćeni fragment praksi koje, uhvaćene u zračnu struju, privlače i ohrabruju nepoznate druge. Usmjerene protiv lažnog i autoritarnog jedinstva koje izbacuje one nepoželjene „dijelove" koje ne može da uskladi, te prakse odbijaju da ih se koristi ili da ostanu jedinstvene sve dok svatko (kao što se to kaže u sloganu AAA „Evo dolazi svatko") ne bude mogao da im se pridruži.

Dodatak: Mitopoetika 2.0

Skorije bujanje himeričnih populističkih pokreta na krajnjoj desnici koji su svoju vidljivost izgradili na popularizaciji ideja i tehnika koje su iscrpli sa ljevice dodaje i notu poniženja ovom istorijskom porazu.[80] Podkultura proizvodnje mema, onlajn anonimnosti, spiskova, humora ponavljanja, seksa i nasilja pomogla je da na vlast dođe novi heterogeni suveren, Tramp, očigledno zbog toga da bi zabranio sav haos koji vidi svuda oko sebe. Njegova amajlija Pepe ili Kek (androgino božanstvo iz drevnog Egipta koje predstavlja primordijalni haos) također ukazuje na to kako ovo može biti samo način da se ubrzaju haos ili kriza koji su već počeli.[81] Ovaj novi desničarski val tako je i selektivno identitetski kao što je i konstitutivan za jednu anti-identitetsku politiku. Njegovo pomirljivo negiranje „kulturnog marksizma" uključuje svođenje manjinskih tužbalica na litaniju prigovora koje upućuju bijelci: okrivite kulturu, ponižavanje protivnika, rasizam i seksizam. Ako su to pokazatelji pokušaja desnice da vodi rat na polju kulture, to isto tako ukazuje i na stanovitu impotenciju, bar ako smo išta naučili od gorenavedenog. Filozofski antiidentitarizam, koji predstavlja intelektualnu posljedicu ovih pokreta, svuda je forma idealizma sem

---

79. „Kako bi ovo utjelovilo referendumski duh, moralo bi u sebe da uključi i povratak suverenosti, kao i značajno, privrevemeno uzdržavanje od slobode da se bude dio pokreta." Paul Mason, 'How the left should respond to Brexit', 17 oktobar 2016, *http://www.newstatesman.com/politics/uk/2016/10/paul-mason-how-left-should-respond-brexit*
80. Dale Beran, '4chan: The Skeleton Key to the Rise of Trump', *https://cominsitu.wordpress.com/2017/02/20/4chan-the-skeleton-key-to-the-rise-of-trump/*
81. Vidjeti: *http://knowyourmeme.com/memes/cult-of-kek*

ukoliko se ne hvata u koštac sa složenošću čovjeka kao subjekta. Svaki izraz kolapsa uslova reprodukcije (života, identiteta, društvenih odnosa) ljutito se drži svoje maske. Njegov identitet predstavljen je amblemom žabe, egipatskog boga, čašom mlijeka, ali je opet rječito da ga ti njegovi pokušaji da se sabere pod ovim simbolima nisu učvrstili.[82] Autoritarni

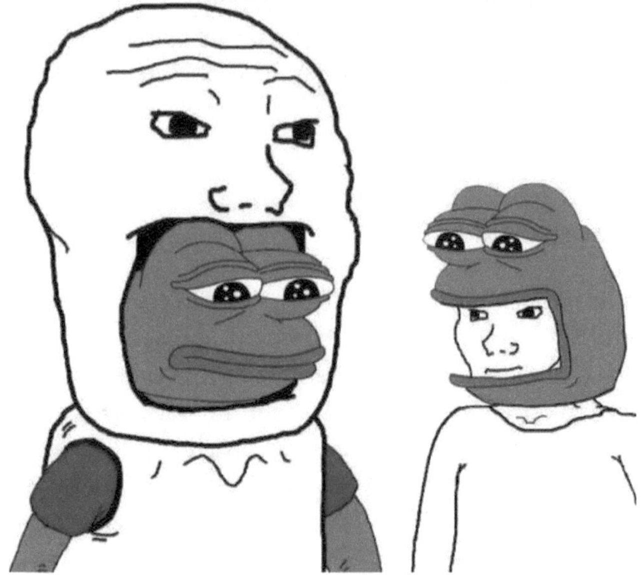

Anon., Pepe i Feels man u Cosplay-u, 2012.

pokreti nastoje da rade u sadejstvu sa kapitalizmom usprkos prikrivanju patnji koje leže u samom srcu kapitalističke društvene reprodukcije. U abjektnim „karakternim maskama" Pepeu i Feels Man-u patnje i poniženja NEETS-a[83] transformiraju se u abjektno-komični duo kojeg čine čovjek koji osjeća previše i žaba koja se samo „osjeća dobro". Kultura gikova ovdje izražava prokletstvo viška života a bolno shvatanje rascjepljuje subjekt na dvoje: na lijevoj strani je gubitnik koji osjeća previše, a na desnoj veliki drkadžija koji ne osjeća ništa. Nesretni par

---

82. Mark Hay, 'A Scientist Explains Why Alt-Right Milk Chugging Is Idiotic', februar 2016, *http://www.extracrispy.com/culture/2167/a-scientist-explains-why-alt-right-milk-chugging-is-idiotic*

83. Pepe i Feels Man (ili Feels Guy, Wojak) – meme, crtani likovi koji kruže netom reprezentirajući određena stanja, stavove, paradoksalne situacije: prvi je lik žapca, drugi ćelavog čovjeka blagog izraza lica, i jedan i drugi nacrtani svedenim linijama u MS paintu; NEETS – kratica: Not in Education, Employment, or Training, koja označava mlade ljude koji nisu ni u programima obrazovanja ni zaposleni niti pohađaju kakvu obuku (prim. prev.).

beskrajno igra u ovom ubistvenom rivalitetu na koji su osuđeni. „[A]ko ljudi više ne moraju da se izjednačavaju sa stvarima, njima više neće biti potrebna ni stvarolika nadgradnja a ni nepromjenjiva slika njih samih koja je napravljena prema modelu stvari.“[84] Suveren pomoću privlačenja i iskazivanjem gađenja sprovodi nasilnu integraciju drugih kao i radikalizaciju sopstva. Koji god put da izabere, on ubija, a Pepe nikada neće moći da se riješi Feels Man-a, jer njih dvojica su odistinski naizmjenični. Subjekt je grupa – mnoštvo – a ne identitet. Porijeklo ovih mema ne leži u bijeloj ili evropskoj moći, već u patnji.[85] Kroz odvratnost spram iskustva kolektivizacije patnje ta patnja prenosi se na druge i to što je moguće nasilnije. Fašizam su također izmislili ljudi. Ipak, što se tiče Pepe-Feelsa (s obzirom da put kojim je moguće pobjeći vodi samo kroz priznavanje postojeće moći i države), njih dvojica ne rastavljaju se na jednog od njih, nego se pretvaraju u ništa – u jedan „lavirint bez središta“.[86] Invaginacija Pepea i Feels Man-a svima na uvid pruža odsustvo bilo kakve posebne ljudske suštine, i upravo tu je zakopana *gola tajna* ne-identiteta ali i forma žaljenja za ljudskom zajednicom koja bi mogla da je raskrije.

---

84. Theodor W. Adorno, *Negative Dialectics*, citirano prema: Marcel Stoetzler, 'Subject Trouble'. *Philosophy & Social Criticism*, 18 avgust 2016, str. 359.
85. Na primer 'green text stories', vidjeti *https://www.reddit.com/r/greentext/comments/31v5m5/anon_is_sad/*
86. '4chan: The Skeleton Key to the Rise of Trump', op. cit.

BEZ PREDSJEDANA

EIRIK ŠTAJNHOF

Sloboda je uvijek sloboda da se misli drukčije.
- Roza Luksemburg

U ranim godinama prve dekade ovoga vijeka zatekao sam se u zatvoru na mjestu učitelja. Predavao sam jedan intenzivni trotjedni kurs pod nazivom „Radionica o jeziku i mišljenju" za one koji su po prvi put pohađali koledž, a koji su bili zatvoreni u muškom zatvoru sa maksimalnim obezbjeđenjem u Grin Hejvenu, država Njujork. Pejzaž oko zatvora bio je pastoralan. Apalački planinski lanac prolazio je nedaleko. Zatvorske zidine probijale su se iz okolnog zelenila, što je bio prizor koji je uvijek izazivao grudvicu straha u mom stomaku. Bilo je kasno ljeto, vrelo i vlažno, a prozori naše učionice nisu se otvarali. Da bismo do nje stigli morali smo da prođemo kroz dugi tunel zidan blokovima od šljake koji su klimu činili samo gorom, ma kakvo vrijeme bilo. Radovao sam se odlasku na taj posao.

Na ovom poprištu poučavanja, u uslovima koji su vladali u jednoj popravnoj ustanovi, mnogo smo čitali i sve vrijeme zajedno pravili bilješke u našim sveskama. Provodili smo po pet sati dnevno, pet dana tjedno, a čitali smo Darvina i Kafku, Hanu Arent i *Antigonu*, „Pismo iz birmingemskog zatvora" kao i dijelove *Strukture naučnih revolucija*. Proučavali smo povezanost riječi i mišljenja, anomalije i paradigme, običaja i navike, preobražaja i revolucije, *poisesisa* i *praxisa*. Tokom našeg drugog tjedna predstavio sam jedan tekst i plan predavanja koji sam preuzeo od svoje prijateljice i koleginice Emili Abendrot (Emily Abendroth), koja je predavala isti taj kurs na drugoj obali rijeke Hadson studentima zatvorenim na istoku.

Predavanje se odnosilo na snažan odgovor Petra Kropotkina socijalnom darvinizmu koji je iznio na početku svoje knjige *Uzajamna pomoć*.[1] Ono što je bio ulog ove Kropotkinove ispravke bio je, ni manje ni više, nego odnos između prirodnih zakona i zakona kulture. On se sa svojim sabesjednicima (među kojima su, pored Darvina, još i Herbert Spenser [Spencer] i Tomas Haksli [Thomas Huxley]) slaže u tome da su ovi zakoni povezani, te da ono što je prirodno i ono što je kulturno nisu toliko odvojene stvari kao što nas to antropocentrična isključivost može nagnati da pomislimo. Ali on se ne slaže, i to veoma snažno, sa opisom prirodnih zakona kakav daju socijalni darvinisti. Zato što su ponudili

---

1. Peter Kropotkin, *Mutual Aid: A Factor of Evolution*, New York: McClure Phillips & Co, 1902.

pogrešan opis prirodnih zakona, oni nisu mogli ni zakone kulture opisati kako valja. U svom predgovoru Kropotkin posebno odbacuje njihovu primjenu „borbe za opstanak" kakvu Darvin opisuje u svijetu prirode na društveni svijet u kom mi živimo. Prema Kropotkinovom mišljenju konceptualni monopol koji socijalni darvinisti pridaju „borbi za opstanak" i preuveličava i iskrivljuje ono što je Darvin nazivao „širokim i metaforičkim smislom" u kom je ovu frazu trebalo razumjeti. Kako Kropotkin kaže, socijalni darvinisti „sveli" su Darvinovu heurističku metaforu na „svijet opetovane borbe između polugladnih pojedinaca, uzajamno žednih krvi onih drugih" (4). Ali, nastavlja on dalje, i sam Darvin je pokazao na koji način je *„borba* zamijenjena *saradnjom,* i na koji način ta zamjena rezultira razvojem intelektualnih i moralnih sposobnosti koje vrstama osiguravaju najbolje uslove za opstanak" (2). Nasuprot uzimanja za uzor gladijatorskog individualizma, što čine socijalni darvinisti, i protiv osiromašujućih ekonomskih opravdavanja koja izvlače iz svog opisa prirode kao bojnog polja, Kropotkin stavlja ono što on naziva „uzajamna pomoć", kolektivnim i kooperativnim procesom koji opisuje kao *„zakon prirode i glavni faktor evolucije",* a svoj argument podupire velikim brojem dokaza kako iz prirodne tako i iz kulturne istorije. (6).

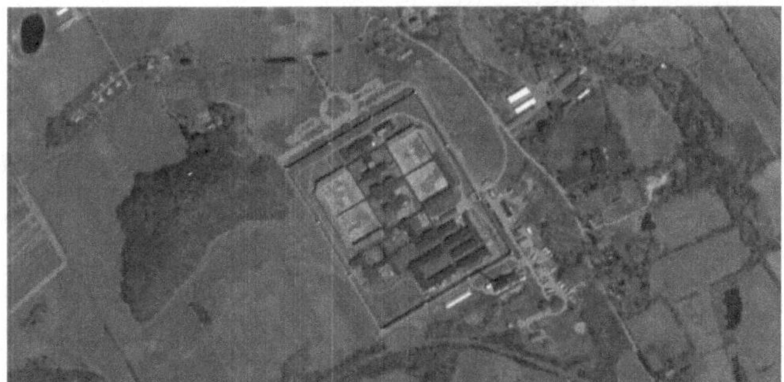

Popravna ustanova Grin Hejven (Bikmen, Njujork)

Mi nismo iščitavali cijelu ovu knjigu u našoj učionici pod maksimalnim obezbjeđenjem, već samo te uvodne polemičke dijelove u kojima smo analizirali i rašlanjavali riječi mnogih redaka na kojima je počivala Kropotkinova argumentacija i sve to vrijeme smo vodili bilješke u našim sveskama. Prvog dana predavanja rekao sam kako shvatam pisanje kao način izgradnje formi mišljenja koje je inače teško izraziti drugim sredstvima. I priznao sam im i to da stvarno jeste donekle čudno kada se to radi u društvu. Ali, isto tako, rekao sam i to kako shvatam da ovo

MUTUAL AID
A FACTOR OF EVOLUTION

BY

P. KROPOTKIN
AUTHOR OF
THE GREAT FRENCH REVOLUTION," ETC.

pisanje na času, koje se tiče kompliciranih tekstova, ujedno predstavlja i način kolektivizacije naše ranjivosti, deprivatizacije nečega za šta nas naša kultura obično uči da iskušavamo sami.[2]

Potanko smo ispitali primjere iz prvog poglavlja knjige o 'Uzajamnom pomaganju među životinjama' do u detalje se zanimajući za Kropotkinov detaljan opis ponašanja prilikom hranjenja kod mrava koji naučnici nazivaju „trofalaksom" (što potiče od grčkih riječi *tropho* [hranjenje] + *allaxis* [razmjena]):

> dva mrava koja pripadaju istom leglu ili istoj koloniji legala prići će jedan drugom, razmijeniti nekoliko dodira antenama i „ukoliko je jedan od njih gladan ili žedan, a posebno ako onaj drugi nosi sakupljen urod [...] on će od njega odmah zatražiti hranu". Onaj pojedinac koji je na ovaj način upitan nikada ne odbija zahtjev; on otvara svoju vilicu, zauzima odgovarajući položaj i izbacuje iz sebe kap providne tečnosti koju gladni mrav liže. To izbacivanje hrane za druge mrave zauzima tako istaknuto mjesto u njihovom životu [...] i ono se toliko često ponavlja, bilo da je riječ o hranjenju gladnih drugova ili hranjenju larvi, da je [entomolog] Forel smatrao kako je kanal za varenje kod mrava sastavljen iz dva odvojena dijela od kojih

---

2. U ovoj posebnoj institucionaliziranoj prilici (predavanje sam držao u ime Inicijative iz Bard zatvora), praksu posvećivanja dijela vremena na predavanju za zajedničko pisanje uveo je Piter Elbou (Peter Elbow), a radikalno ju je proširila i izmijenila Džoan Retalak (Joan Retallack). Tamo gdje Elbou naglašava populistički imperativ projekta poučavanja pisanja, Retalak vidi načine na koje taj imperativ nikako ne smije da bude u nesuglasju (kako se to ponekad pogrešno razumijevalo) sa rigoroznim i razigranim estetskim, intelektualnim i političkim istraživanjima.

jedan, onaj koji se nalazi natrag, ima posebnu namjenu da služi
jedinki, dok drugi, onaj koji je naprijed, uglavnom služi za potrebe
zajednice. (12-13)

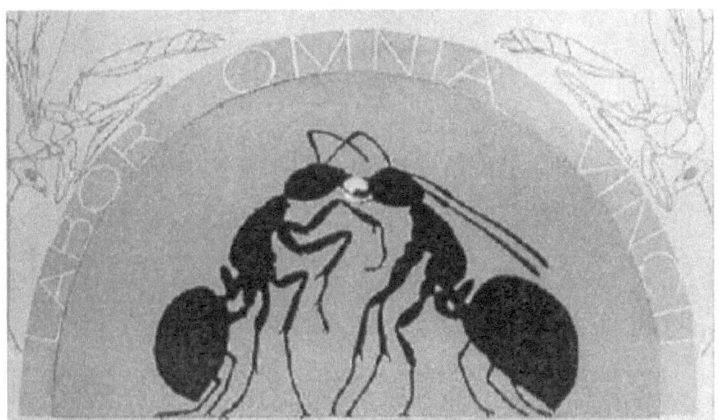

Detalj sa naslovne strane Avgusta Forela, Le Monde Social des
Fourmis (Libraire Kundig 1921)

Od tog trenutka naša radionica o jeziku i mišljenju malo je skrenula
u svojoj izvedbi u odnosu na to kako je zamišljena. Došlo je vrijeme da
se pozabavimo pisanjem – izravno. Brzina promjene podrazumijevala je
jedan misaoni eksperiment koji je uključivao gotovo naučnofantastični
scenario:

> Šta bi se desilo kada bi ljudi, baš kao i ti mravi, bili opremljeni
> jednim takvim podijeljenim organom čija bi jedna polovina, kako to
> opisuje Kropotkin, „uglavnom služila za potrebe zajednice", dok bi
> druga polovina bila namijenjena „za posebne potrebe jedinke".
> Uzmite si pet minuta i napišite ono što ste zamislili.

I dok je većina studenata u Grin Hejvenu spremno dala sebi oduška u
ovlašćenjima koja im je ova vježba omogućila (iznoseći prijedloge o
tronogoj rasi, zajedničkim očima, mozgu, džepovima za hranu na našim
šakama i tome slično), a nekolicina se hrabro borila sa tim zahtjevom
(„*šta* vi to tačno želite da ja zamislim?" upitao je jedan od njih bez
uvijanja, opirući se tako ludosti samog poziva), bio je tu i jedan student
koji je bez teškoća istog trenutka shvatio jednostavnu istinu da je *sam
jezik* ljudski organ koji se najbolje može opisati kao djelimični zaštitnik
pojedinačnog i djelimični zaštitnik onog zajedničkog. I koliko je on
vidio, tu nije bilo ničeg nategnutog; nije se radilo čak ni o metafori.
Štaviše, rekao je, čak je i otvor o kome se radilo, usta, bio isti – iako je
precizna priroda metabolizma u mnogome drukčija.

Kada se danas osvrnem, tačnost ovog uvida potpuno je očigledna, ali me je on u to vrijeme u potpunosti iznenadio. Na koji način bismo mogli smatrati jezik „zajedničkim organom" koji igra operativnu ulogu i u kolektivnom i u pojedinačnom ljudskom metabolizmu?

Hans Džonas (Hans Jonas) određuje „metabolizam" kao „razmjenu materije sa okruženjem"[3] koju sprovodi neki organizam. Marks opisuje „rad" kao „proces između čoveka i prirode, proces u kome čovek svojom sopstvenom aktivnošću omogućuje, reguliše i nadzire svoju razmenu [*metabolism*] materije sa prirodom".[4]

Ono što bismo ovom prilikom mogli nazvati „Kropotkin-Grin Hejvenovom dopunom" ovim određenjima je iskaz prema kome je *jezik* najbolje sredstvo pomoću koga se ovo kolektivno ljudsko reguliranje metabolizma (izbacivanje iz sebe) posreduje, uređuje i kontrolira.

Ako rad predstavlja način na koji mi „omogućujemo, reguliramo i nadziremo" svoju „razmjenu materije sa [našim] okruženjem", onda je jezik način na koji „omogućujemo, reguliramo i nadziremo" svoje međusobne odnose – to jest, naše odnose sa nama samima. Jezik je primarno sredstvo kojim stvaramo i mijenjamo ove odnose: sa svima drugima (kultura) i sa svijetom u kojem živimo (priroda). Ja se brinem da mi ubrzano gubimo trag ove jednostavne činjenice – i da za posljedicu toga imamo brutalnu prisilu kako između sebe tako i u odnosu na prirodu.

Morao sam da odem u zatvor kako bi ova moć jezika privukla moju pažnju.

Pjesma, kako je ja vidim, ono je što nas ponovo povezuje sa ovom moći.

§

Temeljna odgovornost koju ima pjesma jeste da stvori i održi jedan prostor želje u jeziku. „Plod nije *gnosis* već to mora biti *praxis*", kako je još u 1580-im tvrdio Filip Sidnej (Philip Sidney).[5] Ono što poezija proizvodi po ovom iskazu nije znanje nego akcija. Ali daleko od toga da

---

3. Hans Jonas, *The Phenomenon of Life: Toward a Philosophical Biology*, Evanston, Illinois: Northwestern University Press, 1966, str. 79.

4. Karl Marx, *Capital*, vol. 1, (prev. Ben Fowkes), New York: Vintage, 1976, str. 283. [BCHS izdanje: Karl marks, *Kapital*, (prev. Moša Pijade i Rodoljub Čolaković), Beograd: Bigz i Prosveta, 1973, str. 163. – riječ dodata u uglastoj zagradi, *metabolism*, riječ je koja je korištena u engleskom prijevodu, a u našem je to *razmjena*; ostavio sam je kako bi naredni pasusi bili jasniji (prim. prev.)]

se ovdje radi o igri nultog zbira. Elejn Skeri (Elaine Scarry) tvrdi da je „navika ono što podjarmljuje misao i akciju zajedno", a kako ja shvatam Sidneja on *praxis* shvata upravo u ovom smislu.[6] U svojoj najširoj verziji pitanje koje ja ovdje želim postaviti moglo bi glasiti: *kako predstavljamo ono nepredstavljivo?* Pitanje izvedeno iz ovoga bilo bi: *kako usiljavamo to nepredstavljivo?* I, ako mi je dozvoljeno da zloupotrijebim nedavno tvitovani neologizam: *šta bi to značilo biti bez preDsJedana?*

U ovom eseju želim pjesmu zamisliti kao jednu „afordansu"[7] (affordance) u smislu kakav joj daje psiholog percepcije Dž. Dž. Gibson (J. J. Gibson). „*Afordanse* okruženja" (kako ih opisuje Gibson) „su ono što ono *nudi* životinji, ono što ono *obezbjeđuje* ili *isporučuje*, bilo to dobro ili rđavo".[8] Svaka procjena odnosa između nekog organizma i njegovog okruženja tako se transformira isticanjem iznad svega „mogućnosti-akcije" – ili onoga što Sidnej naziva *praxisom*. Rukovodeći se primjerom Donalda Normana, dizajneri su prenijeli Gibsonovu teoriju afordansi i primijenili je u rekonceptualizaciji objekata. U ovom svjetlu, ono što neka stvar jeste može se razumjeti ne više polazeći od onoga što se o njoj može saznati, već uzimajući u obzir ono za šta ona može da se iskoristi.[9] Za one koji kažu „Pjesma ne treba da znači / nego da bude" (kako glasi slavna izjava Arčibalda Mekleiša [Archibald MacLeish]), one koji bi da na pjesmu gledaju kao na odgovor na afordansu, „značenje neke riječi njena je upotreba" (kako tvrdi Vitgenštajn [Wittgenstein]).[10] Umjesto što računamo neku pjesmu samo u kategorijama njenih formalnih svojstava, što je način na koji nas uče još u školi (metrika, rima, dikcija i sl.), trebalo bi da obratimo pažnju i na to koje sve

---

5. Philip Sidney, *An Apology for Poetry, or The Defence of Poesy*, Manchester: Manchester University Press, 1973, str. 94.
6. Elaine Scarry, *Thinking in an Emergency*, New York: W.W. Norton, 2012, str. 80.
7. Pojam *affordance* uveo je psiholog Džejms Gibson (James J. Gibson) u svom članku iz 1977. godine, 'The Theory of Affordances'. On definira *affordances* kao sve „mogućnosti za akciju" koje su latentne u okruženju, objektivno mjerljive i neovisne o umnoj moći jedinke da ih prepozna, ali su uvijek u relaciji prema agensima i samim tim ovisne o njihovim sposobnostima. Pojam se upotrebljava u ekološkoj teoriji i u komunikologiji. Doslovno bi to značilo *donosnost*, u smislu onoga što nam neka sredina donosi, ali kako nisam našao neki adekvatan prijevod odlučio sam koristiti se uslovnim neoanglicizmom *afordansa* dok me naša agilna teorija ne opovrgne (prim. prev.).
8. J.J. Gibson, *The Ecological Approach to Visual Perception*, Hillsdale, N.J.: Lawrence Erlbaum Associates, 1986 (1979), str. 127.
9. Donald Norman, *The Design of Everyday Things*, New York: Doubleday, 1990.

mogućnosti za akciju ona oslobađa, ma kakve da su okolnosti u kojima se trenutno zatiče.

Pinta možda jeste prozirna zasječena staklena kupa zatvorena diskom na svom manjem kraju, ali ono što ona „donosi" jeste mogućnost zadržavanja pića koje netko može progutati kada njen otvoreni kraj nagne ka svojim ustima. Drugim riječima, akcija koju omogućava jedna pinta je pijenje. To je funkcija za koju je ona stvorena. Ali nju također možete iskoristiti i da pomoću nje nacrtate dve kružnice različitih veličina, ukoliko poželite tako što. Kada se razbije, njen dio može postati sječivom. Ali šta je to što može donijeti jedna pjesma, bilo svojim stvaranjem bilo njegovim prekoračenjem? I šta nas to pjesme uče o tome, i općenito ali i nešto posebičnije, o tome kako učiniti nešto sa riječima?

Dž. L. Ostin (J. L. Austin) obznanio je kako se govorni činovi u pjesmama ne računaju: „Ako pjesnik kaže 'Idi i uhvati zvijezdu padalicu' ili šta god drugo da je posrijedi, on ne izdaje neku stvarnu naredbu".[11] Mislim da nisam jedini koji ne razumije zbog čega su naredbe u pjesmama po definiciji „parazitske" ili „izblijedjele", a time i neprikladne.[12] Članak Čarlsa Altijerija (Charles Altieri) o „demonstrativnom iskazivanju" sadrži cijeli niz plodnih uvida o ovom pitanju:

> Pjesme ostvaruju ono što je jezik u stanju kada je riječ o artikuliranju pojedinih stanja (*states*), i to ostvarenje nam zauzvrat omogućava pristup da zamišljamo uslovne identifikacije koje možemo nastojati da usvojimo u okolnostima u kojima se nalazimo – što nije tek posljedica iskušavanja teksta već posljedica prilagođavanja tog iskustva svijetu tako što ćemo iskušati sličnosti i razlike koje nam on dozvoljava da pobliže odredimo.[13]

---

10. Archibald MacLeish, *Collected Poems, 1917-1982*, Boston: Houghton Mifflin, 1985, str. 107; Ludwig Wittgenstein, *Philosophical Investigations,* (prev. G.E.M. Anscombe), New York: Palgrave MacMillan 1958, §43. [BCHS izdanja: Ludvig Vitgenštajn, *Filozofska istraživanja* (prev. Ksenija Maricki Gađanski), Beograd: Nolit, 1980, §43; Ludwig Wittgenstein, *Filozofijska istraživanja,* (prev. Igor Mikecin), Zagreb: Nakladni zavod Globus, 1998, §43]

11. J. L. Austin, *Philosophical Papers,* Oxford: Clarendon Press, 1961, str. 241.

12. J. L. Austin, *How to Do Things with Words,* Oxford: Clarendon Press, 1962, str. 22. [BCHC izdanja: Dž. L. Ostin, *Kako delovati rečima* (prev. Milorad Radovanović), Novi Sad : Matica srpska, 1994, str. 32; J. L. Austin, *Kako djelovati riječima* (prev Andrea Milanko), Zagreb : Disput, 2014.]

Altijeri misli na afektivna „stanja" (*states*), ali ja ne vidim zbog čega ne bismo razmatrali načine na koje pjesme također mogu i da „ostvare ono što jezik može da uradi povodom toga da određene *nacije*-države (*nation*-states) učini *ne*artikuliranim". Ovom Altijerijevom retoričkom ozdravljenju pjesme koji dolazi sa druge strane modernističkog estetskog rascjepa, predlažem da dodamo uvid Stenlija Kavela (Stanley Cavell) o „strastvenom iskazivanju" i da od njih napravimo mješavinu:

> Performativno iskazivanje je jedna ponuda da se učestvuje u poretku zakona. A možda možemo reći: strastveno iskazivanje je poziv na improvizaciju u neredima želje.[14]

Ovaj „poziv na improvizaciju" dozvoljava nam da neko djelo „demonstartivnog iskazivanja" posmatramo prilikom kakvih demonstracija ili u trenutku izbijanja pobune – tim prizorištima političke želje, kako bismo mogli da ih nazovemo.

Sonet Kloda Mekeja (Claude McKay) koji počinje stihovima „Ako već moramo umrijeti, daj da ne umiremo k'o krmad" pruža nam jedan grubi primjer kako demonstrativnog tako i strastvenog iskazivanja. Iako je prvi put ispjevan za vrijeme linčeva i pobuna tokom krvave 1919, sonet je kružio i među zarobljenicima iz Atike prije pobune i masakra iz 1971. godine.[15] Militantna samoodbrana artikulirana u jednom političkom okruženju, koja koristi poetsku formu obično povezanu sa ljubavnim djelima i strastima, doprinosi transformacijama mogućnosti u jednom potpuno drugačijem (iako ne i nepovezanom) političkom okruženju.

Imajući na umu poli-istorijsku afordansu Mekejeve pjesme, kao i transformaciju u afordanse forme koju ona sobom donosi, želim da iz Kavelovog proširenja Ostina ishodujem dozvolu da nadogradim iskaze Gibsona i Normana. Tamo gdje nam koncept afordanse dopušta da odnos između nekog organizma i objekata iz njegovog okruženja razumijemo u smislu mogućnosti koju taj odnos pruža za akciju, koncept *transfordantnosti* (*transfordance*) mogao bi nam omogućiti da u tim mogućnostima za akciju razmotrimo koje bi to transformacije bile

---

13. Charles Altieri, 'What Theory Can Learn from New Directions in Contemporary American Poetry', *New Literary History*, 2012, Br. 43, str. 80.
14. Stanley Cavell, *Philosophy the Day after Tomorrow*, Cambridge, MA: Harvard University Press, 2006, str. 185.
15. Pjesma je rasprostranjena onlajn, ako je niste čitali. O njenim mnoštvenim istorijatima vidjeti: Jordan T. Camp, *Incarcerating the Crisis: Freedom Struggles and the Rise of the Neoliberal State*, Berkeley CA: University of California Press, 2016, str. 74.

poželjne. Afordanse dopuštaju analitičaru da shvati povezanost između organizma i okruženja ne toliko u smislu formalnih osobenosti koliko u smislu mogućih aktivnosti; transfordantnosti pružaju agentu da transformira uslove tih mogućnosti na prvom mjestu transformiranjem te povezanosti između organizma i okruženja. To je jedna vrsta djelovanja za koje bih volio da mislim da ga je pjesma kadra izvesti: da transformira uslove za sreću. „Iznošenje iskazivanja", dakle, otuda postaje ne tek „performiranje akcije" (kako to opisuje Ostin) već također i transformiranje uslova koje govorenje i činjenje čine jednakima.[16]

Otuda i kažem da je pjesma jedna afordansa, kako je definira Gibson: potencijal za akciju. Ali na ovom mjestu htio bih obrazložiti da to znači i stvaranje afordansi, ali i njihovu transformaciju. I – i. I umjesto da pjesmu razmatrmo samo u pogledu njene forme – njenih unutarnjih i vanjskih elemenata koji samo leže i čekaju da ih se analizira – trebalo bi da obratimo pažnju i na ono što neka pjesma čini mogućim, na vrstu akcije koju njena forma izvodi, djela koja njene riječi sugeriraju, ma koliko implicitno ili eksplicitno to bilo. Ovo čini pjesmu ne samo nekim „performativnim", „demonstrativnim" ili pak „strastvenim" iskazivanjem u smislu koji joj pripisuju Ostin, Altijeri i Kavel, već se tu također radi i o jednom *transformativnom iskazivanju*.

Jedno ime za vrstu studije u koju se upuštam je i „poetika", što se može razumjeti ne samo u standardnom smislu studije o činjenju (korijen riječi „pjesma" potiče od grčkog glagola *poiein*, „učiniti"), već i u proširenom smislu studije o transformaciji (kako je to predložio Statis Gurguris [Stathis Gourgouris]).[17] U mjeri u kojoj činjenje podrazumijeva formiranje, ono isto tako zahtijeva i transformiranje. Vrsta poetike kakvu ja ovdje predlažem, dakle, računa i sa transformacijom našeg shvatanja poetike. I dok jedna estetika i poetika koja je usmjerena na formu nužno u svojoj analitičkoj i interpretativnoj alatnici sadrži i morfologiju, estetika i poetika usmjerena na formu *i* transformaciju sadrži kako morfologiju tako i ono što bismo mogli nazvati

---

16. *How to Do Things with Words*, op. cit., str. 6. (Kako delovati rečima, op. cit., str. 16-17)
17. Stathis Gourgouris, 'The *Poiein* of Secular Criticism', u: Ali Behdad, Dominic Richard and David Thomas (Ur.), *A Companion to Comparative Literature*, Chichester, West Sussex; Malden, MA: Wiley-Blackwell: Blackwell, 2011, str. 78-80.

metamorfologijom, koju uvodim kako bih naglasio značaj teorije i prakse transformiranja uslova mogućnosti.

§

Ovaj esej dotiče se polja istraživanja koje sam otvorio sa svoja tri eseja objavljena pred kraj 2015. godine kojima sam pokušao da promislim definiciju sabotaže koju je ponudila Elizabet Gerlej Flin [Elizabeth Gurley Flynn] prema kojoj je ona „svjesni opoziv industrijske učinkovitosti radnika", s jedne strane, i analizu Generalnog štrajka Roze Luksemburg, sa druge, a sve u vezi sa shvatanjem V. H. Odena [W. H. Auden] prema kome „poezija čini to da se ništa ne desi" i definiciji pjesme Paula Celana prema kome je pjesma „ono što ne odgovara mjeri".[18] Motivacija za pisanje ovih eseja bila je šarolika: placibo efekt, stihovi poezije koji su uzvikivani kao slogani na Trgu Tahrir 2011. godine, ponovno uprizorenje štrajka iz 1913. ovoga puta kao predstave. A na koji bi to tačno način jedna pjesma mogla „učiniti da se ništa ne desi", ako je njeno izvođenje usmjereno na drugu stranu od one koju nam nudi ustaljena forma, kultivirajući tako i čineći održivim ono što je prema standardnim ocjenama smatrano za nemoguće? Eseji su crpli dosta toga iz mojih iskustava iz blizine buntovne Ouklandske komune (iliti Ocuppy Oakland) sa kraja 2011. i početka 2012. godine, gdje sam bio zauzet na prvom mjestu sastavljanjem i širenjem pamfleta pod nazivom *Gnjevni leteći valjak* (*A Fiery Flying Roule*).

Jedan od eseja iz ove trilogije o sabotaži zaključujem naliježući na riječ „difolt" ('default'):

> U jednu ruku (nazovimo ovu finansijskom) biti „u difoltu" znači ostati nekako kratak, izostajući, na primjer, sa redovnim izmirivanjima svog studentskog zajma. U drugu ruku (nazovimo ovu tehnološkom), „postavka po difoltu" je ono stanje koje je prvotno: to vaš mobilni telefon prije nego što ste ga sjebali svim silnim škart aplikacijama. „Difolt" tako može značiti i pogrešno stanje kao i ono koje je postojalo prije greške. Drugim riječima, djeluje kako biti „u difoltu" znači naći se na suprotnom mjestu od onoga u kom se

---

18. The Anomaly Contains the Homily: Placebo & *Poiesis'*, *Floor: A Journal of Aesthetic Experiments*, 2015; 'Making Nothing Happen: poetry and sabotage', *Postmedieval*, vol.6, br.4, 2015, str. 417-428; 'The Difference is Spreading: Sabotage and Aesthetics', *Black Box: A Record of the Catastrophe* Br.1, 2015, str. 71-80.

Fiery Flying Roule:

TO

All the Inhabitants of the earth; ſpecially to the rich ones.

NEXT TIME A NEW RIOT ACT WILL BE READ :

We hereby declare this to be a most awesome assembly. In the name of the people of this place — which is to say: IN OUR OWN SOVEREIGN NAME *— we command you to immediately* LEAVE US THE FUCK ALONE. *If you do not do so, your violence may be repelled, your authority will be mocked (which may result in a permanent feeling of humiliation), and we know for a fact that the injuries you inflict upon our persons shall afflict each of your souls for the remainder of your days. We prohibit you from fucking with our most awesome assembly. If you attempt to arrest us, history shall prove your folly absolute. If you do not leave,* LYRICAL AGENTS *will be used, which may result in unmitigatable sensations of bliss.* GO HOME. *We liberate you in the power of, well: in the power of* YOU *declared by* WE *in our sovereign autonomy.* WE COMMAND YOU TO BE FREE OF YOUR COMMANDS *& remind you above all to* LEAVE US THE FUCK ALONE.

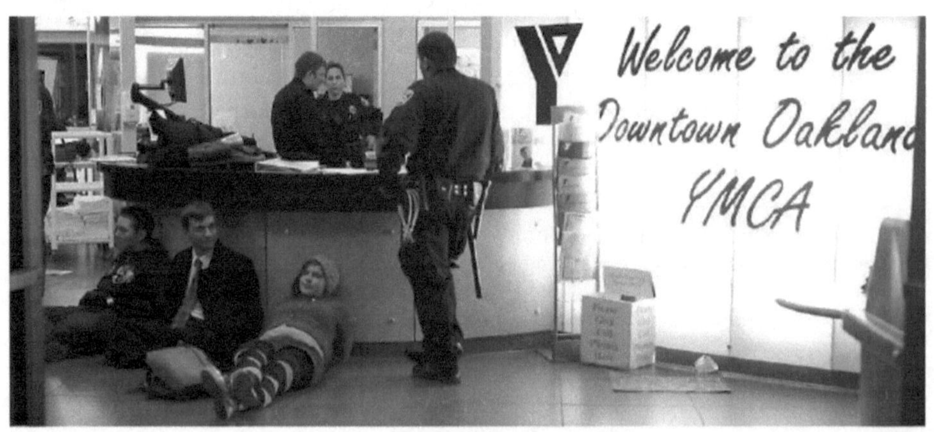

nalazite kada ste „po difoltu". Prilično sam siguran da se u ovoj dvosmislici krije jedan radikalni potencijal samo ako shvatimo kako da zajednički do njega dođemo.

Pitanje sa kojim bih da vas ostavim je: *koje – ili gdje – su naše difolt postavke?*[19]

Kropotkin-Grin Hejvenova dopuna – prema kojoj je *jezik* sredstvo kojim naš kolektivni ljudski metabolizam (iliti „rad") omogućen, reguliran i nadziran – pojavljuje mi se sada kao veoma jak kandidat za odgovor na to pitanje.

U jednom skorijem eseju na koji su mi pažnju prvi skrenuli urednici ovog izdanja, Endnote pišu

U slučaju greške, sredstvima kojima raspolažemo manjka projektovanih krajnjih ishoda, pa greška sa kojom se suočavamo imenuje i ovaj manjak mogućnosti. [...] [I] čim netko pokuša nešto što nije dato afordansama svijeta, stanje greške – kao mjerilo za ovu nesposobnost – obavezno se pojavljuje. Ali, jednim rekonstruktivnim naporom, grešku je možda moguće postepeno potisnuti natrag u njene granice, oslobađajući time prostor mogućnosti.[20]

Ono na šta se ja ovdje kladim je da pjesme mogu biti naprave za stvaranje prostora mogućnosti koji se pojavljuje kao posljedica grešaka kako ih opisuju Endnote – za izmještanje našeg *difolta*, a također i za njegovo resetiranje.

§

U ovoj tački, zreli smo za primjer, za ono „na primjer", kako bismo ove apstraktne propozicije učinili nešto konkretnijima. Dozvolite mi onda da ubacim žeton u poker-aparat:

Ovo je bio jedan od na hiljade novčića koji su kružili po Engleskoj prije otprilike jednog vijeka, što je bila samo trunka u zajedničkoj borbi za opća prava glasa. Evo malog prikaza atmosfere, kako je opisuje Etel Smit (Ethel Smyth):

---

19. 'Making Nothing Happen', op. cit., str. 424.
20. Endnotes, 'Error', *Bad Feelings*, London: Bookworks, 2016, bez broja str.

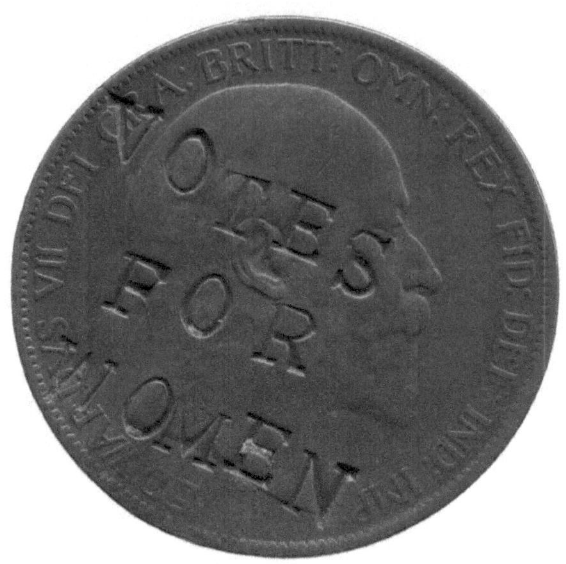

Tačno u 5.30 jedne večeri za pamćenje 1912. godine, grupe žena načinile su čekiće od svojih mufova i ručnih torbica, i metodično počele da razbijaju izloge na svim velikim londonskim saobraćajnicama – na Pikadiliju, u Ulici Ridžent i tako dalje. One su na taj čin bile inspirisane spoznajom da je baš u tom trenutku gca Pankherst (Pankhurst) otvorila bal jednim kamenom kojim je naciljala prozor u Ulici Dauning na broju 10.[21]

Ovo nam govori ponešto o okruženju u kome su novčići kakav je bio ovaj kružili. Druge akcije i događaji u ovoj epizodi uključuju i bombe u poštanskim sandučićima, masovna hapšenja, štrajkove glađu i mučeničku smrt Emili Dejvidson (Emily Davidson) koja je skončala pod kopitama kraljevog konja na Derbiju.

Ali ja bih se ovom prilikom skoncentrirao na sa sam predmet, a posebno na riječi koje su i urezbarene (crtežom) i utisnute (protiv zakona) na njegovoj površini.

Jezik duž oboda prikazuje čitavu jednu političku kosmologiju podržanu božanskom sankcijom. Skraćeni latinski ovdje se prevodi kao „Edvard VII milošću Boga Kralj cijele Britanije branitelj vjere Imperator

---

21. „Novčić koji su nagrdile sifražetkinje" ('Suffragette-defaced penny'), 95. epizoda BBC-jeve emisije *A History of the World in 100 Objects*, 2010, transkript arhiviran na: *http://www.bbc.co.uk/ahistoryoftheworld/about/transcripts/episode95/*

Britanije“: moćne titule i gorda prava koja kombiniraju drevnu privilegiranost, na jednoj strani, sa imperijalnim širenjem, na drugoj.

Pa šta je onda na stvari sa tim jezikom koji je dodan na novčić?

T. Dž. Klark (T.J. Clark) kaže, „Novac predstavlja temeljnu formu reprezentacije u buržoaskom društvu. Prijetnje monetarnoj vrijednosti prijetnje su onome što one označavaju“.[22] Ureži „V“ u bakar juvelirskom presom za slova. „Novac je neka vrsta poezije“, kako Volas Stivens (Wallace Stevens) kaže u svom djelu *Adagia*.[23] Podesite dršku svog čekića dok ubadate „O“. Šta se dešava ukoliko ovaj novčić shvatimo kao pjesmu? Udari „T“ tik iznad njegovog uha. Mogli bismo prvo poželjeti da razmislimo malo o rodnim konvencijama. Unesimo jedno „E“ na njegovu sljepoočnicu. Marks u *Osnovama kritike političke ekonomije (Grundriesse)* definira novac kao društveni odnos maskiran u metalu. Neka se „S“ ureže u njegov obraz. Vrijednost novca u ovoj prilici potiče iz mreže društvenih odnosa kojima se on prihvata i u kojima se proizvodi kao oblik vrijednosti. „F“ ide u potiljak. Zar nije ono što predstavlja prijetnu značajnosti urezano na površinu tog komadića metala? Poravnaj „R“ sa čeljusti. Zbog jezika koji joj je pridodat, ova posebna novčana jedinica predstavlja neskrivenu strukturu sporazumā na koje smo zaboravili da smo ih uopće i napravili. Ako ti drška sklizne u trenutku kada bi da dodaš jedno „W“, moglo bi to biti i jedno „OMEN“.[24]

Nekoliko ljudi kojima sam u proteklim godinama pokazivao taj novčić, ukazali su mi i na ono „T O O“[25] koje se može vidjeti ako se ima navika slovkanja riječi vertikalno (kao u križaljki ili slovnoj slagalici). Jedan takav nenamjerni ekses činio se veoma prikladnim. Sirova snaga koja je ukucala slogan prekida autoritet latinskih slova izdignut duž ivice čineći mogućim i nehotično i strateško iskrivljeno čitanje riječi slogana. „Pjesma je“, kako kaže Paul Celan, „ono što ne odgovara mjeri“.[26] Ali taj manjak uklopivosti ne predstavlja nikakvu podložnost, i

---

22. T.J. Clark, *Farewell to an Idea: Episodes from a History of Modernism*, New Haven: Yale University Press, 1999, str. 10.
23. Wallace Stevens, *Opus Posthumous*, New York: Knopf, 1989, str. 191.
24. Neprevodiva igra riječi: autor sve vrijeme u ovom pasažu ispisuje krilaticu W.O.T.E.S. F.O.R. W. – OMEN, s tim što ostatak posljednje riječi, kada čekić već sklizne, ima samostalno značenje *„omen“ – znamenje, slutnja, predskazanje* (lat.) (prim. prev.).
25. „Također“, „isto tako“, (prim. prev.).
26. Paul Celan, *The Meridian: Final Version - Drafts - Materials*, (prev. Pierre Joris), Stanford: Stanford University Press, 2011, str. 165.

u ovom slučaju korespondira sa onim *le part sans part* (*dio bez dijelova*) koji Žak Ransijer identificira u središtu „politike": „Politika postoji kroz činjenicu veličine koja izbegava običnoj meri, kroz udeo onih koji nemaju udela i koji je ništa i sve".[27] Takozvane „sifražetkinje" bile su baš to: nužni izuzetak bez kojega nema države-nacije i čijim prezrenjem muškarci određuju politiku.

Slogan sa ovog novčića mogao bi biti pjesma one transfordantne vrste kakvih vjerujem da moramo pisati više – vrsta teksta koji nam dopušta da rekonstituiramo niše koje stvaramo i u kojima živimo skupa. Transformativno iskazivanje. Nije li upravo pogrešno čitanje slogana kao naslova – to jest, uzimajući GLASOVI ZA ŽENE više kao opis nego li zahtjev – sankcionirano istorijskom transformacijom čijem je ubrzanju doprinijelo upravo ponovno štancanje tog novčića? Grešamov (Gresham) zakon tvrdi kako „loš novac crpi dobra". Ali šta se dešava kada „loš novac" prebaci natpis koji nosi i uspije da reorganizira društvene odnose maskirane metalom? Prije stotinu godina ovaj slogan predstavljao je zahtjev; danas u mnogim zemljava on predstavlja opis. Novembra 2016. godine, 65,844,964 građanina SAD glasalo je za ženu.

Ali nemojmo se pretjerano zanositi. Ostavljajući po strani pitanje jačih strana i ograničenja izborne politike, koja je i pored toga takorekuć postignuće tog „glasovi za žene", dobro ćemo uraditi ako primijetimo jednu stvar koju ovo postignuće skriva: razliku u primanja među rodovima. Najbliži grad mjestu u kojem živim (Sijetl) bilježi najveći jaz u primanjima između rodova u Sjedinjenim Državama: žene su plaćene tek 77 centi na svaki dolar koji zaradi muškarac, sa prosječnim gubitkom od 12,000 dolara godišnje po svakoj ženi, čime se ukupni gubitak penje na skoro osam milijardi dolara godišnje. Mogli bismo se pitati zbog čega se naši političari grčevito ne uhvate za ovako nešto. Možda je to i zbog toga što su suviše zauzeti prikupljanjem priloga za kampanju. Članovi Kongresa SAD dnevno provode 2 do 3 sata telefonirajući u pokušaju da prikupe novac. Njihova dnevna kvota koju moraju da ispune je da prikupe između 10,000 i 15,000 dolara – što ugrubo odgovara iznosu *godišnje* razlike u primanjima po glavi

---

27. Jacques Rancière, *Disagreement: Politics and Philosophy*, (prev. Julie Rose), Minneapolis: Minnesota University Press, 1999, str. 15. [BCHS izdanja: Žak Ransijer, *Nesaglasnost: politika i filozofija*, (prev. Ivan Milenković), Beograd: Fedon, 2014, str. 33; Jacques Rancière, *Nesuglasnost: politika i filozofija*, (prev. Leonardo Kovačević), Zagreb: Fakultet političkih znanosti, 2015]

"Here we are" — You can't
hear us without having to be
us knowing everything we

know — you know you can't

Verbal echoes so many ghost
poets I think of you as wild
and fugitive — "Stop awhile"

[Susan Howe, *Souls of the Labadie Tract* (New Directions, 2007), 58]

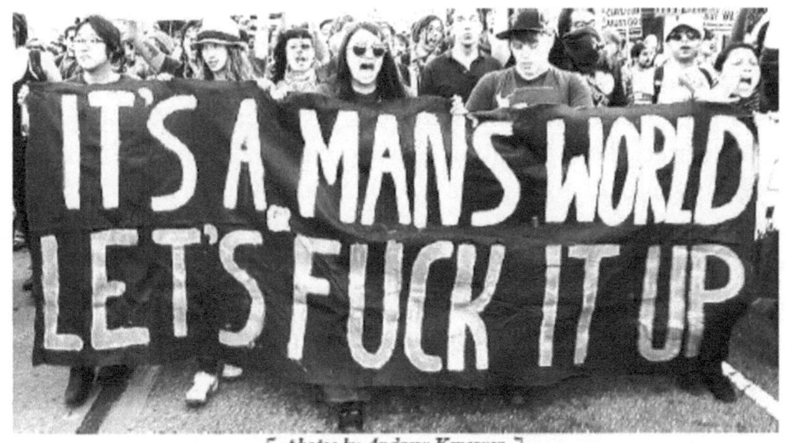

[*photos by Andrew Kenower*]

stanovnika za područje Sijetla... Jeziva podudarnost kao da isplivava. Ima još puno posla. Latite se čekićā.

Ovim želim reći kako mi doprinos ovog sabotiranog novčića u dokazivanju transformacija u uslovima mogućnosti daje za pravo da postavim sljedeće pitanje: kakav bi trebalo da bude vaš slogan koji bi doveo do preobražaja jednog zahtjeva u opis, vaša fraza koja bi pomjerila faze u ovim registrima, koji bi to bio vaš govor koji bi postao jednako vrijedan vašem činjenju?

§

Džejms Risonov (James Reason) „Model švicarskog sira" jedne „putanje udesa"[28] nudi nam vizuelizaciju koja ide protiv naše intuicije, ali koja može da nam pomogne u odgovaranju na ova pitanja:

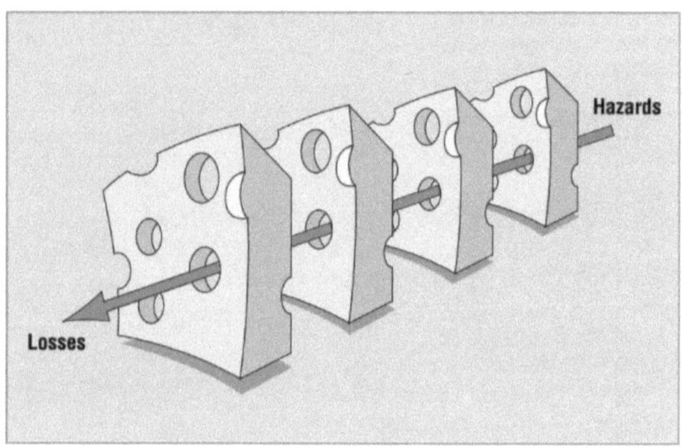

The Swiss cheese model of how defences, barriers, and safeguards may be penetrated by an accident trajectory

Razmotri taj sir. Razmotri kriške. Razmotri sjenke koje se nalaze ispod kriški. Razmotri rupe. Razmotri kako su rupe poslagane. Razmotri kakav je to složen sistem. Razmotri prelom. Razmotri razinu propasti. Razmotri proklizavanja u infrastrukturi, školovanju, pouzdanosti. Razmotri nesreću koja postaje vidljiva kada se naprsline u svakom od tih slojeva pojave u isto vrijeme i poslože jedna uz drugu. Razmotri samo kako se nestručnost, pogreške, bezakonje, loša izrada, loše planiranje svi poravnavaju kako bi uništili tvoj dan, tvoju noć, tvoj tjedan, tvoj mjesec, tvoju godinu, tvoj život. Razmotri kako su

---

28. James Reason, 'Human Error: Models and Management', *British Medical Journal*, Br. 320, 2000, str. 769.

usaglašeni svi aktivni i prikriveni nedostaci. Razmotri bregzit. Razmotri šta si uradio. Razmotri Trampa. Razmotri kako se to desilo. Razmotri kako su se svi sistemi za koje si mislio da će uspješno djelovati kao prepreka protiv slučajnosti zavjerili u stvaranju uslova za mogućnosti baš za onu stvar za koju si bio ubijeđen da ćeš je izbjeći. Razmotri strelicu. Razmotri vektor. Razmotri šiljak. Razmotri penetraciju. Razmotri „Hazarde". Razmotri „Gubitke". Razmotri kako se „Hazardi" pretvaraju u „Gubitke". Razmotri mogućnost koja stvara postojeće. Razmotri transformaciju. Razmotri šta se dešava kada prekrižimo riječ „Gubici" i napišemo riječ „Dobici". Razmotri kako jedna „putanja udesa" može isto tako da posluži za predstavljanje „putanje prilike". Razmotri kako se tvoj zahtjev pretvara u opis. Razmotri kako sada dijagram Razuma postaje izvrstan primjer onoga što su stari Grci nazivali *kairos*. Razmotri neizbježni osjećaj za pravovremenost kojim se raskriva onaj pravi trenutak kada možeš „udjenuti iglu" u atletskom smislu, prohujati mimo ili između odbrane da bi postigao gol, ili u jednom više retoričkom smislu, kada pred publikom konačno zakucavaš slučaj protivno svim šansama. Razmotri filologe koji nam govore kako se za stare Grke *kairos* odnosio ne samo na jednodnevne artefakte poezije ili govorništva, već isto tako i na nešto konkretnije prakse tkanja ili streljaštva.[29]

§

Zahtjev koji u sebi krije opis skrenuo mi je misli na pjesmu Keneta Koha [Kenneth Koch] „Jedan vlak mogao bi sakriti drugi" (za koju je motivaciju dobio od jednog znaka koji je vidio na nekom željezničkom prijelazu u Keniji):

> U pjesmi, jedan stih mogao bi skriti drugi,
> Na prijelazu, jedan bi vlak mogao skriti drugi.
> To jest, ako čekaš da pređeš
> Tračnice, sačekaj za to još jedan tren
> Bar pošto prvi vlak prođe. A i kada čitaš

---

29. Richard Onians, *The Origins of European Thought*, Cambridge, Cambridge University Press, 1951, str. 346. Formu u kojoj je napisan ovaj odjeljak dugujem Metu Longabuku [Matt Longabucco], koji ju je, bar tako mislim, mogao pokupiti od Darvina: „Pogledajte porodicu vjeverica [...]. A sada pogledajte *Galeopithicus* ili letećeg lemura", *On Natural Selection*, New York: Penguin, 2005 (1859), str. 82-3.

Sačekaj dok ne pročitaš naredni stih –
Jer tek tad je sigurno da nastaviš.[30]

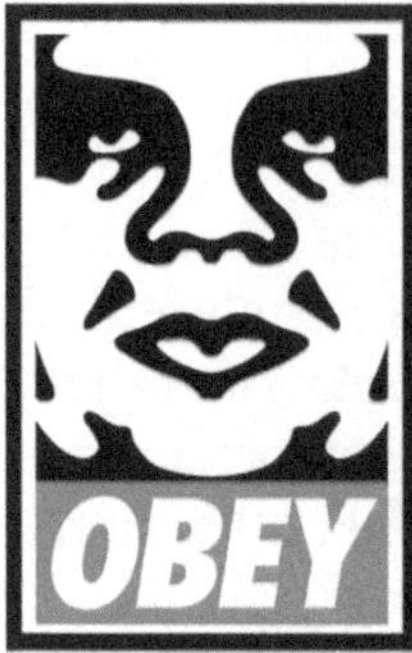

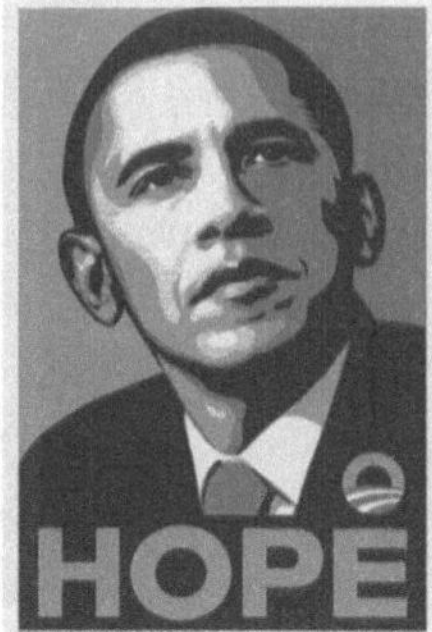

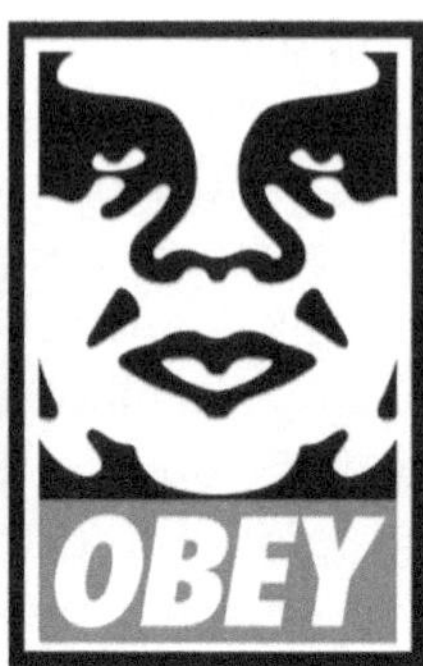

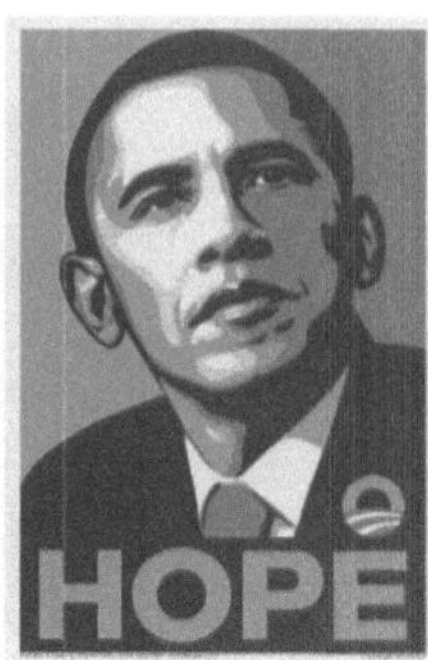

Jedan poster mogao bi da skriva drugi. Slavni poster za kampanju
Baraka Obame iz 2008. godine koji je napravio Šepard Faeri [Shepard
Fairey] ispod sebe ima iscjepanu naljepnicu profesionalnog rvača
poznatog kao Džin Andre. Oba prikazuju stilizirane portrete. Oba su
ispisana riječima od po četiri velika slova. Vjerovatno ste Obamin
poster vidjeli prvi put na internetu. Naljepnica na kojoj je Andre često
se mogla sresti po površinama u Providensu na Rod Ajlendu – po
alejama i „stop" znacima i bilbordima kao i u wc-kabinama po
barovima. Riječ sa dna Obaminog postera predstavlja dvosmislen
termin: imenica koja može skrivati u sebi i glagol. Riječ sa Andreove
naljepnice očigledno je glagol. Ali jedna riječ od četiri slova mogla bi da
sakriva drugu; ono što je Emili Dikinson zvala „pernata stvar" moglo bi
da skriva i jednu naredbu.

   Mogao bi i ovdje biti slučaj da jedan slogan skriva drugi. Iz jednog
pisma prijatelju datiranog na 26. juli 2016. godine:

poslije tjedan dana koje sam proveo udaljen od engleskog jezika,
osjećajući odistinski do koje mjere smo mi 'Meričani osiromašeni
bivajući u svojim hegemonijskim audio-vizuelnim balončićima, bio
sam u stanju da jednu Hilarinu poštapalicu čujem na potpuno novi
način. Ona, sa neumjesnom ontološkom samouvjerenošću, kaže:
„Ljubav pobija mržnju" ('Love trumps hate'). Ali ako niste svjesni da
je riječ pobiti ('trump') glagol, ovaj slogan više bi mogao zaličiti na
naredbu. Drugim riječima, imenice i glagoli lako mogu zamijeniti

---

30. Kenneth Koch, *The Collected Poems of Kenneth Koch*, New York: Knopf, 2007, str.
441-442.

mjesta – što nas dovodi u situaciju da iz ovoga pročitamo jedan posesivni imperativ: „Voli Trampovu mržnju" ('Love Trump's hate'). Slogan nam sada naređuje da obožavamo neprečišćeno preziranje.

Pa šta onda mora da se desi da bi se tvoj opis pretvorio u zahtjev?

§

Roman Jakobson počinje svoje „Završno izlaganje: poezija i poetika" (koje je prvi put pročitano na jednoj akademskoj konferenciji 1958. godine) izjavom „Na svu sreću, akademske i političke konferencije nemaju ništa zajedničko".[31] Ali tek nekoliko pasusa dalje bez ikakvih problema je iskoristio jedan politički slogan kao primjer onoga što je zvao „poetskom funkcijom", sve vrijeme obrazlažući kako bi „Svaki pokušaj da se sfera poetske funkcije svede na poeziju ili da se poezija suzi na poetsku funkciju predstavljao tek varljivo pojednostavljivanje" (356). Ne bih se mogao više složiti sa ovim, ali se već kod istih ovih redaka pitam nije li razgraničavanje akademskog od politike po sebi još jedna greška. Zar ne bi trebalo da je akademska funkcija – činjenje znanja zajedničkim dobrom – biti središnja za političku funkciju – činjenje moći zajedničkim dobrom? Kao da je ovdje promašena putanja prilike koja bi vodila ka otvorenom izvoru sa jednakim pristupom za sve.

Džil Lepor [Jill Lepore] je nedavno uspostavila političko okruženje iz kakvog je Jakobson iščupao svoj nezaboravni primjer:

[G]lasači vrlo lako mogu da budu ošamućeni reklamnim sloganima koji se emituju sa svih strana iz noći u noć. U jednoj televizijskoj reklami iz 1956. godine – koju su napravili politički savjetnici koji su se oslanjali na istraživanja javnog mnijenja – jedan glasač u crtiću očajava „Poslušao sam sve. I na TV-u i na radiju. Pročitao sam novine i časopise. Stvarno sam se potrudio! Ali i dalje sam zbunjen. Tko je u pravu? Šta je ispravno? U šta bi trebalo da vjerujem? Šta su činjenice? Kako da ih razlikujem? Ali partije su vrlo jasno napravile svoj izbor: „Riječi te obasipaju brzo i žestoko", javlja se glasaču iz crtaća utješni glas koji razmatra sve dokaze i na kraju zaključuje, „Meni? Meni se sviđa Ajk!" ('I? I like Ike!')[32]

---

31. Roman Jakobson, 'Closing Statement: Poetry and Poetics', u: Thomas A. Sebeok (ur.), *Style in Language,* Cambridge MA.: MIT Press, 1960, str. 350.
32. Jill Lepore, 'The Party Crashers', *The New Yorker,* 22. februar 2016.

Jakobson svoju pažnju usmjerava upravo na ovaj džingl i koristi ga kako bi izdvojio ono što naziva „empirijskim lingvističkim kriterijumom poetske funkcije." Do nje dolazi oštrom analizom odnosa koje proizvodi zvučna matrica slogana:

> Politički slogan „Meni se sviđa Ajk" ('I like Ike') /aj lajk ajk/, strukturno sažet, sastoji se od tri jednosložne riječi i zbraja tri dvoglasa /aj/, a svaki do njih simetrično je praćen jednim suglasničkim fonemom, /... I ... k ... k/. Izgovaranje ove tri riječi predstavlja varijaciju: bez suglasničkih fonema u prvoj riječi, sa dva koji se nalaze oko dvoglasa u drugoj i jednim završnim suglasnikom u trećoj. [...] Obje kolone trosložne formule 'I like / Ike' rimuju se jedna sa drugom, a druga od dvije riječi koje se rimuju u potpunosti je uključena u prvoj (rima odjeka), /lajk/ – /ajk/, paronomastička slika osjećaja koji u potpunosti opkoljava svoj objekt. Obje kolone ponavljaju jedna drugu, a prva od riječi koje se ponavljaju uključena je u drugu: /aj/ – /ajk/, što je paronomastička slika voljenog subjekta opkoljenog voljenim objektom. Sekundarna poetska funkcija ove izborne parole spaja svoju impresivnost sa učinkovitošću. (357)

Ovdje mi se posebno sviđa ova „paronomastička slika osjećaja koji u potpunosti opkoljava svoj objekt", i dodao bih samo to da je, u ovom posebnom slučaju, „voljeni objekt" izvršni direktor, štaviše on i jeste Glavni i izvršni direktor kako je nadimkom obilježen još od djetinjstva. To nije Dvajt D. Ajzenhauer (Dwight D. Eisenhower), Vrhovni komandant savezničkih snaga za Evropu tokom Drugog svjetskog rata (odgovornog za Dan-D itd.), koji je u svojoj „Završnoj riječi" upućenoj iz Ovalnog kabineta (dvije godine pošto je Jakobson pročitao svoje predavanje) upozorio svoje drage sugrađane o opasnostima ogromnih vojnih troškova i privatizacije za koju je prozvao „vojno-industrijski kompleks". Ne, dakle, ta osoba, već radije „Ajk". Također je interesantno primijetiti zvučnu matricu koja uređuje jedno sasvim posebno osjećanje koje se obznanjuje. Ne „Ja *volim* Ajka", nego „sviđa mi se". Sadašnji predsjednik (koji je svečano proglašen na dan kada je ovaj esej izašao: hvala vam, urednici) nema nikakav problem sa tim da priča o onome što voli. „Volim loše obrazovane" objavio je, na primjer, prilikom osvajanja stranačke predizbore u Nevadi.[33] Kladim se da je tako.

Jakobson svoju formalnu analizu zaključuje zapažanjem da „poetska funkcija izborne parole spaja svoju impresivnost sa učinkovitošću". U ovom slučaju, dejstvo slogana bitni je dio njegove forme. Operacija „učinkovitosti" ovdje je od posebnog značaja u svjetlu uvida Čarlsa Sandersa Persa (Charles Sanders Peirce) o tome kako neki lingvistički znak operira (ovo potiče iz jednog od njegovih pisama gospođi Velbi [Welby]):

Djeluje mi kako je suštinska funkcija znaka da neučinkovite relacije učini učinkovitima – ne da ih stavi u dejstvo, već da ustanovi naviku ili neko opće pravilo pomoću kojega će oni ponekada djelovati.[34]

Prema ovoj procjeni, znak stvara putanju prilike, jedan kanal „učinkovitosti", sredstvo za jednu praksu, mogućnost djelovanja i činjenja. Znaci pod uticajem poetske funkcije kako ovu opisuje Jakobson u prvi plan ističu svoj status stvari:

Skup [...] koji se odnosi na PORUKU kao takvu, usmjeren na poruku za svoj račun je POETSKA FUNKCIJA jezika. [...] Ova funkcija,

---

33. Kada već govorimo o sadašnjim događajima i prošlosti koju oživljavaju, oni koji su pravili slogan za Ajzenhauera pokušavali da pronađu način da i njegovog satakmaca Ričarda Niksona [Richard Nixon] uključe u trku, da bi na kraju završili sa jednim „Meni se sviđaju Ajk i Dik" ('I like Ike and Dick'). Nije da on nije u sazvučju, ali njime se ponavljanje koje sadrži original razbija zvukom koji zahtijeva od nas da svoja usta namjestimo kao da isturamo svoje očnjake gadeći se. I kako to biva, sam izraz završio je na Zefirovim slikovitim naljepnicama koji nam pomaže da islovkamo rebus:

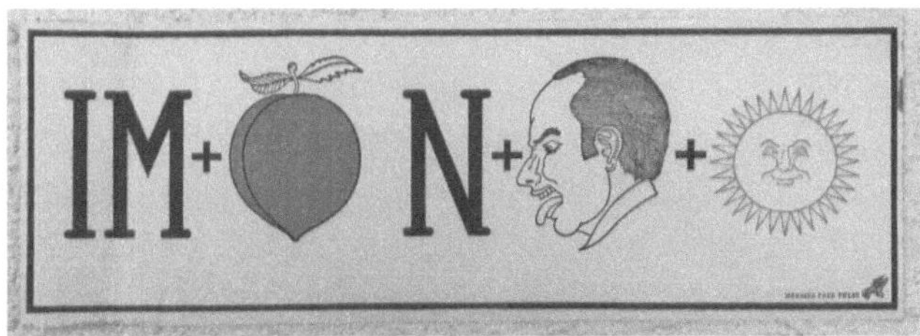

Kad već govorimo o Lukavom Diku, prvo značajnije pojavljivanje senatora Niksona u javnosti bilo je na mjestu pomoćnika senatora Džozefa Mekartija [Joseph McCarthy] u Domu komiteta za antiameričku djelatnost. U timu istog tog komiteta bio je i advokat Roj Kon [Roy Cohn], alijas mentor za ulične političke borbe Preznit Combover McTweeta. E da, prije nego što zaboravim: kao što „Meni se sviđaju Ajk i Dik" ('I like Ike and Dick') baš i ne zvuči baš tako dobro, i Kris Kraus [Chris Kraus] je otkrio da isto važi i kada knjigu nazovete *Ja volim Dika* (*I Love Dick*). (u doslovnom, slengovanom prijevodu: *Ja volim kitu*; prim. prev.).
34. Charles Sanders Peirce, *Selected Writings*, New York: Dover, 1966, str. 390.

promovirajući opipljivost znakova, produbljuje fundamentalnu
dihotomiju znakova i objekata. (356)

Ili kako to Koh kaže u „Jedan vlak mogao bi sakriti drugi":

I tako uvijek ispred nečega stoji nešto drugo
kao što riječi stoje ispred objekata, osjećanja i ideja.
Jedna želja možda krije onu drugu.

Možemo li onda reći da ono što Jakobson naziva „učinkovitošću"
poetske funkcije omogućava da svjesno odbacimo „učinkovitost" čiji
nam opis nudi Pers, i da pjesma može da nastane zarad sabotaže
„navika ili općih pravila" – društvenih normi i društvenih formi, alijas
„želja" – koja su zamke za naše uviđanje želje da moć učinimo
zajedničkom? Ovo pitanje dugujem koncepciji sabotaže, kao „svjesnog
opoziva industrijske učinkovitosti radnika" koju nudi Elizabet Flin. U
tom smislu shvatam da je funkcija sabotaže da uvede taktiku opozivanja
učinkovitosti ne zbog same sebe, već kao dijela šire strategije
transformiranja odnosa između rada i vrijednosti na prvom mjestu. Na
sličan način i pjesma opozivanjem semantičke ili spoznajne
učinkovitosti transformira odnos između riječi i stvari.[35] Tako pjesma
„čini da se ništa ne desi" ponovo tvoreći načine na koje mi opisujemo
kako se ne dešava ništa sa čime bismo mogli početi.

Jakobsonova poetska funkcija naglašava ono što, iz perspektive
normalnog diskursa, liči na pogrešnu vrstu ekvivalencije. Ističući u prvi
plan materijalni sastav poruke, poetska funkcija transformira naš odnos
prema poruci kao takvoj. Prestajući da bude transparentnim, medij
ističe organizacionu snagu iznad iskazivanja: *„Poetska funkcija projicira
princip ekvivalencije sa ose selekcije na osu kombinacije"* (359; njegovo
naglašavanje). Čineći to, poetska funkcija transformira hijerarhije
usađene u naše semiotičke reflekse. „Ekvivalencija je izdignuta na
razinu konstitutivnog gesla poretka", piše Jakobson, nagovještavajući i
to da su hijerarhije koje su implicirane u „selekciji" stavljene van snage
kada je poetska funkcija na djelu; *„borba"*, kako Kropotkin kaže, „je
zamijenjena *saradnjom"*. Za posljedicu toga, arbitrarna veza između
označitelja i označenog, kako je opisuje Sosir (Saussure), transformirana
je u nužnu vezu – ili je u najmanju ruku u igru uvedena mogućnost za

---

35. Elizabeth Gurley Flynn, *Sabotage: The Conscious Withdrawal of the Workers'
Industrial Efficiency*, Chicago: I.W.W. Publications Bureau, 1917.

jednu nužnu vezu. Mi ćemo ipak dodati da se tu ne radi o sredstvima za pasivno predstavljanje objekata označenih u poetskom iskazivanju, već prije o aktivnim sredstvima transformacije povezanosti između ovih objekata. Poetska funkcija transformira hijerarhiju predstavljanja i tako, a to bih želio istaći, ima moć da na prvom mjestu transformira ono šta predstavlja.

§

Kad već Jakobson opisuje i definira poetsku funkciju na primjeru političkog slogana, postoji li način da mu uzvratimo uslugu? Drugim riječima, šta je to čemu nas poezija može naučiti po pitanju „političke funkcije"? Premisa Žaka Ransijera je da je političko zasnovano na i ubrzano „pretpostavkom jednakosti bilo koga sa bilo kim".[36] Ili, kako je to nedavno rekla Džudit Batler (Judith Butler): „Biti političkim glumcem je funkcija, lik koji igra na temu jednakosti skupa sa drugim ljudima [...]. Jednakost je stanje i karakter same političke akcije, a u isto vrijeme ona je i njen cilj".[37] To liči na moguće polazište: od činjenice da se i političko (kako ga određuju ovi mislioci) i poetsko (kako ga određuje Jakobson) tiču jednakosti i ekvivalencije – koje, naravno, nisu potpuno jenake niti ekvivalentne jedna sa drugom, ali skapirali ste. (Sjećajući se novčića koji smo posmatrali nešto ranije, vrijedno je zapaziti makar u prolazu da novac, za Marksa, operira kao „opći ekvivalent" na čemu se zasniva jedna posebno postojana ekonomska logika.)

Šta onda mora da se desi kako bi tvoj zahtjev postao jednak opisu, ili da tvoj opis bude pretvoren u ekvivalent jednog zahtjeva?

§

Svi znaju kako završava pjesma iz 1926. godine 'Ars poetica' Arčibalda Mekleiša („Jedna pjesma ne bi trebalo da znači / Nego da bude"), ali tek nekolicina zna kako počinje njena posljednja strofa:

Pjesma bi trebalo da bude jednaka onom:
Nije tačno.

---

36. *Disagreement*, op. cit., str. 17. (*Nesaglasnost*, op. cit., str. 36)
37. Judith Butler, *Notes Toward a Performative Theory of Assembly*, Cambridge, MA.: Harvard University Press, 2015, str. 52.

Zong! #4

<pre>
                                        this is

                not was

                                            or

                                        should be

                this be

                                            not

                should be

                                            this

                should

                                            not

                be

        is
</pre>

Obožavam preciznost ovog kontrafaktičkog dvostiha. Pogledajte šta se desi kada ga prevedete na jezik matematike:

$$\text{„pjesma“} = \text{„} \neq \text{“}$$

Ovo je odličan parnjak Celanovoj definiciji: „Pjesma je ono što ne odgovara mjeri“. Ako se sjetimo etimologije naše riječi pjesma u grčkom glagolu *poiein* („učiniti“), smatram da se ono „tačno“ iz Meklejševog dvostiha ne odnosi samo na pridjev koji je suprotan pogrešnom, već također i imenici koju tesari ili popravljači bicikala koriste kada kažu kako je neki štok ili točak „neispravan“ ('out of true'), isto kao što je i glagol koji koriste kada pokušavaju da predmet svog majstorisanja isprave, izglade, i usklade sa ostatkom naprave čiji su dio. „Gubim istinu“ ('I'm losing true'), kako je je jednom, u harmoniji sa svojom sestrom, pjevala Megi Roče (Maggie Roche). Posao pjesme, kao dvostih kaže, je da bude jednak i u nivou ne samo sa onim što je pogrešno, već i sa onim što je nejednako i van tog nivoa.[38]

Razmotrimo onda, u ovom svjetlu, četvrtu pjesmu prvog odjeljka iz zbirke *Zong!* M. Norbese Filip (NourbeSe Philip):[39]

Jezik koji imamo ovdje izvučen je iz pravne odluke u poznatom slučaju *Gregson protiv Gilberta*, koji se odnosio na potraživanje osiguranja povezano sa ubistvom davljenjem 150 robova od strane kapetana i posade broda za prijevoz robova koji se zvao *Zong* 1781. godine. Kako to Filip opisuje u pogovoru:

> Precizno tumačenje osiguravajućeg ugovora, bar prema vlasnicima *Zonga*, za rezultat će imati veliku finansijsku probit za njih: oni će platiti za ubistvo 150 Afrikanaca. U isto vrijeme, oni će biti oslobođeni optužbe za davljenje 150 ljudi zato što se tu nije radilo o ubistvu već jednostavno o odlaganju vlasništva u opasnim uslovima kako bi se osiguralo očuvanje ostatka „tovara" – što je bilo jedno razumljivo tumačenje u skladu sa zakonom kojim su uređivani osiguravajući ugovori. Međutim, čak i da su sudovi donijeli odluku protiv vlasnika *Zonga* i ustanovili da oni nisu mogli polagati pravo na obeštećenje od osiguranja, prema zakonima tog vremena, ni kapetan Kolingvud (Collingwood) niti oni koji su mu pomagali u ovom masakru ne bi mogli biti optuženi za ubistvo, s obzirom da ono što je uništeno, budući da se radilo o imovini, i nije moglo biti ubijeno. (191)

Sedamnaest riječi pjesme *Zong! #4* izvještava nas o tome da ove pravne okolnosti i ekonomske jednačine na koje se ove oslanjaju – ljudi kao stvari, ljudi kao imovina, ljudi kao tovar, ljudi mjereni novcem – nisu tek stvar prošlosti već i sadašnjosti. „Ovo je / a ne bilo je": kapitalističko stvaranje porobljenih ličnosti istorijski je proces koji se i dalje odvija. Ono „ili / trebalo bi da je" uvodi normativni imperativ sa kojim se poigrava i Mekleiš. Te činjenice opstaju iako ne bi trebalo da je tako. Pjesma zvuči tako da ova tvrdnja liči na akord, raspoređujući vremena nagrizajući negacijom u dvije kolone na desnoj strani. Činjenice iz ovog slučaja zaista bi mogle biti dodate pod „nije tačno", ali kao što ono ultimativno „jeste" insistira – čvrstoća pozadine ovog

---

38. Pjesma shvaćena na ovaj način priziva pojam anomalije shvaćen u kunovskim terminima, a koji ja obrazlažem u radu: 'The Anomaly Contains the Homily' (op. cit.).

39. M. NourbeSe Philp, *Zong!*, Middletown, CT.: Wesleyan University Press, 2008, str. 7.

aranžmana u obliku dvostrukog unosa koja određuje i oblik ostatka stranice – činjenice slučaja nisu ono jedino što „nije tačno", već one ostaju operativne i do današnjih dana. Ono „jeste" koje štrči je „ono što ne odgovara mjeri". I ono govori o tome šta je istina.

I dok „novčić koji su nagrdile sifražetkinje" (kako ga naziva Britanski muzej) koji smo vidjeli nešto ranije u ovom eseju, svoj posao radi pomoću jezičkih sredstava čekićem ulupanih u komad novca, pjesma Filip je, suprotno tome, napravljena od jezika koji je izvučen iz i oduzet od jednog pravnog dokumenta koji se tiče „isplate troškova" povezanih sa regularnim poslovnim masakrom porobljenih osoba. U režimu Jakobsonove poetske funkcije, riječi su ovdje tretirane kao stvari; u režimu ropstva, tako su tretirane osobe. Kompozicija slogana utisnutog na novčić i kompozicija pjesme *Zong!* oboje prilježno uključuju upotrebu sile. „Ubila sam tekst", kako Filip kaže u svom pogovoru,

> bukvalno sam ga isjekla na djeliće, kastrirajući glagole, daveći pridjeve, ubijajući imenice, bacajući članove, prijedloge, konjunkcije preko palube, bacajući u more priloge: odvojila sam subjekt od glagola, glagol od objekta – stvorivši semantički kaos, sve dok mi ruke nisu prokrvarile od tolikog sječenja i ubijanja, doprla sam do smrdljivih, rasporenih iznutrica, i poput kakvog vidovnjaka, sangome [iscjelitelja] ili proroka koji, pošto je žrtvovao životinju zarad znakova i predskazanja nekog novog života, ili tek života, čita neispričanu priču koja se sama priča nepričanjem. (193)

§

Gordon Broterston (Brotherstone) piše da je „primarna funkcija klasičnih tekstova da stvore politički prostor i oslonac za istorijski kontinuitet".[40] Uzimam *Zong!* za klasičan tekst u ovom smislu. Šta se dešava kada je politički prostor stvoren klasičnim tekstom iskazan kršenjem političke pouke o univerzalnoj jednakosti? Ili kada oslanjate istorijski kontinuitet na radikalni diskontinuitet kakav predstavljaju otmica, silovanje, ubistvo, prisilni rad i svi drugi oblici otimačine koje je baštinilo ropstvo? Pjesma Filipove obavezuje nas da produbljujemo ova pitanja. Da se difoultujemo prema njima. Primarna funkcija klasičnih tekstova u ovom smislu je da *dekonstruiraju* i *rekonstruiraju* politički

---

40. Gordon Brotherston, *Book of the Fourth World*, Cambridge: Cambridge University Press, 1992, str. 4.

prostor ukotvljavanjem istorijskog *diskontinuiteta.* Želja izgrađena na kidanju. Pjesma performira i opis („ovo je") i zahtjev („ovo / ne bi / trebalo / biti") istovremeno, i ostavlja nas sa pitanjem: *šta bi to moralo da se o-stvari da bi bilo drukčije?*

Acknowledgements

Zahvaljujem se Entoniju Ajlsu, Marini Višmit, Mirandi Melis (Miranda Mellis) i Silohu Radovskom (Siloh Radovsky) za aktivno i angažovano čitanje i reagovanje.

KLASNA PODJELA VS. DIOBNE STREPNJE

DENI HEJVARD

U trećem poglavlju svojih *Razmišljanja o nasilju*, poglavlju koje nosi
naslov „Predrasude o nasilju" francuski revolucionarni sindikalista Žorž
Sorel (Georges Sorel) objašnjava zbog čega je za proletarijat nužno da
sačuva strogu odvojenost od srednje klase. „Sve bi moglo biti spaseno",
piše Sorel,

> ukoliko bi proletarijat, koristeći se nasiljem, uspio ponovno
> uspostaviti podjelu na klase, i na taj način obnoviti nešto od
> prijašnje energije srednje klase; to je veliki cilj prema kojem
> cjelokupna misao svih ljudi – onih koji nisu hipnotizirani
> svakodnevnim događajima, već misle na uslove sutrašnjice – mora
> biti usmjerena.[1]

Uslovi za spasenje kakvi su ovdje zamišljeni postoje u dugoj tradiciji
moderne regenerativne brutalnosti koja se proteže od Voltera Ralija
(Walter Raleigh) sve do njegovog buntovnog antipoda, Franca Fanona
(Frantz Fanon). Ovdje se nasilje začinje isprva kao politički ekvivalent
iznenadnog buđenja. Fanonovim rječnikom rečeno, ono svoje agense
crpi iz stanja ebulije, ili odsustva snage volje,[2] preobražavajući one
„koji su inertni, koji ne mogu da planiraju, koji nemaju nikakvih resursa
[i] koji žive od danas do sutra" u nosioce „nacionalne sudbine i
kolektivne istorije".[3] Sorelovim, pak, jezikom rečeno, ono svojeg agensa
istrže iz stanja „hipnoze", izvlačeći ga iz njegove žalosne
preokupiranosti „događajima dana" i fiksirajući njegovu pažnju na
zastakljeni ormarić sutrašnjice u kojima, umotani u ukrasne vrpce
mističkog okolišanja, jedino i mogu biti izloženi njegovi apokaliptički i
teško opisivi trofejni „uslovi": „uslovi sutrašnjice".

Svaki onaj koji svoje dane provodi izoliran, „pokušavajući da osujeti
ili pak da ugodi snažnim impulsima u svijetu [koga] se boji" i koji se
stalno breca zbog uobičajenog nasilja državne politike, ove „okolnosti"
može shvatiti kao nerealne čak i prije nego što one budu uzete u
razmatranje kao poželjne.[4] Politika regresivne podjele danas je življa
nego što je to bila u bilo kom momentu u proteklih pedeset godina, a
psihološka para-politika straha i odbojnosti oživljava se skupa s njom pa

---

1. Georges Sorel, *Reflections on Violence*, ur. Jeremy Jennings, Cambridge: Cambridge
University Press, 1999, str. 85.
2. Frantz Fanon, *The Wretched of the Earth*, (prev. Constance Farrington), London:
Penguin 1961, str. 228.
3. Ibid., str. 73.
4. Richard Wright, *Native Son*, London: Vintage, 2000, str. 73.

čak i u većoj mjeri od nje. Štaviše, kako to oživljavanje dobija na ubrzanju kroz mnoštvo izbornih ciklusa i posredstvom potpuno medijatizirane atmosfere „javnog mnijenja", sam proces ističe svoje skrivene tendencije u obličju odskora ubrzane, reakcionarne politike prisilnog i odbrambenog jedinstva. Šta bi, dakle, u ovakvim uslovima uopće i mogla značiti radikalna podijeljenost u smislu koji joj daje Sorel (ako je tako nešto zaista ikada i postojalo) i nije li teorija klasne podjele, po kojoj je on postao poznat, oduvijek i bila tek neka vrsta podrobnog opravdavanja estetskog puritanizma, sa svim njegovim sklonostima ka gušenju seksualnosti i deplasiranoj mizogijini koje hrane takve ideologije i koje nezadrživo bujaju tik pored njihovog korjena?

Kratki esej koji slijedi predstavlja pokušaj da se odgovori na to pitanje. Tu se ne radi o istoriji političko-ekonomskih promjena koje su nastale uslijed regresivne podjele ili onih koje su raniju politiku radikalne podjele iscrple do te mjere da od tih promjena više ne bude vidljivo ništa drugo sem njihovih najregresivnijih izdanaka; ovdje se radi o kratkom i provizornom pokušaju da se objasni jedan psihološki *odnos* između fašističkih zahtjeva za rasnom ili etničkom segregacijom i liberalnih zahtjeva za nacionalnim jedinstvom i da na taj način pokaže kako se u oba svjetonazora ta bremenita i bolna *činjenica* podjele pogubno poriče i isključuje iz vitalnog ili podsticajnog izraza. Iz istog razloga, on predstavlja i element šireg uvida u prirodu instinkta za dijeljenjem u jednoj transformativnoj i potpuno otvoreno radikalnoj kulturi.

§

Šest dana prije referenduma o članstvu UK u EU, 16. juna 2016. godine, britanski neonacist Tomas Mer (Thomas Mair) ubio je članicu parlamenta iz laburističke partije i zagovornicu opcije „Ostati" ('Remain') Džo Koks (Jo Cox). Ubistvo je bilo potvrda toga da je istorijski i psihoanalitički značaj potrebe za podjelom nadjačao značaj potrebe za jedinstvom. Objavljeno je kako je Mer bio „usamljenik" sa snažnim simptomima depresije i kompulzivne neuroze.[5] U danima poslije smrti Džo Koks, novine – koje su pored svih skarednih detalja o njegovim navikama da se opsesivno čisti – su zabilježile i to da ispis pretraživanja iz kompjuterā koje je koristio u biblioteci pred kojom će kasnije upucati

---

5. 'Thomas Mair: Extremist loner who targeted Jo Cox', 23. novembar 2016, http://www.bbc.co.uk/news/uk-38071894.

i izbosti Džo uključuju i upite o matricidu,[6] želji koja je u Merovom umu bila povezana sa činjenicom da je njegova majka stupila u vezu sa muškarcem porijeklom sa britanskih Kariba u vrijeme njegove kasne adolescencije.[7] Nasilje pomoću kojega se nadao da će, da se poslužimo sorelovskim terminima, „uspjeti da ponovo uspostavi… podjelu" iscrpilo se isključivanjem fantaziranog povratka u prijašnje stanje, što ukazuje na slične rascijepe između otvorene namjere i djelovanja kakve

---

6. Mržnja prema majkama predstavlja stalnu preokupaciju tipova ličnosti koji naginju fašističkim pokretima (iako je jasno da *državni* fašizam ima mnogo veće uporište u bazi), kako su to pokazali Klaus Tevelajt i Kristina Viland u svojim radovima o institucijama muškosti: Klaus Theweleit, 'Männliche Geburtsweisen', u: *Das Land, das Ausland heisst,* Munich: DTV, 1995, i Christina Wieland, *The Undead Mother: Psychoanalytic Explorations of Masculinity, Femininity and Matricide,* London: Karnac, 2000.

7. Richard Spillett, ''Jekyll and Hyde' assassin was a loner …', *Daily Mail*, 23. novembar 2016, http://www.dailymail.co.uk/news/article-3960988/Jekyll-Hyde-Jo-Cox-assassin-Thomas-Mair.html; Dan Sales and Gemma Mullin, 'He Would Have Killed Again', *The Sun*, 23. novembar 2016, https://www.thesun.co.uk/news/2246112/jo-cox-killer-thomas-mair-planned-more-murders/. U članku koji je izišao u novinama *Mail* citiran je Merov polubrat Dvejn Seint Luis (Duane St Lewis), koji kaže kako: „On nikada nije izražavao bilo kakve stavove o Britaniji, niti je pokazivao ikakvu naklonost rasizmu. Ja sam i sam iz rasno mješovite veze i njegov sam polubrat, a nas dvojica smo se dobro slagali. Nikada se nije ženio. Jedini put koga se sjećam da je bio sa djevojkom bio je u vrijeme dok je još bio vrlo mlad, ali tu mu je djevojku preoteo jedan ortak. Rekao mi je da ga je to odbilo [od žena] zauvijek." Ovdje se, naravno, radi tek o citatu koji je izvučen iz konteksta, a njegova izvorna namjera bila je da se ukaže na to kako Merov čin nije bio „ideološki" već da se radilo tek o „poremećaju", što je bilo u skladu sa željom *Maila* kao i većine britanskih štampanih medija da ne dovode u vezu ubistvo sa općom atmosferom koja je vladala u prilog kampanje da se napusti EU, a za koju su isti taj *Mail* i većina britanskih štampanih medija, naravno, bili direktno pa možda čak i prvenstveno odgovorni. Ali ne čini li se kako ovo bar ukazuje na to u Merovom fantazmatskom životu središnju ulogu ima neka vrsta primalnog bijesa uslijed percipiranog napuštanja, i da njegovo prvo iskustvo napuštenosti od strane partnerke treba tretirati kao da se radi o nečemu nepopravljivom i neiskupljivo pogrešnom, zbog čega se sve žene uopće, bez ikakve razlike, imaju smatrati odgovornima? Ideja kako je to „odvratilo [Mera] zauvijek" jedna je indikacija činjenice da je on, zapravo, već uvelike bio odvraćen, a da je prvo iskustvo „problema u vezi" koje je iskusio kao odrasla osoba bilo nešto što je on samo iskoristio kao sjajnu priliku da racionalizira, i na taj način da oduška nečemu što bi inače ostalo tek na razini jedne uznemirujuće i neoprostive odbojnosti. (Na sličan način, u iskazu Dvejna Seint Luisa primjetno je i to kako muškarac koji je Meru „ukrao" djevojku nije unio nikakvu trajnu promjenu u njegov stavu prema „ortacima". Selektivna dioba srama u skladu je sa nedotupavnim porodičnim obrascem. Ukoliko dijete pati, to mora da je krivica majke, a nikada oca: uvijek je kriva EU, nikada država članica.)

nalazimo u rječniku krajnje desnice u SAD kada ova govori o „terapiji" preobraćanja i „korektivnom" silovanju. Nesvjesni pokušaj da se pasivan, infantilan strah od napuštenosti (ili ekstremne diobne strepnje) pretvori u aktivnu, odrasloj osobi primjerenu želju za uvođenjem režima etničkog aparthejda,[8] samo je posljednji istorijski izraz represivnog stava koji će Sorel tako pompezno slaviti kao herojsku volju-za-podjelom oličenu u „pomirljivom poricanju ljudi koji se upinju da postignu nešto ne žaleći se pri tom".[9]

O ubistvu Džo Koks nužno je govoriti na ovaj način baš usprkos opasnosti patoloških „učitavanja" od strane fašizma, i usprkos rizikā da se mržnjom ispunjeno političko ubistvo pretvori u nekakav portfolio za jednu amatersku studiju slučaja, zbog toga što je važno stalno imati u vidu kako u samom korjenu rasističke „djeljivosti" trepere široko rasprostranjeni zahtjevi za jedinstvom. Ubistvo u ime fašističkog nasilja svoje porijeklo ima u jednom grčevito raširenom protestu protiv uslova koji to nasilje reproduciraju. Ovaj princip tumačenja vrijedan je ne zbog toga što nam pomaže da se sjetimo kako su i ultimativni fašisti povrijeđena i složena ljudska bića, ispunjena neartikuliranom mukom, bića koja će možda jednog dana čak biti podvrgnuta i rehabilitaciji,[10] već stoga što nam pomaže da uvidimo kako ni geste preuranjenog pomirenja za račun „podijeljene" nacionalne zajednice ne stoji nužno *nasuprot* vatrenih moraliziranja o „vrlinama" nasilne segregacije, već

---

8. Čak i u procesu mišljenja svjedočimo jednoj konvencionalnoj inverziji: Mer je bio ubijeđen kako je njegova majka zaslužila da umre zbog toga što je bila „izdajnik rase": bijeli suprematizam služi racionalizaciji prethodno postojeće želje i time joj daje privid smisla. Mogli bismo se zapitati da li nam to pomaže u objašnjenju zašto je Merova želja da ubije majku, iako osviješćena, bila također i neaktivna, tako da su novine mogle da izvještavaju o tome kako je on dan prije ubistva proveo podešavajući TV aparat svoje majke. Naravno, primarna žrtva ovakvih zamjena teza bila je Džo Koks.

9. *Reflections on Violence*, op. cit., str. 228.

10. Očigledno je da ni Tomas Mer, pa čak ni članovi jebene nacističke bande kakva je Nacionalna akcija (National Action), neće biti ti koji će u najvećoj mjeri izvući korist od pretvaranja Ujedinjenog kraljevstva u jedno predimenzionirano sjedište za oslobađanje od poreza, u šta ga, u odsustvu drugih sredstava upravljanja dijelom ukupnog globalnog viška vrijednosti, politička klasa koja danas raspolaže imovinom nastoji pretvoriti. (Nacionalna akcija je prva fašistička organizacija koja je zabranjena u UK. Zabranu je inicirala Amber Rad [Amber Rudd], sekretarka poslaničkog doma torijevaca, dijelom i zbog toga što je organizacija izražavala javno divljenje Tomasu Meru. Jedan od njenih članova zatvoren je prošle godine zbog pokušaja da odsiječe glavu i nanošenja ozbiljnih povreda jednom zubaru iz Lidsa koji je porijeklom Sik.)

predstavljaju jednako učestale *elaboracije identičnog procesa samoizlječenja*, samo što su sada one uzglobljene u jezik čija je svrha nešto istančanija, a forma i izraženi sadržaj su im konzistentniji.[11] Danas je 21. januar 2017. godine. Prošlo je više od sedam mjeseci od ubistva Džo Koks. Jučer je Donald Tramp (Trump) svečano postavljen za predsjednika Sjedinjenih Država i tom prilikom govorio je jezikom nekog losanđeleskog scenariste o nužnosti suprotstavljanja „američkom krvoproliću". Liberalno-parlamentarna štampa sipa kao iz otvorenog kanala svoj beskrajni niz osuda razdora, apela za „ozdravljenje", bogobojažljivih želja za re-uspostavljanjem jedinstva. To prešutno priznaje impotentnost ovih objava, a obznanjuje se ispoljavanjem sopstvene unutarnje strepnje zbog odlazećeg predsjednika Obame, ili pak zbog „njegove žene", čime se aktivni otpor protiv autoritarnog državnog populizma zamjenjuje konformerskim fantazmom o očinskoj neranjivosti, čija je neformalna pristojnost tako vrišteća i u potpunom neskladu sa stvarnošću da to djeluje smiješno:

---

11. Ovdje možda možemo blago izvući iz konteksta jednu rečenicu Lea Bersanija: „brutalnost je istovjetna sa [...] idealizacijom.": *Is the Rectum a Grave?: And Other Essays,* Chicago: University of Chicago Press, str. 29. Uzgred, ako je Bersani u pravu sa ovom svojom tezom i ukoliko se ono što se stereotipno smatra za „pasivnu" seksualnost (tj. ono što se iz pozicije muške heteroseksualnosti odnosi na gej i žensku sekusalnost) poistovjeti sa (a onda i organski ponavlja) zadovoljstvom koje se doživljava u nekim epizodama u djetinjstvu kada se dijete suočava sa gubitkom identiteta, onda ima smisla tvrditi i to da bi osoba koja je iskusila neku posebnu bol zbog bespomoćnosti ili napuštenosti u kasnijem stadijumu djetinjstva, mogla na kraju da se okrene protiv tog svog ranijeg osjećaja gubitka kontrole i to posebno jako, i na taj način može da osudi sve ono za šta može da pomisli da je njihova posljedica po njegov seksualni život kao *odrasle* osobe. Ta odbojnost može biti do te mjere agresivna da može djelovati patetično prenaglašena čak i kada se usporedi sa „uobičajenim" predrasudama dominantnog (tj. heteroseksualnog) društvenog pogleda (*Is the Rectum a Grave?,* str. 24). Povezanost ova dva pogleda u apologetskom tonu sažima brat Merovog inspiratora Dejvida Koplanda (David Copeland) u jednoj epizodi BBC-jeve serije *Panorama,* koja je emitovana 1999. godine: „Mislim da je on [Dejvid Kopland] imao tek odnos zdravog nedopadanja prema gej populaciji, kao što je to slučaj sa najvećim dijelom muškog roda, i nije se radilo o mržnji već o nedopadanju". (Kopland je 1999. godine bio osuđen zbog serije bombaških napada na etničke manjine i ono što je on sam zlobno smatrao za londonsku gej „zajednicu". Mer je naručio prvu količinu priručnika za sklapanje oružja 10 dana po Koplandovom prvom pojavljivanju u sudu). Vidjeti: http://news.bbc.co.uk/hi/english/static/audio_video/programmes/panorama/trans cripts/transcript_30_06_00.txt; i: https://www.theguardian.com/uk-news/2016/nov/23/thomas-mair-slow-burning-hatred-led-to-jo-cox-murder. Posebno članak u *The Guardianu* sadrži neka veoma inteligentna istraživačka obavještenja.

Obama je sišao niz stepenice rame uz rame sa Trampom, čavrljajući i razmjenjujući šale. U podnožju, Obama se široko osmjehnuo. Njegova žena nije mogla da skrije izraz koji je nalikovao melankoliji. On je podigao njenu ruku do svojih usana i poljubio ju upućujući joj umirujući osmijeh.[12]

Na ovom mjestu, kao i u pasažima nalik ovom, liberalni i humani poziv na „jedinstvo" i „ozdravljenje" (Obama i Tramp, rame uz rame!), svojom naglošću ispoljava drugu instancu upravo one vrste lažne odlučnosti kakvom se psihoistoriji jednog neonaciste strah i očaj zbog podjele transformišu u katastrofičnu političku potrebu za njima. To je model koji može poslužiti kao primjer za ono što Frojd naziva „diobom ega u procesu odbrane",[13] koja nije usporena melemima i nesebičnom prvom pomoći od strane nacionalizma srednje klase koja obećava „ponovnu potvrdu" ega u procesu njegovog zgrušavanja. Gdje god da pogledam djeluje kao da se ova vrsta lažne odlučnosti samoreproducira, na svakom sporednom putu i u najmanjem izdanku političkog diskursa. Rasplamsava se na svakom mjestu na kom se bilo kakva istinska politička žudnja ili kakav stvarni istorijski razvoj pojave, ne bi li ih strmoglavio do samog temelja umirujućih općih političkih mjesta.

(Naravno, neće svi liberali eksplicitno podržati Trampa čak i ako nastave da brane političke mjere koje će, na dugi rok, pomoći bujanju desničarskog nacionalizma; zapravo, mnogi će ga prezirati onim osobenim, uzvišenim intenzitetom onih koji se po prvi put u svom životu osjećaju ugroženima. Ali argumentacija koju ovdje želim iznijeti nije ta da liberalizam nije sposoban podržati „podjelu" ili suprotstavljenosti pod bilo kojim uslovima, već da on na jednoj općoj razini pogrešno razumijeva način na koji potreba za podjelom nastaje i kako se razrješava. On drukčije i ne može. Svjetonazor koji implicira prosječan uređivački odbor *New York Timesa*, odbojnost prema analizi psihološke potrebe za jedinstvom upravo su ono što dopušta reprodukciju jedinstva kao politički zahtjev. Bez te odbojnosti politika postaje sumorna i neosjetljiva, zato što samo pomoću ovog mehanizma liberalna misao može osloboditi samu sebe od priznanja da u ovom

---

12. Joanna Walters,'Obama departs White House with a promise', *The Guardian*, https://www.theguardian.com/us-news/2017/jan/20/barack-obama-departs-white-house.
13. Sigmund Freud, 'The Splitting of the Ego in the Process of Defence', u: *Complete Psychological Works of Sigmund Freud*, James Strachey (ur.) i dr., London: Vintage, 2001.

klasnom društvu, apstraktni pokušaj da se postigne pomirenje jednako je malo vjerovatan kao i mogućnost da se neko činom reakcionarnog nasilja može izraziti kao da se radi o nastanku novih odnosa uzajamne podrške. Ili da to kažemo i direktnije: liberalna je misao odbojna spram psihološke potrebe za jedinstvom zbog toga što ta potreba nastaje ne samo u svjetlu prijetnji onim liberalnim privilegijama koje su utjelovljene u konstitutivnoj buržoaskoj državi, već i u svjetlu narastajućeg siromaštva, dezintegracije porodičnih struktura, pod-zaposlenosti ili super-eksploatacije, zemljoposjedništva, srezavanja svih davanja, vijestī koje prikazuju udaljene porodice koje su iskorijenile bombe i milicija koje su do zuba naoružali stranci, a povrh svega toga još i u dubokoj ličnoj spoznaji isključenosti koja je glavni element klasne strukture u društvu koje više ne pretpostavlja formalnu podjelu. Njena posvećenost ograničenim raspravama o jedinstvu koja je strogo u domenu politike, kao i filtriranjima isključivo u domenu ličnog ili „pojedinačnog" iskustva, otuda su, paradoksalno, glavni metod kojim ona zatamnjuje istorijski izraz klasnog iskustva kao takvog, i na taj način ona poriče sopstveno učešće u reakcionarnom nasilju u borbi protiv kojega za samu sebe misli da je posljednji bastion.)[14]

Kuda nas sve ovo vodi? Amaterski entuzijasta neonacizma pokušava da stvarnu individualnu traumu prebrodi presađujući je u jednu političku fantaziju etničko-nacionalne „samoodbrane", dok, nasuprot njemu, profesionalni zagovornik jedinstva pod pokroviteljstvom liberalne demokratije nastoji da smućka individualnu traumu iza niza fantazija o ispunjavanju želja, stojeći rame-uz-rame usred političke inercije srednje klase. Žorž Sorel nije mogao da predvidi duboki integritet ovakvog stanja stvari više nego što su to mogli Marks ili Roza Luksemburg. Ali, šta znači kada se kaže da u oba ova društvena gledišta *činjenica* podijeljenosti ili isključivanja ostaje brižno poreknuta ili potisnuta? Ukoliko je želja da se ostane uzdržano podijeljen od bilo koje kulture sada postala *odlučno* reakcionarna, a u isto vrijeme politički zahtjev za jedinstvom opstaje u postojećim okolnostima neizbježno

---

14. Iz ovoga proizilazi kako je kriterijum jedne progresivne politike jedinstva u tome da pokret uvijek mora da artikulira svoj odgovor na trenutne, defanzivne zahtjeve situacije praktičnim rječnikom koji odgovara iskustvu onih isključenih (koji u empatijskom smislu ne pripadaju samo „bijeloj radničkoj klasi"), ne obazirući se na interese onih koji nikada ranije nisu bili isključeni iz bilo čega i koji bi sada vrlo rado da se stave na čelo „antifašističkog" otpora.

beživotno preuranjen – kako je onda moguće postojeće i instinktivno *iskustvo* podjele radikalizirati i transformirati?

Transformativno političko umijeće mora da prepozna (a gdje god tog umijeća ima, ono to u praksi i čini) da istorija klasne podjele istovremeno u stvarnosti jeste istorija kapitalističkog ujedinjavanja. Gigantsko širenje i integracija kapitalističke eksploatacije širom svijeta i njegovo neumoljivo i silovito prodiranje u svaki domen i na svaki nivo ljudskog iskustva je to što određuje lažnu odlučnost Sorelovog mitskog pogleda u pseudo-svjetskoj istoriji jednog Tomasa Mera, koji iz komforne pozicije za svojim kompjuterom abreagira svoj nesvjesni bijes zbog napuštenosti, transformišući ga u slikovitije, svjesno ispunjenje želje rođene u malom gradu obilježenom tipičnom NSDAP atmosferom. I sada više nema zemlje i oblasti ili regiona u kojima sorelovska politika „klasne podjele" može da poluči poželjne rezultate, s obzirom na to da i najekstravagantnija nacionalistička raskoš i najdivljije podvale u vezi sa „istorijskim pokretom/ima"[15] ne mogu sakriti činjenicu da se iza svjetlucavog znamenja i kiša konfeta kao ni ispod medijskog škrgutanja brojkama, nije dogodila nikakva značajnija *kvalitativna* transformacija koja bi nadmašila veličanstvenu metamorfozu koju je uzrokovao javni kompjuterski terminal Tomasa Mera na glasačku kabinu svakog odraslog građanina sa pravom glasa.

Ono na šta je Sorel mislio pod „energijom" kulture radničke klase sada se stvara ne više čestitim i uzdržanim povlačenjem od buržoaskih vrijednosti i institucija, već gladnim i borbenim grabljenjem sredstava, instrumenata i načina izražavanja za koja je radnička klasa istorijski bila uskraćena. Naime, tako nešto spada u snažnu i istorijski legitimnu potrebu za buržoaskim privilegijama, a to se dodatno *podupire spoznajom krcatom biografske frustracije i zasjenjenom institucionalnim napadima u čemu je glavnu ulogu igrala agresija u prevladavanju sila koje su ovima zabranjivale pristup.* Divlja psihoterapija ove klase ne predstavlja tek neplodnu involuciju fašističkog identitarijanizma ili njegovih praktičnih potvrda pod inertnim rukovodstvom procesa nacionalnog izlječenja; radi se o jedinstvu-pomoću-grabeži, o pokretu u tu svrhu, povredi imovinskih prava, eksperimentalnom prekoračivanju definiranih

---

15. Donald Tramp, „Svi te sada slušaju. Postigao si to da desetine miliona sada postanu dijelom istorijskog pokreta, i svijet do sada ništa slično nije vidio", „Cjelokupan govor Donalda Trampa prilikom inauguracije", http://time.com/4640707/donald-trump-inauguration-speech-transcript/.

granica, samo-rasijavanja, o bijesu pasivnosti, što se sve proživljava posredstvom i protiv neprestane integracije globalnog kapitala i usprkos teoretičarima čiji glas odzvanja sa desničarskog podijuma i uzdiže se iz ljevičarskih vrela ne bi li u jedinstvenom horu objavili njegovu trajnost i neuništivi autoritet.

Pa kako onda da u ovom našem svijetu opstane makar i mali dio nekadašnjeg značaja ideje prema kojoj je zadatak antikapitalističkih *umjetnika* da stvore jedan potpuno odvojen i neovisan svjetonazor, odijeljen od buržoaske stvarnosti ne zidom ili kontrolnim punktovima, već energijom koja je do te mjere prkosna i nesumnjivo svoja da potrošači iz srednje klase uzmiču od nje potpuno dezorijentirani i žalosni? Radikalna teorija koja daje odgovor na ovo pitanje proglašavajući kako je podjelama došao kraj i da je s njom svršeno, zato što je kapital sada „premostio podjelu između zaposlenosti i nezaposlenosti, radnog i neradnog, produktivnog i potpomognutog, prekarnog i neprekarnog" – rječju, sve „podjele na kojima je ljevica temeljila svoje kategorije mišljenja i akcije" – i koja zaključuje kako mi antikapitalisti „moramo da se uzdignemo na [isti] nivo apstrakcije [...] ukoliko ne želimo da budemo zbrisani sa lica zemlje" – takva, dakle, teorija samo je napola tačna.[16] Tačna je zbog puke, sirove činjenice da se istorijski razvoj zaista kreće ka prevladavanju podjela radničke klase i u stvarnosti i kao ideala. Ali ona je i pogrešna, jer samo u leksikonu sitne buržoazije možemo naići na ideje prema kojima je „podjela" uvijek ispod razine razmatranja, dok je apstrakcija nešto na šta se neizostavno primamo. Zaključci koji slijede već su dosadno poznati. Za jednu klasnu kulturu više okrenutu sukobima, u kojoj se prijetnje isključivanjem gomilaju nad našim glavama, a apstrakcija jednako učestalo obznanjuje otvaranje tla pod našim nogama, oni predstavljaju sjajan primjer pomanjkanja osjećaja za realnost, jednu vrstu opsesivno-kompulzivnog pranja ruku u domenu političke misli, čime se produžava uvježbavanje intelektualnog sfinktera sve do kasnih stadijuma antikapitalističke kulturalne teorije. A intuicija od koje se čiste ili je sadistički odbijaju je u ovome: u jednom svijetu čija se potpuna integracija više nego ikada do sada oslanja na apstraktna obrazloženja, ono što je radikalnoj kulturi

---

16. Ovaj citat potiče od Mauricija Lazarata (Maurizio Lazzarato) i njegove knjige *The Making of the Indebted Man: An Essay on the Neoliberal Condition*, Los Angeles: Semiotext, 2001, str. 161; ali ostali njemu nalik mogu se naći i bilo kom od brojnih drugih napisa koji, ugrubo, predstavljaju istu tendenciju.

potrebno da bi se podijelila nije istorija buržoaskih vrijednosti ili mišljenja, već ogromna, narcistička dopadljivost od strane onih koji izjavljuju kako vjeruju u njenu univerzalnu dostupnost. To jest, jedinstvo mogu postići samo oni koji su intimno spoznali ne nekakav rezidualni značaj klasne podjele, nego prodorni šok otkrića da su u ovom društvu oni sami tek od rezidualnog značaja.

I baš zato što i najprogresivnijim pozivima na jedinstvo upućenim od strane srednje klase manjka ovo instinktivno saznanje, oni na nekom dubokom i uglavnom nesvjesnom nivou dijele neprijatnu naklonost ka ubilačkim zahtjevima za podjelom, a što sve potiče iz katastrofalnog neuspjeha da se živi sa, da se razumije ili da iz nje otcijepi neki novi izvor bijesa i nesputane izražajne energije.

OPIS BEZ RASPRAVE

Deni Hejvard

I

Ovu vam poruku emituje slab ud, u čijoj je slaboj šaci,
    jaz koji ne bi ispunio nikakav trud,
    uručen za stolom na rasklapanje, čije se granice iznova povlače za
ono što je prihvatljivo
                              reći
i što je dostupno u konkretnom i apstraktnom iz svih izvora
    života u pasivnim blokovima šest do osam potreba zašivenih skupa
i onda uključenih ili ne, neovisno o tome kako protiču tjedni, godine
potom, bez
    ikakvih smetnji po njih
    ili da se bilo šta učini kako bi se život digao protiv izgriženog
bedema
na margini depresivnog idealizma.
Ali konkretno, to se ljušti u 11:15
Recesija u raspravi kako će se vidjeti nema protivtežu.
A u vremenima sveopće recesije osiguranje polovnih auta je kralj.

II

U nekoj vrsti života
    slabi ud, i u njegovoj šaci
kvadrati trave iz ranijeg doba, bandere,
ograda, kuća bijele fasade sa šest prozora,
drumovi, jesenje mrtvilo na sve strane
    ma šta govorile komšije o vinovoj lozi koja
nemirno buja preko zarasle prilazne rampe
prihvatilišta, i ne smije se biti šokiran ovim,

jer zašto ne biti užasnut time,
napola pješke, napola letom, pokraj radnji kod
kružnog toka jedan znak fantastično zamagljen
ali koji ipak pokazuje strogo i zbog onog
nagore prema nebu najprije.
Nebo kao i obično ima svoje razloge da motri
dok bočna kiša odozgo nadolje čupa kaldrmu u izvornoj tami.
Loše operemljeni su izašli. Sljedeća
scena na koju skrolaš na trenutak pokazuje maj 2015.
I ako je bodljikava žica Društva za industrijsku saradnju
kasnije pitana o ovome šta god da to je
u kanalu iskopanom noktima koji su ga rasparali kao i obično ništa se
ne bi dokazalo
sem da smo
tu u svakom slučaju
i šta god da se sada desi električna varnica može
izbiti iz eksplozivnog kola i
spustiti se na nas, zato što se riječi bez ubjeđenja poništavaju i postaju
                    zakovane;
i bez ubjeđenja pogan se pomazuje u bijesnim stanjima
jer tu iz ma kog razloga nije baš sasvim
jedna aleja u smrznutim blokovima usisana sve do autobuskog skloništa
mogućeg sažaljenja u isplati prljavštine koja bez ubjeđenja jede
s neprijatnom sporošću našu varnicu,
može li se ona otkinuti i spustiti na nas
baš kao što kino ispunjava otrovom odvažnosti,
isjeckana u noći spoljašnjost pada u postelju. Zapravo u kutiju od
stiropora.
A onda i sjedište tvornice. Ono kopni nagore kroz prozor
odakle glib posmatra imajući svoje razloge i usprkos njima maršira
ka gradskom centru obuzdavajući
osjećaje bes-
korisnosti koji budući zajednički čine ovo lakšim; i preko puta ulice
jaz između idealnog i stvarnosti deindustrijaliziran je.

    Guma upada u njega kao i svaki tumor; iza ugla
usta koja se krevelje ne bi li se prisilila da ispune
taj jaz izgurana su.
    Biraš pod kojim uslovima u to stavljaš život.
    U slomljenoj osovini bez ubjeđenja koje je mojim ustima naredilo
    da očajnički tragaju za raspravom usprkos opisu

i u pasivnoj ravnodušnosti spram grubog
proizvoda socijalizma, jaz se ponovo otvara. U Zapadnom
Jorkširu
jedna biblioteka. Život se gega ušutkan poput usta
tromo.
Svi smo pozvani.
Svi smo pozvani
da parkiramo negdje bliže centru ovog opisa
bez jebene rasprave na kišici i da istupimo
bez aplauza dok boje prolijeću a jesu suština stvari
koja je ponovo otvorena kao gastro piksel
koji upada u sopstveni sok u strahu i iznenadnoj
boli na terenu ispod pogleda njegove propale maloprodaje.
Sada se pored picerije pojavljuje novi metež beživotnosti.
Flajer mili pod nokat i tamo se savija.
Koliko parking mjesta za invalide živi za vikend.
Požar je povremen.
Život je puko nagađanje. Život je grubi uvid.
Kod berberina ostaviti sirovi proizvod socijalizma
i iskoračiti u centar grada opisa bez jebene rasprave
bilo bi neodgovorno, kao što sam i sam sada neodgovoran
u glupom obrazovnom filmu o anti-fašizmu
i zato što ću tresnuti o tle
ne znajući kako cijeniti život bez licemjerja.
U izbornoj operaciji
biraš svoj karakter, odlučno se okrećeš jazu između idealnog i
stvarnosti. Jaz je ili opći ili specijaliziran. Stvarnost je revidirana
nizbrdo ili je to ideal. Svako od njih stavlja svoj profit u ono drugo. Jaz
je neodrživ ili to nije. Varnica ulijeće u njega. Likovi koji otkupljuju jaz
svinjski su i didaktični; Korporativna svinja u prvoj sezoni važno se
pridružuje domoljubnoj asocijaciji. Idealizam je zamijenjen safirnim
mjehurom na crijevu i može se koristiti i kao džepni sat.
Jednim okretom Korporativna svinja postaje bliska Deng Ksiaopigu koji
uskače a u sljedećoj sezoni je to general Pigoče. Kako održati jaz
nesmanjeno zjapećim a u isto vrijeme voljeti stvarnost usprkos tome što
to nije dovoljno. Kako učiniti da se ubistvo nikada ne desi u borbi bez
vođe na samom kraju današnje neiskorištene sposobnosti za očajavanje,
isto tako. Ako jaz postaje sve više neprijateljski a potom i izmanipuliran
u zavjeri i još uvek je na tebi da i ti manipuliraš
kao opis bez rasprave ili centar bez periferije,

i kroz sve to elastičnost se jaza baca na noge
stvarnosti i rasteže u krizi do svojih krajnjih granica.
I tada Piter Piguri uskače, Pig Čejni, organizacija Pigida,
Pig Džonson, redom izdani rastegljivošću jaza koji
po naglašavanju svoje poante nestaje.
Pogledaj moj džepni sat.
Mržnja odstupa u jarak i korov u njemu buja.
Kako se stvarnost povlači idealizam ne odumire
već u trodimenzionalnoj strukturi takozvanoj, magla izmješta centar
operacija.
Iz života u opisu bez ikakve jebene rasprave svaki ideal može iskrsnuti
i učiniti ga smislenim.
Komentatori predlažu ovo.
General Pigoče vraća se u kameju i razbija se.
Potom se pojavljuje međučin bolesti i nesposobnosti.
U izbornoj operaciji biraš
dok se jaz između idealnog i stvarnosti širi
kako smisao dati životu
stabiliziranom nebesima i desteriliziranom slobodno
kao što se varnica odvaja i polijeće ka fantomskom ne-jezgru Generala
Pigočea
izbijajući lagano poput ulja na iskidanoj mrežnjači
u minut do ponoći na vlasničkoj mapi
naše zajedničke margine, pojavljujući se u zamućenom razočarenju
u zdravstvenoj
klanici na tvojim rukama i koljenima
sa jednim čamčićem. Pokusna publika sada
na navodno petotaktnom bijelom vozilu zahtijeva jedan 3D udar s
boka
u zaključku. A u zaključku jaz nije njihov da
manipuliraju njime već tvoj, ni sa čim on je tvoj,
fotošopiran iz života on je tvoj,
svih rasa i nacionalnosti on je tvoj,
usiljen on je tvoj,
bez općinskih službi on je tvoj,
počinjući borbu iznova svaki dan on je tvoj
lupajući vratima on je tvoj
probijati se kroz klanicu pješčane oluje sve do obeliska od
piksela
okružen čuvarima bez lica i buditi se sa osjećajem praznine

ili je tupost znati da iza jaza ispod
opisa očišćenog od rasprave jedan zaključak čuči
i na tebi je da imaš i posjeduješ i zgrabiš naposljetku
da izabereš da kažeš odjebi generalu Pigočeu koji jaše svoj džepni sat
sada
već u sumraku smrznute baterijske kiseline, i svima onima koji ga
slijede, vitlajući svojim napuhanim vilama u nove
pogrome, nove veb strane,
u nove praznine neispričane osušenim lišćem uz ogradu bez rasprave
sem one koju ti izabereš zakucati u ćorsokak opscene
i neosigurane briljantnosti čija se nit mjeri dahtavim grudima
način je da se oda počast životu bez licemjerja u haosu.

[IZ] ANTOLOGIJE PJESAMA PIJANE ŽENE

LIZA JEŠKE

Operacija Vanitas Eikonal Heimat Horor pjesma

Zimska operacija u Bad Ajblingu oh putovanje
od dubine srca do srčanog spoja. Mi mala
Govna što samo što se ne sudaramo od dosade na poslu
Sva tijela u drhtavici! U ovom dupetu

Od svijeta u ovoj kadi za popravku loših tijela
Tuševi su bili hladni. Loptice za golf
Marljivih planinskih dimenzija i domašaja,
Uši naćuljene kroz tanku konzervu, slušajte!

S uživanjem se skidate do gola. Svakome
Okolnost čini vašu glavu skeletnom
Glavom u vašoj ruci hehe. I vi ste u njoj je mrak
Poslije podne. Kada umremo, ide li to organ

Po organ ili sve odjednom? Hoće li jedan obraz
Otići prvi a ti, Pinki, drugi hoho?
Bok je beskrajno infra, plus x džinovi
Očaja, glavna cesta vodi ka vani ah

Planeri gradova SRNJ, centar
Rehabilitira neonski blistavu svjetlost u noć.
Ovo je mjesto razboljevanja zdravlja, i ono zove
Samo sebe prelijepim, a akumulira šta? Ono

Globalno crpe, to je njegova stvar, njegov obrt, njegova
Snaga. Jasno na različitim planetama
Huhu mahnula si mi a onda si
Nestala. Iščezla. Timovi za potragu rupa

Ne mogahu proširiti. Je li to kralj pojeo
Čovjeka? Je li to bio Horst S.? E sad, da li si
Ga pojeo iznutra? Može li spavati
Noću? Izgubila sam se. Pronašla ga! Izgubila ga. Hm

„Bolje da se isiječem sama | sebe samu a ne da čekam
Njega da to učini." Ne! Ne mogu to podnijeti: odsjeći
Si jezik. Alpski potočići se zarumeniše, potekoše
Natopljeni krvlju. Krvna slika pogleda nagore

Užasnuta. Eto kako smo živjeli. A
Onda iziđosmo iz kade, i vratismo se u
Minhen sada centar Evrope. I
To je bio obrat godine. A bilo je tu još i

Upozoravajuća najava terorističkog napada za centralnu
Stanicu. I u roku od nekoliko minuta, Pegida-Luc
samozadovoljne face o tome kako bi sada volio vidjeti
Tu one što tapšaše u znak dobrodošlice. Ali naravno

Da ćemo mi biti tamo. Luc Luc Luc Luc Luc.

Pjesma iz jedne rečenice

Ja sam žena i moram da jedem.

Bolje i grupno napastvovana u Kelnu
Nego udata za muškarca
To je moja novogodišnja
Rezolucija.

Da, dobro si čuo,
Jebeni, primjereni AfD mladoženjo,
Koji me braniš, svojim moćima?

Mužjače na položaju, dušu ti je poždrao strah,
Domaća kratice, skloni se:
Dalje ruke od moje zemlje!

Čuvanje blagajne

U mojim leđima i na mojim leđima
Osmooka stvar motri na mene
Odjednom i rotirajući se. Šesnaest
Nogu i ruku drži i grabi,
I muči škakiljanjem nikad ne dodiruje
Od blata mora da sam napravljena.
Ispred mene zjapeća usta vremena.

Blagajna

Napravila sam ljupkom k'o mogućnost
I sad više nemam nikakvu ličnost.

Blagajna

Spora je usporila sve pokrete, sve
misli, sav govor do razine na kojoj kao da se
uopće nije kretala. Ovo je otvorilo jedan skoro beskonačan vrijeme-
prostor. I ako bi je jedne godine vidio *ovdje*, sljedeće godine zatekao bi
je *ondje.*

Blagajna

Svaki sat za sat bilo mi je dozvoljeno da ustanem, da prošetam do usana
zaposlenja. Do jedne strane, ambis, do druge, grkljan flegme. Smijali su
se.

Eurosmeće

25. juna 2016. godine šećući prekrasnom prirodom londonske doline,
Dok su mi misli lutale skupa sa stopalima: lijevo desno i po sredini
Iznenada sam ugledala prizor čudovišne mlade guzičarke koja je pjevala
I koja je očito bila pijana, nesumnjivo negdje iz EU, i slinila
Bila sam opčinjena, i zastala sam, i oslušnula te potplaćene

                                       ajtjunove iz

Koji su lako kuljali iz njenih usta
Pravo u niskobudžetno održavane buđave cjevkaste ulaze mojih

                                       ušnih

Školjki, u ili van,
A evo šta je to pjevala:

Želim piti sa Borisom, želim piti sa Najdželom,
Želim se utopiti u moru!

Ja!

Oni će dobit' poneku pivu
Mi ćemo dobit' more.

Vidiš!

Nastavila sam dalje shvativši
Bila sam to ja koja sam pjevala, svezana njihovim izborom [*sic*], skupa
sa mnogim

                                       drugima

O da, bila sam transportni
Kanal i kilogrami i kamenje od kamenja iz džepova vukli su nadole,
izvan,
Pitaj ti mene kakva je bila moja govedina u Britaniji, bila je organska,
Gdje dan ranije postasmo duhovi mi bio tijela jednog dana

                                       rektalna,

Osmoza postade spektakularno katastrofalna, a smanjenje nikada dobro,
Odumiru plačućeg organa procenti mudrijeg mjehura,

JESEN:
JE LI TO KRIVICA VLADE?

Kako se od bilo koga razumno ili nerazumno
Može očekivati da se spremi, kada je cijena goriva ovolika?
Ovo skupo, hitno, preobilje! Hej! Hej! Hej!

Zar svi ćemo pomrijeti? – Da! Svi ćemo
Pomrijeti! Od ubistva! I odavde, kao da je niotkud,
Vlak ulazi u stanicu, i glas i

Glasovi (gdje to bi?) bili su podavljeni, ali koga
Je bilo briga? Gomilu, ali ne i nas. Mi smo se smijali i pravili belaj i
Kikotali se. Mora da je bio vlak smrti taj

Metro mišljenja. Dobro znani jesenji ušni crv
Šapućući, i to, na platformi, dahće da upozori
Na svoj način da upozori tamu kraj ivicu, ogromnog

Sela, i drugih. Ja, žena, rodila sam
Ovo mrtvo, koje mi prethodi, u utrobi,
Godinama. Stvar ili više od onog „to" mora doći da dođe

**Treba li da se ubije onaj što gleda na
NIŠTA sem ARBAJTA pred sobom?**

Ti, doktorice moje zemlje
Frauke Petri

Ne želim da čitaš
Uh, moje tinejdžerske dnevnike!

Jer ako to uradi
Ona će znati

Da nemam
Genitalije, i to bilo koje vrste.

Da li, uh?
Frauke Petri

Bit će veoma ljuta.
Horst Zehofer će reći da takva osoba

Ne može postojati huhu. Donald Tramp
Će dati da me ubiju, ali

Neće to uraditi sam no će
Poslati nekoga. Nekoga iz tima

Tim, tim.
Kakve ribe! Ljubav

Tokeni za pregovaranje
Sada znam da ćemo proći

Draga Engleska Hobson Džobson smrtnić mužić
Ćuko sumnjiv, pedes' supernova

Progonjena, ja, kamena lica
Kurva, jezik na rukavima i slična sranja

Žena čovjek – sastavi tinejdžerske dnevnike!
Da ih sakrijem prije nego što me ščepaju,

Bježi van, ja sam još unutra, imaš izbora
Brdo na kom je vunonosna

Ovca bee ili bus. Bruji.
Gomila ujeda raskošno. Osvrnula sam se, pogledala sam

Naprijed, osvrnula se, pogledala naprijed,
Osvrnula se, pogledala naprijed,

Osvrnula se,
Pa ja sam mesnata

Jebeni proteinski anđeo istorije,
Ne moći dočekati da umreš, da plačeš, da kupiš, da
uzdahneš,

Da osušiš, da ispržiš. Počelo je godinama
Unatrag, ali zaborava si da paziš na svoje kožne

Pore! Hoće li pomoći ako odsiječem svoje šake?
Hanse, Hanse, odsjekla sam šake!

Glupe neophodne šake.
Ja li je ovo još uvijek Zapadna Njemačka?

Preko palube. Naš dogovor bio je
Razuman, rečeno mi je da sam ostala bez daha

Sad progutaj. Horst Sehofer, moj glavni
Zubar, shvata to kao pristanak.

Što me navodi da pomislim da i jesam pristala. I
Tako on shvata moj pristanak na njegovo mišljenje kao moj

Pristanak na to da potvrdim njegovu pretpostavku
Mog pristanka. Pa tako i ja shvatam njegov pristanak

Na moje pristajanje na njegovo mišljenje
Da sam pristala kao na moj pristanak.

I tako sam pitala da to uradim sama. A oni su rekli da će
Uraditi to za mene. Tako su oni mene da NAPUSTIM ovaj posrani

Svijet. I ispostavilo se da sam za njih
Tek dečko sa postera kada se rado o slobodnoj VOLJICI.

Treba li da se ubije onaj što gleda na NIŠTA sem ARBAJTA pred sobom?

Izbor koji imam je strogo između A, udati se za
Donalda Trampa ili B, udati se za Donalda Trampa. Ako
Se odlučim za A, ako se odlučim udati za Donalda Trampa,
Bit će to odluka uperena protiv B, protiv udaje za

Donalda Trampa. Ako se odlučim za B, odlučim udati se za
Donalda Trampa, međutim, onda će to značiti
Ne-A, to jest, neću se udati za Donalda Trampa.
Odlučila sam: Da-A, odlučila sam se za A, udat ću se za

Donalda Trampa, dakle to je odluka protiv B. Neću se
Udati za Donalda Trampa. Posljedice
A, udaje za Donalda Trampa su, citiram, život, kraj citata.
posljedice ne-B, ne udati se za Donalda

Tramp(a) je grob. Ova odluka će biti moj grob
Hehe. Znam da

      more

          sada znamo šta učiniti, biti
Više od njega, potpuno skeletno-celularne olupine. Klice,
Mi urlamo, u svjetlost! I rastemo. I rastemo! 50

Metara, prešišasmo oblake (ograničena izdanja, vlagom obrubljeni
Akumulirani nizovi malokostih podataka), potom
Dostižemo prosječnu tjelesnu dužinu: 149.597 miliona
Kilometara. Glava je bistra, laž raspršena širom

Univerzuma. Mi cjevčimo, vrući sok. A on? Oh
Jadan on, kad uporedi svoju maleckost, on čupa
Prekrasnu plavu kosu, izražavajući duboku bol koju osjeća.
A onda? Zove djevojke za koje nisam mislila da to vole.

A mi? Smijeh, priprema. A onda? A poslije?

Budućnost

Postavila buduće vjerovatnoće kao da su tekuće
Vjerovatnoće – i to je sve? Provjerila verifikacijski kod.
Pozvala polstere, postere, utvrđene
Minimum je bio hiljadu. Univerzum
Metode pouzdanosti. Nijedan se nije javio. Oni
Su se okrenuli: zabrinuti zbog zvonjave koja najavljuje
Kreditore. Pokušala pozvati Samarićane.
Super duša se javila, ispovijedili su se zbog curenja
Nafte. Pokušala objasniti hehe iskustvo
Samoubilačkih osjećanja, između ostalih. Ne. Slušala,
Čvrsto, koliko je bilo moguće (ali da li sam?). Rekoh da ću nazvati
ponovo
Narednog dana (godine). Spustila slušalicu, pogledala
Gore, opazila porodični dron, raširila noge i
Omirisala.

Budućnost

Hihi,
Kada bih imala dijete,

a odakle
God

Ono moglo da se pojavi
Ni nalik meni! Ni nalik bilo kome od nas! (npr.

Audi!) hihi
Jebiga, iza čega

Frankenštajn i njegove imitacije, pih!
O da! Lajk, anlajk

Ovo, potpuno menuetski drukčije
Možda šišteći, kao čudovišno,

Šiš šiš (iščezavajući eho),
Pojavnosti kakve ne mogu ni zamisliti

Bez ikakve sličnosti u koži, očima, ušima, licu, ne,
Bez kože, očiju, ušiju, lica! Oni neće (neće htjeti da)

Pitanja transrodnosti nisu "skretanja teme." Ona su preteča onoga što slijedi. A kada se to desi vama, onda to neće biti skretanje teme.

(Čelzi Mening)

MJESTO KLETVE: POETIKE I POLITIKE KLETVE U SAVREMENOJ BRITANSKOJ EKSPERIMENTALNOJ POEZIJI

BENDŽAMIN NOJS

Kletva je vradžbina ili prokletstvo. Riječ potiče od njemačke riječi „hexen" koja znači vještičarenje, a korištena je kako bi se odnosila na čin čaranja gestovima ili jezikom. Kazivanje kletve ima poguban uticaj na objekt na koji se odnosi. Poetska kletva je govorni čin koji se nalazi negdje između vjerovanja, fantazije i želje. Također, poetske kletve, bar što se tiče snage poezije, često se smatraju najneučinkovitijom i najnižom formom pisanja.[1] Kletva će prevladati taj nedostatak uticaja i učiniti da se nešto dogodi. Na kletvu može da se gleda i kao na polaganje prava na moć, na magijsku moć, moć riječi, od strane onih koji moć nemaju, pa čak i kada se radi u priznavanju same te nemoći. To je, da se poslužimo naslovom jednog britanskog akademskog časopisa i jedne odavno izgubljene teorijske struje, pokušaj jedne naročite i neobične „tekstualne prakse". Tako kletva oscilira među ovim granicama – između fantazije i proizvodnje, između fantazije i njenog ukinuća, između fikcije i stvarnosti.

Svoju pažnju usmjerio sam na upražnjavanje kletve u savremenoj britanskoj eksperimentalnoj poeziji – poeziji koja se „tradicionalno" određuje kao neo-modernistička.[2] Posebno sam se usredsredio na pjesnike Šona Boneja (Sean Bonney), Kestona Saterlenda (Keston Sutherland) i Veriti Spot (Verity Spott). Dvoje među ovim pjesnicima, Bonej i Spot, u svojim poetskim praksama kletve koriste eksplicitno, usmjeravajući ih – kako ćemo već vidjeti dalje – protiv određenih britanskih političara. Sve troje pjesnika od kletve prave formu pomoću koje se nose sa problemima savremenog kapitalizma, a posebno problemima kapitalističke krize i iz nje proizašlim programima štednje.

---

1. Džudit Balso (Judith Balso) ističe:
„Ja ne dijelim dijagnozu prema kojoj postoji tako nešto kao iskvarenost poezije u savremenom dobu. Rad pjesnika se nastavlja; on nije ni manje ni više pod opsadom od rada istinskog pozorišta ili inventivne politike, one koja nije prisvojena od strane partija. On se događa."
– Judith Balso, *Affirmation of Poetry*, (prev. Drew S. Burk), Minneapolis: Univocal, 2014, str. 9.
2. To je tradicija koja se javlja u Britaniji počev od 1960-ih, a posebno je povezana sa figurama kakvi su bili Dž. H. Prin (J. H. Prynne) u Kejmbridžu i Bob Kobing (Bob Cobbing) u Londonu, koji su bili pod uticajem američke modernističke poezije, a posebno Ezre Paunda (Ezra Pound) i Vilijama Karlosa Vilijamsa (William Carlos Williams). Zbirka koja je služila kao smjernica bila je ona koju su sastavili Endrju Krozijer i Tim Longvil: *Drukčija umjetnost* (Andrew Crozier and Tim Longville (ur.) *A Various Art*, London: Paladin, 1990).

Anonimne apstrakcije

I dok se kapitalizam često smatra upravo kao *taj* model bezlične i anonimne moći, koji operiše posredstvom slijepog imperativa svođenja ljudi i ne-ljudi na izvore vrijednosti, on je također i opredmećen. To opredmećenje poprima formu onoga što Marks naziva „karakternom maskom" (*Charaktermaske*), što je koncept koji je teško ispratiti u engleskim prijevodima *Kapitala* koji je bio podvrgnut mnogim i veoma različitim prevođenjima.[3] Ovim konceptom on se služi tek nekoliko puta, mada stalno ističe da su nosioci odnosā društvene uloge i ljudi. U predgovoru prvog njemačkog izdanja *Kapitala* (1867) Marks napominje:

> Još jednu reč kako bi se izbegli nesporazumi. Kapitalistu i zemljoposednika ne slikam ni najmanje u ružičastoj svetlosti. Ali se ovde o ličnostima radi samo ukoliko su one oličenje ekonomskih kategorija, nosioci (*Träger*) određenih klasnih odnosa i interesa.[4]

Ova konstatacija ukazuje na Marksovu perspektivu u kojoj pojedinci dobijaju na važnosti upravo kao *nosioci* ekonomskih odnosa. Moja, možda isuviše očigledna, polazna tačka je prijedlog po kome bi okretanje kletvi bio jedan pokušaj da se uzme mjera „bezličnoj" moći kapitalizma pomoću bajanja ili zaklinjanja pojedine „ličnosti" koja nosi i izražava zloćudnu moć kapitalizma.

I dok na kletvu možemo gledati kao na nešto što cilja upravo na te apstrakcije, moramo istovremeno biti pažljivi kako ne bismo tek tako sugerirali da su takve poetske strategije uvijek osuđene na promašaj i kako uvijek ciljaju *pogrešnu metu*. Deni Hejvard je, razmatrajući djelo Lusi Bejnon (Lucy Beynon) i Lize Ješke *Dejvid Kameron: Teatar pjesama noža* (*David Cameron: A Theatre of Knife Songs*) iz 2015. godine, i u njemu izraženu fantaziju o silovanju tadašnjeg britanskog premijera iz redova konzervativne partije Dejvida Kamerona, istakao kako navođenje na takva djela može samo ukazivati na to da su političari „karakterne maske" i da se tako poništava stvarno iskušenje i nasilje u njima.[5]

---

3. Vidjeti stvarno odličan unos na Vikipediji:
https://en.wikipedia.org/wiki/Character_mask
4. Karl Marx, *Capital Vol. 1*, uvod: Ernest Mandel, (prev. Ben Fowkes), Harmondsworth: Penguin, 1990, str. 92. [BCHS izdanje: Karl Marks, *Kapital*, (prev. Moša Pijade i Rodoljub Čolaković), Beograd: Bigz i Prosveta, 1973, str. 17. – riječ u zagradi, njemački original dodao sam prema citatu iz engleskog prijevoda; u BCHS izdanju je nema (prim. prev.)]

Možemo dodati, a Hejvard bi se nesumnjivo složio s tim, kako se time potcjenjuje i način na koji Marksova analiza povezuje stvarne ljude, stvarna tijela, sa apstraktnim odnosima nasilja. Koncept „karakterne maske" može i mora da bude iščitan na oba načina: kao oznaka pojedinca kao „pukog" nosioca kapitalističke moći i kao oznaka za pojavljivanje te moći u njenom utjelovljenom obliku. Dakle, ovaj esej predstavlja neku vrstu isprobavanja niza poetskih strategija, jedno inicijalno usmjerenje ka procesima nasilja i gubitka, koje se kreće unatrag od apstrakcije ka tijelima, a sve posredstvom jezika. Tu se naročito ističe – a to ćemo kasnije i vidjeti – pojavljivanje usta i oralnosti kao prizorišta jezika i nasilja, materijalnosti i apstrakcije. Usta su ona iz kojih potiče kletva i iz kojih ona polaže svoja prava na materiju.

ACAB

Nevidljivi komitet je u svojoj objavi *Našim prijateljima* primijetio da „sama epoha u kojoj živimo ostavlja fraze na svojim javnim mestima – počevši od grafita *All Cops Are Bastards* [ACAB/Svi panduri su ološ] koje pripadnici jedne čudnovate internacionale orno ispisuju po zidovima gradova prilikom izbijanja svakog nereda, u Kairu i Istanbulu, u Rimu i Parizu ili Riju."[6] Zbirka pjesama Šona Boneja iz 2015. godine, pod nazivom *Pisma protiv nebesa* (*Letters Against the Firmament*) u sebi sadrži i njegovu možda najpoznatiju pjesmu, koja je izvorno objavljena kao „ACAB: rima za djecu" na njegovom blogu *abandonedbuildings*.[7] Ta pjesma, sa svojim refrenom „Jebeš policiju", referira na pjesmu venecuelanskog pjesnika Miguela Džejmsa (Miguel James) 'Against the Police' („Protiv policije") koja počinje stihovima „Cijelo moje Djelo protiv je policije"[8], a možda i na numeru NWA[9] „Jebeš policiju".[10] Tako Bonejeva pjesma počinje sa „umjesto 'volim te' reci policijo, jebem te" a

---

5. Danny Hayward, 'Strong Language: Beynon & Jeschke's *David Cameron: A Theatre of Knife Songs*', *Hix Eros Poetry Review* 6, 2015, str. 99–108, str. 99.
6. The Invisible Committee, *To Our Friends*, (prev. Robert Hurley), South Pasadena, CA: Semiotext(e), 2014, str. 12. [BCHS izdanje: Nevidljivi komitet, *Našim prijateljima* (prev. Đorđe Čolić), Beograd: Fakultet za medije i komunikaciju, 2016, str. 14 – izmijenjen prevod].
7. Sean Bonney, 'ACAB: A Nursery Rhyme', *abandonedbuildings* blog, 31. decembar 2014: *http://abandonedbuildings.blogspot.co.uk/2014/12/acab-nursery-rhyme.html*
8. Miguel James, 'Against the Police', *Typomag* 18: *http://www.typomag.com/issue18/james.html*

završava sa „reci nema pravde, nema mira policija kurcu svira."[11] U vrijeme krize svjedoci smo povećane militarizacije policije kao i njihove militantnosti prilikom razbijanja protesta. To je postalo naročito vidljivo u strategijama kakva je „kotao", kada se protestanti okružuju u ograničenim javnim prostorima na dug vremenski period prije nego što ih se procesuira bilo hapšenjem bilo oslobađanjem.[12] Iako postoji duga tradicija nepovjerenja radničke klase prema policiji (što je i porijeklo ACAB slogana), ovakve su strategije samo intenzivirale doživljavanje policije kao utjelovljenja državne moći u procesu usiljenog uvođenja krize kao načina života. Upotreba kriminalizacije masa, kakvu pamtimo prilikom britanskih pobuna iz 2011. godine, koje su uslijedile poslije policijskog ubistva Marka Dagana (Duggan),[13] generisala je novi oblik masovnog kažnjavanja. Osude koje su trebale poslužiti za primjer, upotreba kamera iz sistema javnog nadzora (CCTV) i doušnika poslije pobuna, sve je to prethodilo hapšenjima, podizanju optužnica i zatvaranju, a ovo je, opet, sve skupa bitno ohladilo dalje proteste.

Policija, dakle, ostvaruje apstrakciju ekonomske krize u formi utjelovljene nasilne državne moći. Na taj način ona je postala faktorom i dijelom, često anonimnim, nove i militarizirane opreme za razbijanje protesta, koja ostvaruje apstraktno nasilje. U Bonejevim pjesmama ta forma apstraktnog nasilja prodire u poetsku i umjetničku formu: „policijsko nasilje sadržaj je cijele / zvanično sankcionisane umjetnosti" (12). Tako su onda i sva umjetnička djela ispunjena ovim nasiljem, koje se obično negira ili potiskuje. Od ključnog je značaja i to da to nasilje poprima apstraktnu formu: „neprijatelj je ne-materijalan / mi nismo" (18). Iako je očigledno nasilno materijalno, policijsko nasilje također je viđeno i kao forma „nematerijalnog nasilja" – plutajuće nasilje koje je naneseno našoj materijalnoj ličnosti.

---

9. NWA (Niggaz Wit Attitudes) – američka hip-hop grupa iz Komptona, SAD. Pionirska hip-hop grupa aktivna u periodu od 1986. do 1991. godine, poznata po svojim kontroverznim stavovima i stihovima, posebno onima koji se odnose na policijski sistem i brutalnost policije (prim. prev.).
10. *https://www.youtube.com/watch?v=c5fts7bj-so*
11. Sean Bonney, *Letters against the Firmament,* London: Enitharmon Press, 2015, str. 29. Dalje u tekstu navedene su stranice koje se odnose na ovo izdanje.
12. Šon Bonej piše „kameni krugovi policijski su kotlovi, i ne možeš me ubijedit' u drugo"
13. O čemu piše i Veriti Spot u svom *Gideonu* (Verity Spott: *Gideon*, London: Barque Press, 2014, str. 7. Dalje u tekstu navedene su stranice koje se odnose na ovo izdanje).

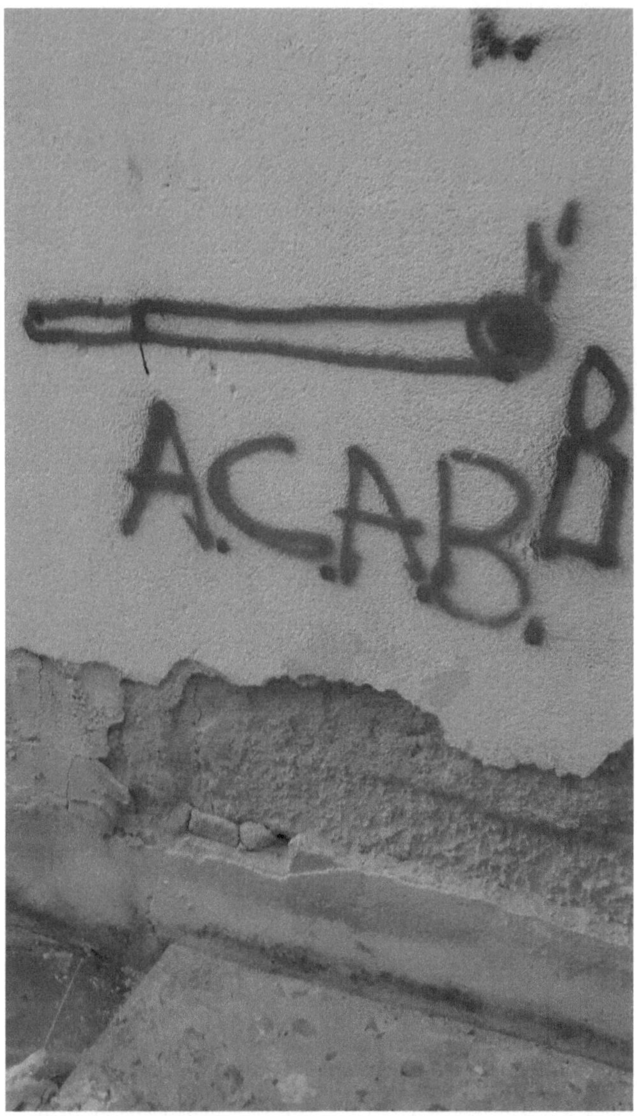

Grafit, Cefalù, Sicilija, 2016, autorova fotografija

Bonejeva *Pisma protiv nebesa* također uključuju i jedno pismo koje je „kletva" bačena na Ijana Dankan-Smita (Ian Duncan-Smith) (111-12). Dankan-Smit je britanski torijevski političar koji je, tokom svog rada u Državnom sekretarijatu za rad i penziono osiguranje, bio odgovoran za nasrtaje na primanja socijalne pomoći namijenjena radno nesposobnima i nezaposlenima. Bonejeva kletva oživljava napade romantičarskih pjesnika na Lorda Kastlriga (Castlereagh), još jednoga arhitekte reakcije.

Šeli (Shelly) je, u pjesmi „Maska anarhije" ('The Mask of Anarchy') iz 1819. godine – koja je napisana poslije masakra kod Piterloa, kada su protestanti koji su se borili za parlamentarne reforme napadnuti konjicom – napisao: „Na putu sretoh Ubistvo / Imalo je masku nalik Kastlrigu –".[14] Bajron je, poslije samoubistva Lorda Kastlriga ovoga nazvao „intelektualnim evnuhom" nabacivši u svojoj posveti za *Don Žuana* (1824)[15] i ovo: „Budući naraštaji vidjeti neće / Groba plemenitija neg' što je ovaj / Kastlriga tu kosti sada leže / Zastani, putniče i slobodno pi... !" Pišaj, u slučaju da imate bilo kakvu dvojbu. Također, ovdje je od velikog značaja i nešto skorija figura Margaret Tačer (Thatcher), konzervativne premijerke i inicijatorke neoliberalnog projekta u Britaniji. Iza praznih obličja trenutnih političara, obično okarakterisanih mnogim besmislicama od strane njima naklonjenih medija, stoji otvoreniji i sukobima skloniji lik Tačerove. Bonej Tačerovu, koja je tada još bila živa, eksplicitno povezuje sa proganjanjima poslije pobuna iz 2011: „Margaret Tačer i njena čudnovata povezanost sa kombiniranim centralnim nervnim sistemima svih ljudi koji su pokupljeni u nedjeljama koje su uslijedile poslije pobuna, njih oko 3000" (37). Veriti Spot osvrće se na „Tačerkina brojna ubistva" (8) kada raspravlja o oslobađajućoj presudi za policiju koju je sud doneo za ubistvo Marka Dagana. Tom Rejvort (Raworth) u svojoj pjesmi 'Rip Rep' također psuje Tačerovu:

orgrejv
tvoj grob[16]
Margaret Hilda Tačer[17]

Orgrejv je bio poprište nasilnog napada policije na rudare 18. juna 1984. godine.

U Bonejevom slučaju pjesma direktno vrijeđa „kandžu koja govori", to jest Ijana Dankan-Smita (111). Međutim, pjesma također pokušava i „da ga definiše, da recitira, opiše i da se bavi njegovim konstelacijama" (111). Ona se ne bavi samo ličnošću političara već i time što je on utjelovljenje zakona. Mjere, koje su dovodile do samoubistava i smrti korisnika socijalne pomoći, bile su *legalne* mjere. Dankan-Smit nudi

---

14. *http://www.bl.uk/learning/langlit/poetryperformance/shelley/poem3/shelley3.html*
15. *http://www.gutenberg.org/files/21700/21700-h/21700-h.htm*
16. Neprevodiva igra riječi: Orgrave – *Your* (tvoj); *Grave* (grob) (prim.prev.).
17. Tom Raworth, *Average Cabin,* Cambridge: Face Press, 2015.

jedan „pakosni alfabet" (111), njegov sopstveni jezik, njegovu psovku, upućene najranjivijim članovima društva. Splin pjesnika prepoznaje tu zlonamjernu i materijalnu moć koja „nadgrobnim spomenicima razbija djeci zube" (111). Bonej pokušava uzeti mjeru „samodržačke tame" (112) koju je izumio i koju širi Dankan-Smit.

Pored toga što je, kao ličnost, utjelovljenje figure mržnje, Dankan-Smit isto tako predstavlja i sam arhetip političara kao *sive eminencije* (*éminence grise*), onoga koji metaforički stoji iza scene, manipulatora, ali i bukvalno „sivog", ispranog, potpuno praznog. Pa kako onda prokleti samu sivost sivih eminencija? Kako se suprotstaviti političarima štednje koji se ponose svojom uvlakačkom zlobom? U Bonejevim poetikama, u ovom primjeru, kletva smjera da ustima introjicira Dankan-Smita. Riječima samog Boneja „držat ćemo vas u ustima, i tu ćete / recitirti prljavštinu vaših života" (112). Ovo me podsjetilo na Frojdove uvide o negaciji prema kojima izricanje negativnih sudova ima porijeklo u „primitivnom", oralnom nagonu i odbijanju nečega što ne može da se jede tako što će ono biti izbačeno iz usta.[18] Ovdje nešto loše uzimamo u usta, ali ono ostaje u našim ustima, i upravo odatle političari recitiraju i na taj način čak i govore u naše ime ali tako da osuđuju sami sebe i raskrivaju svu svoju prljavštinu. U ovom položaju političar je abjekt, objekt gađenja koji leži negdje između subjekta i objekta.[19] Abjekt ovdje nije jednostavno ispljunut, već je natjeran da govori. Na ovaj način ostvareno je djelimično gospodarenje nad ovim apstraktnim legalnim nasiljem, ali je istovremeno ostao okus bespomoćnosti s obzirom na to da abjekt i dalje govori umjesto nas.

U narednom pismu Bonej primjećuje da njegov dopisnik tvrdi kako on napada samo „lake mete" (113). I mada se pismo tiče odbrane Bonejevog slavljenja „forme pobune" kao načina rastrzanog govora, možemo se zapitati i to da li se ta preptostavljena fikcionalna razmjena odnosi i na „laku metu" u vidu Ijana Dankan-Smita. Zar nije lako ciljati političare kao zamjenu za kapitalizam i državu? U „Pismu o radu i harmoniji" ('Letter on Work and Harmony') Bonej će napisati:

---

18. Sigmund Freud, 'Negation' (1925), u: P.F.L. 11. *On Metapsychology*, ur. Angela Richards, (prev. James Strachey), Harmondsworth: Penguin, 1984, str. 435-442.
19. Julia Kristeva, *The Powers of Horror: An Essay on Abjection*, (prev. Leon S. Roudiez), New York: Columbia University Press, 1982. [BCHS izdanje: Julia Kristeva, *Moći užasa: ogled o zazornosti*, (prev. Divina Marion), Zagreb: Naprijed, 1989.] O društvenoj logici abjekcije u savremenom kapitalizmu vidjeti: Endnotes, 'An Identical Abject-Subject?', *Endnotes* 4, 2015, str. 277-301.

„Činjenicu da je Ijan Dankan-Smit i dalje živ smatram ličnom uvredom, ok BENG svakoga jutra a on je još uvijek živ BENG BENG BENG" (47). Pa ipak, ja želim naglasiti kako ova kletva ipak nije tako „laka". Nijedno od ovih proklinjanja ili psovanja, koja ovom prilikom želim da ispratim, ne pretpostavlja da za jednostavan cilj ima to da bude puko premoštavanje gubitka. Kletva nije namijenjena tome da nadoknadi pretrpljene patnje ili nasilje ili čak da nadomjesti nastojanje da se to nasilje utjelovi ili predstavi sinegdohalnim činom. Ovdje se ne pretpostavlja kako taj dio, Ijan Dankan-Smit, može zamijeniti cjelinu, kapitalizam. Prije će biti da ovdje dio može da se uzme u usta kao način da se uzme mjera zakonu koji prerasta u akt neprestanog nasilja. Ta mjera i sama je abjekt, kao što smo vidjeli: nešto što ne može da bude introjicirano ili ispljunuto. Kletva je, dakle, privremena tačka nasilja koja negira samim činom očuvanja i time pokušava da uzme mjeru „pravnom" nasilju.

Fetiški karakter

U pjesmi Kestona Saterlenda iz 2011. godine pod nazivom *Vrući bijeli Endi* (*Hot White Andy*), „Endi Čeng" (Andy Cheng), stvarna osoba, tretiran je kao „Čeng *Fetischcharakter*" (riječ kojom je Marks opisao prirodu robe u čuvenom odjeljku *Kapitala* koji se bavi fetišizmom robe).[20] Već u ovom djelu Saterlend se bavi ventrilokviranjem kapitalizma,[21] kada je „nijema" roba prisiljena da progovori. Ovdje bih želio da svoju pažnju usmjerim na njegove *Ode TLP61P-u* (*Odes to TLP61P*), koje predstavljaju ode (lirske poeme koje se obraćaju određenom subjektu) jednom kodu za naručivanje Hotpointove veš mašine i sušilice, tipa TLP61P koji se više ne proizvodi.[22] I ovo je jedna ljubavna pjesma upućena izgubljenoj robi, iščezlom artiklu beskonačnog ciklusa kapitalističkog zastarjevanja izuzetom iz „luka / razmjenske strasti" (18). Ova duga pjesma

---

20. Keston Sutherland, *Hot White Andy*, London: Barque Press, 2011, bez paginacije. Za Saterlendovu raspravu o dvojnoj prirodi 'Fetischcharaktera', vidjeti: Keston Surtherland, 'Fetish and Refuge: A Mock Pastoral', 'Crisis Inquiry', posebno izdanje *Damn the Caesars,* ljeto 2012, str. 243-254.
21. Za analizu različitih slučajeva ventrilokviranja kapitalizma pogledati studiju Alberta Toskana i Džefa Kinkla: Alberto Toscano and Jeff Kinkle, *Cartographies of the Absolute*, Winchester and Washington: Zero Books, 2015, str. 40-48. Za kritičku raspravu o ulozi robova kao „robe koja govori" vidjeti: Fred Moten, *In the Break,* Minneapolis: University of Minnesota Press, 2003, str. 8-22.
22. Keston Sutherland, *The Odes to TL61P*, London: Enitharmon Press, 2013, str. 18. Dalje u tekstu navedene su stranice koje se odnose na ovo izdanje.

predstavlja složeno djelo koje u sebi sadrži mnogo formi, a sačinjeno je od pet oda čiji se sadržaji kreću u rasponu od savremenih političkih pregleda do seksualnih iskustava iz djetinjstva. Metju Ebot (Matthew Abbott) hrabro se upušta u pokušaj sumiranja primjećujući da „tekst artikulira (i/ili ne uspijeva artikulirati) političke polemike, posljedice ekonomske krize, poslovična (gnomska) kazivanja i aforizme, lirske meditacije o ljubavi itd."[23] *Ode* su često pisane u formi „proznih blokova" a Saterlend to obrazlaže tvrdnjom kako pjesma postoji pod pritiskom koji prisiljava ili svodi poeziju na te „blokove".[24] Iako se u *Odama* kletve ne koriste eksplicitno, mislim da je upotrebom nekih drugih formi (kakva je, na primjer, zaklinjanje) u ovom tekstu moguće vidjeti nešto što kletvi nalikuje.

Treba napomenuti i to da je Saterlend napisao nekoliko veoma značajnih eseja o Marksu, među kojima posebno mjesto zauzima onaj koji se bavi temom razmišljanja o Marksovom *Kapitalu* kao satiričnom djelu.[25] Saterlend se bavi Marskovom upotrebom termina *Gallerte* (koji se na engleski obično prevodi sa „zgrušani") kada je riječ o apstraktnom radu, a koji se odnosi na životinjske supstance (meso, kosti i vezivna tkiva) stopljene ili smiješane kako bi se dobilo ljepilo.[26] Dakle, za Saterlenda engleski prevodi služe neutralisanju odvratnosti na koju je Marks mislio upotrebljavajući baš taj termin u sagledavanju apstraktnog rada kao nečeg što je sačinjeno ili napravljeno od dijelova kako bi se napravilo nešto nalik ljepilu ili želatinu.[27] Marksov *Kapital* nije tek puko djelo „čiste teorije", niti je djelo koje je neminovno apstraktno već se, bar po Saterlendu, radi o djelu koje je usko povezano sa tim na koji način su te apstrakcije materijalno izražene. Na taj način on ukazuje na uski krug ustaljenih lingvističkih ili strukturalnih čitanja Marksa koja

---

23. Matthew Abbott, 'The Poetry of Destroyed Experience', *3AM Magazine* (2013): *http://www.3ammagazine.com/3am/the-poetry-of-destroyed-experience/*
24. Keston Sutherland, 'Email to Josh Stanley', 'Crisis Inquiry', posebno izdanje *Damn the Caesars*, ljeto 2012, str. 205-6, str. 206.
25. Keston Sutherland, 'Marx in Jargon' *World Picture* Br.1, 2008, str. 1-25, *http://www.worldpicturejournal.com/WP_1.1/KSutherland.pdf.* Preštampano u: Keston Sutherland, *Stupefaction: A Radical Anatomy of Phantoms*, Calcutta: Seagull Books, 2011.
26. Ibid.
27. Možda je vrijedno spomenuti i skorašnju kontroverzu oko upotrebe loja, životinjske masti, prilikom proizvodnje novih britanskih novčanica od pet funti sterlinga: *http://www.telegraph.co.uk/news/2016/11/29/new-5-notes-contain-animal-fat-says-bank-england-drawing-anger/*

ignorišu ovu zbijenu materijalnost kao i odvratnost i satiru koju Marks razvija kao oružje upravo *protiv* apstraktnih formi kapitalističkog društva.

I baš zbog toga, prilikom čitanja *Oda TL61P-u*, koje se olako smatraju za visoko apstraktna djela, moramo da obratimo pažnju na Saterlendov pokušaj da uhvati apstrakciju kao jedan proces usmjeren ka materijalnom. Na nivou forme, Saterlend je tvrdio kako su „blokovi" teksta sami po sebi „svođenje" poetskog na isti onaj način kao što je to i miješanje u onom *Gallerte* robne forme.[28] Druga oda počinje razmatranjem preklapanja između kapitalističkog menadžmenta i menadžmenta policije kojim je potonja suzbijala okupaciju trga Trafalgar u Londonu 2011. godine. Ovdje Saterlend isprobava „ustosjećaj" „želatinastog suflea" kojim ga snabdjevaju „brujalice"[29] (buzzword) tog menadžerskog diskursa (19). Taj „gnjecavi" i odvratni diskurs materijalizira se u policijskom nasilju namijenjenom „čišćenju" trga. Oda završava riječima: „Spoznaj svog jebenog / neprijatelja" (22), u još jednom pokušaju da se uđe u trag baš ovoj materijalizaciji riječi, policijskom nasilju i apstrakcijama robne forme.

Posebni odjeljak na koji bih ja da se usmjerim je onaj u kome se nalazi litija različitih formi bojazni i užasavanja iz djelokruga profesija povezanih sa finansijskim uslugama i djelatnostima a koji je sačinjen od jedne rečenice koja se prostire na cijele tri stranice (38-40). Navest ću samo njen početak:

Vrtoglavo gnušanje nad višim menadžerima likvidnosti, snažna odbojnost prema strateškim savjetnicima, duboka odvratnost spram glavnih kontrolora, rastuće nestrpljenje za direktore industrijskih odnosa, spazmično grčenje od finansijskih modelara, racionalni strah od izmiritelja poslovnih gubitaka, blaga sumnjičavost u korporativne računovođe, psihodelično nepovjerenje u službenike žalbenog odjeljenja... (38-9)

Ovdje imamo niz ponavljanja i modulacija nesviđanja, razvlačenje jezičkih resursa u jednom činu ili seriji činova, što „cilja" na sva ta silna

---

28. 'Email to Josh Stanley', op. cit., str .205.

29. Engleska riječ *buzzword* označava riječ iz nekog ograničenog i uskostručnog polja koja je ušla u svakodnevnu upotrebu i postala pomodna do te mjere da je izgubila svoje prvobitno značenje; adekvatnog prijevoda nema, a nailazio sam još i na rješenja tipa *pomodnica, zujalica* ili *inriječ*. Opredijelio sam se za 'brujalica' jer riječ zadržava nešto od pčelinjeg zujanja ili brujanja (prim. prev.).

utjelovljenja formi finansijskog menadžmenta koje su se namnožile. To, na kraju, smjera na izazivanje odvratnosti: izvlačenjem ovih apstraktnih i naizgled besmislenih poslova u nešto nad čime treba da se zgadimo i čime bi trebalo da se pozabavimo. I tu je huljenje usmjereno ka nekoj drugoj materijalizaciji, koja je ovoga puta uperena protiv „nosilaca" kapitalizma u obličju širenja finansija, prije nego protiv utjelovljenja državne moći.

Ode prave jedan čudan luk između ovih formi nasilja prema jeziku i tijelima – nasilja koje stvari čini mekim i ranjivim – i seksualnosti. *Ode* istražuju i seksualno eksperimantiranje u djetinjstvu (i to na autobiografski način) kao jednu od „polimorfnih perverzija". Seksualnost se izlaže na složen način, i kao „neukrotiva oralna žudnja za uzbudljivim kontrolisanim uništenjem vrijednosti" i kao apsorpcija seksualnosti unutar kapitalističkog vrijednosnog poretka (29-30). Iako bi se moglo učiniti da se na ovaj način sugeriše urušavanje robnog fetiša u seksualni, zapravo se radi o tome da se Saterlend zanima za ono što se opire i zadržava svoje osobenosti unutar robne forme.[30] Razmatrajući seksualno iskustvo iz djetinjstva, kada je oralno zadovoljio svog prijatelja Kristijana, Saterlend piše: „Htio sam da svako dobije nešto iz mojih usta. Ono što sada iz njih izlazi je ova oda, jasno poništenje apatogeneze" (45). „Apatogeničko" znači ono koje uzrokuje bolest, pa bi „apatogeneza" predstavljala procese kojima se sprječava razvoj bolesti. Oda ovo poništava, pa se čini da se time ponovo vraća bolest ili raz-lakšanje.[31]

Usta ne služe samo za introjekciju kapitalističkih vrijednosti, već izgleda da ona igraju i ulogu odbacivanja ili abjekcije tih vrijednosti. Metju Ebot, međutim, iznosi jedan dublji uvid u samu stvar kada kaže kako ova upotreba dječije seksualnosti nije puki odraz prisile da se prizna, već isto tako predstavlja i jedno idilično prizorište:

> Ona dvosmisleno postavlja nježnost koja je uvijek oposredovana sa moći i pornografijom, jeftino uzbuđenje zbog sticanja prve sumorne slike muške seksualnosti čak i pošto potonja izjava ljubavi dolazi kao nešto što je uglavnom iskreno i dirljivo.[32]

---

30. Vidjeti: Sutherland, 'Fetish and Refuge', op. cit.

31. Ponovo teško prevodiva igra riječima/značenjem: *disease* na engleskom znači *bolest, zarazu*, a rastavljeno na prefiks *dis-* (*raz-*) u kombinaciji sa *-ease* (*lako, mirno, olakšati, umiriti*), najpribližnije (značenjski) vuče na *od-lakšavanje, raz-lakšavanje*, iako se time gubi prizvuk rime koji je, svakako, u jednom ovakvom radu bitan (prim. prev.).

Za Ebota pjesme ne polaze od seksualnosti kao isključivog mjesta nasilja. *Ode* se ne bave pukim prepričavanjem trauma, ispovijedanjem i analiziranjem kodiranja seksualnosti u formama kapitalističke potrošnje. Utopijski element *Oda* upravo je u insistiranju na izvornom iskustvu unutar ovih formi komodifikacije i nasilja. I opet, kao i u slučaju Bonejevog djela, *Ode* podastiru složenu introjektivnu dinamiku u kojoj su libidinalna i ekonomija krize savremenog kapitalizma internalizirane u samom srcu (lirske) subjektivnosti. Još jednom, „ustosjećaj" apstraktnog nasilja, napravljen kao i želatin komodifikacijske forme, okus je kako nasilne apstrakcije tako i osobenog momenta otpora unutar robne forme. Moment „izuzeća" ili „otpora" postoji, ali nije izvan robe već je unutar – metaforično rečeno – usta.

Pročišćenje

Pjesma Veriti Spot iz 2014. godine pod nazivom *Gideon* sama po sebi je kletva: Gideon je ime za jednu kletvu, za „napis mržnje" (8). Konkretno, pjesma je kletva usmjerena protiv britanskog političara Džordža Ozborna ([Georges Osborne] rođenog kao Gideon Oliver Ozborn) konzervativnog poslanika u parlamentu, ministra finansija od 2010. godine i osobe odgovorne za program štednje koji je sprovodila torijevska vlada. Pjesma predlaže „kao što netko traži nečiju glavu mi to sad možemo / uraditi sa utrobom Džordža Ozborna" (8). U jednoj zgodnoj prilici, koja je doduše kratko trajala, Džordž Ozborn bio je otpušten sa posla neposredno poslije izglasavanja bregzita i izbora nove predvodnice torijevaca Tereze Mej (Theresa May) pa je vraćen na klupu za rezervne igrače. Pjesma se sastoji od odjeljaka pisanih u tri 'glasa': Gideonovom glasu, glasu Ištar (boginje prirode i magije, čiji simbol označava „blagostanje" i „život") i glasu Eris (grčke boginje sukoba i nesloge). Pjesma je kletva protiv „zle ništice" (3) političara koji, ponovo, predstavlja modernu verziju političara kao šupljeg nasljednika golih privilegija. Ozbornov otac, ser Piter Ozborn (Peter) osnivač je fabrike za proizvodnju visokokvalitenih tkanina i tapeta, firme pod nazivom Osborne and Little. Džordž Ozborn je pohađao oksfordski Magdalenski koledž i bio član Bulingdon kluba. To je bio elitni isključivo muški klub i

---

32. 'The Poetry of Destroyed Experience', op. cit.

restoran koji se nalazio u Oksfordu i koji je postao svima znano mjesto za štancanje nebrojeno mnogo vodećih konzervativnih političara.

Kao osoba koja je stajala iza sprovođenja mjera štednje koje su natovarile bijedu za vrat tolikom broju Britanaca, dok su u isto vrijeme finansijske institucije ostale netaknute, ili su im se čak i dugovi otplaćivali, Džordž Ozborn bio je još jedno oličenje nasilja finansijske apstrakcije. U ovoj kletvi Spot pokušava da ocrta „konceptualno / neprijateljsko poremećeno tijelo (5). 'Kletva grgolji' 'jer zubi niču' pa moramo da 'ponovo provjerimo / ravnotežu gutanja'" (3); još jednom kletva radi u i pomoću usta kako bi ocrtala jedno „poremećeno" tijelo. To se posebno odnosi na odjeljak u kojem progovara Eris, i u kojem se prikazuje kult koji slijedi ovu „Boginju nesklada" (13), gdje pjesma koristi pojam pročišćenja kog shvata kao primjenu kletve. Pročišćenje, koje ima kako oralni tako i politički smisao, sprovodi jedna zaista „imaginarna partija", da se poslužimo terminom koji su proslavili Tikun (Tiqqun).[33] Ovo pročišćenje izvodi se u tri ili četiri oblika. Prvi se izvodi na lukav način, a sastoji se od različitih naizgled imaginarnih figura (iako nisu baš sve imaginarne) koje nose imena koja ukazuju na privilegije: „Džordži Hajgrejd-Midlton Čenej", na primjer, koja se možda odnosi na Kejt Midlton (Kate Middleton, vojvotkinju od Kejmbridža i ženu princa Vilijama), Dika Čejnija (Dick Cheney, potpredsjednika Sjedinjenih Država za vrijeme Džordža V. Buša [George W. Bush]), a možda čak i na Midlton Čejni (jedno selo u Južnom Nortemptonšajru u Engleskoj).

Drugo pročišćenje je „zabavno", pročišćenje od „primijećenih javnih/slavnih neprijatelja" (15). Njime je obuhvaćen širok raspon slavnih ličnosti koje bi se velikodušno moglo nazvati „javnim intelektualcima", uključujući i profesora Brajana Koksa (Brian Cox, voditelj popularnih naučnih programa), Melvina Braga (Melvyn Bragg, aktuelni voditelj serijala sa radija BBC 4 pod nazivom „U naše vrijeme" ['In Our Time'], koji je posvećen diskusijama o velikom broju intelektualnih tema) i Teri Iglton (Terry Eagleton) (dvaput), koji se obično predstavlja kao vodeći marksistički književni kritičar u Britaniji. „Sljedeće pročišćenje" predstavlja autodestruktivno pročišćenje u kom „Ispaljujem metke u skoro sve moje drugove ubijajući najveći broj njih"

---

33. Tikun su bili prethodnica Nevidljivog komiteta, iako ove dvije grupe nisu u potpunosti identične. Vidi: Tiqqun, 'Theses on the Imaginary Party', 1999, 25. avgust 2009, *https://libcom.org/library/theses-imaginary-party*

(16). Ovdje se radi o „samorazdiranju", koje dolazi poslije pročišćavanja od „aristokratije i nebitnih slavnih ličnosti" (16), i tu se parodira konzervativna kritika revolucijā počev od Terora iz Francuske revolucije pa sve do samoubistva partije pod boljševicima i rušilačkog nasilja Crvenih Kmera. Isto tako, ovo se može smatrati i za još jednu od involucija kletve kojom se potkopava njena vanjska pozicija i nudi jedan proces koji bi pomeo sve pred sobom.

Ali unutar ovog pročišćenja nalazi se još jedna kletva upućena firmi IBEX Global Solutions plc, „vodećem provajderu za pružanje usluga kontaktnog centra i drugog autsorsinga poslovnih procesa / rješenja" (16). Ovo nas vraća natrag na kapitalizam, na „autsorsovanje" i pozivne centre koje kao da dominiraju zapošljavanjem u savremenoj Britaniji. IBEX je stvarna kompanija koja samosvjesno gaji „hip" sliku o sebi, opisujući se kao „SLUŽBU koja pravi rez u svijetu autsorsinga poslovnih procesa".[34] Njihov aktivni sajt prikazuje slike multietničkih i rodno ravnopravnih radnika u odijelima i sa sunčanim očalama sa crvenim okvirima, negdje u rasponu između *Uličnih pasa* i Džejms Bonda. Prema namučenim marksistima, kakav sam i sam, tako se samo tipizira užas savremenog kapitalizma sa „ćaknutim" licem. Na kraju tu je i „Konačno" pročišćenje koje se odnosi na „partije i mislioce", iako se na tom mjestu pjesma razliva na nebrojeno mnogo spiskova imena (u tekstu manjeg formata) da bi se kasnije „vratila" u okvire očiglednije poetske forme.

Ova različita pročišćenja pobrojavaju subjektivnosti savremenog kapitalizma kao ekvivalente „živućim nulama" i na taj način ih prazne. Pjesma je, kao i sva ova djela, svjesna ograničenja takvih strategija, a njihovim sprovođenjem „KLETVA je ta koja nas sve čini beskorisnima" (8). U isto vrijeme, kletva i pročišćenje također su nešto što je uprizoreno. To uprizorenje je ono koje označava fantaziju i želju, raskrivanje nasilja apstrakcije i kontra-nasilje usmjereno protiv te apstrakcije. Na ovaj način nasilje apstrakcije učinjeno je vidljivim u svoj njegovoj raspomamljenoj zbiljnosti – neka „ništica" koja je još i „živa", nešto što je nesklad koji se predstavlja u modusu legalnosti. Pročišćenje također priziva i sredstvo za čišćenje, kao i političku metaforu. Ovo je još jedan čin proklinjanja koji, spiskovima koje stvara, drži pročišćene na oku (ili u ustima) u isto vrijeme dok ih proklinje.

---

34. *http://www.ibexglobal.com/company.php*

Pomenuta pobrojavanja govore i o mnoštvenosti karakternih maski i njihovih različitih oblika i struktura. I dok spisak smjera da poravnava i ujednačava, nešto skorašnjiji rad Spot pod nazivom „Ugao menadžerske okrutnosti" ('An Angle on Management Cruelty') iz 2016. godine također govori o slojevima i hijerarhijama koje te maske podrazumijevaju.[35] U pjesmi „menadžer" postaje lik umješten u rastući veliki lanac bivstvovanja savremenog kapitalizma. Hijerarhija se odnosi na strukture u kompaniji, na uloge i „vještine", dakle sve te fetišističke objekte savremenog kapitalizma: „Zdravstvo, Bolnice, Promjena, Menadžment, Biznis, Strategija, Tim bilding, Trening, Biznis, Razvoj, Koučing, Menadžment, Mentalno zdravlje, Performanse, Menadžment, Liderstvo, Razvoj, Razvoj organizacije i Regrutiranje". I ovdje se na okrutnost menadžerskih odluka gleda kao na nešto prazno, što je diktirano sa vrha, ali i stvarno, koje se uprizoruje kao želja da se bude dobrim menadžerom koji sprovodi ono što se od njega zahtijeva. Dopunjujući Gideonovu kletvu o jednom i svemu, ova pjesma izgovara kletvu koju kapitalizam izvodi svojom sopstvenom okrutnošću – plutajući ali istorvemeno utjelovljen i stvaran, posebno u obličju menadžera. Na taj način možemo vidjeti kako je strategija bacanja kletve također i odgovor na mnogo veću moć bacanja kletve koju posjeduje kapitalizam, kao i odgovor na zloćudnost kapitalističkog čarobnjaštva – na moć kapitalizma da začara, proklinje i osudi.[36] Kletva je mjera i odgovor, proždiranje, abjekcija i odbijanje.

Zaključak

Iako ne polažem prava na konačni uvid u namjere autora niti prava da nudim neki iscrpan pregled ovih djela, ipak u poetskom ili bilo kojem drugom smislu kletvu vidim kao praksu poetskog jezika koji istodobno imenuje, proklinje i pokušava da stvori sam objekt kletve. Pred nosom sila i formi apstraktne moći, koje su sve brutalno ostvarene u pojednim tačkama, praksa proklinjanja uprizoruje scenu na kojoj su nemoćni tu apstraktnu moć *natjerali da se pojavi*, i to identifikacijom poezije sa nemoćnima, utoliko bolje što je više proklinju. Ovo smo imali prilike da

---

35. Verity Spott, 'An Angle on Management Cruelty', 5. decembar 2016, *http://twotornhalves.blogspot.co.uk/2016/12/an-angle-on-management-cruelty.html*
36. Vidjeti: Philippe Pignarre and Isabelle Stengers, *Capitalist Sorcery*, (prev. Andrew Goffey), Basingstoke: Palgrave, 2011.

vidimo na primjeru djelovanja usmjerenih na oralnost – i to ne tek na jezik, nego isto tako i na jedenje i povraćanje objekta koji se poriče. Pojavljivanje ili materijalizacija spajaju se u jedno u ustima i pomoću usta. Oralno je to koje sažima tijelo i jezik u otvaranju spram spoljašnjosti koja je ujedno i prizorište govora i prizorište potencijalnog vršenja nasilja. Ukoliko je, za Frojda, negacija bila čin izbacivanja iz usta, ove pjesme zadržavaju objekt kletve u ustima, i to upravo na jednom ambivalentnom mjestu između introjekcije i ispljuvavanja. Derida (Derrida), u jednom drugom konktekstu, zapaža da se: „Haos odnosi baš na ambis ili na otvorena usta, kako ona koja govore tako i na ona koja označavaju glad."[37] Usta, opet, obavljaju dvostruku funkciju: govorenja i jedenja, što sve može da se odnosi i na tenziju koja postoji između apstraktnog nasilja i materijalnog otpora. Ovaj „haotični" ambis je ambisni moment kojem se obraća kletva pokušavajući registrirati taj haos ili ambis koji apstraktna nametanja uravnoteženosti i razmjene poništavaju i satiru.

Kao odgovor na pokretljivost kapitalističke apstrakcije i bezličnu pojavu državne moći, kletva je performans koji pravi stvarnost od tih formi fiktivnog kapitala i državne fikcije. Ova djela leže na samoj ivici fantazije i njenog ispražnjivanja i ona istodobno sadržavaju i fantaziju kao modus kletve (ne bi li se tako uočila slabost) dok u isto vrijeme i predlažu izbjegavanje fantazije (ne bi li se ono apstraktno privelo svojoj supstancijalnosti). Pa opet, slabost nije nešto što mora biti obznanjeno, ona ne obustavlja kletvu, kao što ni privođenje supstancijalnosti objekta kletve ne predstavlja kraj stvarī. U ovim tekstovima tijela se bacaju o druga tijela: tijela o poetska djela, tijela pjesnika *protiv* tijela kapitala, tijela o državu, tog utjelovljenog neprijatelja. Ovi činovi ukazuju na nasilje apstrakcije i suprotstavljaju se mišljenju da su takvi činovi protiv-nasilja uvijek iznova osuđeni da promaše svoju metu ili da biraju samo lake mete. Jedno prekomjerno naglašavanje apstraktne forme kapitalizma i jedno prekomjerno naglašavanje nužnosti neuspjeha činova osvete kao forme ničeanskog resantimana su, kao što sam to ranije napomenuo,[38] načini da se neutraliziraju političke mogućnosti.

---

37. Jacques Derrida, *The Gift of Death*, (prev. David Wills). Chicago: Chicago University Press, 1995, str. 84. Bonejeva knjiga *Letters Against the Firmament*, op. cit., na poleđini ima ispisan tekst 'Žao mi je zbog svega onoga što sam rekao dok sam bio GLADAN'.
38. Benjamin Noys, 'Theses on Revenge: Knee-Jerk Nietzsche and Abstract Marx' u: *Bad Feelings*, ur. Nina Power, London: Bookworks, 2015, bez paginacije.

Nasuprot tome, kao što kaže Deni Hejvard, ova djela proklinju kako bi iscrpila jezik, kako bi taj iscrpljeni jezik gurnula do tačke iscrpljenog radnog tijela; ona svojim litijama i ponavljanjima stvaraju kletvu kao strategiju iscrpljivanja i to u oba smisla: iscrpljivanjem jezičkih resursa i nagovještajem kako je naš jezik već iscrpljen.[39]

Međutim, ona u isto vrijeme šire i umnožavaju jezik i mete. Moglo bi biti suviše jednostavno otpisati kletve kao djela fantazije i fikcije. Dijana di Prima (Diane di Prima) u svom „Revolucionarnom pismu #46" ('Revolutionary Letter #46') piše: „I kao što si naučila magiju, nauči i da povjeruješ u nju / nemoj da te 'iznenadi' ako radi, time potkopavaš / svoju moć."[40] U kletvama i dalje ima moći, i ta moć možda nije samo moć jezika ili moć da se jezik gurne do tačke njegovog iscrpljivanja. „Magija" opstaje u želji da se ide dalje, onkraj granica apstrakcije, onkraj upletenosti u načine na koje apstrakcija obuzima tijela. U ovom trenutku opstajanja kletve upisana je i želja da se tijelo učini pojavnim – i to ne samo tijelo kao meta, već i tijelo svih onih koji se opiru. I iako je najlakše smatrati ovo „pukom" fikcijom (da se još jednom vratimo na trope poezije kao beskorisne i izlišne), nešto i dalje nastavlja da se dešava u pojavljivanju mjesta sa kojeg je moguće pružiti otpor.

Zahvale

Želio bih se zahvaliti Veriti Spot, Entoniju Ajlsu i Marini Višmit na njihovim komentarima ovog eseja.

---

39. Hayward, 'Strong Language', op. cit., str. 108.
40. Diane di Prima, *Revolutionary Letters,* San Francisco: Last Gasp Press, 2007, str. 59.

BIOGRAFIJE UČESNIKA

Grupa za konceptualnu politiku (GKP) je nastala iz onoga što bismo mogli nazvati *sukobom na levici našeg vremena* (2011), u Novom Sadu, Srbija. GKP je grupa koja se bavi politikom *na strani ljudi*, teorijom i umetnošću. Pokrenula je projekat „Lokalne politike i urbana samouprava" u okviru kojeg radi sa ljudima na rešavanju problema vezanih za stanovanje i lokalnu samoupravu. Od svog osnivanja grupa je sarađivala sa kuda.org na brojnim projektima i zajedničkim poduhvatima. Među njima je prevodilački i izdavački projekat, važan za mišljenje i delanje GKP-a, u okviru kojeg je sa francuskog na srpsko-hrvatski jezik prevedeno i objavljeno nekoliko naslova: *Antropologija imena* Silvena Lazarisa i *Teorija subjekta* Alena Badiua. Trenutno radi na prevodu *Cartographies schizoanalytiques* Félixa Guattaria, koja treba da bude objavljena tokom 2017. godine.

Liza Ješke je pesnikinja i prevoditeljica i bavi se teatrom. Njen dosadašnji rad uključuje *Nine Drugs* (prevod Ulf Stolterfohtove *holzrauch über heslach*; Cambridge: Face Press, 2016) i, zajedno sa Lusi Bejnon (Lucy Beynon), *The Tragedy of Theresa May.* (https://www.youtube.com/watch?v=djwyIRJ3DWE).

Deni Hejvard živi u Londonu i povremeno učestvuje u osporivoj medijskoj imperiji No Money <n-o-m-o-ney.tumblr.com>

Entoni Ajls trenutno radi na doktoratu na Školi za umetnost & dizajn, Univerzitet Midlseks (Middlesex University) i jedan je od urednika u časopisima *Mute* / Metamute i *Cesura* / *Acceso*. Zajedno sa Džozefinom Beri-Slejter (Josephine Berry-Slater) autor je knjige *No Room to Move: Art and the Regenerate City* (Mute Books, London 2011), urednik publikacije *Language: writing and crisis* (Archive Books, Berlin, 2015), i učesnik u *Brave New Work: A Reader on Harun Farocki's Film A New Product.* Njegovi skorašnji eseji objavljeni su u časopisima *Radical Philosophy, Rab-Rab: Journal for Political and Formal Inquiries in Art and Logos.*

Bendžamin Nojs predaje na Univerzitetu Čičester (University of Chichester). Njegova poslednja knjiga je *Malign Velocities* (2014).

Eirik Štajnhof živi u Olimpiji (Vašington), gde drži predavanja o temama „Kako raditi s rečima", „Imperijalizmi" i „Novi Bliski Istok?" na Evergrin državnom koledžu (The Evergreen State College). Kolekcija pamfleta koju je distribuirao tokom kasne 2011. godine i rane 2011. godine, pod nazivom *A Fiery Flying Roule*, uskoro objavljuje Station Hill

Press iz Beritauna (Barrytown), a trenutno radi na knjizi o značenju slučaja u engleskoj renesansi.

Marina Višmit je urednica, kritičarka i spisateljica iz Londona, koja se uglavnom bavi pitanjima vezanim za umetnost, rad i vrednost. Autorka je knjiga *Speculation as a Mode of Production* (Brill, rana 2016) i *A for Autonomy* (sa Kerstin Stakemeier) (Textem, kasna 2014). Često sarađuje sa umetnicima i objavljuje svoje tekstove u časopisima poput *Mute, Afterall, Texte zur Kunst, Ephemera, Kaleidoscope, Parkett,* i *OPEN!* Takođe je ko-uredila zbornike i katalog, među kojima je poslednji *Anguish Language* (anguishlanguage.tumbr.com). Autorka je poglavlja u *The Routledge Companion to Art and Politics* (Routledge, uskoro izlazi) i *The ECONOMY Reader* (University of Liverpool Press, uskoro izlazi).

www.ingramcontent.com/pod-product-compliance
Lightning Source LLC
La Vergne TN
LVHW041309180726
843489LV00001BA/14